Radioactive Ghosts

posthumanities

Cary Wolfe, Series Editor

61 *Radioactive Ghosts*
    Gabriele Schwab

60 *Gaian Systems: Lynn Margulis, Neocybernetics, and the End of the Anthropocene*
    Bruce Clarke

59 *The Probiotic Planet: Using Life to Manage Life*
    Jamie Lorimer

58 *Individuation in Light of Notions of Form and Information Volume II Supplemental Texts*
    Gilbert Simondon

57 *Individuation in Light of Notions of Form and Information*
    Gilbert Simondon

56 *Thinking Plant Animal Human: Encounters with Communities of Difference*
    David Wood

55 *The Elements of Foucault*
    Gregg Lambert

54 *Postcinematic Vision: The Coevolution of Moving-Image Media and the Spectator*
    Roger F. Cook

53 *Bleak Joys: Aesthetics of Ecology and Impossibility*
    Matthew Fuller and Olga Goriunova

52 *Variations on Media Thinking*
    Siegfried Zielinski

51 *Aesthesis and Perceptronium: On the Entanglement of Sensation, Cognition, and Matter*
    Alexander Wilson

50 *Anthropocene Poetics: Deep Time, Sacrifice Zones, and Extinction*
    David Farrier

49 *Metaphysical Experiments: Physics and the Invention of the Universe*
    Bjørn Ekeberg

48 *Dialogues on the Human Ape*
    Laurent Dubreuil and Sue Savage-Rumbaugh

(continued on page 340)

RADIOACTIVE GHOSTS

GABRIELE SCHWAB

posthumanities 61

University of Minnesota Press
Minneapolis
London

Copyright 2020 by the Regents of the University of Minnesota

"Children of the Nuclear Age" copyright 2017 Gabriele Schwab and Simon J. Ortiz

All rights reserved. No part of this publication may be reproduced, stored in a retrieval system, or transmitted, in any form or by any means, electronic, mechanical, photocopying, recording, or otherwise, without the prior written permission of the publisher.

Published by the University of Minnesota Press
111 Third Avenue South, Suite 290
Minneapolis, MN 55401-2520
http://www.upress.umn.edu

ISBN 978-1-5179-0782-2 (hc)
ISBN 978-1-5179-0783-9 (pb)

Library of Congress record available at https:/lccn.loc.gov/2020024768.

Printed in the United States of America on acid-free paper

The University of Minnesota is an equal-opportunity educator and employer.

UMP BmB 2020

*For Leon and Lucia
and in memory of all those who died
after nuclear wars or catastrophes*

CONTENTS

PREFACE	On Three-Eyed Fish and Other Ghostings	ix
INTRODUCTION	Why Nuclear Necropolitics Today?	1

PART I. NUCLEAR SUBJECTIVITIES

ONE	No Apocalypse, Not Now: Derrida and the Nuclear Unconscious	39
TWO	Nuclear Colonialism	57
THREE	Critical Nuclear Race Theory	85
FOUR	The Gender of Nuclear Subjectivities	105

INTERLUDE: CHILDREN OF THE NUCLEAR AGE with Simon J. Ortiz		133

PART II. HAUNTING FROM THE FUTURE

FIVE	The Afterlife of Nuclear Catastrophes	151
SIX	Hiroshima's Ghostly Shadows	187
SEVEN	Postnuclear Madness and Nuclear Crypts	217
EIGHT	Transspecies Selves: Intimacies, Extimacies, Animacies	237
CODA	Postnuclear Ecologies—Language, Body, and Affect in Beckett's *Happy Days*	267

ACKNOWLEDGMENTS	285
NOTES	289
INDEX	319

PREFACE

ON THREE-EYED FISH AND OTHER GHOSTINGS

BLINKY, THE THREE-EYED FISH

On November 1, 1990, FOX aired "Two Cars in Every Garage and Three Eyes on Every Fish," season 2, episode 4 of the iconic American television show *The Simpsons*.[1] The episode opens with Bart and Lisa Simpson fishing in a river downstream from the Springfield Nuclear Power Plant, where their father, Homer, works as an employee. Just as a reporter for the *Springfield Shopper* arrives for an unrelated story, Bart hooks a three-eyed fish. Soon after, the story of Blinky the three-eyed fish makes headlines across the state. Suspecting radioactive contamination as the cause of the fish's mutation, Springfield governor Mary Bailey calls for an investigation into the Springfield Nuclear Power Plant and the dumping of nuclear waste into the town's water supply. To avoid a shutdown, the plant's owner, Mr. Burns, runs against Bailey for the office of governor. To dispel the community's fears, Mr. Burns stages a highly publicized dinner at the house of an ordinary employee, Homer Simpson—a choice that causes a rift between Homer as an employee of the Springfield Nuclear Power Plant, on one hand, and his wife, Marge, and daughter Lisa, on the other, who belong to an antinuclear coalition of Springfield residents. The highlight of the episode occurs when Marge serves Mr. Burns Blinky for dinner. Unable to swallow his bite, Mr. Burns spits out the mutant fish in front of a live audience, effectively ending his campaign for governor.

In its simplicity, "Two Cars in Every Garage and Three Eyes on Every Fish" speaks to a number of concerns found in *Radioactive Ghosts*. One of my goals in the pages to come is to understand how the multiple and entangled legacies of the Manhattan Project generate a "haunting from the future" that is specific to nuclear politics, and that profoundly impacts the very formation of subjectivity. Psychically, this haunting frequently manifests in what I refer to as "phantasms of the mutant body."

FIGURE 1. Screen capture from *The Simpsons,* "Two Cars in Every Garage and Three Eyes on Every Fish," season 2, episode 4.

People affected by radioactive contamination, or the fear thereof, often express living with the terror of transgenerational genetic damage—or, more specifically, the fear of having mutant children and grandchildren. Similar to Lacan's "phantasms of the fragmented body," phantasms of the mutant body manifest a specific state of ontological insecurity. Blinky the three-eyed fish registers such phantasms, quickly becoming a veritable cultural icon that embodies the specter of nuclear mutations.[2] Mr. Burns, moreover, attempts to co-opt the specter of mutation, hiring a Darwin impersonator to declare Blinky's mutation a beneficial step in evolutionary progress. After all, is it not better to have three eyes than two? This particularly insidious form of denial, which enlists the natural sciences as a form of political legitimation, invokes the rhetoric of natural selection to naturalize the genetic damage caused by nuclear contamination.

Defensive strategies like those employed by Mr. Burns help to illustrate what I refer to as a *will to deceit and denial,* one of the most widespread responses to nuclear fears. Designed to conceal the risks and impacts of nuclear damage, the will to deceit is part and parcel of the infrastructure generated by the nuclear–military–industrial complex. Often, the victims of nuclear damage collude with official strategies of deceit, embracing a complementary will to denial aimed at warding off overwhelming feelings of fear and, sometimes, even conflicting interests. In fact, the divisiveness of nuclear politics, as well as the corrosive effects it has on local communities and families, is often the result of a conflict of interest.³ The rift caused in the Simpson family, for example, between Homer, whose income depends on the nuclear power plant, and the work Marge and Lisa perform to expose Mr. Burns's attempt at covering up the river's contamination dramatizes a rather common and simultaneous dependence on and refusal of the nuclear–military–industrial complex. The episode's conclusion, though, also highlights the power of antinuclear activism to expose the corruption, deceit, and denial at the heart of nuclear politics.⁴ "Two Cars in Every Garage and Three Eyes on Every Fish" thus provides an apt example not only of a nuclear haunting in popular culture but also of cultural production's ability to intervene in the formation of a collective nuclear imaginary.

TRAJECTORIES OF INTERVENTION

Radioactive Ghosts draws on a wide range of examples from literature, the arts, and popular culture to theorize the multiple legacies of the Manhattan Project and the far-ranging impact of nuclear politics in its wake. Rather than dealing with the history of nuclear politics as such, I read a range of cultural objects from literature, film, television, oral history, and ethnography to trace the effects of nuclear trauma in the political and sociocultural imaginary—or, more specifically, the nuclear imaginary. I read these traces as manifestations of a new type of subject-formation that came into being at the dawn of the nuclear age, the early twentieth century. The ontological insecurity generated by the invention of the Bomb and enforced by the proliferation of nuclear power plants establishes a qualitative leap in the formation of subjectivity. Whether or not we are aware of it, we are constituted as nuclear subjects, endowed with a nuclear unconscious that profoundly shapes our being in the world. Moreover, the ontological insecurity generated by what I call *nuclear necropolitics* has defining and lasting consequences not only for psychopolitics but also for biopolitics and the larger ecology of mind and planetary life that molds the formation of subjectivity.

Radioactive Ghosts proposes that nuclear necropolitics requires a sustained conversation between biopolitical, psychopolitical, and ecological thought. In this context, I see psychopolitics as a foundational part of a larger ecology of mind in the sense outlined by Gregory Bateson.⁵ During the past decades, we have seen a systematic repression of public nuclear debates. While biopolitics and ecology intersect in debates about climate change, the entanglement between climate change and the nuclear threat is all but eclipsed from these debates.[6] *Radioactive Ghosts* aims to remobilize earlier works on nuclearism—both theoretical and literary—in light of the impasses of our contemporary moment, forcing a theoretical return to the repressed nuclear threat to assess its relevance for today's nuclear politics and theory. In the following, I trace various rhizomatic trajectories of intervention that inform the nuclear theory developed in *Radioactive Ghosts*. Reiterated from different oscillating perspectives, the topics and concepts I identify in the following pages permeate all chapters, creating links and feedback loops between them that deepen the overall theoretical framework in the context of shifting material manifestations of nuclearism.

Nuclear Necropolitics

Bringing Achille Mbembe's work on necropolitics in conversation with debates in nuclear criticism, I use the introduction to develop a concept of "nuclear necropolitics" that highlights the specific nuclear "work of death." Integrating biopolitical, psychopolitical, and ecological thought, this concept prepares the ground for a sustained theoretical encounter between these fields in critical theory. Against the current marginalization, if not silencing, of the continued threat of nuclearism in ecological debates, I insist that nuclear necropolitics must be added to climate change as one of the foremost challenges to the survival of planetary life. *Radioactive Ghosts*, I hope, conveys the need to see nuclearism as absolutely central to the debates about the Anthropocene or Capitalocene. Radioactive contamination is, after all, arguably the most destructive footprint humans have left on the planet. Within this larger framework, my focus on nuclear subjectivities also counters the current neglect of psychopolitics in political as well as ecological debates about nuclearism. *Radioactive Ghosts* presents steps toward a first comprehensive psychological theory of nuclear subjectivities with the hope to inspire further work in this direction.

A Critique of Nuclear Reason

Two chapters, "Nuclear Colonialism" (chapter 2) and "Critical Nuclear Race Theory" (chapter 3), trace crucial features and historical moments in the deeply racialized colonial genealogy of nuclear necropolitics. Expanding Mbembe's *Critique of Black Reason*, I develop a *critique of nuclear reason*, showing that nuclear necropolitics has remained firmly embedded in its colonizing practices, including not only the subjection and sacrifice of lands and peoples but also the colonization of mind and psychic space. What emerges in response to the formation of nuclear subjectivities is the urgent imperative to both decolonize and denuclearize the mind. It is from this perspective that *Radioactive Ghosts* also makes a contribution to discussions about environmental racism and environmental justice.

Nuclear Trauma Studies
Following my work in *Haunting Legacies*, *Radioactive Ghosts* starts from the assumption that the genocide in the German concentration camps and the atomic attacks on Hiroshima and Nagasaki embody the twin horrors of World War II. Focusing on the haunting legacies of the Manhattan Project, *Radioactive Ghosts* explores the specificity of nuclear trauma, including transgenerational trauma, from the perspective of a double nuclear haunting from past and future. Generating a profound ontological insecurity, this haunting impacts the very formation of subjectivity from within. Nuclear subjects are traumatized subjects, haunted by memories of nuclear catastrophes while also harboring the invisible ghosts of a future nuclear disaster in a sealed-off crypt within the core of their selves.

Nuclear trauma also presents a challenging conundrum to the formation of a collective nuclear memory. Ranging from splitting to amnesia, trauma-induced defenses relegate unbearable and overwhelming aspects of nuclear encounters to the unconscious. This, I insist, happens at both the individual and the collective levels. In relation to the nuclear threat, familiar psychic defense mechanisms, such as splitting, doubling, dissociation, denial, moral inversion, deceit, psychic encryption, forgetting, and, in some cases, even traumatic amnesia, have become common conditions of human functioning in everyday life. Drawing on nuclear criticism, trauma studies, and psychoanalysis, including Abraham and Torok's theory of the crypt, I develop a concept of a traumatic nuclear unconscious as the core of a theory of nuclear subjectivities.

Ontological, Epistemological, and Psychological Rupture
With its unique focus on nuclear subjectivities, *Radioactive Ghosts* theorizes the ontological, psychological, and epistemological break inaugurated by the nuclear age. The most profound epistemological crisis triggered by the nuclear has to do with its extreme scalar challenge. While

the nuclear threat can be assessed scientifically (at least to a large extent), it can never be fully experienced. Understanding the impact of radioactive contamination on life on earth by far exceeds the boundaries of the human imagination, at the large scale of deep time and its material manifestations as well as the small scale of molecular materiality and being. *Radioactive Ghosts* addresses this problem methodologically by developing a multiscalar nuclear theory replete with resonances, feedback loops, and diffractions. Within this theoretical framework, the book particularly emphasizes the effects of the ontological, epistemological, and scalar challenges of the nuclear on the formation of nuclear subjectivities.

The Molecular as a New Episteme

Radioactive Ghosts theorizes the impact of molecularity on nuclear subjectivities within the larger context of the molecular turn in the life sciences. Drawing on Michelle Murphy's concept of chemical infrastructures and Mel Chen's concept of animacies, I discuss nuclear reproductive politics from the perspective of nuclear infrastructures. Owing to the haunting from the future of molecular and genetic damage, nuclear reproductive politics is transgenerational, challenging the very formation of subjectivity within familiar (and imaginable) spatiotemporal coordinates. There is to the best of my knowledge no other study of the nuclear that has theorized this molecular turn in the formation of nuclear subjectivities.

Transspecies Being and Transspecies Ethics

Radioactive Ghosts demonstrates the need for a new ethics linked to the nuclear challenge. Expanding Marx's concept of "species being" and Robert J. Lifton's concept of the "species self," I argue that we need to replace these concepts with new ones that are less anthropocentric, namely, "transspecies being" and "transspecies self." The latter are able to address the danger of the nuclear to planetary life and the related guilt and responsibility humans need to face and translate into action. Ultimately, this involves a new ethics of transgenerational care for living species with whom we share the planet, now and for generations to come. Striving to transcend environmental speciesism, such an ethics must also develop steps toward an environmental transspecies justice.

The Role of Literature and the Arts

Radioactive Ghosts highlights the role of literature and the arts in shaping nuclear psychopolitics and in addressing the mnemonic, psychological, and scalar challenges of the nuclear. Literary and artistic works counter the politics of splitting, denial, and deceit at the heart of nuclear necropolitics, thus actively intervening in the formation of a nuclear unconscious. Moreover, using experimental forms that provide imaginary extensions of the boundaries of human experience, artistic figurations may convey a sense of deep and molecular time that targets affects and emotions, especially ones related to suffering at extreme distances. In this context, many literary and artistic works engage in "a politically committed work of mourning"[7] the victims of the nuclear work of death, including those who died as a result of nuclear catastrophes as well as those who will suffer or die as a result of transgenerational nuclear legacies. Finally, literary and artistic works have produced a dazzling range of transspecies imaginaries that provide emotionally embedded aesthetic experiences of transspecies care and responsibility. In this respect, they form experimental systems for exploring the new transspecies ethics needed to address the nuclear threat to the survival of planetary life.

DESIGN

I have divided *Radioactive Ghosts* into two parts with a particular logic and compositional architecture in mind. It is by no means a hard division. I continually construct feedback loops between chapters to revisit a particular issue in light of new perspectives drawn from different, yet interrelated theoretical debates. Concepts like "phantasms of the mutant body," "transgenerational nuclear trauma," and "haunting from the future" (to name only a few) are threaded throughout different chapters and further developed in shifting contexts. One reader suggested that *Radioactive Ghosts* is structured like a constellation or satellite system with particular anchors that take hold as the chapters unfold. Most often, these anchors are theoretical, but sometimes they are political, historical, psychological, or literary. I have taken great pains to create resonances between these anchors, as well as between recurring themes and concepts, and hope doing so will inform the reading process.

In other words, *Radioactive Ghosts* is not a linear text. Neither is it chronological. When I began visualizing the book's organization, a map emerged in my mind with specific concepts serving as landmarks and rhizomatically distributed arrows moving back and forth between the chapters to create feedback loops and resonances. Given the prominent role molecularity plays in my theory of nuclear necropolitics, I hope that readers will become aware of the book's molecular flows beneath its molar organization into discrete chapters.

The two parts of *Radioactive Ghosts* form a dialogical relationship with each other. Part I, "Nuclear Subjectivities," develops an overarching framework for theorizing the nuclear today, with chapters emphasizing how the nuclear-military-industrial complex has been entangled from the very beginning with both histories of colonialism and the politics of race and gender. Part II, "Haunting from the Future," focuses on literary texts, films, and works of art to closely read specific aspects of the nuclear imaginary. Here I introduce and develop a number of concepts, including postnuclear madness, the nuclear crypt, nuclear infrastructures, transspecies selves, and multiscalar ecologies of mind, which are meant to add depth and nuance to the overall theory of nuclear subjectivities developed in part I. While the theory of nuclear necropolitics outlined in part I informs each of the close readings and case studies in part II, each chapter in the latter, in turn, expands the scope, scale, depth, and boundaries of the theory.

OVERVIEW OF CHAPTERS
Introduction: "Why Nuclear Necropolitics Today?"
Drawing on Achille Mbembe's seminal 2003 essay "Necropolitics," as well as a range of critical nuclear theories, I develop a concept of nuclear necropolitics that serves as the project's overall theoretical framework.[8] Outlining the specificity of nuclear necropolitics, as compared to other necropolitical forms of violence and destruction, I explore how the nuclear turn impacts the parameters and reach of both sovereignty and subjectivity. The legacy of the Manhattan Project, I insist, continues to impact the formation of nuclear subjectivities today. This much is obvious in the contemporary resurgence of debates around the viability of "limited nuclear war in the 21st century."[9] Several proponents of this notion argue openly that one of the prime tasks is to prepare the American public emotionally for nuclear war to avoid a new wave of antinuclear activism. This is a stunningly—and, I think, symptomatic—overt intervention in the formation of nuclear subjectivities at the very level of policy.

Part I: "Nuclear Subjectivities"
Chapter 1, "No Apocalypse, Not Now: Derrida and the Nuclear Unconscious," juxtaposes Derrida's essay "No Apocalypse, Not Now"

(1984) with Jonathan Schell's classic study of nuclear war in *The Fate of the Earth* (1982). Focusing on the role of imagining extinction within the psychodynamics and rhetorical condition of the nuclear imaginary, my revaluation of Derrida and Schell pursues two goals: first, it actualizes two foundational theoretical and critical interventions that, never brought in conversation with each other, have subsequently been repressed, most pointedly after the end of the Cold War; second, it provides an entry point for developing the concept of the nuclear unconscious that will inform subsequent chapters. Theorizing the role of the nuclear unconscious, I argue, is crucial in light of today's large-scale repression in public debates of the monumental threat the nuclear continues to pose to the health and, indeed, the survival of much of planetary life.

Chapter 2, "Nuclear Colonialism," interrogates the legacies of the Manhattan Project from the perspective of the Indigenous nuclear borderlands in the American Southwest and the Second Wounded Knee at Pine Ridge. I revisit the work of Valerie Kuletz, Ward Churchill, Joseph Masco, and Traci Voyles to accentuate that it was the colonization of Indigenous lands and peoples in the interests of corporate and military nuclearism that facilitated the inauguration of the nuclear age. Linking the history of resource extraction, especially uranium mining, to the colonization of Indigenous lands, I again mobilize a seminal work of the 1980s, namely, Peter Matthiessen's *In the Spirit of Crazy Horse* (1983). The latter allows me to draw an arc to the current protests and struggles over water rights and the Dakota Access Pipeline at Standing Rock, emphasizing the inextricable entanglement of nuclear politics and water politics. Understanding the legacies of the Manhattan Project from the perspective of the colonization of Indigenous lands, resources, and peoples is crucial to expose the continued creation of sacrifice zones and disposable populations for the sake of the profit economy of the nuclear–military–industrial complex.

Chapter 3, "Critical Nuclear Race Theory," shifts the focus from the impact of nuclearism on Indigenous peoples to the role of antinuclearism in the civil rights movement. The chapter outlines steps toward a critical nuclear race theory, tracing the largely forgotten genealogy of African American antinuclear resistance and its internationalist orientation. Black writers, public intellectuals, and activists have emphatically insisted on the inextricable link between the civil rights movement and the antinuclear movement. Together, chapters 2 and 3 trace a trajectory from the critique of nuclear colonialism to the current global antinuclear politics. Expanding the theory of nuclear necropolitics developed in the introduction, "Critical Nuclear Race Theory" draws on Achille Mbembe's recent work in *Critique of Black Reason* to outline a proposal for a *critique of nuclear reason.*

Chapter 4, "The Gender of Nuclear Necropolitics," analyzes the gendering of nuclear culture, politics, and discourses, emphasizing the entanglement of nuclear politics with a politics of reproduction. Drawing on Michel Carrouges's concept of the "bachelor's machine," I analyze male fantasies of the Bomb as a sublime object of male reproduction. The bachelor machine emerges in these fantasies as a nuclear war machine that heralds the triumph of masculine technology over both nature and the feminine. By contrast, women's antinuclear activism embraces a radically different politics of reproduction, stressing a politics of survival and responsibility for future generations in opposition to the reigning hypermasculinist militarism. Drawing on Michelle Murphy's concept of "distributed reproduction," the chapter ends with theorizing the role of nuclear infrastructures in initiating a molecular turn in women's reproductive politics.

Interlude: "Children of the Nuclear Age"
A piece of collaborative nonfiction I wrote with Acoma poet, writer, and critic Simon J. Ortiz, the interlude presents a tapestry of interwoven bits of memory that describes scenes of how, as children growing up in different parts of the world, we gained our first knowledge about radioactivity: X-rays and the atomic bomb. Belonging to entirely different cultures—the Acoma reservation in New Mexico and a small German town bordering Switzerland and the Black Forest—we were both mesmerized by the mystique of X-ray machines and terrified by stories of the atomic bomb. Rather than creating a dialogue, our alternating memories mirror intimately personal and local stories in the global imaginary. The collage thus creates an experimental syncretistic memory of two children born at the very onset of the nuclear age.

Part II: "Haunting from the Future"
Developing symptomatic readings of a wide range of literary texts, works of art, documentaries, ethnographies, oral histories, and case studies, the second part of *Radioactive Ghosts* zooms in on specific manifestations of nuclearism. Chapter 5, "The Afterlife of Nuclear Catastrophes," ana-

lyzes the refashioning of subjectivities in the aftermath of both nuclear war and disaster. Drawing on Robert J. Lifton's *Death in Life,* I trace the subjectivities of survivors of Hiroshima, Nagasaki, Chernobyl, and Fukushima to analyze the precarious remaking of personhood in the wake of nuclear war and catastrophes as well as the material and psychic fallout of the continued cover-up, deceit, and corruption in nuclear energy politics.

Chapter 6, "Hiroshima's Ghostly Shadows," opens with readings of the "shadowgraph," left on the stone steps of a Hiroshima bank, of a human incinerated by atomic heat rays. As a memento mori that allegorizes the work of nuclear death, this ghostly trace of a human foreshadows the extinction of the species, serving both as reminder of Hiroshima's past catastrophe and as material embodiment of a perpetual haunting from the future left in its wake.

I then discuss the transgenerational legacy of slow nuclear violence. Readings of Ray Bradbury's "August 2016: There Will Come Soft Rains" and Jorge Luis Borges's "Library of Babel" foreground the early nuclear imaginary of a world without humans through shadow archives of destruction that no longer have any witnesses. Turning to the art of Adrian Villar Rojas and Michael Madsen's documentary *Into Eternity,* I address the social, cultural, and political challenges these works present as they imagine extinction by thinking across scales that transcend the boundaries of human temporality and experience, if not imagination. Moving from the deep time of millennial histories to the small scale of molecular micropolitics, I end by examining the implications of the "molecular turn" in nuclear micropolitics for a theory of nuclear subjectivities.

Chapter 7, "Postnuclear Madness and Nuclear Crypts," focuses on the famous case of bomber pilot Claude Eatherly, described in his correspondence with German philosopher Günther Anders. Tormented by guilt over his role in the first atomic attack, Eatherly suffered a psychotic breakdown, which, in tandem with his turn to antinuclear activism, led to his forced prolonged confinement in a psychiatric hospital. I am reading the exchange between Eatherly and Anders in the context of Robert J. Lifton and Greg Mitchell's *Hiroshima in America,* establishing a psychological link between the legacies of Hiroshima and the rise of fundamentalisms, including nuclear fundamentalism, in the United States.

Chapter 8, "Transspecies Selves: Intimacies, Extimacies, Animacies," expands the reflections on the molecular turn in the life sciences and its impact on the nuclear imaginary. In particular, it theorizes the role of phantasms of the mutant body and the concept of a transspecies self in the formation of nuclear subjectivities. I explore the challenge of Cornelia Hesse-Honegger's science art of mutant insects and her nonanthropocentric ethics of care and transspecies responsibility for addressing nuclear haunting from the future and related transgenerational responsibilities. Using Mel Chen's concept of "animacies" and "molecular intimacies," I suggest that the molecular turn reaches beyond the life sciences, generating a new episteme attuned to the increasing toxification of the planet and its organisms. In this respect, the critique of nuclear reason becomes part and parcel of a more encompassing critique of environmental reason.

Radioactive Ghosts ends with a coda on Samuel Beckett's *Happy Days*, a play Beckett originally set in a postnuclear landscape. I read *Happy Days* as a conceptual metacritique of environmental reason. Replete with references to catastrophic climate conditions, the play opens a unique perspective on planetary extinction. Invoking classical texts as rem(a)inders of the ruinous archive of a past civilization, *Happy Days* exposes the ability not to see what is right in front of one's eyes. We can't go on. We'll go on, not seeing what we do not want to see. Perhaps the most sinister diagnosis we may glean from a reading of Beckett's play is that, in facing the nuclear threat, humans are trapped in an ecology of denial and fear, the very hallmarks of negative hallucination.

It's November 26, 2018. As I write, a nuclear missive arrives in my inbox: "California Wildfire Likely Spread Nuclear Contamination from Toxic Site."[10] With a series of wildfires raging throughout California, the so-called Golden State is living its latest state of emergency. In Southern California, the Woolsey fire has burned nearly one hundred thousand acres in Los Angeles and Ventura Counties, causing excessive damage and resulting in three deaths. While the fire has received extensive news coverage, both nationally and internationally, a warning voiced by the group Physicians for Social Responsibility–Los Angeles (PSR-LA) has been largely ignored: the Woolsey fire may have started at the Santa Susana Field Laboratory (SSFL) site and released large amounts of radiation and other toxic substances into the air.[11] The SSFL, a nuclear research facility and former rocket engine test site, is located a mere one thousand yards from a reactor that experienced a partial nuclear meltdown in 1959. Burning through this site, the Woolsey fire has likely exposed millions of people living and working within a one-hundred-mile radius to airborne radioactive waste and toxic chemicals. The University of California, Irvine, where I work and live, falls well within this radius. PSR-LA's warning once again drives home the urgency of both revisiting nuclear politics and reviving a dormant antinuclear movement in our contemporary moment.

The Atomic Energy Commission was successful in its efforts to cover up the 1959 partial meltdown at SSFL, until students working with Daniel Hirsch, director of the Program on Environmental and Nuclear Policy at the University of California, Santa Cruz, discovered it in 1979. Hirsch and his students contended that lax oversight of the site resulted in widespread radioactive and toxic chemical contamination of soil and water. Meanwhile, the California Department of Toxic Substances Control (DTSC) issued a statement suggesting that the organization does not believe the Woolsey fire would have caused the release of hazardous materials. We are, of course, all familiar with similar official statements in the aftermath of nuclear-related catastrophes, including the disasters in Chernobyl in 1986 and Fukushima in 2011. Systematic cover-up is standard practice for the nuclear–military–industrial complex, even as studies like the one conducted by the Agency for Toxic Substances and Disease Registry in 1997 found a greater than 60 percent increase in cancer rates among communities surrounding the SSFL site.[12] Melissa Bumstead formed the grassroots organization Parents vs. SSFL after her daughter was diagnosed with a rare and aggressive form of leukemia and after meeting other families in the area also battling childhood cancer. On the matter of the DTSC's negligence in overseeing the SSFL site, Bumstead called the state agency a "disgrace to democracy." To this day, the findings and warnings of groups like PSR-LA and Parents vs. SSFL are largely ignored in mainstream media outlets. The silence that continues to envelop the dangers and risks posed by the nuclear–military–industrial complex is part and parcel of the sociopolitical and psychic infrastructures that shape planetary energy politics in the twenty-first century. And it is that silence—understanding it, interrogating it—that has animated me in developing this book.

INTRODUCTION

WHY NUCLEAR NECROPOLITICS TODAY?

SCIENCE FICTION: H. G. WELLS'S IMAGINARY ETHNOGRAPHY OF NUCLEAR WAR

> There are stories of puffs of luminous, radioactive vapor drifting sometimes scores of miles from the bomb centre and killing and scorching all they overtook. [. . .] Such was the state of Paris, and such on a larger scale was the condition of affairs in Chicago, and the same fate had overtaken Berlin, Moscow, Tokyo, the eastern half of London, Toulon, Kiel, and two hundred and eighteen other centres of population or armament. [. . .] In the map of nearly every country of the world three or four or more red circles, a score of miles in diameter, mark the position of the dying atomic bombs and the death areas that men have been forced to abandon around them. Within these areas perished museums, cathedrals, palaces, libraries, galleries of masterpieces, and a vast accumulation of human achievement, whose charred remains lie buried, a legacy of curious material that only future generations may hope to examine.
>
> —H. G. Wells, *The World Set Free*

The stories of these "spinning boiling bomb centres"[1] from which the above passage is drawn describe a world in the aftermath of nuclear war, a world of infernal toxicity and glowing ruins in which the dispossessed urban population lives in "blank despair."[2] It is a world replete with warnings that alert passersby to a "zone of imminent danger," that is, a "zone of uproar, a zone of perpetual thunderings, lit by a strange purplish-red light, and quivering and swaying with the incessant explosion of the radio-active substance."[3] The world these images evoke is captured in an "imaginary ethnography of the future,"[4] a speculative fiction written by H. G. Wells, the man who allegedly was the first to envision the fission of the atom and who invented a fictional atomic bomb more than two decades before the explosion of the first actual atomic bomb at the Trinity Test Site in the Jornada del Muerto desert. Published in 1914, *The World Set Free* is said to have inspired physicist Leo Szilard, a prominent member of the Manhattan Project, in conceiving the idea of the neutron chain reaction. The novel, which Szilard read in 1932, describes a uranium-based hand grenade the size of an orange that continues to explode indefinitely. Szilard asserted that it was Wells's novel that gave him a sense of what the liberation of atomic energy on a large scale would mean. Becoming increasingly obsessed with the possibility of chain reactions and the development of atomic bombs, Szilard regularly discussed his ideas with Winston Churchill, also an avid reader and acquaintance of H. G. Wells. Finally, in 1939, Szilard convinced Albert Einstein to sign a letter he had written to U.S. president Franklin D. Roosevelt warning him of the danger that Germany might develop an atomic bomb. Recommending that the United States start its own nuclear program, the letter was sent in August 1939 and resulted in the birth of the Manhattan Project.

Among the physicists participating in the Manhattan Project, Szilard was the first to promote the idea of building an atomic bomb. Szilard, Churchill, and Einstein were eventually tormented by their role in devising a weapon with such destructive potential. Einstein later declared that signing Szilard's letter to Roosevelt was the greatest mistake he had made in his life. After the dropping of the first atomic bomb on Hiroshima, Szilard tried to convince policy makers and fellow scientists that the world must forever abandon the idea of securing political goals by military means. Accurately predicting the arms race between the United States and the Soviet Union, he developed a vision of "permanent peace" that was once again inspired by Wells's *The World Set Free*, in which, in response to the horrors of atomic destruction, a world government is formed to guarantee international security.

The origins of the Manhattan Project can thus be traced to a fateful entanglement of science, speculative fiction, technology, politics, and psychology. From early on, there was a mystique about the atom and the ability to split it in order to release a truly superhuman amount of energy. Early atomic psychopolitics reveals people's speculative—if not entirely phantasmatic—capture by the idea of the bomb. There is a messianism in the Benjaminian sense of redemption that characterizes emergent fantasies about the atomic bomb's impact on world politics. Mobilizing the cliché of a redemptive rebirth from the ashes, scientists and politicians embraced the phantasm of the atomic bomb as a supreme instrument so terrifying that waging war would have to be outlawed forever. Wells's idea of a "world set free" in the aftermath of atomic destruction is symptomatic of a psychological reaction formation, if not moral inversion, that would come to mark the idea of the "war to end all wars" more generally.

In this context, however, we must recall that Wells's vision arises from the meticulous description of a nuclear death world in which atomic bombs continue to explode in perpetuity. What he calls a "zone of imminent danger" is reminiscent of the "zones of exclusion" created in the aftermath of Chernobyl—or, more recently, Fukushima—and indeed of what we might call "zones of exception" formed under the rule of a sovereign's work of death more generally. Wells's "world set free" evolves in a transitional space of survival within the ruins of nuclear devastation that harbors the buried archives of human achievement and holds out hope for perpetual peace.

Radioactive Ghosts traces the multifarious entanglements of nuclear psychopolitics from the beginning of the Manhattan Project to today's renewed debates about limited nuclear war.[5] Using a wide range of nuclear archives, the book's particular emphasis lies in the politics of representation; the role of literature, film, and the arts; and more generally the fantasies and phantasms that form the nuclear imaginary and the vicissitudes of the nuclear unconscious. In close readings of a paradigmatic selection from these archives, *Radioactive Ghosts* explores affects and emotions, fears and desires, denials and messianic hopes, fantasies and phantasms, all of which aggregate to generate new types of embodiment, subjection, and capture that I refer to as *nuclear subjectivities*.

What distinguishes my inquiry from the thousands of books on nuclear politics is its focus on the impact of the nuclear age on psychic life. While I trace this impact in relatively broad terms, I do so by pinpointing paradigmatic instances that are symptomatic of a traumatic formation of subjectivity by the nuclear. In certain respects, *Radioactive Ghosts* falls within the genealogy started by Robert J. Lifton's pioneering book *Death in Life,* which was originally published in 1968. While Lifton conducts extensive interviews with survivors of Hiroshima and Nagasaki to provide empirical evidence for the pervasive nuclear trauma in the aftermath of the first atomic attacks, *Radioactive Ghosts* expands this focus, highlighting a diverse array of nuclear violence that impacts psychic life and leads to the shaping of nuclear subjectivities at a much broader level. Apart from actual sites of nuclear colonialism, war, or catastrophe—the nuclear borderlands in the American Southwest, Hiroshima, Nagasaki, Maralinga, Hanford, Three Mile Island, Chernobyl, and Fukushima—I also include sites of slow or structural nuclear violence.[6] I consider the latter to be virtually ubiquitous because the risks nuclear contamination poses to health—including cancers, reproductive damage, and pervasive nuclear trauma—inevitably affect psychic life in myriad ways, albeit, as I will show, disproportionately.

One of my basic assumptions is that the very invention and use of the first atomic bomb and the haunting knowledge of its power to annihilate planetary life have generated a rupture in "the order of things" that leaves a profound mark on psychic life.[7] We know that our species has invented a weapon with the capacity to contaminate the entire earth, including air, water, soil, and food. We know of this weapon's ability to destroy the human as well as other species. How can this knowledge not affect people in their entire existence? How can it not change their sense of who they are, their very sense of being in the world? How can it not affect how humans think about their place in the universe? And yet, we rarely think, let alone feel, this way. This blindness at the heart of the gravest danger humans have ever faced is part of what I want to explore. It is a blindness that entails diverse psychic mechanisms, such as denial, splitting, inversion, and reaction formation. It is this blindness that generates what I call the *nuclear unconscious*.[8] I indeed believe that the very knowledge of a possible nuclear annihilation, even if split off from conscious awareness, generates a qualitative leap in the collective shaping of subjectivities. It is also in this sense that I speak of nuclear subjectivities.

Philosophers and theorists like Günther Anders, Theodore W. Adorno, Georges Bataille, Michel Serres, Jacques Derrida, Jonathan Schell, and R. J. Lifton all assume that nuclearism (Lifton's term) affects every facet of our lives and psyches. The far-reaching implications of this assumption for the restructuring of subjectivity, however, have yet to be fully explored. Moreover, regarding the production of public nuclear knowledge, there is ample ground to speak of a *nuclear episteme* linked, as I argue, to an epistemology of deceit and denial. However, denial is a complicated issue. The official denial at the heart of nuclear politics forms only one side of a larger denial that includes self-deception.

Many do not want to think or even know about the full extent of the nuclear threat. And we would indeed not be able to live our daily lives, let alone enjoy them, if we did not succumb to a fair amount of psychic splitting. This means that we go on living as if the nuclear danger were not there. As a result of the splitting off of nuclear fears, living in a mode of *as if* is an essential feature of nuclear subjectivities. Ultimately this type of splitting is an adaptive feature that facilitates living in a nuclear world. But as a coping mechanism, splitting also creates a scarring psychic rift that is potentially threatening, not only because it causes the ontological insecurity of divided selves,[9] but also because it reduces the felt urgency for political action and resistance.

Eclipsing the nuclear threat from consciousness, splitting thus helps one to live without becoming paralyzed by fear. At the same time, however, splitting exiles those very fears into the nuclear unconscious, generating a haunting from within, thereby unconsciously impacting both people's sense of being and their actions. The nuclear unconscious, I argue, profoundly shapes the cultural, political, and indeed economic unconscious in the nuclear age. Most of us know, but do not necessarily act as if we knew, that even against our will, we structurally participate in the nuclear–military–industrial complex that extends its reach—again disproportionately—across the globe. Most of us do not want to know or think about how many of our tax dollars feed the nuclear war machine or the nuclear energy industry. Thus we become involuntary—and for many, indeed, voluntary—participants in nuclear violence, if not complicit bystanders in support of the nuclear war machine. How can this knowledge not affect our psychic lives? How can it not shape the very structuring of our subjectivities? And yet, this very fact remains largely shielded from public awareness.

Whenever I make this claim about the ubiquitous reach of the nuclear age and the qualitative leap it generates in the formation of nuclear subjectivities, I am asked about those people who never even think about, let alone worry about, the Bomb, or—to take the most extreme case—those who, like the disenfranchised people from remote areas in India mentioned by Arundati Roy in *War Talk*,[10] have never even heard about the atomic bomb and the first atomic war that destroyed Hiroshima and Nagasaki. Of course, one cannot say that all subjectivities are directly shaped by the nuclear age. However, one can say that their very lives are profoundly affected by it, even without their knowledge. The entire world has become part and parcel of the global nuclear economy and war machine. The people in India whom Roy recalls live in a country that faces a nuclear arms race with its neighbor Pakistan. While, in the age of global media, the number of people who are remote enough to remain "protected" from the knowledge of the nuclear threat is relatively small and shrinking, it is also true that even people who may have never heard of Hiroshima are already significantly impacted by the nuclear, be it at the level of nuclear geopolitics or at the material level of bodily harm through the increase in the planet's radioactive contamination.

Those, on the other hand, who are exposed to the media but brush their fears aside or succumb to trauma fatigue are all the more affected by the nuclear unconscious. The images of nuclear catastrophes from Hiroshima to Fukushima remain burned into people's minds, even if they do not consciously recall or feel affected by them. It is virtually impossible not to become numb, at least to a certain extent, to the now almost daily news of nuclear war talk or the frequent reports about irresolvable problems of nuclear reactors and the nuclear waste they generate. While one may split off these nuclear threats from conscious awareness, the images and words will leave their trace in the unconscious. Without knowing it, people may thus be haunted by unconscious nuclear fears, both individually and collectively.

Attending to the nuclear unconscious, therefore, is not just important mentally and psychologically; it also becomes a political task, because the nuclear unconscious contributes to removing the barriers to political awareness and action. To the extent that the nuclear provokes a genuine trauma, the formation of resistances, defenses, and denials is inevitable. This pertains to both the individual and the collective levels. Taking the nuclear unconscious into account thus means being attentive to the unsaid, to ellipses, catachreses, inconsistencies, and contradictions, in the rhetoric of nuclear discourses. It also means exploring the unconscious resonance that may be hidden at the surface of words and images. Finally, it means methodologically to telescope in and out from the particular to the general to assess how this unconscious manifests itself in specific geographic regions or geopolitical contexts, in gendered or racialized phantasms, or in the political unconscious of imaginary nuclear ethnographies of the future.

At a more general level, *Radioactive Ghosts* is also framed by the question of why it has become imperative to reconsider the centrality of nuclear politics and its work of death today. One of my basic assumptions is that nuclear politics has been haunted by denial, deceit, and forgetting. Forgetting plays a central role at both the individual and collective levels. Yet, we forget at our own peril. In his pathbreaking work on the rise of forgetting in the digital age, Andrew Hoskins traces instances of a pervasive forgetting of the nuclear threat, pointing out that in the public media, the consciousness of nuclear war has been displaced and forgotten three times: first, after the bombing of Hiroshima and Nagasaki; second, after the Cuban Missile Crisis; and third, after the Second Cold War and the fall of the Soviet Union.[11] Hoskins argues that these dangerous forms of forgetting lead to complacency: "namely, the removal of a widespread perception of the threat of nuclear war actually makes that war more likely."[12]

By recalling resistance movements as well as antinuclear theories and philosophies developed in the 1980s, *Radioactive Ghosts* counters the history of this triple forgetting that Hoskins identifies. But at the same time, I also ask why the concern with nuclear politics is reemerging with such urgency after having been eclipsed from public debate—if not relegated to the political unconscious—since at least the end of the Cold War? Why are scientists, politicians, and concerned citizens from all reaches of the globe beginning to fear the new nuclear turn in world politics, if not the specter of nuclear war? Finally, what does it mean in this context that, as I discuss later, this new nuclear turn is predominately cast in terms of a "limited nuclear war"? As a preliminary answer, I propose that, in addition to the politics of forgetting, there is also a politics of displacement at work in current discourses about limited nuclear war, a displacement designed to cover up the ongoing threat of total war, if not nuclear annihilation.

MATERIAL AND PSYCHIC LEGACIES OF NUCLEARISM

Emphasizing the suicidal madness of an all-out nuclear war is not to suggest that the vision of limited nuclear war was ever a viable alternative. Henry Kissinger, in "Force and Diplomacy in the Nuclear Age," had already insisted that wars could only be limited by political decisions that "define objectives which do not threaten the survival of the enemy."[13] And to this day, experts continue to insist that there is no guarantee that nuclear war could ever be containable.[14]

Since Hiroshima, when the United States was the only country in possession of the atomic bomb, the geopolitical terrain of nuclear politics has completely changed. As one of the protagonists put it in the 1983

ABC television film *The Day After*, "we are not talking about Hiroshima anymore. Hiroshima was *peanuts*."[15] To cite just one example among many, in *Thermonuclear Monarchy*, Elaine Scarry reports that, after the fall of the Berlin Wall, the United States added eight new Ohio-class nuclear submarines to the six already in existence, each of them carrying the equivalent in injuring power to four thousand Hiroshima blasts. Scarry depicts the alarming scale of this power: "the eight ships built since the fall of the Berlin Wall carry sixty-four times the total blast power expended by all sides in WWII. The launching, christening, and commissioning of these ships was not covered in news reports."[16] The politics of secrecy and deception thus includes the sheer unimaginable injuring power of nuclear weapons. The fact that these submarines spend most of their time under the surface in open oceans and thus become largely invisible and secluded from public scrutiny turns them into an almost perfect metaphorical embodiment of the nuclear unconscious.

As Scarry, among others, has pointed out, the Bomb's vast capacity to injure is utterly disproportional to the relative lack of public information,[17] including information about the myriad voices of dissent and antinuclear protests both at home and abroad. Insisting on the illegality of nuclear weapons both constitutionally and according to international law, Scarry reminds her readers that "in 1995, seventy-eight countries from the U.N. General Assembly asked the International Court of Justice to provide a judgment about the illegality and inhumanity of nuclear weapons."[18] The mainstream media in the United States silenced the voices of these foreign populations through sheer omission. Similarly, when the International Court of Justice debated the legal status of nuclear weapons on the basis of the United Nations charter and its "rules of proportionality" for international warfare, it did so, Scarry writes, by rejecting international protocol as inapplicable to nuclear weapons.[19] The days-long debates in the international court, she argues, never made the front-page news in the United States, just as the resistant voices of affected foreign populations as well as the occasional protest at home remain ignored.[20]

As the debates in the International Criminal Court about "rules of proportionality" reveal, the nuclear problem is also about scale. Speaking of "out-of-ratio weapons," Scarry concludes that weapons designed to kill millions of people cannot but fail to elicit proportional emotional responses. In part, she writes, "this reflects the nature of compassion:

public health scholars differentiate between our ready ability to feel 'compassion' for a solitary person and our inability to feel 'statistical compassion' when a large multitude undergoes far more excruciating forms of suffering."[21] As a consequence, Scarry argues that nuclear weapons have ceased to "have any interior psychological content. [. . .] It is as though they have ceased to be a center of suffering or a center of gravity."[22]

This complex psychological condition is, I argue, part of the psychological trauma that structures nuclear subjectivities. Scarry's analysis demonstrates how U.S. citizens have been disempowered for the last sixty years, becoming like the global population more generally, "frozen in structures of thermonuclear subjugation."[23] This subjugation is further aggravated by a collusive routinization of the fear and horror of a possible new nuclear war, a collusion that reinforces the repression of nuclear trauma—and the pervasive trauma fatigue—that marked the later decades of the twentieth century.

What Scarry only indirectly addresses, however, is the pervasive operation of the nuclear unconscious, that is, the capture by the nuclear in a mode of repression. We could indeed speak of a nuclear colonization of the mind, which, like all forms of mental colonization, operates at a largely unconscious level. Moreover, the nuclear state of exception and the subjugation that Scarry notes extend beyond the parameters of nuclear weapons and war to include the nuclear energy empire that generates radioactive contamination of the environment, ozone depletion, and the unmanageable proliferation of nuclear waste. In response to the growing global resistance, nuclear energy industries have developed a widespread politics of cover-up, deceit, and outright lies.

Since their earliest formation, antinuclear movements have been systematically mischaracterized as antinational and alarmist, if not pathological, and, most efficiently, as communist. Prominent leaders have faced investigations and discrimination, including the refusal to grant nuclear scientist Linus Pauling a passport to lecture abroad. Outspoken opponents of the nuclear war who criticized the atomic attacks on Hiroshima and Nagasaki were silenced. Claude Eatherly, for example, the pilot who took part in the atomic attack on Nagasaki and later became a prominent antinuclear activist, was, owing to the intervention of the U.S. Air Force, kept in a mental institution in violation of his psychiatrist's initial diagnosis that he was ready to be released.

In recent years, the nuclear industry has pushed a new myth that threatens to be more effective than the previous strategies of concealment: the myth that nuclear energy can help to save the planet from climate change and global warming. This myth has not only divided the scientific community, at least in the United States, but also taken hold of the public nuclear imaginary. When I lectured on nuclear politics in recent years, I was on various occasions confronted with the same question: "So, would you rather die of climate change?" The controversies about nuclear power's ability to reduce the pace of climate change are enormous, including among scientists.[24] While a full analysis of the relationship between nuclear energy and climate change is beyond the scope of *Radioactive Ghosts*, I want to address at least why the claim about nuclear energy as a safer form of energy is a myth. For this purpose, I will rely mainly on research commissioned by the World Information Service on Energy located in Amsterdam, the Netherlands. The report, titled *Can Nuclear Power Slow Down Climate Change?*, was published by Jan Willem Storm van Leeuwen in 2015; sponsored by the Greens in the European Parliament;[25] and supported by several organizations, including Sortir du Nucléaire (France), Women in Europe for a Common Future, Nuclear Information and Resource Service (United States), Ecodefense (Russia), Global 2000 (Friends of the Earth; Austria), Bürgerinitiative Lüchow-Dannenberg (Germany), and Folkkampanjen mot Kärnkraft-Kärnvapen (Sweden). Van Leeuwen first dispels the claim that nuclear power emits no greenhouse gases. Nuclear power in fact emits presently 88–146 grams of carbon dioxide per kilowatt-hour, and the emissions are bound to grow from the current level to values approaching fossil fuel generation within the lifetime of new nuclear facilities.[26] The nuclear industry does not currently report emissions of other greenhouse gases. As van Leeuwen states, "krypton-85, discharged by all nuclear power as well as reprocessing plants, generates greenhouse gases in the troposphere; in addition it causes other weather and climate changing effects."[27]

Another problem results from the predictable unrealistically high construction rates of nuclear power plants. As van Leeuwen reports,

> by 2060 nearly all currently operating nuclear power plants (NPPs) will be closed down because they will reach the end of their operational lifetime. [. . .] To keep the global nuclear capacity at the current level the construction rate would have to be doubled. [. . .] In view of the massive cost overruns and construction delays of new

NPPs that have plagued the nuclear industry for decades it is not clear how the required high construction rates could be achieved.[28]

Van Leeuwen also addresses the nuclear industry's promise to develop advanced nuclear systems, arguing that they would all have to rely on reprocessing uranium and plutonium to fabricate nuclear fuel. He insists, however, that "reprocessing is a complicated, highly polluting, and very energy-intensive process. Decommissioning and dismantling of a reprocessing plant after it has to be closed down requires massive investments of materials, energy and financial resources and likely will take more than a century of dedicated effort."[29]

Van Leeuwen affirms that "future nuclear power depends exclusively on the availability of natural uranium resources."[30] Moreover, since the average ore grade declines with time, "the nuclear system becomes an energy sink instead of an energy source: nuclear power falls off the energy cliff."[31] Van Leeuwen's report concludes with the following assessment: "Due to the *après nous le deluge* culture of the nuclear industry the health hazards posed by radioactive materials in the human environment will increase with time, in addition to risks of Chernobyl-like disasters and of nuclear terrorism."[32]

While van Leeuwen's report could not specifically consider additional economic factors that contribute to nuclear energy's unfeasibility as a viable alternative to fossil fuels, this is a point Helen Caldicott has repeatedly made in her work. The most fervent critic of claims that we need nuclear energy to offset climate change, Caldicott had already argued more than ten years ago—in her book *Nuclear Power Is Not the Answer*[33]—that the claim is unsustainable, even from the point of view of merely economic considerations. The money allocated to nuclear energy corporations, she argues, is systematically diverted from the mass production of renewable energy technologies, and "only these renewable technologies will have a positive effect to reduce global warming gases. As we know, the nuclear fuel cycle substantially adds to global warming."[34]

Caldicott makes the further point that global warming itself poses a serious problem for nuclear energy. Extreme weather events can heat up the rivers and lakes from which nuclear power plants extract their cooling water, while the extrusion of very hot water from reactors, in turn, poses a serious threat to aquatic life. Moreover, designed forty to fifty years ago, nuclear regulations do not even take global warming into account. As temperatures rise, so does the need for more electricity, thus creating a vicious cycle.[35] Finally, critics also argue that any debate about nuclear energy must consider the increased health hazards from the discharge of radioactive materials into the environment, the increasing chance of large nuclear accidents, the hazards from nuclear waste storage, and the risks of nuclear terrorism. I have discussed these arguments in detail here because the myth that nuclear energy can be used to offset climate change belongs, I argue, to the dangerous epistemology of deception, denial, and cover-up that marks nuclear politics.

The overall dangers posed by the nuclear energy industry and the nuclear weapons industry, which together form the nuclear–military–industrial complex, are affecting not only physical health but also mental health. The latter is rarely explored in the vast literature on nuclear politics. Accordingly, *Radioactive Ghosts* places its central focus on the nuclear impact on psyche and mind, or what I call *nuclear psychopolitics*, a politics that emerges from the entanglement of the political and the psychological in nuclear matters. Nuclear dangers, including the dangers resulting from the threat of nuclear wars, generate a chronic collective nuclear trauma. Usually concealed within the pervasive politics of denial, the risks from the already existing planetary radioactive contamination include not only skyrocketing levels of various cancers and other health problems like reproductive damage but also the transgenerational persistence of major forms of physical and psychological trauma. The psychic afterlife of the Bomb has, in fact, led survivors to question whether the damage done by the nuclear destruction of Hiroshima and Nagasaki can ever be repaired. Indeed, as Takashi Nagai, a survivor of Nagasaki, wrote, "today, we of Nagasaki, living on in the atomic wasteland, apply our energies to reconstruction. [. . .] Does it seem, then, that the deadly work of an atom bomb can be repaired? [. . .] We carry deep in our hearts, every one of us, stubborn, unhealing wounds. [. . .] It is this spiritual wreckage, which the visitor to Nagasaki's wastes does not see, that is indeed beyond repair."[36]

This "spiritual wreckage" is closely linked to another feature of nuclear politics and its "out-of-range weapons," namely, the sense that the kind of death faced by the victims of nuclear attacks is, in the words of the Hiroshima survivors interviewed by Lifton, a "false death."[37] The notion of a "false death" resonates with the experience of a "false dawn" described by an Acoma elder who witnessed the glaring light of the first nuclear test at White Sands. For the Hiroshima survivors, the sense of a false death emerges from the feeling that, in a nuclear world whose entire order has been shaken, the unprecedented possibility of total annihilation leaves the notion of natural death behind. Similarly, for the Acoma elder, the false dawn of atomic light competes with the natural dawn created by the rising sun. Humans have thus irrevocably dislodged the natural order of things. According to Robert J. Lifton, the most prominent theorist of psychic damage left in the wake of Hiroshima, the completely annihilating death encounter in an atomic attack prevents *hibakusha*—that is, the survivors of an atomic attack—from integrating the catastrophic experience as part of their ongoing self-process.[38] At the psychological level, nuclear politics thus includes an irreparable sense of annihilation at the core of psychic life. If Lifton calls this a "false death" or "double death," it is because it is an entirely unnatural psychic death that happens before the actual death of the body. This death will henceforth haunt the survivors of nuclear attacks from within like an uncanny double of natural death.

As historian Kate Brown argues in her seminal book *Plutopia,* at the material level, one of the legacies of the Manhattan Project is a rise of cancers in the United States by 85 percent, a fact that is hardly ever mentioned. This legacy affects not only the survivors of Hiroshima and Nagasaki but the survivors of the reckless nuclear tests in the American Southwest as well. Brown notes that this cancer spike constitutes a health epidemic: "Taken as a complex, the militarized landscape also helped produce health epidemics. In the United States from 1950 to 2001, the overall age-adjusted incidence of cancer increased by 85 percent. Childhood cancer, once a medical rarity, has become the most common disease killer of American children."[39] Reminding us that children are the most vulnerable targets of slow nuclear violence,[40] Brown also reports that in Russia, where cancer rates increased from 115 to 150 per 100,000 people between 1960 and 1985, only one-third of the infants are born healthy.[41] While radioactive contamination is not the only substance that has contributed to the planet's increasing toxicity, it is certainly the most crucial component in the rise of certain cancers, including blood and thyroid cancers. That this health crisis remains eclipsed from public debate is particularly scandalous now that we are witnessing a new push toward modernizing and increasing the stockpiled nuclear weapons and, concomitantly, as I discuss in chapter 2, toward resuming uranium mining in the American Southwest and elsewhere.

The systematic downplaying and silencing of the dangers that subtend nuclearism belong to the larger political history of secrecy and deceit that has from its very inception marked nuclear politics. During the Manhattan Project, for example, nuclear experts had already worked frantically to protect the secrecy of their attempts to manufacture the first nuclear weapons, including with such means as cover-up, willful deception, and corruption. This political history and epistemology of deception has also shaped governmental and corporate reactions to the major nuclear disasters of our time, Chernobyl and Fukushima. Public information often depends on alternative modes of knowledge production that include awareness generated by antinuclear activism or leakages by investigative journalists like Christopher Steele, who investigated the notorious assassination by radioactive poisoning of Alexander Litvinenko in 2006.[42] Steele is, incidentally, the former spy who also leaked the Russian government's attempts to influence the 2016 U.S. elections. According to a report in the *Telegraph,* an ex-KGB chief who allegedly helped Steele to compile his dossier on Trump was found dead in his car in Moscow.[43] If these stories read like nuclear crime fiction, it is because they illustrate how, at the level of both macro- and micro-politics, this history and its mechanisms of covert operation continue to form the very center of nuclear politics. Not surprisingly, it was crime fiction that first predicted assassinations with radioactive poison. Published just two years before Litvinenko's murder, Martin Cruz Smith's nuclear detective novel *Wolves Eat Dogs,* which I discuss in chapter 5, tells the story of a series of murders by radioactive poisoning in the aftermath of the Chernobyl nuclear disaster.[44]

More generally, the highly precarious leakages that periodically disrupt the nuclear politics of secrecy reveal how easily the secrets of nuclearism can travel across dangerous boundaries. Under the Trump administration, the explosive dynamic of secrecy and leakage plays itself out at the highest level of government. On May 24, 2017, media outlets reported that Trump revealed the locations of nuclear submarines near North Korea to Philippine president Rodrigo Duterte.[45] Obviously, this revelation goes against the U.S. Defense Department's interest in protecting the secrecy about the location of its submarines. Leaking the location of nuclear weapons therefore poses a potentially major threat to national security at various levels. As is blatantly obvious from the president's action, the volatility of nuclear secrets and the related dangers can no longer be considered merely accidental side effects but must be seen as part and parcel of what defines nuclear politics more generally.

However, one must also consider the broader context of this recent conflict with North Korea, which includes the role of China in what Aijaz Ahmad has called the "inauguration of an arms race on the Asian continent."[46] The latter, of course, involves long-term U.S. goals in Asia. With India and Pakistan as emergent Asian nuclear states, the Chinese—if not also the Western—nuclear monopoly has been challenged. While discussing the complexities of the Asian arms race goes beyond the scope and focus of *Radioactive Ghosts,* it warrants mentioning as part of an increasing nuclearization of the globe. This global expansion vastly increases the degree of planetary nuclear danger, environmental contamination, and ecological costs as well as the nuclear subjugation of ever more people worldwide.

One more incident warrants attention: in August 2017, the tension between North Korea and the United States escalated sharply after President Trump threatened to unleash "fire and fury like the world has never seen" against North Korea.[47] In more rational times, investigative journalist Allan Nairn argues, Trump's threats against North Korea would be an article of impeachment. Provoking North Korea and thereby risking destruction of part of the United States, Nairn affirms, is "violating the system's rules on its own terms. He's committing an actual threat against U.S. national security."[48] This development is, Nairn suggests, fully in line with what he calls a "rightist revolution" in the Trump administration designed to roll back racial justice and civil rights to pre-Reconstruction. Regarding the emphasis in *Radioactive Ghosts* on nuclear subjectivities, Trump's statement seems both crucial and frightening, because it brings the nuclear unconscious to the surface of a belligerent discourse: "fire and fury like the world has never seen" uses the specter of annihilation as a political weapon, thus openly revealing the fear (or desire) that usually remains covered up in discourses of limited nuclear war. Moreover, as I show later in my discussion of critical nuclear race theory, Nairn's assessment confirms the insistence of prominent African American antinuclear activists, including W. E. B. Du Bois, Paul Robeson, and Martin Luther King Jr., that the fight against nuclear weapons and war is inextricably bound up with the fight against racism and the fight for civil and human rights.

NUCLEAR NECROPOLITICS

Ranging from single events, such as leaks about the location of nuclear weapons, to the global threat of an all-out nuclear war, the aforementioned examples are designed to illustrate the need to revisit the legacy of the Manhattan Project to understand more fully its hold on the psychopolitical landscape of today's nuclearism. By 1942, the Manhattan Project was in full force under the direction of Major General Leslie Groves of the U.S. Army Corps of Engineers and employed more than 130,000 people.[49] The earliest discourses about the Bomb exhibited a messianic tone, offering a veritable mythology of salvation designed, even if unconsciously, to cover up its deadly force. Oppenheimer and his fellow scientists famously propagated the atomic bomb as the bomb to end all wars. Its invisible power was celebrated as a source of fascination, as if the bomb were able to blur the boundary between a lifeless material object and a living being. As Joseph Masco writes in *The Nuclear Borderlands*:

> nuclear materials are sources of invisible power. Radiation is colorless and odorless, yet capable of affecting living beings at the genetic level. In this sense, nuclear materials produce the uncanny effect of blurring the distinction between the animate and the inanimate, and between the natural and the supernatural.[50]

Analyzing the ghostly quality of plutonium as a metal that, in the minds of those who encounter it, assumes the animistic quality of organic life, Masco speaks of the "nuclear uncanny."[51] The nuclear uncanny forms the core of a proliferating imaginary that emerges as a long-term effect of living in the shadow of a global plutonium economy. It is part of the uncontainable psychosocial fallout that shapes the very structure of subjectivity by creating a haunting from the future for generations to come, if not the rest of planetary time. Being haunted by the knowledge of invisible yet potentially lethal toxins in one's body and those of future generations forced to live on toxic lands also creates a psychic toxicity[52] that often remains unacknowledged but becomes firmly anchored in the political unconscious.

This interplay between material and psychic toxicity and its impact on emergent nuclear subjectivities generates, in Masco's terms, "a new kind of trauma, one that corrupts the possibility of an everyday life outside the plutonium economy."[53] This is true not only for the Indigenous people Masco interviews but also for people worldwide, even those who have been kept in the dark about the nuclear threat. Today, the entire world lives inside the plutonium economy, an economy that affects everything, including not only the air people breathe, the water they drink, and the food they eat but also their psychic lives with their fantasies and fears. The hold the plutonium economy has over energy production (including psychic energy production) and the military-industrial complex worldwide generates diverse forms of slow nuclear violence[54]—contamination of air, water, and soil, with its health risks for generations to come—that profoundly affect major aspects of people's lives. At the same time, however, this global existential enclosure in an irreversible plutonium economy remains under erasure, as a persistent epistemology of deceit and denial causes most people to live their lives in a mode of *as if*—they live *as if* the danger of the plutonium economy were a thing of the past, or they live *as if* there still were a sustainable shared world free from the threat of nuclear annihilation. In "Wallace Stevens's Birds," Cary Wolfe analyzes this mode of "as if" as part of an "ecological poetics."[55] Recalling Derrida's assumption that art and poetry's function in a world without ontological security is to "make *as if* there were just a world," Wolfe links this poetic world-making to an uncanny hauntology that marks "our responsibility to those spectral ones who are not here, either already departed or not yet arrived."[56] This is precisely how I would describe the psycho-ontological position of major nuclear trauma in terms of a double haunting from the past—the spectral ones who have been incinerated in Hiroshima—and a haunting from the future: the spectral ones who have not yet arrived but might be born as mutant children or die in a future nuclear war. This, in other words, is the double haunting that we try to escape when we embrace living in a mode of *as if* or, as Stevens calls it, the "malady of the quotidian."[57]

The psychic splitting that facilitates a mode of living *as if* allows people to remain largely oblivious to the damage done by innumerable atomic tests in the United States and around the world, by the virtually irresolvable problems posed by nuclear waste and the real long-term dangers that threaten the survival of the human species. Psychic splitting and denial are the most pervasive defense mechanisms against nuclear fear. Exploring such defenses requires seeing them as part and parcel of a collective formation of new subjectivities that began to emerge with the specter of Hiroshima and Nagasaki.

One of my central goals in *Radioactive Ghosts* is to demonstrate that, in the shaping of the nuclear imaginary, the psychological is inextricably intertwined with the political. To understand more fully how nuclear culture has radically transformed the ways of being in today's world, one needs to analyze and understand the entanglement between politics and psychology in the shaping of nuclearism. Drawing on Achille Mbembe's seminal work,[58] I argue that nuclearism's work of death generates the psychopolitical formation that I call *nuclear necropolitics*.

The concept of necropolitics provides a productive framework for analyzing the new type of violence introduced by the invention of the atomic bomb. Necropolitics in general is defined by the relationship between sovereignty and the power over life and death. The nuclear age, I argue, adds a new and sinister dimension to this power. The power of nuclear weapons can now be used to dictate not only who may live and who must die from a nuclear attack but also how some people must live with and die a slow death from the lingering effects of nuclear contamination. Moreover, the haunting generated by the knowledge of a possible all-out nuclear war with the power to turn the entire planet into a huge necropolis extends nuclear necropolitics not only into psychic and mental life but also into the deep history of the future. Ever since the atomic bomb was first used on Hiroshima and Nagasaki at the end of World War II, we have lived under the shadow of nuclear necropolitics. Heralding the advent of the nuclear age, this new form of violence is in many ways similar to the necropower Mbembe theorizes in his essay "Necropolitics." Given that the ultimate expression of sovereignty resides in the power and capacity to dictate who may live and who must die,[59] we may ask how this necropower works specifically on a collective level in nuclear politics. While nuclear forms of necropolitical violence—for example, the creation of "sacrifice zones" for the testing of nuclear weapons or extraction of resources—do not necessarily target specific individuals or populations to die, as in genocide, they nonetheless use sovereign power to designate certain populations and the lands they live on as disposable. Such designations open both people and land for nuclear exploitation, even though it is well known that many of them will die as a consequence. This is why—as I discuss in detail in chapter 2—many Indigenous people consider nuclear politics to be a new variant of genocidal politics.

Military, corporate, and political powers act in these contexts like sovereigns, taking control over certain territories and domains of life (biopower). Valerie Kuletz, Ward Churchill and Joseph Masco analyze the use of this neocolonial power in the United States as a form of "radioactive colonization"[60]—a designation that highlights the predominate victimization of the country's Indigenous peoples living in what Masco calls the nuclear borderlands. In the United States, Indigenous peoples are disproportionately impacted by radioactive contamination that affects their lands, water, crops, and livelihood as well as their health with increased rates of cancer and reproductive problems, including birth defects. Finally, as I mentioned earlier, it affects their mental health with what Pueblo tribal leader Herman Agoyo calls the "psychic toxicity" that emerges from living in toxic environments. At a psychopolitical level, nuclear colonialism thus also entails a new colonization of the mind, establishing what Mike Davis refers to as a pervasive ecology of fear,[61] linked here not only to the threat to communal health but also to new forms of economic exploitation, oppression, and expropriation. And while nuclear colonialism affects Indigenous peoples more than other populations, this ecology of fear is also a ubiquitous feature of the global nuclear colonization of bodies and minds. Again, I maintain that this ecology of fear operates even in cases where the fear remains largely unconscious.

"War, after all, is as much a means of achieving sovereignty as a way of exercising the right to kill,"[62] writes Mbembe. Nuclear war extends this sovereign right to kill to encompass the entire globe so that nuclear necropower is ubiquitous, affecting not only the entire human species but other species as well. At its most extreme, it arrogates the right to kill life on earth. At the same time, however, nuclear necropolitics also shares with other necropolitical abuses of sovereignty the formation of states of exception that operate under suspension of the law.[63] Nuclear necropower thus operates simultaneously at two levels: on one hand, the large-scale level of deep history that culminates in the colossal and ultimately incomprehensible threat of the annihilation of planetary life, and on the other, the level of slow nuclear violence with its more specific targeting of particular populations, whether by design or by accident.

In a certain sense, both levels operate outside the scale of human comprehension. The threat of a possible global nuclear annihilation undoubtedly transcends the boundaries of human imagination, rendering a proportionate emotional response impossible. But what must also be taken into account is slow nuclear violence, which, while imaginable and even subliminally present as a threat, remains commonly—and to an extent inevitably—split off from the immediate concerns of everyday lives. Moreover, at both levels, the threats posed by nuclear necropolitics remain largely under the radar of public debates.

During the Manhattan Project, for example, an entire population was recruited under conditions of absolute isolation and secrecy to do the groundwork for the research of nuclear weapons. These workers themselves had no idea of the project's purpose, let alone that they were contributing to the manufacture of the first atomic weapons or that they were at their own risk handling one of the most toxic substances on earth, often without any protection. Moreover, few people know that, during the Cold War, to conduct research on the effects of radiation on the human body, eighteen human test subjects—all American citizens—were injected with plutonium without their informed consent. Detailed knowledge about these covert human plutonium experiments only became available in 1993 with the publication of Eileen Welsome's articles in the *Albuquerque Tribune*.[64] Moreover, as Kate Brown's research has revealed, both the U.S. and Soviet governments conducted secret radiation experiments throughout the Cold War. Scientists at the Hanford nuclear weapons complex in Washington State, for example, subjected 131 volunteer prisoners to X-ray experiments that damaged their sperm. At the end, they had to undergo compulsory vasectomies to prevent the fathering of mutant children.[65] Just as the Indigenous peoples living in the nuclear borderlands, these human test subjects had been designated as disposable, fit for unaccountable use as radioactive guinea pigs.[66]

Mbembe details the ways in which necropolitical sovereignty aims at "the generalized instrumentalization of human existence and the material destruction of human bodies and populations."[67] Nuclear necropolitics, as I understand it here, extends this sovereignty to target human bodies for killing in nuclear wars or to sacrifice them for the extraction of uranium, the manufacture of nuclear weapons, secret radiation experiments, pervasive radioactive contamination, or even covert political assassinations. Inextricable from the interests of neoliberal global capitalism and its modes of instrumentalization, as well as its more specific investment in nuclear power, nuclear politics is thus obviously deeply involved in the work of death. While the large-scale material effects of nuclearism operate on a transhuman, geological timescale, such effects are also transgenerational, as nuclear destruction encompasses damage to biological reproductive capacities and genetic heredity. This means that, beyond killing instantly, or slowly through radiation sickness or cancers, nuclear weapons also threaten long-term survival at the most basic material level, that is, the genetic makeup of organic life. In addition, the psychic transgenerational effects include a pervasive, if often unconscious, nuclear fear, a fear linked to what I call nuclear necropolitics' haunting from the future. In contrast to the transgenerational trauma caused by traditional war, where the trauma originates in a past violent history, transgenerational nuclear trauma encompasses past, present, and future. People live with the knowledge not only of the threat of future nuclear attacks but also of the devastating effects of nuclear contamination that extend over many generations into the distant future.

Nuclear necropolitics thus emerges from a particular negation of nature that by far exceeds the Hegelian reduction of nature to human needs. By splitting the atom—that is, the smallest constituent unit of matter—to release unfathomable energies of destruction, humans have irreversibly altered the entire planet and its atmosphere. While humans have throughout history created their world by transforming nature, the violence entailed in transmogrifying the atom to create a nuclear world simultaneously transforms the very parameters of life and death. If we follow Hegel's claim that the human being becomes a subject in the struggle and work through which he or she confronts the inevitability of death, we might similarly claim that, by confronting human beings with the possibility that they might become the agents of the ultimate death of planetary life, nuclear politics transforms the human species itself. As the only species that arrogates nuclear power, human beings are turned into nuclear subjects. In the aftermath of this transformation, all life, including psychic life, is subjugated to nuclear necropower. This is true even though this subjugation often operates only at an unconscious level. Moreover, the knowledge of a possible annihilation of planetary life as an effect of human action manifests as a psychopolitical reality that shapes humans even if it were never to happen. Because we, as the generations that inaugurated the nuclear age by inventing the technology capable of such destruction, possess the knowledge that human-induced extinction of planetary life is a possibility, subjectivity will always bear traces of the nuclear. Such knowledge will forever shape psychic life and burden humans with a hitherto unimaginable responsibility for the destiny not only of their own species but of other species as well. In this respect, the boundaries of subjectivity will henceforth necessarily also encompass the boundaries of other forms of planetary existence. (I unfold the implications of this claim in chapter 8.)

Mbembe elaborates his analysis of necropower through a comparison of Hegel and Bataille, writing that "Bataille firmly anchors death in the realm of absolute expenditure (the other characteristic of sovereignty) whereas Hegel tries to keep death within the economy of absolute knowledge and meaning."[68] Bataille's concept of expenditure and excess is helpful for understanding how nuclear necropower and its attendant forms of nuclear sovereignty are nourished by the fantasy of an expenditure so extreme that it is forever irreversible, a fantasy that ultimately culminates in the last death, the complete annihilation of life. In other words, the most defining characteristic of nuclear sovereignty is that it risks the entirety of planetary life. In "No Apocalypse, Not Now," Derrida went even further, asking whether we might not desire this all-out annihilation, even if only unconsciously. We may thus wonder whether the drive toward annihilation is not part of the cultural unconscious that propels the unrestrained militarism of the world's most powerful nations. As psychoanalyst Edward Glover has already warned in 1946, Hiroshima and Nagasaki have actualized the most extreme fantasies of world destruction, thus establishing a psychic—if not psychotic—breach in the boundaries between reality and fantasy, feeding into totalitarian fantasies of omnipotent power as well as, and paradoxically, immortality: "We will outlive them all!"[69]

Something of this absolute expenditure resonates in Oppenheimer's famous invocation after Hiroshima of the line in the Bhagavad Gita: "Now I am become death, the destroyer of worlds." It is this absolute expenditure with its excess, exuberance, and superabundance that contributes to generating the intensely overwhelming feeling of awe and horror that has been called the "nuclear sublime."[70] In light of this fascination with the Bomb as the ultimate expression of nuclear sovereignty and our species' capacity for destruction and self-destruction, it is hard not to link Bataille's concept of expenditure with the Freudian death drive. The nuclear sublime and the concomitant fantasies of the Bomb as a superhuman power able to transcend the boundaries of the human lie at the operative core of today's nuclear world. At its outer limits, nuclear necropower is an almost orgiastic embrace of the death of all life.

Indeed, if, as Mbembe argues, sovereignty requires the strength to violate the prohibition against killing, nuclear necropolitics radicalizes this logic. Mbembe defines the Bataillian notion of sovereignty as the "refusal to accept the limits that the fear of death would have the subject respect,"[71] so that the sovereign is "he who is, as if death were not."[72] Interestingly enough, such a refusal is precisely what Bataille called for as early as 1947 in "Concerning the Accounts Given by the Residents of Hiroshima."[73] Framed as a response to John Hersey's *Hiroshima*,[74] Bataille develops a concept of "sovereign sensibility" that raises fundamental questions about nuclear sovereignty and subjectivity. Asserting the "primacy of the instant" against being ruled by a concern for the future and a fear of atomic annihilation, Bataille proclaims categorically, "The man of sovereign sensibility is not unrelated to the birth of the atomic bomb."[75] Bataille makes this link precisely because the atomic bomb is a weapon of terror that for the first time in human history threatens with the specter of an all-out annihilation. The "man of sovereign sensibility" emphatically embraces the only way to escape nuclear terror: becoming he who is as if nuclear death were not. Trying to escape the limits imposed by the fear of nuclear death by performing a radical psychic splitting, the man of sovereign sensibility becomes, paradoxically, the supreme embodiment of nuclear subjectivity.

The primary goal and, indeed, ethics of Bataille's nuclear philosophy is thus "freeing the world from fear."[76] "A movement that carries me beyond limits is more helpful than an oppressive worry and a fear of the future," he states. "The powerlessness of this world, established by the primacy of action, and by the atomic bomb, the latest expression of this powerlessness, is obviously detestable."[77] We must keep in mind that Bataille's statements are made in response to the accounts given by the victims—or, as he calls them pointedly, the "residents"—of Hiroshima. In an almost shocking eclipse of conventional forms of compassion, Bataille also rejects sensory representations of the disaster, equating them with weakness and sentimentality. Regarding what he calls the "atomic effect" and its essential disproportionality, he resorts to a form of comparative victimhood, maintaining that whether we consider those killed by the atomic bomb or those dying of natural causes, "horror is everywhere the same."[78]

The difference is, of course, as Bataille acknowledges, that nuclear horror is preventable, while human mortality is not. Precisely this preventability then raises the question of evil. According to Adi Ophir's philosophical ontology of evil, the latter can be defined by the infliction of unnecessary suffering.[79] Bataille, however, would not subscribe to such an ontology. Placing his philosophy beyond good and evil, for Bataille, the only suffering that counts is one that is "quite close to pure animal sensibility,"[80] free from the limits of reason, fear, and concern for the future. This suffering—we could perhaps call it "bare suffering"—emerges from the liberation that comes for Bataille with the suppression of all hope for a world trapped in a corner, a world "doomed to abrupt metamorphosis."[81] Only this bare suffering is capable of creating the blending of extreme misery, ecstasy, and joy that, for Bataille, marks sovereign sensibility. It is a suffering that embraces the "Buddhist meditation on the boneheap"[82] with its fearless "morality of the instant": "I am. In this instant I am. And I do not want to subordinate this instant to anything."[83]

Ultimately, Bataille's sovereign refusal to accept the limits imposed by the fear of death is grounded in a relinquishing of any hope for a better future. This is of course also the end of political action. As he asserts, the sensibility that "enters the path of politics is always of cheap quality."[84] First and foremost a refutation of the ecology of fear generated by the atomic bomb, Bataille's resistance embraces a paradoxical morality of inhabiting the horror: "Let us lift, in the instant, a form of life to the level of the worst."[85] In the last instance, Bataille must embrace, paradoxically, "the level of the worst," that is, nuclear annihilation, if only to escape the regime of terror it imposes on the here and now.

Bataille's voice remains unique among the philosophers who have addressed what he calls the "atomic effect." One may wonder, however, if by embracing an attitude of inhabiting the horror, Bataille is truly able to escape the contradictions of what I have earlier called with Mbembe *nuclear sovereignty*. After all, the "man of sovereign sensibility" is confronted with the different sovereignty of the nuclear state. The latter, in fact, becomes his supreme adversary. Bataille's defiant rejection of fear thus requires more than inhabiting contradiction or even surviving in the ruins. It requires what Gayatri Chakravorty Spivak calls a "rearrangement of desire."[86] For Bataille, the latter is grounded in the liberation of desire from any future-oriented (affective) politics. If the renunciation of the limits imposed by the fear of death is indeed the hallmark of sovereignty, Bataille's concept of "sovereign sensibility" thus displaces sovereignty from politics to psychic life. Thus internalized, sovereignty marks the very structure of subjectivity and affect.

How, then, can this sovereign sensibility confront the devastating conditions of the sovereignty of the nuclear state, that is, nuclear sovereignty proper? The latter, we could say, not only refuses to accept the limits imposed by fear of death but also extends this refusal by rejecting even the limits that the fear of an all-out nuclear war and the death of all life would impose. Nuclear sovereignty, in other words, ultimately refutes the prohibition against killing the entirety of life on earth. Yet, "he who is, as if death were not" is, I argue, a sovereign in a position of radical psychic splitting, one who lives in denial of death, including his own work of death.[87] As a precondition, the latter requires relinquishing the concern for the future. Bataille's concept of sovereign sensibility is thus designed to master nuclear terror by refuting fear.

There is, however, a form of sovereignty that is born from a resistance of a different kind, one that refutes and conquers fear *because* of a concern for the future. Interestingly, this form of sovereign sensibility emerged from the black resistance movement in response to the history of slavery, continued racist and racial oppression, and infringement on civil rights. African American poet and activist Jayne Cortez writes, "Death, you are death no more. [. . .] Liberation in my head. Liberation in my eye. [. . .] I have killed fear and my soul is on fire."[88] For this impassioned resistance, the path of politics is not always of cheap quality as it is for Bataille. On the contrary, it is an unruly mode of survival that refutes the fear of death to embrace a fight for life and liberation. As Ayi Kwei Armah avows, the latter inevitably entails a deep concern for the future: "What are we if we see nothing beyond the present, hear nothing from the ages of our flowing, and in all our existence can utter no necessary preparation of the future way?"[89] This resistant politics beyond despair requires a sovereign sensibility of a different kind, one which—as I discuss in detail in chapter 3—will actually lead black and Indigenous activist leaders to a forceful conjoining of the civil rights movement with a global antinuclear resistance. Perhaps these resistance movements offer steps toward the "different principle of sovereignty" Bruno Latour is calling for when he returns to the question "in the name of what supreme authority have we agreed to give our lives—or, more often, to take those of others?"[90]

If I have argued that Bataille's "man of sovereign sensibility"—he who is as if death were not—presupposes a position of radical psychic splitting, we need to acknowledge, however, that living in the nuclear age inevitably generates such a position. It is, in other words, foundational for the formation of nuclear subjectivities. Melanie Klein, the psychoanalyst who developed the first fully fledged theory of splitting, distinguished a first stage in infant development marked by what she calls a "paranoid-schizoid position." In this stage, in which the infant internalizes good objects and externalizes bad (persecutory) objects, a

Manichean horizontal splitting becomes the basis for dividing the world into good and evil. As Robert Meister argues in *After Evil: The Politics of Human Rights,* Klein's theory generates a "moral psychology of splitting."[91] By contrast, we could say that the psychology of splitting that facilitates Bataille's sovereign sensibility is a vertical temporal and affective splitting between present and future.

The latter, in fact, marks nuclear subjectivities more generally. To go on living in the everyday, the threat of a possible future nuclear annihilation needs to be split off, at least temporarily. The nuclear subject "is, as if (nuclear) death were not." Only thus can the minimal sovereignty required for everyday life be maintained. Radical psychic splitting therefore defines not only the condition of nuclear sovereignty but also the condition of living in today's nuclear world. As I will demonstrate, *all* humans have become nuclear subjects, including those left in the dark about the dangers of nuclearism. Short of utter despair and paralysis, nuclear subjects need to live as if the specter of all-out nuclear war and destruction were not (or no longer) imminent. No one can live in today's world without a massive amount of splitting and psychic numbing. On one hand, such psychic splitting is politically necessary to sustain nuclear—as well as other forms of—necropower. If successful, this splitting cuts subjects off—even if only temporarily—from fear, compassion, love, anger, or grief. On the other hand, splitting is also psychically necessary to live within an ecology of nuclear fear. We would no longer be able to function in our quotidian lives if our emotions were proportionate to the violence, cruelty, and danger of a nuclear world. The nuclear has contaminated the most basic emotions, either numbing them completely or replacing them, as the *hibakusha* Lifton interviews insist, with "counterfeit" ones. The "false dawn" or "false death" experienced in the wake of nuclear explosions also "falsifies" psychic life. Apart from chronic fear, this falsification too is a central aspect of "psychic toxicity."

The nuclear age has further refashioned the boundaries of human subjectivity and communal relationality by increasing the power of death on earth and, more specifically, by introducing what Jonathan Schell famously calls "the second death."[92] Schell insists on the crucial importance of a qualitative distinction between two forms of death, namely, the natural death of an individual within a species, on one hand, and the death of a species by extinction, on the other. For humans—the species responsible for creating the conditions that propel extinction and the only one capable of imagining it—this second death entails facing the death of mankind.[93] In the event of a nuclear holocaust, however, the two forms of death merge:

> In extinction by nuclear arms, the death of the species and the death of all the people in the world would happen together, but it is important to make a clear distinction between the two losses; otherwise, the mind, overwhelmed by the thought of the deaths of the billions of living people, might stagger back without realizing that behind this already ungraspable loss there lies the separate loss of the future generation.[94]

Nuclear necropolitics thus performs a double work of death, namely, mass killing and the potential extinction of the species. Or, to put it differently, nuclear necropolitics doubles the work of death with the work of extinction. As Schell writes, "death is only death; extinction is the death of death."[95] To think this way, however, entails posing the question, what do future generations mean to those of us among the living? This question concerns the currently living because, as Schell puts it, "no generation before ours has ever held the life and death of the species in its hands."[96] Within the parameters of nuclear necropolitics, sovereignty thus means more than arrogating the right to decide which individuals, communities, or nations will live or die. It also means deciding, by design or accident, whether the human species, if not planetary life, will live or die.

In the context of imagining extinction,[97] it is important to remember that nuclear necropolitics is only part of a much more encompassing environmental necropolitics. As Schell argues, nuclear danger is an *ecological* danger that has to be considered in its entanglement with other ecological threats to planetary life: "The nuclear peril is usually seen in isolation from the threats to other forms of life and their ecosystems, but in fact it should be seen as the very center of the ecological crisis."[98] The reason Schell insists on the centrality of the nuclear crisis, however, is its "unique combination of immensity and suddenness."[99] It is this feature, the potentially annihilating power of nuclear war, that challenges the limits of human imagination and emotional comprehension. And, I argue, it is this challenge that engenders denial, including the denial inherent in the wishful fantasy that humans can remain in control of the power they have unleashed with the splitting of the atom.

LIMITED NUCLEAR WAR AND THE LEGACIES OF THE MANHATTAN PROJECT

> The technetronic era involves the gradual appearance of a more controlled society [. . .] dominated by an elite, unrestrained by traditional values. [. . .] Persisting social crisis, the emergence of a charismatic personality, and the exploitation of mass media to obtain public confidence would be the stepping-stones in the piecemeal transformation of the United States into a highly controlled society.
>
> —Zbigniew Brzezinski, *Between Two Ages*

This passage taken from Brzezinski's 1970 study of the United States' role in shaping twentieth-century technocratic global culture provides an alarming framework within which to situate the rise of a new phase in U.S. nuclear politics. As I am writing, we are on the verge of another arms race, if not another Cold War. In an article titled "We're 30 Seconds Closer to 'Doomsday,'" published after the fateful election of Donald Trump, Stephen Schwarz, a nuclear policy expert and editor of the *Nonproliferation Review*, told the *Los Angeles Times*, "I lived through the tense and dangerous early to mid-1980s; it's the reason I made understanding, controlling and eliminating nuclear weapons my career. [. . .] I have no desire to go backward to that era."[100] Doomsday predictions have long been part and parcel of nuclear politics. Every year, the *Bulletin of the Atomic Scientists*, a journal founded in 1945 by the very scientists involved in the Manhattan Project,[101] publishes an assessment of the so-called Doomsday Clock, which is purported to measure how close the world is to midnight, that is, to global nuclear catastrophe. In 2017, the clock was moved ahead to two and a half minutes before midnight, the closest it has been since 1953—the early days of the aboveground testing of nuclear weapons. Among the reasons given for moving the Doomsday Clock forward, the group of atomic scientists mentioned that President Trump's "intemperate statements, lack of openness to expert advice, and questionable Cabinet nominations have already made a bad international security situation worse."[102] Kingston Reif, director for disarmament and threat reduction policy at the Arms Control Association in Washington, added, "Put simply, the fate of tens of millions depends in part on the good judgment and stability of a single person. The president, and the president alone, has the supreme authority to order the use of nuclear weapons. Responsible leaders understand that the use of nuclear weapons is a terrible and likely catastrophic game-changer. There can be no winners in a nuclear war."[103]

When I started this project on nuclear politics a few years ago, I still assumed that I would need to open with a detailed discussion about why the threat of nuclear war, the dangers of nuclear power, and the damaging effects of storing nuclear waste belong to the most pressing political issues of our contemporary moment. I thought I would have to make a case for why the concern about nuclearism[104] needs to be included among today's various and vital ecological concerns, including climate change; the contamination of environmental resources; the devastation of lands, livelihoods, and health; the new water wars; the skyrocketing of abject poverty and social abandonment; and the increasing global production of disposable peoples, species, languages, and forms of life. It was not that the nuclear danger had ever disappeared—indeed, far from it. But it had gradually disappeared from the center of public awareness and debate, increasingly so after the fall of the Soviet Union in 1989. As Elaine Scarry, for example, meticulously documents in *Thermonuclear Monarchy,* nuclear politics and the dangers of nuclearism have been systematically silenced. Until the recent resurgence of the threat of nuclear war, now widely discussed in the media, the omission of nuclear issues from U.S. news reports was virtually ubiquitous. For example, as Scarry reports, the antinuclear resistance of foreign populations, including a 1995 petition to the International Court of Justice by seventy-eight countries to illegalize nuclear weapons, has received virtually no coverage in the U.S. media.[105] But the silencing also includes a pervasive epistemology of denial manifested, for example, in the "population's collective, nearly tour-de-force ability to abstain from mentioning aloud our own nuclear weapons."[106]

At a deeper level, the silencing of nuclear debates in the media is linked to delusional fantasies of control over both nuclear war and nuclear power. Related debates about limited nuclear war, which first emerged in the 1950s, have been revived with full force today. World War II was the first war that forced the enemy into total submission. In dropping the atomic bombs on Hiroshima and Nagasaki, the United States targeted civilian populations directly, introducing hitherto unimaginable terror and killing on a mass scale. These first nuclear weapons killed both instantly and slowly. Yet, we need to remember that, despite the unfathomable magnitude of material and lethal destruction, this was what policy makers call *limited* nuclear war.

In their preface to the edited volume *On Limited Nuclear War in the 21st Century*, Jeffrey Larson and Kerry Kartchner open with the following statement: "While the threat of all-out nuclear war has diminished, the likelihood that nuclear weapons may be used in some way is increasing. This assessment is widely shared, and has become almost axiomatic among policy makers and within the strategic studies community."[107] In his contribution to the volume, titled "Post-Cold War US Nuclear Strategy," Paul Bernstein further invokes a "'flexible, globally focused war-planning process' designed to respond to 'spontaneous threats which are more likely to emerge in a new international environment unconstrained by the superpower standoff.'"[108] A new specter is haunting global strategic planning communities, namely, the specter of nuclear rogue states and nuclear terrorism. Specialists argue that enhanced types of nuclear capabilities are needed to confront adversaries armed with weapons of mass destruction. This has led to a call for a "nuclear transformation" that entails modernizing the nuclear weapons production and enhancing the readiness for new underground tests.[109]

While the Obama years initially brought a paradigm shift in post-Cold War thinking, with Obama arguing for "peace and security of a world without nuclear weapons,"[110] this vision did not last very long. In light of so-called regional nuclear flashpoints, such as India–Pakistan, Israel–Iran, and, more recently, North Korea, as well as the possibility of new nuclear weapon states and nuclear terrorism, the pressure toward modernizing nuclear weapons and preparing for the viability of a limited nuclear war continues to increase. Nuclear policy and research expert George Quester pointedly wonders whether we are witnessing the end of the "nuclear Taboo."[111] Larson and Kartchner actually go so far as to speak of "the implications of US strategic culture for psychologically readying the country"[112] for a limited nuclear war.

Larson and Kartchner's book was published before the presidency of Donald Trump changed the discourses on limited nuclear war. Soon after his election, on December 23, 2016, Trump made his infamous statement on a new nuclear arms race that reverberated around the globe: "Let it be an arms race, because we will outmatch them at every pass and outlast them all."[113] He uttered these shocking words on MSNBC's *Morning Joe* after cohost Mika Brzezinski asked him to clarify his stance on expanding the U.S. nuclear arsenal. As Michael Walsh of the *New York Post* reported, Trump's reply indicates that, rather than restricting himself to upgrading the existing weapons system, he in fact considers the amassment of more nuclear weapons to be a top national priority. With his further assertion that nothing was off the table when it comes to nuclear weapons and the boastful threat mentioned earlier—"They will be met with fire and fury like the world has never seen"—he openly embraces a politics that fuels a new global nuclear arms race, vastly increasing the possibility of nuclear war.[114] Needless to say, Trump's policy on nuclear weapons undermines the decades-long U.S. policy regarding nuclear weapons, including the Treaty on the Nonproliferation of Nuclear Weapons (NPT), which went into effect in 1970 and includes commitments from almost two hundred countries.[115]

The debates about limited nuclear war and the need to modernize the nuclear weapons arsenal mark a new turn in the assertion of nuclear sovereignty. To maintain its necropolitical power, nuclear sovereignty needs to generate conditions of exception and emergency and a fictionalized notion of the enemy. Today the paradox resides in the fact that the countries that have nuclear power need to invoke other countries' nuclear capacity to maintain and expand their own arsenals. Ever since the fall of the Soviet Union, the U.S. rhetoric, once divorced from Cold War politics, has targeted a more diffuse, dispersed, and, importantly, racialized enemy. The specter of terrorism, including nuclear terrorism, and the fabrication of nuclear weapons by so-called rogue states are endlessly invoked to legitimize nuclear sovereignty.

We are indeed living in a phantom-like world of racialized terrorism, fashioned at the intersections of race and religion around the figure of the Muslim terrorist.[116] Mbembe refers to the Nazi state as the most complete example of a state exercising the right to kill. The project of the Final Solution, he argues, became the "archetype of a power formation that combined the characteristics of the racist state, the murderous state and the suicidal state."[117] The feasibility of an all-out nuclear war raises the specter of an entirely different "final solution"—that is, a nuclear one that would simply exterminate most planetary life. In an all-out nuclear war, the murderous state merges seamlessly with the suicidal state. Indeed, the very concept of an all-out nuclear war is built on the premise of mutual suicide or mutually assured destruction (MAD). In a world order where politics is "the warlike relation par excellence,"[118] sovereignty is based, Mbembe argues, on the will to kill in order to live. Nuclear politics anchors this will in a precarious hope of survival, namely, the hope that we will, in Trump's infamous words, "outlast them all." The very fantasy of outlasting all other nuclear nations, however, is built on the delusional belief that—paradoxically—at least one of the perpetrators of nuclear aggression will survive and that it will not be the enemy.

In these omnipotent phantasms of annihilation, nuclear necropolitics radicalizes the links between modernity and terror. The two kinds of nuclear terror—the haunting from the future of nuclear war and the "slow terror" of the ubiquitous radioactive contamination of land, water, air, foods, and bodies, as well as the danger of nuclear accidents—operate in tandem. Slow nuclear terror is intimately tied to radioactivity's invisibility, that is, its role as a silent killer that affects bodies in hidden ways at the molecular level of cells and genes. In this respect, nuclear terror functions as a new instantiation of the biopolitical experimentation so central to sovereign power. The survivors of Hiroshima and Chernobyl, for example, experienced a state of exception that hit them, like the victims of slavery in the earlier times of global imperial modernity, with a triple loss: loss of home, loss of rights over their bodies, and loss of social and political status. Ultimately, this form of social abandonment and social death resembles an expulsion from humanity. In the case of the Chernobyl disaster, survivors with radiation sickness—especially those who were dying—were forcibly isolated. More generally, radiation victims were often shunned as potential carriers of radioactive contamination. Outcast, survivors lived a form of death-in-life, harboring a silent killer inside their bodies and nuclear fear in their minds and hearts. When Alexievich states after her interviews with Chernobyl survivors "I felt like I was recording the future,"[119] she alludes to the fact that today's zones of exception may well become the norm in a world of perpetual war.

Zones of sacrifice and exception are zones of radical abandonment in which people and lands are treated as disposable. This aspect of nuclear sovereignty implements a racial politics based on the calculus of disposability. In a nuclear world, the specific terror formation Mbembe calls necropower operates more subliminally than early modern colonial violence, partly because it is a power that operates within a culture of invisibility and secrecy. Just as radiation itself operates as an invisible killer, nuclear necropower seeks invisibility, concealing, if not denying, its status as power and colonizing force.

Mbembe's analysis of resource extraction and exploitation in African states is helpful for understanding similar processes in the Indigenous U.S. Southwest as well as around Pine Ridge. According to Mbembe, the concentration of activities connected with the extraction of valuable resources resulted in the generation of privileged spaces of war and death. "War itself is fed by increased sales of the products extracted. New linkages have therefore emerged between war making, war machines, and resource extraction."[120] Nuclear war machines emerge from the collaboration between governments, the police apparatus, and the secret service as well as corporations involved in mining uranium and producing nuclear weapons. Often these corporations have their own private security apparatus. Nuclear war machines, therefore, combine the features of corporations with those of political and military institutions and organizations. In the United States, most nuclear war machines operate on Indigenous lands where labor and uranium become coerced resources. While the conditions in Africa on which Mbembe focuses are different from those in the United States—especially regarding the generation of economic enclaves with financial support from transnational networks—the so-called Second Wounded Knee in Pine Ridge in 1973, which was initiated by members of the American Indian Movement as they occupied the town of Wounded Knee in South Dakota, is, as I discuss in chapter 2, an example of the mobilization of a nuclear war machine within the United States.

Part of the occupation at Wounded Knee was related to the targeting of the Pine Ridge Reservation for uranium mining.[121] If Hiroshima and Nagasaki were the first global nuclear death worlds, then Pine Ridge can be seen as one of the first regional nuclear death worlds in the United States. To fuel the extraction of uranium, nuclear war machines forge connections with transnational nuclear power networks. In *Hiroshima in America,* Robert J. Lifton and Greg Mitchell write, "Nuclear weapons thus take their place in the dominant technology of a permanent, self-propelling American megamachine that seems almost independent of human control."[122] This American nuclear megamachine defines, in short, the core of nuclear necropolitics. The fact that this machine tends toward becoming independent of human control should make it abundantly clear that nuclear necropolitics is inseparable from a psychopolitics that deals with nuclearism's pervasive psychic damages in the present as well as the haunting from the future of its multifold transgenerational legacies.

To face such haunting requires people today not only to imagine extinction while at the same time resisting the lure of apocalypticism but also to learn to imagine thinking and communicating across immense scales that extend over millennia. To think and care about planetary futures ultimately requires humans to relinquish their anthropocentric rootedness in a temporal thinking that focuses on conceivable human life-spans. This challenge has profound implications for the formation of psychic life within the parameters of nuclear subjectivity. In *Deep Time*, Gregory Benford writes, "Tempocentric notions of 'the human condition' do not survive."[123] Nuclear waste alone demands, he argues, "that we mark sites for times longer than the age of our civilization."[124] To think about the condition of human and planetary life in the nuclear age thus requires the formation of nuclear subjectivities trained to think across such vast temporal scales. Not surprisingly, it is the technology of "radioactive dating" that has helped scientists to enhance such scalar imaginings. What I call *haunting from the future* supplements Benford's analysis of the chasm that has opened in modern history, a chasm between the deep longing for perpetuity that is ubiquitous across the diverse histories of civilization, on one hand, and a fundamental fear that emerges with the awareness that human civilization now has the power to annihilate most, if not all, life on earth, on the other. It is a tension, Benford writes, between a longing to "extend across time some lasting shadow of the present"[125] and an "anxiety about the passing of all referents, the loss of meaning."[126]

The "passing of all referents" is—as I further develop in chapter 6—a deeply rooted fear that marks nuclear literature and criticism and has become a staple of the nuclear archive. In Nevil Shute's apocalyptic novel *On the Beach*,[127] for example, the few remaining survivors of a nuclear holocaust spend their last days planting a garden or rebuilding an old Ferrari. These activities are no longer destined to satisfy human needs for food or transportation; they are monuments of sorts, testimonies to their lives, albeit not addressed to future generations. Planting and building become mute gestures, cast into the abyss of a planet void of life. And yet, the last humans continue to build. They continue to live in a mode of *as if* there were no end to the world. Building itself has become the sole purpose, the only remaining consolation for the humans awaiting the annihilation of life on their planet.

In my most apocalyptic moments, I see nuclear necropolitics as having created a brave new world of thanatocracies, a world that depends on instantiations of governance in which policies lead, directly or indirectly, to death or an increased risk of death. However, unlike the Egyptian thanatocracy built by the pharaohs, who organized society around death to hold open a portal to eternity, today's thanatocracy—that is, nuclear necropolitics—emerges from the specter of nuclear annihilation, that is, the enactment of policy organized around mass killing, if not extinction, through the imminent possibility of nuclear war.

Let me end with a few reflections on the profound ambivalence that marks the apocalyptic imaginary. Like an all-out nuclear war, the apocalypse can only be imagined within the parameters of a rhetorical condition. The apocalyptic imaginary can all too easily be co-opted for all kinds of purposes. Moreover, as the rich history of literatures, artworks, films, and popular culture that imagine extinction demonstrates, the lure of the apocalypse reaches deep into the unconscious. Nuclear disaster sites have become popular tourist attractions. Hollywood continues to mesmerize its audiences and saturate the cultural unconscious with racialized tales of apocalyptic war machines and what Mike Davis calls the "fascist apocalyptics of survival fiction."[128] These fictions combine racial hysteria and xenophobia with anxieties about the decline of empire.[129]

This said, however, we also need to acknowledge the political urgency of imagining extinction. The latter generates a haunting from the future that can only be ignored by a denial operating in collusion with the epistemology of (self)-deception that marks nuclear politics. The challenge, then, is to imagine possible forms of extinction without succumbing to the lures of an apocalyptic imaginary. While the latter looms large in the formation of nuclear subjectivities, it remains confined to a paranoid-schizoid world that precludes a politics of mourning. The world before the nuclear age is not mourned because the ontological break that ended it remains eclipsed from consciousness, and possible future worlds cannot be mourned because the ontological insecurity generated by nuclear fear and the specter of extinction is relegated to the political unconscious. Such splitting feeds not only denial but also a psychologically inevitable widespread disaster fatigue, if not disaster amnesia.[130] In this context, apocalyptic phantasms propel a return of the repressed, albeit one that often comes in the domesticated form of either illusory survival or melancholic attachments to omnipotent visions of extinction. Both, I think, are fueled by the autoimmune logic of the death drive that finds its ultimate satisfaction in species suicide.

By contrast, most of the works that initially theorized the psychology of the nuclear age and the specter of extinction without succumbing to the lures of an apocalyptic imaginary were written between the late 1940s and the 1980s. Many inspired both philosophical debates and antinuclear activism. Those that profoundly shaped the theoretical framework of *Radioactive Ghosts* include Robert J. Lifton, Jonathan Schell, Günther Anders, and Jacques Derrida. While they will figure prominently in laying the foundations, I will also revise and/or expand them in light of a broader range of theoretical perspectives as well as relevant contemporary critical theories, including most prominently those related to the molecular turn in the politics of life.

Part I

NUCLEAR SUBJECTIVITIES

ONE

NO APOCALYPSE, NOT NOW

Derrida and the Nuclear Unconscious

> The breaking of the mirror would be, finally, through an act of language, the very occurrence of nuclear war. Who can swear that our unconscious is not expecting this? Dreaming of it? Desiring it?
> —Jacques Derrida, "No Apocalypse, Not Now"

Derrida's provocative invocation of the nuclear unconscious may serve as a stepping-stone toward a larger exploration of the legacies of the Manhattan Project and its impact on the formation of subjectivity. The nuclear age, and especially the memory of Hiroshima and Nagasaki, the Cold War, and the antinuclear resistance movements, as well as nuclear disasters like Chernobyl and Fukushima continue profoundly to mark the cultural imaginary and nourish the fantasies and phantasms that structure nuclear subjectivities. Nuclearism marks the formation of subjectivity so pervasively that it presents a challenge to reconceptualize all notions of the subject and its environment, including psychoanalytic ones. My goal in this chapter is to outline some initial steps toward a psychoanalytic theory of nuclear subjectivity and the nuclear unconscious.

"Just as the unsuspected reality of the subatomic world contributed to changing science's conception of itself, so the reality of environmental processes must lead psychoanalysis to change its own conception of itself as both scientific and therapeutic,"[1] writes Alan Bass in his analysis of Loewald's "Psychoanalysis in Search of Nature." Insisting that a psychoanalytic theory of unconscious processes needs to be grounded in a theory of nature, Loewald states, "Nature is no longer simply an object of observation and domination by a human conscious mind, a subject, but an all-embracing activity of which man, and the human mind in its unconscious and sometimes conscious aspects, is one element or configuration."[2] If Freud demonstrated that the conscious mind couldn't directly perceive psychic reality, the concept of nuclear subjectivity requires one to extend the limits of perception to include material reality. While the materiality of radioactivity is literally invisible, those affected by it, and especially those who die from it, experience it as deadly vibrant matter.[3] Moreover, the scale of possible nuclear destruction and the half-life of nuclear waste are so magnanimous that they transcend the very boundaries of human time and imagination. In this respect, nuclear subjectivities assume an almost allegorical function in relation to the transindividual subject-formation in today's precarious ecologies. The material world, including nature as well as technoscientific objects, can no longer be seen as an outside to this subject-formation. Rather, the boundaries between the subject and the material and immaterial forces that it encounters are continually renegotiated in processes of dynamic exchange.

These processes also challenge conventional notions of objectivity in psychoanalysis. Seen from the perspective of Loewald's theory and its elaboration by Bass, conventional assertions of objectivity appear as a defensive attempt to control the dynamic exchange between inner and outer nature by rendering it static.[4] In this respect, the traditional objective sciences follow the genealogy of the (Western) colonizing project of dominating and domesticating nature. According to Bass, the mind's substitution of static objects for differentiating processes to create perceptual certainty is a form of fetishism. Psychoanalysis, Bass argues, offers by contrast a "powerful theory of the intersection of mind and nature."[5] As he points out, this ecology favors *natura naturans* (nature as active process) over *natura naturata* (nature as the assembly of created objective entities). In other words, this ecological theory, which indeed forms a dynamic "ecology of mind" in the Batesonian sense, belongs to the genealogy of postmodern and fluid onto-epistemologies.[6] Matter and, more specifically, material objects, including textual or artistic materialities, are endowed with an impersonal agency that becomes as formative of the ego and the unconscious as the fantasies and phantasms that emerge from the subject's encounter with them. We know about nature and reality, argues Loewald, by "being open to their workings in us and the rest of nature as unconscious life."[7] According to Loewald's notion of nature as unconscious life, the traditional subject–object opposition belongs to a prepsychoanalytic conception of mind. The origin of individual psychic life is a transindividual field that includes not only others but also nature more generally.[8] Arguing that Loewald supersedes the oppositions of psychic and material reality, Bass writes, the "psychotic 'core' of preoedipal dynamics opens psychoanalysis on a psychological level to the kind of subatomic world that was opened up for physics."[9]

In a similar vein, I am using a dynamic psychoanalytic theory of nature to inform my understanding of nuclear subjectivities, including the phantasms engendered by the nuclear imaginary. At the same time, however, the concept of nuclear subjectivity also requires rethinking the psychoanalytic theory of life and death in the context of today's nuclear necropolitics. To the best of my knowledge, it was Jacques Derrida who first addressed the issue of a "nuclear unconscious." In his rarely discussed and early essay "No Apocalypse, Not Now," published in a 1984 special issue of *Diacritics* entitled *Nuclear Criticism,* Derrida speaks of the possible future occurrence of nuclear war, asking the pointed question, "Who can swear that our unconscious is not expecting this? Dreaming of it? Desiring it?"[10]

I recall, when I first read "No Apocalypse, Not Now," stumbling over the provocative "desiring it?" Could there truly be an unconscious desire for the occurrence of an all-out nuclear war? Then I recalled having found a possibly related fantasy about nuclear annihilation a few years prior in Jonathan Schell's *The Fate of the Earth,* in which he wondered whether "there might actually be something consoling in the idea of having so much company in death."[11] I asked myself whether we could have truly reached a point where the idea of our extinction as a species might be perceived as a consoling fantasy. Are such fantasies symptoms of our subjection to the nuclear sublime, or do humans try desperately to construct consoling objects to ward off apocalyptic fears? Most of us have also heard the assertion that, if humans were to become extinct, the planet and other species would be much better off.[12] Does such a fantasy generate a comparable form of consolation? On the other hand, wouldn't the unconscious desire for nuclear annihilation be the ultimate manifestation of the death drive? Insisting that we can only apprehend nuclear war as a rhetorical condition, Derrida emphasized its function as a fantasy, a phantasm. What role does the nuclear imaginary play in the formation of subjectivities and subjections after World War II and the inauguration of the so-called nuclear age with the bombing of Hiroshima and Nagasaki? If these and similar questions have lost nothing of the urgency they had more than three decades ago, they may provide an indication as to why it behooves us to return to some of the debates and movements about nuclearism from the 1980s—if only because at that time in history the psychopolitical awareness of the nuclear threat was so much more pronounced and alive than it is today. Derrida's claim, made in the 1980s, still rings true even after the end of the Cold War arms race that engendered and was engendered by the nuclear imaginary he invokes: "No single instant, no atom of our life (of our relation to the world and to being) is not marked today, directly or indirectly, by that speed race."[13]

More than three decades later, we still live with the legacy of the Manhattan Project and the fantasies and phantasms of nuclear destruction. While the overt Cold War has ended with the collapse of the Soviet Union, we now live in the shadow of debates about limited nuclear war, fears of rogue nuclear attacks, and nuclear disasters like those at Three Mile Island in 1979, Chernobyl in 1986, and Fukushima in 2011. Revisiting Derrida's essay helps to raise a series of questions regarding the psychopolitical impact and transgenerational legacies of the Manhattan Project and the nuclear necropolitics that emerged in its wake. The current nuclear age is marked by global nuclear power industries; the irresolvable problems and dangers of storing nuclear waste and stockpiling as well as modernizing the nuclear weapons arsenal; and finally, the specter of the production of nuclear arms by so-called rogue or terrorist states. More recently, during the Trump presidency, the time is once again marked by the ghostly rhetoric of nuclear war, if not threatened by his hubris of boasting with "fire and fury like the world has never seen."

More than thirty years ago, Derrida reminded us that not only does the phantasm of nuclear war trigger the "senseless capitalization of sophisticated weaponry" but it also affects "the whole of the human socius today, everything that is named by the old words culture, civilization, *Bildung, schole, paideia.*"[14] Not much has changed in this respect, only that, except in the immediate aftermath of nuclear disasters, or more recently, in the wake of nuclear posturing by Donald Trump and Kim Jong-un, the discourses of nuclear war and catastrophe have been largely, if not systematically, eclipsed from public debate. Why, for example, does the important global antinuclear movement of Indigenous peoples, which I discuss in chapter 2, not gain more traction in the public media? Why are the voices of concerned scientists, doctors, scholars, writers, and public intellectuals muted in the mainstream media? It is hard not to suspect a deliberate politics of secrecy, concealment, and deceit. Have we managed, as Derrida feared, to domesticate the terror of the death-machine?[15]

The present is defined by a need to face the legacies of a world in which peace has often meant the continuation of war by other means.[16] To the extent that the notion of peace can even be maintained, it has become inextricably entangled with the threats of nuclear war, nuclear disasters, and the nuclear imaginary that emerges from these threats. Yet, as shown in the testimonies of those for whom such nuclear threats have become a reality, namely, the survivors of Hiroshima, Nagasaki, Chernobyl, and Fukushima, even those who have gone through the horrors of nuclear disaster cannot escape the phantasmatic relationship to the nuclear that Derrida places at the center of his analysis. Looking at such phantasms highlights the impact of the nuclear imaginary in sharper profile. The very testimonies of survivors of nuclear catastrophes, for example, can be read as paradigmatic for the formation of postnuclear subjectivities more generally.

I use the term *postnuclear subjectivity* in reference to the subjectivity of survivors of nuclear attacks or disasters. This particular subject-formation pertains to survivors of Hiroshima and Nagasaki just as it does to survivors of Chernobyl and Fukushima or other nuclear disasters. However, this is not to say that the condition of these survivors is exclusively postnuclear. Rather, in addition to their nuclear trauma from the past, they inhabit an enhanced haunting from the future generated by the fear of a repetition of the horror they have already experienced in the past.[17] Just as the postcolonial condition does not mean the complete end of colonialism, the postnuclear condition does not mean the end of nuclearism. The necropolitical violence that characterizes both colonialism and nuclearism continues, even after the demise of the official colonial regime of occupation, after the end of a nuclear war, or in the aftermath of nuclear disaster. The term *postnuclear* is crucial, however, to marking the specific condition of actual victims whose transgenerational nuclear trauma is different from that of potential future victims. The haunting from the future, however, affects both—the immediate victims of nuclear catastrophe and those who witness it from a distance, that is, all those who live in the nuclear age. Everybody born after 1945 lives in a world haunted not only by the ghosts of past nuclear violence but also also by the ghosts of the radioactive contamination that haunts

FIGURE 2. Michael Light, *061 HURON*, in *100 Suns*, 2003. Photograph courtesy of Michael Light.

lives and bodies as well as the specter of looming future nuclear disasters. A nuclear hauntology thus needs to be part of a comprehensive theory of nuclear subjectivities. The objects and phenomena that pertain to such a hauntology are manifold, entangled, and multiscalar. They are material and immaterial, invisible, mobile, and invasive. The ghostly material matter, moreover, is endowed not only with a deadly vibrancy but also with such a threatening longevity that it exceeds the boundaries of human imagination and will in all likelihood outlast the lifetime of the species. No one has grasped the haunting materiality of the nuclear better than Michael Light in his photo series *100 Suns*. In the picture titled *061 HURON*, atomic light appears spectral and unearthly in its terrifying fusion of beauty and annihilation.

Regarding the spectral qualities of the nuclear imaginary, even the very stockpile of nuclear weapons and the growing masses of buried yet undead nuclear waste take on a ghostly quality themselves. Nuclear weapons that are decommissioned but not destroyed are called "zombie bombs." Antinuclear activists call the abandoned uranium mines "zombie mines." Traci Voyles writes, "The notion that the uranium industry could be seen as zombie-like—as *undead*—provides a compelling metaphor that suggests connections to larger systems of threat. [. . .] Environmental and social ruin have turned the planet into a visceral kind of haunted house, a closed ecosystem haunted by cyborgs, ghosts, cannibals, zombies, and the dead."[18] She then concludes, "We are indeed haunted by the ghosts, zombies, and monsters inherent in these apocalyptic technologies and they do not stay put—they radiate out from polluted geographies in ways that insist on drawing new maps of toxicity."[19] With Karen Barad, we could add that "our atomic past not only haunts the present but is alive in the thickness of the here and now. [. . .] Hauntings are not immaterial, and they are not mere recollections of reverberations of what was. Hauntings are an integral part of existing material conditions."[20] The atomic past, then, is doubly alive: in the material haunting of the land, the water, the air, and the bodies of humans and other species by radioactive toxicity and in the immaterial psychic haunting or psychic toxicity, which, in turn, often manifests in material effects, including psychosomatic and mental illnesses. It is this characteristic of radioactivity, namely, that it will remain materially alive in the here and now as well as in the future—its being ontologically an "undead" materiality—that distinguishes nuclear hauntings from the haunting of other violent histories. This very quality creates what I have been calling "haunting from the future."

Hauntings are thus extremely complex psychic manifestations. Nuclear haunting from the future provokes a highly ambivalent oscillation between apocalyptic fears and their counterpart, a reaction formation that inverts the disaster by refashioning the aftermath of catastrophe as a rebirth, if not—as the testimonies of Chernobyl survivors, for example, illustrate—a creation of a postnuclear Eden. The oral histories of nuclear survivors reveal that the phantasms that aggregate around the nuclear imaginary range from apocalyptic to idyllic scenarios. The power of an apocalyptic imaginary is related to a haunting from the future that comes from the global destruction of sustainable ecologies. By contrast, the fantasies of a postnuclear idyll are survival fantasies, designed to ward off the fear of the devastating short- and long-term effects and the fear of repetition. While such fantasies are, of course, the product of powerful denial, they also have the adaptive function of splitting off the fear to carve out a living under the most threatening and precarious conditions.

At the same time, however, it is necessary to disentangle the apocalyptic imaginary from notions of a haunting from the future. "No Apocalypse, Not Now" was written at the height of the nuclear arms race. Derrida insists that the massive stockpiling and capitalization of nuclear weaponry and the (apocalyptic) fantasies of a nuclear war are not two separate things.[21] Calling the nuclear war "an event whose advent remains an invention,"[22] Derrida invokes a haunting from the future that requires one to rethink the relationship between knowing and acting. Imagining nuclear war seems to become a precondition for (collective) actions that may be able to avert it. Yet, the imagination of a remainderless destruction depends on the performative and persuasive power of texts, discourses, and figurations. As Derrida writes, "the worldwide organization of the human *socius* today hangs by the thread of nuclear rhetoric. [. . .] The anticipation of nuclear war (dreaded as the fantasy, or phantasm, of a remainderless destruction) installs humanity [. . .] in its rhetorical condition," concluding that a remainderless destruction forecloses any cultural or symbolic "work of mourning, with memory, compensation, internalization, idealization, displacement, and so on."[23]

In fact, apocalyptic fantasies can, as Karen Barad warns, be mobilized to cover up the undeclared nuclear war on the planet that has been going on since 1945: "In our 'postatomic age,' time is synchronized to the apocalypse-to-come, and the present is caught in a pose of holding its breath in an attempt to forestall the onset of nuclear war, as if it had ever been a thing of the past. This singular sense of temporality is fixed and fixated on the event horizon of total annihilation, calibrated to fear and the elision of the ongoingness of war in our hypermilitarized present."[24] Apocalyptic fantasies can also contribute to a pervasive foreclosure of mourning the losses and injuries already incurred by nuclear attacks or disasters. It is precisely the unavoidable and apocalyptic undertones of nuclear rhetoric that make it so immensely vulnerable to commodification. The uncanny attraction to the nuclear imaginary has generated its own rhetorical and figurative history. Thirty years after the catastrophic events at Chernobyl, for example, the site has been exploited for astounding waves of disaster tourism, as more than fifteen thousand people a year visit Chernobyl and the nearby town of Pripyat. The areas have become the sites of films, novels, and an apocalyptic imaginary that draws on the lure of the "nuclear sublime."[25] This imaginary is marked by a fundamental ambivalence. On one hand, there is the voyeuristic fascination with emergent forms of life in Pripyat's postnuclear zone of exclusion, with the ruins of a repopulated nuclear ghost town, and even with the mutant bodies of humans and animals. On the other hand, there are survivors—often the poorest of the poor— who return to Pripyat with a pervasive desire to recast the disaster zone as an idyll of freedom, survivors who refashion and reappropriate the zone of exclusion outside the law on their own terms, generating a new conviviality with other species and a flourishing of new life philosophies. Francesco Cataluccio speaks of a "postnuclear optimism,"[26] expressed in assertions that, around Chernobyl, plant life seems to thrive, the fields are planted again, and people have moved back to the contaminated areas.

Both the commodification of a nuclear aesthetic of ruins and the phantasmatic reconstruction of the disaster zone as an idyll of freedom bear upon Derrida's insistence on the "fabulously textual"[27] nature of the nuclear and the question of how to get speech to circulate under the conditions of life in zones of nuclear toxicity and/or overshadowed by the threat of a stockpile of nuclear weapons that could destroy planetary life. "Nuclear weaponry depends," Derrida writes, "more than any weaponry in the past, it seems, upon structures of information and communication, structures of language, including non-vocalizable language, structures of codes and graphic decoding."[28] We may ask, then, how literary or artistic works, or even oral histories and "ethnographies of the future,"[29] relate to apocalyptic phantasms and the foreclosed mourning of the loss of life, health, and communal infrastructure in nuclear zones of exception, on one hand, and the threat of a remainderless destruction, on the other? What kind of intervention does the figuration of nuclear disasters in literary and artistic works or in oral histories make in shaping the nuclear imaginary? Derrida links literature and nuclear war through the "paradox of the referent." Like nuclear war, literature is "constituted by the same structure of historical fictionality, producing and then harboring its own referent."[30] Derrida concludes that, because literature and nuclear war share this self-referentiality, literature and literary criticism must be obsessed with the nuclear, albeit not in a naively referential sense: "If, according to a structuring hypothesis, a fantasy or a phantasm, nuclear war is equivalent to the total destruction of the archive, if not of the human habitat, it becomes the absolute referent, the horizon and the condition of all the others."[31] While, according to Derrida, the symbolic work of culture and memory, their work of mourning, limits and softens the reality of individual death, the "only referent that is absolutely real is thus of the scope or dimension of an absolute nuclear catastrophe that would irreversibly destroy the entire archive and all symbolic capacity."[32]

Remainderless destruction is, of course, part of the pervasive yet deeply ambivalent apocalyptic imaginary of nuclear war. The ambivalence results from the fact that, given the destructive potential of nuclear weapons, we can't afford not to imagine extinction; yet we can also not afford to succumb to the lures of the apocalyptic imaginary. This ambivalence creates an inescapable double bind: the refusal to imagine extinction would amount to buying in to the politics and epistemology of denial and (self-)deception; succumbing to the apocalyptic imaginary, on the other hand, would amount to buying in to the ecology of fear and annihilation that enables nuclear necropolitics in the first place. The challenge therefore consists in imagining extinction while at the same time avoiding the secondary gratifications of sensationalizing apocalypticism. Since there seems to be an almost instinctual attraction to the apocalyptic, not unrelated to the death drive, changing the modalities of imagining extinction may well require a rearrangement of desire and unconscious attachment to visions of the end times.

Under the paradoxical compulsion to imagine the unimaginable catastrophe of extinction, literature's most primordial impulse seems to be to produce "concord fictions,"[33] that is, fictions that convey the sense of such an ending in ever-new modes of indirection by inventing, as Derrida describes it, "strategies of speaking of other things, for putting off the encounter with the wholly other."[34] Because of this paradox of referentiality, Derrida believes that the "nuclear epoch is dealt with more 'seriously' in texts by Mallarmé, or Kafka, or Joyce, for example, than in the present-day novels that would offer direct and realistic descriptions of a 'real' nuclear catastrophe."[35] Just as in the case of the Holocaust, survivors and critics of nuclear disaster have invoked the trope of unrepresentability. The question of indirection as a response to the limitations, if not inadequacy, of quasi-realistic representations profoundly shapes debates about nuclear fiction.

More specifically, apocalyptic texts and films, and the apocalyptic imaginary in general, inevitably entail a symbolic domestication of the ultimate threat of nuclear destruction. They may perform a displaced anticipated mourning of the end of our planet and of human life along with that of most other species, but they cannot convey the horrors that Derrida describes in terms of an "absolute self-destructibility without apocalypse, without revelation of its own truth, without absolute knowledge."[36] Perhaps the difference between the more narrowly referential works about nuclear disasters and the experimental texts Derrida invokes lies in the fact that the former try symbolically to contain the terror of remainderless destruction, while the latter try to evoke them via structural approximations, indirections, and displacements. Samuel Beckett, for example, uses indirection to evoke a possible nuclear catastrophe in such works as *Endgame, Happy Days, The Lost Ones,* and *Catastrophe.* He traces the nuclear imaginary as it manifests in the dark comedy of humans who are haunted by the vague and brittle knowledge of the likelihood of catastrophes that would end the precarious lives on their planet. Evocative rather than referential, and performative rather than conclusive, Beckett's visions thus radically undercut the familiar thrills and consolations the apocalyptic imaginary is able to offer. It is the very darkness of Beckett's texts and plays that is replete with a haunting from the future. *Happy Days,* which will be the subject of a coda to end *Radioactive Ghosts,* might be the play that comes closest to grasping the rhetorical condition of the nuclear and its impact on the formation of nuclear subjectivities. Pushing the sense of the nuclear as a rhetorical condition to its limit, Beckett explores the contagion of language by the nuclear, a contagion that affects speech and communication, revealing that they have become obsolete in a world in which the old "wonderful lines"[37] are trapped in catachresis yet are the only language that remains.

Beckett's *Happy Days,* however, is also a play that offers a paradigmatic ethnography of the future. *Radioactive Ghosts* is more broadly concerned with how the nuclear as a rhetorical condition affects not only the oral histories of survivors or, for that matter, the process of writing in theory about the nuclear but also the formation of nuclear subjectivities in the nuclear age more generally. Nuclear subjectivities emerge within the larger context of today's increasingly spreading necropolitical spaces around the globe. Nuclearism may well be the most radical instantiation of necropolitics, not only as far as the technologies and scope of nuclear weapons and their destructive potential are concerned but also in the immediate as well as transgenerational psychological impact of the nuclear threat. In this context, nuclear fictions assume allegorical valence in relation to a haunting from the future and a world to come that, while anticipated by a nuclear imaginary, has entered the space of the real with catastrophes such as Hiroshima, Nagasaki, Chernobyl, and Fukushima. To understand the connection between necropolitics and a neoliberal economy based on resource extraction, we need not merely a "political ecology," as Latour has described, but also an ecology that encompasses economy and psychology.[38] Only such a psychopolitical ecology can account for the rhetorical condition of the nuclear that forms the center of Derrida's reflections.

To return to the chapter's epigraph, referring to nuclear war, Derrida asks, "Who can swear that our unconscious is not expecting this? Dreaming of it? Desiring it?"[39] This seminal provocation reminds us that the question of the death drive looms large in theories of nuclear subjectivities, just as it looms large in Mbembe's theory of necropolitics. In the closing chapter of *Rogues,* entitled "To Arrive—At the Ends of the State (and of War and of World War)," Derrida returns to a reflection on sovereignty's right to exception, including the "right to decide on the exception and the right to suspend rights and law."[40] The "zones of exception" established in the wake of Chernobyl and Fukushima testify to the workings of nuclear sovereignty in states of emergency. Derrida also addresses the tendency to annul or neutralize the eventfulness of an event in order to immunize oneself against it. From this perspective, the pervasive denial of the danger of nuclear annihilation might be seen as an attempt to immunize oneself against apocalyptic nuclear fears. In an age of nuclear necropolitics, to "free not only thought but scientific research from the control or conditioning to which it is subjected by all sorts of political, military, technoeconomic, and capitalist powers or institutions"[41] undoubtedly requires a sustained critique of nuclear reason. In this respect, it seems no coincidence that Trump opposes both scientific research and intellectual labor in his attempt to consolidate his necropolitical sovereignty. As far as nuclear nations are concerned—and the United States is foremost among them—nuclearism has always been mobilized to protect the sovereign power of the nation-state. However, the sovereignty of nuclear nations, that is, nuclear sovereignty, is also deeply affected by what Derrida describes as the fragility and precariousness of "nation-state sovereignty." If, for the latter, "tense, sometimes deadly, denials" are "manifestations of its convulsive death throes,"[42] then we must ask what role the politics of denial that marks nuclear culture plays in relation to national sovereignty. Wouldn't it seem that, to secure their already precarious sovereignty, nuclear nations would have to renounce the denial, deceit, and outright lies that have marked nuclear necropolitics from its very inception?

Derrida argues that, in the age of globalization, concepts such as war, world war, enemy, and even terrorism should be losing their pertinence. Unfortunately, they are currently reasserting themselves on the stage of world politics with a vengeance, doing so despite the new forms of autoimmune violence that Derrida describes:

> Air or surface missiles, chemical, bacteriological, or nuclear weapons, covert infiltrations into computer networks ("cyber attacks")—all these weapons can destabilize or destroy the most powerful apparatuses of the state. Yet such weapons now escape all control and all state oversight. They are also no longer at the sole disposal of a sovereign state or coalition of sovereign states that protect one another and maintain a balance of terror, as was the case during the Cold War [. . .] so as to exclude [. . .] any suicidal operation. All that is over. A new violence is being prepared and, in truth, has been unleashed for some time now, in a way that it is more visibly suicidal or autoimmune than ever.[43]

It is in this context that Derrida introduces the death drive and the logic of unconscious desire. His reflections in *Rogues* allow one to return once again to his question whether we might not unconsciously desire an all-out nuclear war. In *Rogues,* Derrida links the death drive to "this poisoned medicine, this *pharmakon* of an inflexible and cruel autoimmunity."[44] Derrida's insistence on the death drive begs the question whether there is a truly autoimmunitarian logic at work in nuclear necropolitics. To put it differently, the sought-after immunity of nuclear nations, exemplified most succinctly by its radical manifestation in the (short-lived) establishment of the United States as the one and only nuclear nation, would, under conditions of nuclear necropolitics, spiral out of control. The alleged immunity would eventually collapse into an autoimmunitarian logic that is, I would argue, ultimately already at the heart of the idea of mutually assured destruction (MAD).

Derrida argues that "the indivisible sovereignty of the nation-state is being more and more called into question, along with the immunity of sovereigns."[45] Highlighting the indissoluble connection between sovereignty and war, Jonathan Schell, in *The Fate of the Earth* and *Abolition,* names the invention of the nuclear weapon as the single most important force that calls sovereignty into question. Nuclear weapons were born into the sovereignty system, he insists, but have become the most profound challenge to the system of sovereign nation-states:

> One might say that they appeared in the world in military disguise, for it has been traditional military thinking, itself an inseparable part of the traditional political thinking that belonged to the system of sovereignty, that has provided those intentional goals—namely, national interests—in the pursuit of which extinction may now be brought about unintentionally, or semi-intentionally, as a "side effect." The system of sovereignty is now to the earth and mankind what a polluting factory is to the environment. The machine produces certain things that its users want, in this case national sovereignty—and as an unhappy side effect extinguishes the species.[46]

Tied to the nuclear threat, sovereignty becomes the internal enemy, that is, a systemic form that propels self-destruction. We need to understand, Schell insists, "what nuclear weapons have done to war, and, through war, to the system of sovereignty of which war has traditionally been an indispensable part."[47] But we also need to understand, Schell adds, that the nuclear "peril comes from our own actions—from within us. [. . .] The peril of extinction by nuclear arms is doubly ours: first, because we have it in our power to prevent the catastrophe, and, second, because the catastrophe cannot occur unless, by pursuing our political aims through violence, we bring it about."[48] Given that, in the nuclear age, nations live in terror of annihilation, Schell finally concludes, "The world now has to decide whether to reject sovereignty and 'war' [. . .] and institute global political arrangements that would arbitrate international disputes or to try to shore up sovereignty with the use or deployment of nuclear weapons."[49]

The choice Schell describes here bears a distinct resemblance to the one H. G. Wells presents in *A World Set Free*. We recall, however, that in Wells's science fiction scenario, humans only gave up the sovereignty of nation-states in favor of a world government after a nuclear world war had already destroyed all major cities and much of the planet. Given the destructive force of today's nuclear weapons, the likelihood that humans will still have a chance to renounce the sovereignty of nation-states after a nuclear war is minimal. Schell points out that so far humans have historically opted to risk extinction rather than giving up the sovereignty of nation-states. Consequently, he sees only one solution for the work of survival: "global disarmament, both nuclear and conventional, and the invention of political means by which the world can peacefully settle the issues that throughout history it has settled by war."[50] If this sounds utopian, it is, according to Schell, the only way to pursue at all costs the "desire that the species survive."[51]

Schell's vision would presuppose both a political revolution and a rearrangement of desire. To juxtapose the desire for the survival of the species and the unconscious desire for nuclear annihilation that Derrida invokes in his essay has far-reaching implications not only for the reshaping of the boundaries of nuclear subjectivities but also for the psychopolitical implications of living within the structures of national sovereignty. From a psychodynamic point of view, the agonistic entanglement of the desire for both survival and annihilation forms the very paradoxical structure of nuclear subjectivities. In other words, it places the most elementary existential conflict at the heart of the nuclear subjectivities that are now defining not only individuals but also the human species.

The psychic tension between a survival instinct and a death instinct finds its parallel in two opposed schools of thought about handling the nuclear threat: one that insisted—like Albert Einstein after 1946—on the surrender of sovereignty, complete disarmament, and the formation of a world government and another that accepted the unwillingness of nations to relinquish sovereignty and opted for a politics of deterrence. According to Schell, deterrence is designed to maintain and is therefore inextricably linked to national sovereignty.[52] Those who, in the name of political realism, opt for a politics of deterrence to protect national sovereignty cannot do so without accepting the risk of extinction. By contrast, those who favor complete nuclear disarmament must be willing to renounce national sovereignty and the freedoms and benefits that come with it. The political question of sovereignty is thus, according to Schell, "central to the nuclear predicament."[53] Our present system, he insists, has become inimical to life because political realism is not biological realism but biological nihilism."[54] So far, because of the structural violence inherent in the system of national sovereignty and the political realism that opts for holding on to it, history has sided with biological nihilism. Opting instead for biological realism would require a hitherto unimaginable radical change in world politics, including psychological changes based on the will to relinquish the consoling illusions of denial as well as certain "values," economic and technological comforts, and perhaps even freedoms that have been firmly embedded in neoliberal capitalism.

Needless to say, these "sacrifices" require a profound and radical "rearrangement of desire."[55] Since many of the required changes do not only demand the relinquishing of engrained ways of living but must also occur at an unconscious level, such a rearrangement is all the harder to achieve. Among other things, the rearrangement of desire requires considerable sacrifice, mainly the sacrifice of the full political control by people of their own territory as well as the liberties guaranteed by many democratic sovereign nations. For Schell, this dilemma boils down to a simple question: is upholding liberty worth the risk of extinction?[56] And yet, most people still refuse fully to imagine extinction, let alone accept that the choice between letting go of neoliberal lifestyles and values and nation-state sovereignty might be the only alternative. Denial and deception, including self-deception, continue, after all, to be at the center of nuclear necropolitics.

As we have seen, both Schell and, later, Derrida insist that international institutions, ranging from the International Criminal Court to NGOs, and even a utopian world government, encroach on nation-state sovereignty. Yet, Derrida also insists on the fundamental ambivalence that characterizes nation-state sovereignty: "one cannot combat, *head-on, all* sovereignty, sovereignty *in general*, without threatening at the same time, beyond the nation-state figure of sovereignty, the classical principles of freedom and self-determination."[57] Moreover, Derrida reminds us that under certain conditions, nation-state sovereignty can provide protection against certain "international powers, certain ideological, religious, or capitalist, indeed linguistic hegemonies."[58] Derrida's reminder is crucial because capitalism and global corporate interests are at the center of nuclear necropolitics and the nuclear war machine. Schell, I think, sidelines the question of economy too hastily when he argues that "many discussions of nuclear attacks on the United States devote considerable attention to their effect on the nation's economy, but if the population has been largely killed off and the national environment is in a state of collapse 'the economy' becomes a meaningless concept."[59] While this may be true from the perspective of an imagined

FIGURE 3. Enrico Baj, *Figura atomica,* 1951. Oil on canvas. Reprinted with permission from Roberta Cerini Baj.

all-out nuclear war, Schell sidesteps the crucial role of global corporate capitalism in any decision about future planetary governance, including the role of nation-state sovereignty and a possible world government. While Schell considers the latter to be the only possible solution to the nuclear dilemma, for nation-states to agree to give up national sovereignty in favor of supranational governance, they would, short of a radical revolutionary overturn of capitalism, need the support of global capitalist corporations. In other words, the question of political realism needs to include the question of economic realism. Moreover, under certain conditions, global corporate capitalism itself may provide a challenge to national sovereignty. At the same time, however, capitalism continues to form the center of the war machines that were established to protect this very sovereignty. Any vision that pursues nuclear disarmament, as well as international oversight and control of nuclear weapons and energy programs, will thus have to address the power of global corporate nuclearism. It will also have to address the psychopolitical implications of revisiting the sovereignty of the nation-state in relation to the sovereignty of the individual and the species. Finally, today, more than three decades after Derrida's and Schell's reflections, we cannot address the question of nuclear disarmament without placing it in the context of recent debates, mainly within the military and its scientific advisors and policy makers, about so-called limited nuclear warfare in the twenty-first century. These debates, which have yet to make headlines in the public media, are inseparable from the global war economy and the nuclear war machine that sustains it.

Will a newly invigorated antinuclear movement turn the nuclear economy around in time to save the planet? Or is it too late, as Rosalie Bertell worried more than two decades ago, to reverse human extinction or "species suicide"?[60] Will we become skeletal atomic figures like Enrico Baj's *Figura atomica*? Could we end like Samuel Beckett's last humans, buried like Winnie in a desert under a merciless sun on an earth that has lost its atmosphere? Are we indeed straddling the boundaries between denial and resilience by conjuring the inverse idyll of *Happy Days*? Or will some "lost ones" survive, hovering in a cylinder in outer space, looking down on a dead earth? Perhaps Sergei Gurin, the cameraman from Chernobyl, was right when he said, "We're all—peddlers of the apocalypse."[61]

NUCLEAR COLONIALISM

> Is there a sense of temporality that could provide a different way of positioning these markers of history and understand 1492 as living inside 1945, for example, and even vice versa?
> —Karen Barad

INDIGENOUS NUCLEAR BORDERLANDS

When I began working on radioactive colonization, I contacted Acoma leader and political activist Petuuche Gilbert to ask him about his antinuclear work. This was his answer:

> It's true some of us are involved in anti-nuclear work and mainly because we are intensely impacted by it. I've been advocating that we, *everybody*, are all nuclear radiation victims because it is so pervasive and we're unaware of it. I was in Japan last year for a forum on nuclear radiation victims and the plenary wanted to educate people about hibakushas and to tell we're all such victims. Lately I've been telling how this state, New Mexico, is addicted to nuclear money as such; we neglect the dangers of the nuclear fuel chain. The state depends on nuclear money for jobs and revenues. Nuclear fuel affects Indigenous peoples but it's a problem for all. That's where I stand. I want us to collaborate on the entire nuclear fuel chain. I work with a small group, Multicultural Alliance for a Safe Environment, against uranium mining and I've said we can't stop it until America and the rest of the world opposes nuclear energy. It's more often that nation-states concentrate on atomic bombs, but the real attention must be on nuclear power and its dangerous effects all along the way, from uranium mining to nuclear waste storage.

I had met Gilbert before at various conferences in Los Angeles and Albuquerque and knew he was one of the founders of the Laguna and Acoma Coalition for a Safe Environment (LACSE), a core group in the

Multicultural Alliance for a Safe Environment. I had also corresponded with him when he was a delegate who represented Indigenous people at the United Nations when the Declaration on the Rights of Indigenous Peoples was ratified in 2007. For decades, Gilbert has been part of the continuing Indigenous fight against nuclear colonialism, representing predominately Indigenous communities adversely affected by more than half a century of uranium mining and milling in the Grants Uranium Belt in New Mexico. In his statement at the Environmental Protection Agency (EPA) stakeholders meeting in Gallup, New Mexico, in 2013, Gilbert explained that,

> combined with uranium mining on the Navajo Nation, uranium mining in the region has degraded the environment and left a legacy of over a thousand abandoned uranium mines. [. . .] Thirty-three years ago, an unlined earthen dam at the United Nuclear Corporation mill tailings facility near Churchrock, New Mexico, collapsed and released 1,100 tons of radioactive tailings and 94 million gallons of toxic waste water to the Puerco River. [. . .] Environmental impacts remain today and communities are still living in a radioactive impacted zone.[1]

Gilbert concluded his statement with several recommendations from LACSE to the EPA, a list that included preventing deep drilling and pollution of groundwater; promoting public welfare by protecting the human right to a safe, clean water supply; encouraging states to prevent new uranium and milling sites; phasing out nuclear reactors; developing nuclear-free zone petitions and declarations for a nuclear-free world; regulating and holding accountable extractive industries, as well as establishing jurisdiction over radioactive contamination; removing radioactive tailings into permanent repositories; implementing a Native American public health uranium impact study; and, finally, establishing lines of communication between the EPA and the Nuclear Regulatory Commission, New Mexico Environment Department, Navajo Nation EPA, and federal congressional delegations so that lawmakers can understand and remove regulations blocking the full cleanup of radioactive contamination.

By revisiting these recommendations now, especially after the recent attacks against the EPA by the Trump administration, I hope to convey a sense of the devastating impact of this administration's anti-environmental stance on Indigenous communities. As with Trump's move

FIGURE 4. Indigenous activists at the Climate March on April 29, 2017. Left to right: June Lorenzo, Petuuche Gilbert, Leona Morgan. Haul No! protests hauling uranium ore from the Grand Canyon in Arizona to the White Mesa mill at Blanding, Utah. Photograph courtesy of Petuuche Gilbert.

to allow the construction of both the Keystone Pipeline and the Dakota Access Pipeline (DAPL), the attack on the EPA marks a new phase in environmental and nuclear colonialism that masquerades under the guise of energy independence and security. Since the Keystone Pipeline is designed to go through the Diné and Creek Nations, it galvanized resistance before Standing Rock. The planned construction of pipelines through Native lands constitutes a qualitative leap in the continued colonization of Indigenous peoples linked to energy politics. Thus the resistance to the Keystone Pipeline and DAPL must be seen in the context of an ongoing energy war against Indigenous peoples that can be traced back at least to the Second Wounded Knee in 1973, where nearly two hundred Oglala Lakota and members of the American Indian Movement (AIM) stood against several U.S. law enforcement agencies. Apart from uranium mining and the nuclear politics surrounding it, this energy war also includes, more generally, mineral extraction and processing, resource transport, conveyance, and dumping. In the nuclear politics on Native lands, the fight for the protection of clean water, air, and soil and the fight against radioactive contamination are inextricably entangled. At the forefront of this struggle, Indigenous activists and writers work toward protecting not just their own communities but also all communities living in the precarious environments of our nuclear age.

FIGURE 5. Screen capture from "Indigenous Delegation to DC: Radioactive Pollution Kills," February 8, 2016.

The nuclear colonization of Native lands in the Southwest began in the 1930s and 1940s with the establishment of the Manhattan Project in 1939 and the Los Alamos National Laboratory in New Mexico in 1943. When the first nuclear weapons test was conducted in 1945 at the Trinity Test Site in the Jornada del Muerto desert, peoples of the nearby Indigenous communities described a "false dawn." Petuuche Gilbert's brother, the acclaimed Acoma poet Simon Ortiz, explains:

> I was only a few years old when the false dawn happened in 1945, rising out of the southeastern New Mexican plains. Some people recall the strange dawn as a tremor of light they could feel passing through them. [. . .] Although the people have known the experience and difficulty of loss, they did not understand the meaning of that strange dawn in 1945 and in some ways they still don't. And it is because U.S. society doesn't understand either and refuses to deal with it. [. . .] Although the people had felt the tremor of light and knew that it was strange, they did not know what it meant. The great majority of U.S. society did not know what it meant either, because knowledge was kept away from them just as effectively, and in many ways more so.[2]

The culture of secrecy and deception at the heart of nuclear necropolitics, described in Ortiz's observations, affected Indigenous peoples all the more deeply. As the corporate capture of uranium began on reservation lands, these communities were already living in a system of economic dependency created by earlier encounters with American settler colonialism. Late nineteenth- and early twentieth-century industrialization, in conjunction with the construction of the railroad, had destroyed the agricultural economies of southwestern Indigenous communities, forcing many young Acoma, Laguna, and Navajo men to find employment in uranium mines or the military. Ortiz tells of how he worked at the Kerr-McGee mill site, mainly in "crushing, leaching, and yellow cake,"[3] but also underground in the mines. None of the workers knew that they were handling the most toxic material on earth. In a private conversation, Ortiz told me that they were handed out protective suits to go into the mines, but these were so tedious to wear that many workers went underground without any protection. When they took a shower after work, he remembers, the water was visibly full of yellow cake. A few decades later, Ortiz explained, many of the Acoma men working in the mines, as well as many others in the Acoma community, died of various forms of cancer.[4] Beyond the radioactive contamination of soil and water, he mentioned another reason: after the Kerr-McGee mining company abandoned the mine without sealing it off, people from Acoma and Laguna went there to take the wood used inside the mine as floorboards for their houses, as nobody in the community knew of the dangers of radioactive contamination.

Many critics have called the nuclear borderlands in the Southwest "sacrifice zones."[5] Like the zones of exception created under sovereign rule, these nuclear sacrifice zones are a manifestation of national sovereignty that continues the legacy of colonialism. Ortiz writes,

> It was not the safety or health or lives of the miners there was concern for. In the national interest, mine operators, oil corporations, utility companies, international energy cartels, and investors sacrificed these men and women. In the Grants Uranium Belt area, which is the area between Albuquerque and Gallup, there was a miner killed every month. At home in Aacqu, there are former miners who walk around crippled, as maimed as if they had been wounded in wartime.[6]

In the wake of the anticolonial Indigenous movements in the United States during the 1970s and 1980s, people became increasingly informed about the contamination of their lands and the risk to their health. Ortiz describes his increased paranoia about his health during this time. Like many residents of the nuclear borderlands, he began to fear the slow nuclear violence of radiation-induced cancers developing in the body over decades before they kill.

Ortiz intersperses his creative nonfictional account of nuclear colonialism in the Southwest with deeply mournful poetry:

> This land yearns
> for us.
> The people yearn
> for the land.[7]

People mourn and yearn for the land they have lost. They yearn for their traditional way of life, free from economic dependency. Earlier in the same work, and shifting between the perspective and time of autobiography, family, and culture, Ortiz explains the drying up and contamination of important water resources for the Acoma.[8] The land is still there, still familiar, but traces of destruction are everywhere. The most lethal form of destruction, the damage to cells that results in cancer, remains hidden until it strikes after a long period of latency. Uranium's deadly force is invisible. It knows no boundaries. It nests itself deeply inside the body, the blood, the earth, the water, and the winds.

Ortiz, however, resists writing a narrative of pure victimhood and defeat. Attachment to injury, he knows, is part of a pervasive colonization of the mind. It is a surrendering to victimhood to the point that injurious states are the only ones left that can be felt. We could even say that, analogous to the false dawn, the attachment to injury is a false emotion that comes with the fracturing of the self. In this respect, the colonization of the mind is also a stealing of emotions. Psychic numbing comes not only as traumatic numbing but also as an effect of stolen emotions. Another poem in Ortiz's book *from Sand Creek* about the Sand Creek massacre of Cheyenne and Arapaho women in 1864 ends with the following lines:

> They should have seen
> the thieves stealing
> their most precious treasure:
> their compassion, their anger.[9]

Beyond a certain point, the numbing of emotions will approximate a state of death-in-life, reminiscent of the one R. J. Lifton describes in some of the victims of Hiroshima. Yet, when Ortiz writes "I was being overcome by some force I did not know," he insists, like in so much of his poetry, on ambiguity. The unknown force may allude to the haunting presence of invisible traces of nuclear destruction. But it may also invoke the force of resilience and resistance that sears like wind into the mind. Ortiz's mourning thus counters the colonial story of "the vanishing Indian," vanishing ways of life, vanishing lands, and even vanishing emotions. We are still here, his poems insist, our traditions, our ceremonies are alive, and we can still walk "those miles on the dry stony floor of the hot canyon," yearning for the land. In this, too, is resilience and resistance.

Ortiz traces his narrative back to the early roots of colonial oppression and destruction and to the many histories of Indigenous resistance, not only in the Southwest, but also across the country. He tells the story of Juan de Oñate's colonization of New Mexico, dating back to 1598, and of the Pueblo uprising against the Spanish oppressors in 1680. He tells the story of the American Indian Wars and the Sand Creek massacre of 1864, and he invokes the Wounded Knee Massacre, which occurred in 1890 on the Lakota Pine Ridge Indian Reservation. For Indigenous people, he insists, colonialism has never ended. Indeed, nuclear colonialism is but a continuation of this history, albeit with a more lethal force. Economic dependency is at the core of nuclear colonization. It made people vulnerable enough to agree to uranium mining on reservations during the Manhattan Project, and it makes people vulnerable now to allow not only more mining but also the storage of nuclear waste on reservation lands. In addition to the hazards of radioactive contamination, nuclear politics on reservation lands divides Indigenous communities. Controversies about the storage of nuclear waste have emerged at Yucca Mountain as well as among the Goshutes in Skull Valley, Utah, where former tribal chair Leon Bear has agreed to store four thousand steel and concrete canisters of radioactive waste on the Skull Valley Goshute reservation for the tribe to reap tens of millions of dollars. The Bureau of Indian Affairs (BIA) approved the lease, but members who oppose the waste storage, such as Margene Bullcreek, call it environmental racism.[10]

And yet, Ortiz stresses survival rather than despair. Resilience in Ortiz's poetry emerges from a vision of larger scale, that is, a vision of humans mindful of their place in the universe. In *from Sand Creek,* Ortiz asks if colonialism did not create a fracture in the universal order, thus rendering human history, memory, and survival unpredictable. Indian astronomers, he says, defined the place of humans in all creation by studying the stars and setting them in their memory. In the past, generations and generations of Indigenous people had tied themselves to stars and insects:

> When they didn't,
> star light fractured,
> became unpredictable.[11]

Once people broke the ties to stars, to insects, to generations, starlight became unpredictable. "Memory was not to be trusted."[12] The fracturing of starlight is reminiscent of the "false dawn" the Acoma people witnessed during the first atomic explosion at White Sands. With the fracturing of the atom, humans removed themselves even further from the order of the universe and their ties to stars, insects, and future generations. They abdicated what many Indigenous people call their responsibility for the Seventh Generation. They entered the false dawn of the nuclear age.

THE SEVENTH GENERATION:
FROM WOUNDED KNEE TO STANDING ROCK

The Seventh Generation plays an important role in the prophesies of different Indigenous peoples, most prominently the Lakota and Mohawk. According to the apocalyptic Mohawk prophecy of the Seventh Generation, which some have traced as far back as the foundation of the Iroquois confederacy in the twelfth century, a time will come when, seven generations after contact with Europeans, huge stone monsters will tear open the face of the earth; elm trees, grass, and corn will die, and trees will lose their leaves. Strange animals will be born, deformed and without proper limbs, and strange bugs and beetles will crawl from the ground. Rivers will burn and the air will singe the eyes of humans. Birds will fall from the sky and fish will die in the water. Wars will become so violent that mountains will crack open. A light many times greater than the sun will blind those who see it. Nothing will grow, and water will become too toxic to drink. As the end of the world nears, new diseases will emerge that eat people up inside. Finally, a great wind will come that will make a hurricane seem like a whisper. It will cleanse the earth and return it to its original state. Human life on the planet will come to an end.

In light of the prophecy predicting a threat of apocalyptic proportions, Leon Shenandoah addressed the General Assembly of the United Nations as Tadodaho (or spiritual leader) of the Haudenosaunee (or Iroquois), a confederacy of Six Nations that includes the Cayuga, Mohawk, Oneida, Odondoga, Seneca, and Tuscararo peoples. The address was both a warning and a plea:

> Excessive exploitation [of resources and people] can only lead to our own destruction. We cannot trade the welfare of our future generations for profit now. [. . .] We must abolish nuclear and conventional weapons of war. [. . .] We propose, as a resolution for peace, that a world cease-fire take place in honor of our children and the Seventh Generation to come.[13]

According to the Mohawk, the Seventh Generation mentioned in the prophecies is living today and has inherited the task and responsibility to protect and save the earth. Change must come from within, Shenandoah explains, and the foremost task is "to recognize the enemy—the one within us." The prophecy's challenge to know the enemy within us resonates with Ortiz's notion of a need to restore humanity's sense of place in the universe, as the fracturing of this sense has turned humans, unbeknownst to themselves, into their own worst enemies. Wars are the most destructive external manifestation of this imbalance. The challenge to know "the enemy within" also resonates with the insistence of Jonathan Schell, discussed in the previous chapter, that the nuclear "peril comes from our own actions—from within us."[14] Antinuclear resistance then requires a collective psychopolitical action. From the perspective of Indigenous peoples, the enemy within is directly linked to the violation of the cosmic order. The atomic blast at White Sands fractured not only the starlight but also the place of humans in the universe and their sense of cosmic connection. This fracturing was, of course, imposed on Indigenous peoples, as they had no choice but to live within the nuclear age. This is part of nuclear colonialism. From this perspective, all humans were henceforth affected by the fracturing of communal selves, carrying their enemy within. The false dawn has created false lives and false selves. Fracture. Splitting. Alienation. In this context, the notion of the Seventh Generation establishes a sense of cosmic temporality that measures transgenerational time. It calculates not only the place of the present generation within a history of colonial fracture but also this generation's responsibility for future generations. The Seventh Generation Principle, which mandates the responsibility for and of the Seventh Generation to come, has its origins in an ancient

Iroquois philosophy according to which the decisions we make today should result in a sustainable world seven generations into the future. It dates back to the oral composition of the Great Law of the Iroquois Confederacy, also called the Great Law of Peace (dated anywhere between A.D. 1142 and 1500).[15]

The Seventh Generation is also a prominent feature for the Lakota, dating back to Black Elk's decidedly more hopeful prophecy, recorded in the 1932 as-told-to autobiography *Black Elk Speaks*.[16] Translated from Lakota to English by his son Ben Black Elk, and transcribed by John Neihardt, Black Elk's work predicted that the Seventh Generation of Lakota would not only restore the continuity of the Lakota people that had been severed by the massacre at Wounded Knee in 1890 but also bring about an alliance of all races. Some of the Lakota spiritual leaders identified the current generation living on the Pine Ridge Reservation as the Seventh Generation. For many, the recent demonstrations against the DAPL at the Sacred Stone Camp at Standing Rock, in which members from approximately sixty tribes as well as people from across the globe participated in solidarity, rekindled the hope of Black Elk's vision.

Being part of a 125-year-old prophecy thus added to the cultural importance of the resistance movement for the protection of water at Standing Rock. Elders have identified the black snake that, according to the prophecy, would be overcome by the Seventh Generation with the pipeline. They gave the youth a ceremonial pipe and deputized them as *akicita*, that is, warriors for the people. The great hope placed on the Seventh Generation that carries this movement, the activists assert, will not be dashed by President Trump's recent attacks on Indigenous water rights when he authorized the pipeline's construction.

On January 27, 2017, the *Los Angeles Times* featured a cartoon by David Horsey in which President Trump appears with a group of soldiers on horseback in the uniform of the Seventh Cavalry Regiment of the U.S. Army (Figure 6). Trump stops to ask a young Indigenous man at the side of the road, "Boy! Which way to the Dakota Access Oil Pipeline?" The boy replies, "I'm not sure, Yellow Hair, but I hope you take the shortcut through the Little Bighorn."[17] In response to Trump's almost instant reversal of Obama's decision to halt the construction of the DAPL, the cartoon makes a significant historical connection to the Indian Wars and the colonization of Indian land. Inspired by visions of Sitting Bull, the Battle of the Little Bighorn or, as it was named by the Indigenous people, the Battle of the Greasy Grass, constituted the

FIGURE 6. David Horsey, *Trump as Custer,* featured in the *Los Angeles Times* article "Standing Rock May Be the First Battle Site in Trump's War on the Environment," January 25, 2017.

major event of the Great Sioux War of 1876 and resulted in the defeat of the U.S. Seventh Cavalry by the Lakota, Arapaho, and Cheyenne during which General Custer was killed. "Custer's Last Stand," as it is commonly called, plays an iconic role in the collective memory of the Indigenous peoples of the United States.

Considering that the new wars that President Trump is threatening to prepare include a new energy war on Indigenous land, the historical reference in Horsey's cartoon to Custer's defeat at Little Bighorn is right on target. It was at the Little Bighorn River in Montana that the Lakota Sioux, Cheyenne, and Arapaho set up camp to protest their displacement by the U.S. Army. At that time, the displacement was caused by another resource extraction, namely, that of gold. It was the protest movement against the displacement and sacrifice of Indigenous peoples for gold mining that culminated in the battle at Little Bighorn and the defeat of General Custer and the U.S. Seventh Cavalry.

In 1973, almost a century after the battle at Little Bighorn, a few hundred Native American people occupied the town of Wounded Knee on the Pine Ridge Reservation in South Dakota, the historical site of the 1890 massacre at Wounded Knee. This armed occupation in 1973— in which members of AIM played a crucial role after tribal elders had asked for their support—is commonly called the Second Wounded Knee. At the center of the conflict was another resource extraction, this time, of uranium. The protest targeted the uranium mining on the Pine Ridge Reservation that contaminated the reservation's aquifer and established yet another sacrifice zone on Indigenous lands.

Debra White Plume, a Lakota water and land rights activist who lives near the Wounded Knee Creek, was part of the occupation of the Second Wounded Knee in 1973. In 2016, she also participated in the protests over the DAPL at Standing Rock. In an interview with Amy Goodman, she commented on the connection between AIM and the 2016–17 conflicts over the DAPL.[18] In 1973, the conflict broke out when BIA representative Dick Wilson tried to sign away one-eighth of tribal lands to the government. These were the lands that were rich in natural resources, including coal, gas, oil, and, above all, uranium. White Plume points out that by the time of the conflict over the DAPL, decades of uranium mining had already badly contaminated the drinking water from the Ogallala aquifer. Residents now have to mix the local water with water from the Missouri River to make it potable. Installing the DAPL, the local Indigenous people insist, would pose the risk of an oil leak that would further contaminate the water.

President Trump's authorization of the construction of the pipeline is a devastating blow to the local Indigenous people whose water and sacred sites are threatened by the DAPL. The callous contempt this move reveals for the Indigenous people is, of course, not surprising. After all, it goes hand in hand with the contempt for nature that underlies Trump's environmental policies. As a climate change denier, he shuns not only the indisputable evidence of scientists worldwide but also the disastrous consequences of extreme weather conditions, namely, storms and floods of a hitherto unknown scale, and the disappearance of islands and coastlines that destroys the livelihood of millions of people and the habitats of abundant animals and plants.[19]

Moreover, this new incarnation of environmental colonialism goes hand in hand with the age-old colonizing metonymic alignment of Indigenous peoples, nature, and—not to forget—women in the words and actions of the man who holds the most powerful office in the world. It inaugurates an era of governance that revives some of the nation's most violent foundational moments. Moreover, the fact that this man, who also embraces the fantasy of a new arms race and the expansion of the nuclear weapons stockpile, is also the only one to authorize their use further expands the radioactive colonization of Indigenous lands to a nuclear colonialism of planetary proportions.

This is why it becomes all the more urgent to remember that, historically, what has been labeled the "new Indian Wars," namely, the occupation of Wounded Knee in 1973 and the retaliatory, fierce attempt to destroy the AIM, was already a battle over nuclear colonialism. As is well known, the occupation of Wounded Knee ended with the ill-fated shootout on the Pine Ridge Reservation during which one of the Native residents and two FBI agents were killed. Eventually, Leonard Peltier was convicted of the killing and has been in prison ever since. Already in 1983, Peter Matthiessen's 645-page-long book *In the Spirit of Crazy Horse* presented a meticulous case for the retrial of Peltier, who continues to claim his innocence in the shooting. Despite a forceful worldwide solidarity movement for Peltier, and even though a different man has identified himself as the one who shot the agents, the FBI has to this day resisted the retrial of Peltier as well as his possible pardoning by then president Bill Clinton. Nor did the worldwide solidarity movement—including a plea by the pope—move President Obama to grant clemency to Peltier.

At the time, the FBI did everything to prevent the publication of *In the Spirit of Crazy Horse*, trying to challenge the evidence Matthiessen accumulated. Countering this attempt at censorship—which was certainly not only directed at Peltier's exoneration but also at Matthiessen's antinuclear politics—Matthiessen won the legal battle against blocking the book's publication. In a landmark decision, the U.S. Supreme Court upheld the right of an author "to publish an entirely one-sided view of people and events."[20] Meanwhile, gravely ill, Leonard Peltier is still languishing and dying a slow physical and social death in prison.

Beyond documenting the circumstances surrounding the Leonard Peltier case, *In the Spirit of Crazy Horse* also presents a meticulous documentation of the new Indian Wars and their connection to the extractive economy of U.S. energy politics: "By the mid-1970s, according to the Federal Energy Commission, Indian lands had already produced nearly $4 billion worth of oil, gas, coal, uranium and other minerals, and the corporate state did not intend to allow Indians to get in the way."[21] Legally, according to John Redhouse, "the Department of Energy is allowed to enter into a pact with the Department of Defense to seize unilaterally and hold areas of strategic mineral significance if such action is justified as being in the 'national interest.' For Indian nations [. . .]

to defy the national policies of the U.S. government and multinational corporate interests is to defy the two most powerful forces on the face of the earth. To do so is to invite possible military intervention."[22]

In this context, it is important to remember that nuclear politics—and energy politics more generally—has, as the protests at Standing Rock illustrate, long been inseparable from water politics. This continues also to be the case in the new water wars. These include the numerous power plant leaks that have contaminated the Great Lakes as well as the use of the Great Lakes as a nuclear waste dump.[23] (The disastrous water contamination in Flint that affected the local community is yet another example of the water wars that have been going on for decades.) The construction of power plants and strip mining in Montana during the 1970s, for example, threatened to dry out the water in the Yellowstone River. According to Matthiessen, the proposed "nuclear-energy park" with twenty-five reactors also damaged the water supplies throughout the Black Hills and the western states: "The waste and ruin of precious water throughout the western states is a calamity that few public servants have yet found the courage to deal with."[24] In a similar vein, the energy industry's seizure of water from the lakes and streams of the Black Hills adversely affected these states' agriculture and economy.

The radioactive colonization of the Black Hills and the Lakota territory by the energy empire is thus directly related not only to the country's nuclear politics but also to its water politics. Matthiessen portrays a vivid picture of the change of these territories under the "shadow of the energy empire":

> In a few decades, perhaps less, a dry, poisoned, and eroded waste would transform this gold-green country, and to no good purpose: the uranium to be produced far exceeded all domestic nuclear demand. Despite all the patriotic rhetoric by politicians and energy executives, the uranium was not intended to resolve the pumped-up and immensely profitable "energy crisis" but to add to the grotesque accumulation of weapons for the formerly unthinkable World War III. In the clamor of so-called "serious discussion" of "nuclear options," "limited nuclear war," and other half-cocked concepts by men of stunted imagination and no vision, it was difficult to forget the great destroying fire of Indian prophesy."[25]

This was the situation in the late 1970s. It seems as if, for complicated economic and political reasons, after a temporary hiatus that stalled the madness of nuclear necropolitics, we have now, four decades later, become involved in a frightening return to these fateful debates about nuclear options and "limited nuclear war." Like Matthiessen, we are in tandem also facing a new attack on the First Amendment and new efforts at government-supported censorship of dissenting views, including views based on internationally supported scientific evidence. Such attempts at censorship are particularly alarming because they belong to the much more pervasive culture and politics of secrecy and deception that has marred the Manhattan Project and the ensuing nuclear necropolitics from the very beginning.

THE MANHATTAN PROJECT AND ITS LEGACIES

It is worthwhile, therefore, to revisit these beginnings on Indigenous lands to draw out their bio- and psychopolitical implications. Whether or not we acknowledge it, nuclearism continues to profoundly shape our biological, political, and psychic lives. Jacques Derrida's declaration, more than three decades ago, regains its validity in light of the threat of a new arms race today: "No single instant, no atom of our life [. . .] is not marked today, directly or indirectly, by that speed race."[26] The concerted efforts we witness to eclipse precisely this pervasive impact of nuclearism from public debates, however, are also designed to reframe the nuclear imaginary after the end of the Cold War.

Almost two decades ago, in her pathbreaking book *The Tainted Desert: Environmental and Social Ruin in the American West*, Valerie L. Kuletz wrote, "Why has the 'nuclear crisis' become old news? Perhaps because the collective fear engendered by the alarming arms escalation at the height of the Cold War in the Reagan era has dissipated. Mutual assured destruction is held momentarily at bay. The nuclear era is not yet over, however, and in some ways it has just begun." Writing after the end of the (first) Cold War, Kuletz—whose father was involved in the Manhattan Project and who grew up in the Los Alamos area—was concerned with the emergence of a global nuclear geopolitical era and, most prominently, the haunting crisis in nuclear waste management that severely impacts the life of future generations for at least 240,000 years. As Kuletz pointedly states, many Indigenous people of the American Southwest see the desecration of their homelands as sacrifice zones and nuclear wastelands as "a form of twentieth century genocide."[27]

Rereading *The Tainted Desert* today reveals its continued uncanny and haunting timeliness. None of the issues Kuletz raises have been solved. Many are returning with a vengeance as they pierce the defensive screen of our collective negative hallucination, that is, our ability not to see the dangers that are right in front of our eyes. And while, after 1989, the specter of an all-out nuclear war had been temporarily relegated to the political unconscious, it was replaced, in the wake of Chernobyl and Fukushima, by the specter of nuclear accidents as well as limited nuclear war and nuclear terrorism. As I argued earlier, things changed again when President Trump resurrected the specter of a "nuclear holocaust" that returns us full circle to the threat of the complete annihilation of life on earth. And yet, nuclear politics and culture are systematically kept out of public debate and eclipsed, if not used, by the specter of climate change. It is therefore an adamant political task to push for a public debate about the inextricable entanglement of nuclear war and disaster as two major threats to planetary survival.

The enormous controversies about nuclear power's impact on climate change are ongoing. As I discussed in the introduction, Helen Caldicott's *Nuclear Power Is Not the Answer* makes a strong case for the position that only renewable technologies will have a positive effect on climate change because the nuclear fuel cycle substantially adds to global warming.[28] Any debate about nuclear energy must furthermore consider the health hazards from radioactive emissions, the increasing threat of large nuclear accidents, the hazards from nuclear waste storage, and the looming specter of nuclear terrorism. As the work of Kuletz, Masco, and Churchill, among others, has amply demonstrated, the negative effects and health hazards of nuclear energy disproportionately affect Indigenous peoples.

Nuclear politics, I argued earlier, radicalizes the biopolitical power of the sovereign to create zones of exception in which people can be injured, if not killed, with impunity. In the United States, nuclear necropolitics has, as the previous examples demonstrate, designated entire areas, mostly in the American Southwest, as sacrifice zones. These consist mainly of the homelands of local Indigenous peoples that have become unsafe because of radioactive contamination from nuclear tests, uranium mining, and nuclear waste disposal. The lands of the Western Shoshone, for example, have already been contaminated by nuclear waste. Indigenous people rightly identify this slow biopolitical violence as radioactive colonization or nuclear colonialism, if not as a form of nuclear genocide. After all, governmental and corporate powers execute the hidden sovereignty to allow the release of lethal radioactive toxins that attack the livelihoods and lives of predominately Indigenous populations who are chosen as sacrificial victims.

More generally, the knowledge that, after the invention of the Bomb, humans must continue to live with an invisible power able to destroy the planet and its diverse species inevitably transforms one's anchoring in space and time as well as one's sense of a future to come. Indigenous peoples, whose epistemologies are grounded in a keen awareness of their place in a vast environment that includes cosmic belonging, feel this most painfully because the knowledge of the Bomb's destructive potential cannot but create a complete rupture in human epistemologies and subjectivities, a rupture that affects the very mode of being in the world. This is precisely what Simon Ortiz invoked when he spoke of the fracturing of starlight that broke the order of the universe.

Yet, as if such awareness were intolerable, the culture at large covers it up by large-scale denial, including the denial of our generation's responsibility for the Seventh Generation that is symbolic of a sustainable future of the planet. How can one responsibly live with the knowledge that the long-term effects of the Manhattan Project will extend over ten thousand years or four hundred generations, and that the half-life of plutonium 244 is eighty million years? Denial is often entangled with, if not enforced by, a politics of secrecy. Silencing, denial, and secrecy were already so central to the Manhattan Project that even the existence of plutonium was only made public after the announcement of the first atomic bomb tests. Similarly, the effects of the blast on the nineteen thousand people who lived within a fifty-mile radius of the Trinity Test Site were never publicly discussed. Elias Canetti once wrote that "every secret is explosive, expanding with its own inner heat. [. . .] It does not so much matter what happens, as long as it happens with the fiery suddenness of a volcano, unexpected and irresistible."[29] I can hardly think of an image more apt to capture the culture of secrecy and the male fantasies at the heart of the Manhattan Project and nuclear necropolitics more generally. As I will describe in more detail in chapter 4, in these fantasies, nuclear missiles and the explosions of nuclear bombs are routinely described in phallic images, often with a decidedly messianic undertone and always shrouded in a veil of secrecy.

"The most important truth about Los Alamos National Laboratory is that it has always been and still is a secret; a center whose work has always been kept utterly shrouded from the view of the world; a place with no public memory," says Herman Agoyo from San Juan Pueblo in "Who Here Will Begin This Story?"[30] For the Indigenous Pueblo peoples, the Manhattan Project meant a radical change in their economy; their use of land, including sacred sites; their ways of living; and their public health. This profound and traumatic rupture affects the formation of subjectivity and interpersonal relationships as well the transgenerational transmission of heritage and culture, including spiritual and religious beliefs and practices.[31] When Agoyo speaks of Los Alamos as a "place with no public memory," he refers not only to its official politics of secrecy but also to a systematic deception about the destructive impact of the Manhattan Project on local Indigenous peoples, who were forced to negotiate between the work opportunities that mitigated poverty and the costs to their land, health, and ways of life.

This destructive impact was compounded by the fact that the Pueblo had their own cultures of secrecy. Secret knowledge pertained, for example, to the sacred Pueblo locations on the Pajarito Plateau now threatened by the Manhattan Project. How to convey such danger and avert it without compromising secret tribal knowledges? Masco describes this collision of "dueling cultures of secrecy": "as physicists worked to unlock the power of the atom [. . .], Pueblo leaders sought to manage the ecological balance in their universe through the ritual maintenance of a complex system of shrines and sacred sites. [. . .] The untold story of the Manhattan Project involves this collision between regimes of knowledge, concepts of nature, definitions of security, and secrecy societies on the Pajarito Plateau."[32]

Alfonso Ortiz argues that Northeastern Pueblo oral traditions commonly frame historical events through a reiteration of the founding mythopoetical charters. In sacred ceremonies, *ka'tsina* clowns use caricature to incorporate intruders into Pueblo life and thus contain them within the Pueblo universe.[33] Many of these ceremonies enact the secret knowledge of Pueblo communities that is only accessible to those initiated in the culture. As Masco argues, the Pueblo culture of secrecy collided in many respects with the culture of secrecy surrounding the Manhattan Project. This collision of the two cultures of secrecy forms the center of Martin Cruz Smith's *Stallion Gate*, the first Indigenous novel about the Manhattan Project.

NUCLEAR FICTION: MARTIN CRUZ SMITH'S *STALLION GATE*

In 1986, Martin Cruz Smith published *Stallion Gate,* a fictional exploration of the origins of the Manhattan Project in Los Alamos. The plot of *Stallion Gate* depicts the events that lead to the explosion of the first atomic bomb from an intercultural perspective, according a central role to Indigenous characters. In a portrayal of the secretive *ka'tsina* ceremonies in which Pueblo performers stage a mock disruption of the Manhattan Project, the novel stages a clash of the two cultures of secrecy that marks the onset of the nuclear age in the Southwest borderlands.

Cruz Smith is of Pueblo, Spanish, Seneca del Sur, and Yaqui ancestry. (His father and mother were both jazz musicians, and his mother, Louise Lopez, was a well-known Pueblo Indigenous rights activist.) In *Stallion Gate,* Cruz Smith shows that the shroud of secrecy that veiled the Manhattan Project affected its participants with an operational paranoia that fueled their politics of deception. Blurring the boundaries of genres, *Stallion Gate* is a historical novel that reads like crime fiction or, more specifically, a spy novel.

It is June 1945. Joe Pena and Ray Stingo, two Indigenous sergeants hired as guards at the Los Alamos test site for the Manhattan Project, are driving an ambulance from Utah to New Mexico. The ambulance contains top-secret cargo, a canister with a "ten-gram lead-coated, stainless steel capsule of jellylike plutonium nitrate that drivers called the slug."[34] The nickname "slug" aptly captures plutonium as vibrant matter that uncannily collapses the distinction between the animate and the inanimate: "The slug [. . .] seemed, in Joe's mind, alive. It was an interesting concept: metal that was alive. Not only a mineral capable of some sort of chemical reaction, but so alive with alpha activity that the water around the slug was warmed to a hundred degrees."[35]

Stallion Gate focuses on the weeks preceding the Trinity test on July 16, 1945, near Alamogordo, New Mexico. The test was designed to explore the viability of using the first uranium and plutonium bombs, with code names Little Boy and Fat Man, on Japan. The project ended, as we know, with the nuclear attacks on Hiroshima and Nagasaki. Rather than focusing on the familiar historical events surrounding the Manhattan Project, however, *Stallion Gate* exposes the stories and mythologies people generate around it. These stories reveal the project's impact on the subjectivities of both the scientists involved and the populations affected by it. It was mostly the Indigenous peoples from the surrounding Pueblo reservations whose land was appropriated who were left in the dark about the operations at Los Alamos that would forever change not only their own lives but also those of all living beings on the planet.

In *Stallion Gate,* the collision of two cultures of secrecy propels the action. On one hand there is the culture of secrecy that involves the U.S. government, the CIA, and the crew of the Manhattan Project, who all conspire to protect the secret of the invention of the first atomic weapon. On the other hand, there is the secret culture of the Indigenous Pueblo communities, who are trying to protect not only their tribal secrets but also their clandestine conspiracy to derail the Manhattan Project. The attempt at a mythopoetic incorporation of the Manhattan Project by Indigenous peoples forms the center of action. At a ceremonial dance with *ka'tsina* clowns, attended by the scientists who work on "the Hill" at Los Alamos, a fictional Oppenheimer says, "The Hill isn't a place; it's a time warp. We are the future surrounded by a land and a people that haven't changed in a thousand years."[36] Defying this infamous stereotype of the timelessness or "prehistory" of Indigenous peoples, one of the six clowns begins by impersonating General Groves, the director of the Manhattan Project, while others mimic the scientists' construction of a bomb. When the local policeman complains to Joe, Oppenheimer's Indigenous driver and bodyguard, about a serious breach in security, Joe invokes tribal secrets to withhold information. At the same time, Joe reveals to Oppenheimer that the policeman planted a microphone in his house because the head of intelligence believes him to be a "Red Spy."[37] The development of the novel's plot is thus propelled by a complex game of deceit, denial, and covert activities of spying between the two secret societies.

It is well known that historically, because of his longtime membership in the Communist Party of the United States, Oppenheimer was under suspicion of being a Soviet spy. In *Sacred Secrets: How Soviet Intelligence Operations Changed American History,* Jerold L. and Leona P. Schecter argue that in 1942, Oppenheimer's membership in the Communist Party was concealed because he was used by the Communist Underground as a Soviet intelligence asset to obtain secrets about the atomic bomb. While he was never formally recruited as a Soviet agent, his cooperation would potentially have qualified him as a spy under U.S. law. However, there is no conclusive proof, because the Oppenheimer files in the Soviet Intelligence Archives and the

Presidential Archives remain under seal. On September 8, 2000, Putin admitted on CNN's *Larry King Live* that American scientists cooperated in Soviet atomic espionage, albeit without naming Oppenheimer. It is also well known that in 1954, Oppenheimer's interrogation at a security hearing by the U.S. Atomic Energy Commission resulted in the revocation of his top security clearance (Q clearance). Later, both John F. Kennedy and Lyndon B. Johnson partly rehabilitated Oppenheimer.

Without focusing on these historical details, Cruz Smith chooses Oppenheimer as the central character among the scientists involved in the Manhattan Project. The suspicion raised by his affiliation with the Communist Party and his alleged collaboration with the Soviets propels the novel's plot and highlights the culture of secrecy surrounding the Manhattan Project. The impact of this culture of secrecy was, however, not limited to issues of espionage or the attempt to conceal the project of constructing an atomic bomb from the American public and the world at large. It also deeply affected the Indigenous communities in the vicinity, who were the first to suffer from radioactive contamination without having any knowledge of the dangers of this entirely new form of slow violence to which they had been exposed. The devastating effects of this slow nuclear violence continue to this day, most dramatically manifested in the disproportionately high rate of cancers among the Indigenous peoples in the nuclear borderlands. "No one was told, everything was top secret, and that's the mistake," said Marian Naranjo, Santa Clara Pueblo, director of Honor Our Pueblo Existence, an area community group.[38]

In a certain sense, *Stallion Gate* is thus also a crime novel. Crime in Cruz Smith's narrative is exposed indirectly in the paranoia around suspicions of espionage as well as less formal forms of spying among the affected communities, all related to the secrecy surrounding the construction of the nuclear bomb and concomitant Indigenous acts of sabotage. But crime also figures at the deeper level of radioactive colonization experienced by the novel's Indigenous communities. Finally, crime figures in the very construction of a weapon so deadly that it kills in hitherto unimaginable proportions, a crime so toxic that it also inflicts almost infinite transgenerational damage on the earth and its species.

Radioactive colonization and nuclear necropolitics are, of course, not crimes against the law. They are not crimes at the scale explored, for example, in Jean and John Comaroff's *The Truth about Crime*.[39] But what *Stallion Gate* highlights is that the truth about crime is also about scale. There are crimes that are committed at a scale that transcends the boundaries of the law, crimes that threaten the politics of life itself. While there are international laws about war crimes and "crimes against humanity," these don't include the use, if not construction, of nuclear weapons. By fictionalizing the very inauguration of the nuclear age, *Stallion Gate* exposes the fact that the arbitrariness of the boundaries between law and crime the Comaroffs have identified also pertains to the (missing) laws that affect large-scale ecological futures and the survival of planetary life.

The dynamic of secrecy, spying, and deception that marks the world of *Stallion Gate* is further complicated by the intervention of a third secret force, namely, the infiltration of the Manhattan Project by Soviet atomic spies. The covert interaction of the unholy triad of these secret forces—the culture of secrecy among the involved scientists, the secret culture of espionage, and the Indigenous culture of secrecy—creates an operational paranoia where, during the frantic preparations for the Trinity test, everyone places everyone else under suspicion. At the height of tension during the night of the planned first atomic test explosion, two Indigenous antinuclear activists use their secret knowledge about the bomb in an attempt to derail the experiment. This very attempt was, we learn, inspired by oneiric knowledge reminiscent of the Mohawk prophecies. Indigenous peoples from different tribes had the same dream, Joe says, in which the scientists on the Hill were making a gourd of ashes that would fall and cover the ground, poisoning clouds, water, earth, and everything that lives on the land: "I had the dream in Taos. Two Hopi men had the same dream—two elders. A woman in Acoma had the same dream."[40] In response to this shared dream vision, two Indigenous activists are using sacred lightning rods to interfere with the Trinity test. While they create a massive thunderstorm that forces the scientists to delay the test, they are not able to stop it indefinitely. The novel ends with the dramatic countdown to the detonation of the bomb. The outcome, however, is left ambiguous. We know that the explosion happened but remain uncertain whether Joe, who was trapped trying to help the activists, was able to escape.

Cruz Smith thus ends his novel at the dawn of the nuclear age. We recall that the people at Acoma witnessed the explosion of the first nuclear bomb as the strange light that brought about a "false dawn." Ending his novel with this explosion, Cruz Smith indirectly mobilizes his readers' collective memory of the dropping of the first atomic bombs on Hiroshima and Nagasaki that would forever change the face of the world and herald the nuclear economy. Some of his Indigenous readers will also read the ending as an announcement of the world's "false dawn" that changed the order of things and the place of humans in the universe. To this day, few people know the extent of the Manhattan Project's impact on Indigenous peoples. It is not part of public memory. *Stallion Gate* belongs to a series of works by Indigenous writers designed to break this silence—including Leslie Marmon Silko's *Ceremony*, Linda Hogan's Hiroshima poems, Simon Ortiz's *Woven Stone*, and Jimmy Santiago Baca's "Choices."[41]

Joseph Masco insists that, in the zones of radioactive colonization in New Mexico, "a nuclear subtext informs everyday life [. . .] linking trauma and apocalypse—past and future—in a specific constellation."[42] The very proximity of the Los Alamos weapons laboratory to the Pueblo reservations and the knowledge of their radioactive contamination constitute a perpetual psychic intrusion, even when it remains unconscious in daily life. The psychic toxicity that emanates from New Mexico's nuclear economy generates a nuclear fear that shapes the managing of life within a radioactive biosphere. Those most conscious of the threat experience it as a colonization of psychic space: "A core project of many activists is thus to register the psychosocial and cultural effects of the bomb on their lives, replacing a discourse of national security with a quotidian experience of nuclear terror."[43] To contribute to this cultural and psychopolitical work is the place and function of literary and artistic works that engage and support this activism.

HIROSHIMA BUGI

The quotidian experience of nuclear terror not only concerns the here and now of actual fears and threats; it also contributes to the long-term psychic fallout experienced by survivors of nuclear attacks or accidents. Beyond the more local perspective of the radioactive colonization of nuclear borderlands, Indigenous writers and activists also engage the global legacy of Hiroshima and its role in antinuclear struggles. Their stories explore nuclear fear as a transgenerational trauma, passed down from generation to generation, even across national and geopolitical boundaries. Nuclear trauma constitutes a double haunting from both past and future, a haunting that conjures the ghosts of Hiroshima, the ghosts of ongoing nuclear contamination, and the ghosts of future annihilations into the here and now. Moreover, for Indigenous peoples, the trauma of nuclear colonialism compounds the transgenerational effects of the old trauma of their original colonization and of those earlier wars fought for the sake of extractive economies, including Wounded Knee:

> Children without names.
> Death stories.
> . . .
> Nuclear ghosts in the rain.
> The lonesome souls.[44]

Lifted from Gerald Vizenor's *Hiroshima Bugi*, this poem invokes a transgenerational haunting by nuclear ghosts and the effects it has on the formation of nuclear subjectivities. Hiroshima appears as a death world, full of nameless children, nuclear ghosts, death stories, and an unfathomable loneliness at the core of being. One of the most prominent Native American writers, Gerald Vizenor is of Anishinaabe and Danish American descent and a member of the Minnesota Chippewa Tribe, White Earth Reservation. He served as part of the American occupation forces in Japan in the aftermath of the nuclear attacks on Hiroshima and Nagasaki until he returned to the United States in 1953. Half a century later, he published *Hiroshima Bugi*, which he calls his "kabuki novel."

Hiroshima Bugi addresses the transgenerational legacy of the Manhattan Project from a highly experimental perspective. It is a polyvocal novel with two Indigenous characters, one of mixed heritage, whose narratives are interwoven in intersecting chapters. Ronin Browne, the main character, is of mixed heritage with a Japanese mother, a *bugi* dancer, and an Anishinaabe father from the White Earth Reservation who served as a translator in Japan at the end of World War II. Abandoned at an orphanage in Japan as one of the outcast mixed-race children, Ronin was adopted by the White Earth Reservation and raised there until, as an adult, he returned to Japan and filled several notebooks describing his experience of postnuclear Hiroshima. In search of the father he never knew, Ronin meets Manidoo Envoy, the other Indigenous character, only to learn that his father had recently passed away. Ronin decides to enlist Envoy, a scholar and intellectual, as his editor and commentator. Envoy facilitates the publication of the notebooks with Nebraska University Press under the title *Hiroshima Bugi*, a framing in which Vizenor thus posits himself as a double of Envoy.

As the doubling of narrator and author suggests, *Hiroshima Bugi* is a book about shadows and simulacra, about death and survival or, as Vizenor calls it, "survivance." It is a book about mourning and ghosts, about black rain and mutant bodies. Finally, it is a book about literature and art as well as philosophy, critical theory, and "nuclear aesthetics." Commenting on the poem quoted earlier, Ronin writes in his journal,

> The black rain exposed thousands of people to radiation. The natural fear of thunder, and that pure pleasure of the rain, was lost forever on that ghastly morning of the atomic bomb. Hiroshima was incinerated by a nuclear thunderstorm, and the hibakusha were poisoned by the rain. The dead were resurrected in museums, in the wretched name of peace. Listen, you can hear the undertone, the hints of their sudden, lost breath in the rain.[45]

This passage testifies to yet another fracturing of the universal order, namely, the nuclear transmutation of rain, thunder, and lightning that will forever change the survivors' experience of these elemental forces. "Fake rain," as it is called in another poem in *Hiroshima Bugi,* is reminiscent of the "false dawn" the Acoma people saw and the "fake peace" that Ronin decries as a psychic legacy of Hiroshima's museum culture and "nuclear commerce." The psychic fallout of the fracturing of the natural order of things is a world of perpetual war, Ronin suggests, covered by a simulacrum of "fake peace."

As a transgenerational nuclear legacy, the broken mirror of nature—one of *Hiroshima Bugi*'s central metaphors—also entails a fracturing of both language and psychic space. The cover art by R. W. Boeche features the centerpiece of the Kabuki play *Night Scene Lit by a Lantern,* in which samurai Abe no Sadato fights with a tiger in a broken mirror. The fracturing of bodies in broken mirrors conjures phantasms of the fragmented body that, according to Lacan, signal anxieties about physical and psychic fragmentation. Earlier I argued that, in the nuclear imaginary, phantasms of the fragmented body assume the specific form of phantasms of the mutant body. Another of the Ronin poems places such phantasms within the framework of transgenerational legacies:

> Miko on my mind.
> Look, atomu waists.
> Wispy genes,
> Mutant generations.[46]

Miko is Ronin's lover, a painter whose work poses the question of representation after Hiroshima. How can art or literature represent a violence whose scale fractures the very boundaries of human imagination? Any attempt at aesthetic realism or naturalism, Vizenor suggests, is doomed to fail since it cannot but create simulacra that generate a fake closure, reminiscent of the fake peace that Ronin tries to fight. Miko's paintings portray "nuclear children" in painted mirrors with bent faces folded as origami cranes. "Miko painted the obake, the ghosts of children, in simulated mirrors, and the real mirrors embodied in the canvas were broken."[47] Envoy comments, "The images of the kami are 'forever fragmentary, a nuclear aesthetic,' wrote an art historian for the New York Times."[48] In the Shinto religion, a *kami* is a sacred spirit in nature that can be caught in a mirror.[49] Miko's nuclear aesthetics uses broken mirrors and mutant images to invoke both the violation of the *kami* and the transgenerational haunting of Hiroshima by nuclear ghost children. One of the cryptic scenes in Ronin's stories, in which an old man talks about the *atomu* destruction of Hiroshima, ends with the statement "Didn't it rain children."[50]

The question of nuclear aesthetics is also posed on the level of *Hiroshima Bugi*'s implicit aesthetic self-reflection. The novel relies on a rare density of references to literature, art, film, and historical scholarship on Hiroshima as well as an abundant arsenal of philosophical and aesthetic theories drawn from both Japanese and Western traditions. Envoy's sections provide not only the biographical references about Ronin's life but also in-depth commentaries on the historical, philosophical, literary, theatrical, and aesthetic background that is relevant to understanding his notebooks. Mediated by Envoy's commentary, this uniquely dense intertextual network generates a polyvocal novelistic form that straddles the boundaries between literature, philosophy, and critical theory. Not surprisingly, given the body of Vizenor's work, *Hiroshima Bugi* is another highly experimental postmodern novel. With Hiroshima as its subject matter, the novel's unique experimental form constitutes in itself a forceful intervention into the collective memory of Hiroshima.

Memory, however, as Simon Ortiz states in *from Sand Creek*, is "not to be trusted." In *Hiroshima Bugi,* Ronin profoundly distrusts the public memory of Hiroshima as it is monumentalized in the Peace Museum and other forms of commemoration that he calls "nuclear commerce."

By contrast, *Hiroshima Bugi* offers a countermemory that relies on the ambiguities of muted and mutant emotions—Ronin calls them "spectral moods." Vizenor's text is almost Brechtian in its didactic use of theoretical commentary and reflection and its refusal of emotional pathos. Even though it is replete with painfully beautiful poetic passages, *Hiroshima Bugi* is deliberately not a readerly text. What the novel offers instead is an entirely syncretistic countermemory, built on precarious phantasms of the mutant body, fractured mirrors, images and stories, and a nuclear aesthetics of shadows and artistic transmutations. Perhaps the most viable and vital art after Hiroshima, Vizenor's text suggests, lies in the aesthetic transmutation of Hiroshima's wounded bodies. Kitsutsuki, a wounded lieutenant, who had lost a leg and an eye on a land mine on the same day that his wife and son were incinerated by the atomic bomb, becomes a master of aesthetic transmutation. After receiving seven wooden legs, he fills them with artistic carvings that tell the story of Hiroshima's hauntings by its nuclear ghosts:

> Kitsutsuki carved the faces of the nuclear dead on his wooden legs. Twisted faces, airy bodies, chinked bones, the haunting pouts and frowns of death undone forever. One leg is covered with wild, uncertain eyes, the jumpy eyes of terror, and on another leg he carved a flock of scorched, disunited birds with huge eyes, puny feet, and feathers turned under, melted away at the stump."[51]

Haunted by the eyes of terror found in nuclear ghosts, Kitsutsuki suggests with his carvings that art after Hiroshima must be spectral and visionary. In Miko's watercolor paintings, the children are "almost transparent."[52] Permeable to atomic light, their bodies lost the stability of boundaries, the protection from intrusions by the outside. Nuclear stories—visual or narrative—thus reflect the permeable boundaries of a nuclear world. Ronin's and Envoy's exchanges draw on a creative eclecticism, a syncretism of images and texts drawn from multiple reflections and refractions of Hiroshima in stories, texts, and images that are spread out over the entire world. In this vein, *Hiroshima Bugi* also performs a historical, cultural, and aesthetic encounter between the Japanese and Anishinaabe cultures. Ronin, the outcast mixed-race postwar child, was abandoned in an orphanage. Racism turned him into the living dead, a ghost child of Hiroshima. As he reveals in his stories, he later died seven more deaths, only to come back each time to haunt the living. At the end of *Hiroshima Bugi,* Ronin vanishes once again. Rumors and stories abound around the mystery of his death, stories that he drowned in the lagoon or flew away. His last words are "I am a crane, and you readers who want to know more about me must search in the clouds."[53] Nuclear aesthetics lives under the shadow of ghost children.

CRITICAL NUCLEAR RACE THEORY

> I was born under the shadow of the atomic bomb.
> —Ngũgĩ wa Thiongo'o, *Secure the Base*

> volt crackle and electricity it has invented
> buchenwald nagasaki and napalm
> it is the frozen first atomic bomb.
> —Edward Kamau Brathwaite, "Mont Blanc"

BEGINNINGS

By insisting on the crucial role of race in post-Hiroshima nuclear politics, Gerald Vizenor's *Hiroshima Bugi,* which I discussed in detail in the last chapter, highlights the entanglement between nuclearism and racism. Any in-depth analysis of nuclear necropolitics needs to address the role of race as exceeding the parameters of nuclear colonialism in the nuclear Indigenous borderlands of the American Southwest. While the problem of race undoubtedly propels nuclear colonialism, it is essential to open up a broader historical and theoretical perspective on the entanglement of race and nuclearism. The following reflections are designed to develop steps toward a critical nuclear race theory.

The facts that uranium mining started in Africa and that most of the uranium for the atomic bombs the United States dropped on Hiroshima and Nagasaki came from a uranium mine in Congo, located in a place called Shinkolobwe,[1] already position race at the very origins of the nuclear age. Moreover, uranium production is to this day central to the African economy, with South Africa, Niger, and Namibia producing 18 percent of the world's annual uranium supply. In *Uranium: War, Energy, and the Rock That Shaped the World,* Tom Zoellner describes his visit in 2007 to the now defunct uranium mine in Shinkolobwe that in the 1940s had yielded most of the uranium for the first atomic bombs. Because of the illegal mining trade in Congo, during which local miners had dug out radioactive materials from the pit and sold them on the black market, the abandoned mine is now heavily guarded by a squad of United Nations soldiers. Shinkolobwe is considered an official non-place, its dilapidated traces covering up the central contribution this mining town made to the world that inaugurated the nuclear age and changed planetary life forever.

Zoellner reports that high-grade uranium had already been found in Shinkolobwe in 1915, a time when radium was the most valuable substance on earth, selling at thirty thousand times the price of gold. More than a thousand Congolese were ordered by Union Miniere to perform forced labor in the mine. Racial and colonial oppression thus facilitated the nuclear venture from its very inception. During World War II, the United States became the world's largest user of Congo cobalt. In 1942, Kenneth D. Nichols, administrator for the Manhattan Project, arrived at Shinkolobwe to buy the waste uranium.[2] In addition to colonial racism, a pervasive politics of secrecy and deception shaped the early formation of the emergent militarized nuclear economy. On the basis of a secret contract between the United States and Union Minière, the mine ended up supplying the vast majority of uranium and plutonium used for the Manhattan Project. It also continued to supply uranium for the massive American buildup of nuclear weapons during the Cold War.

The story Zoellner tells reads like a piece of nuclear crime fiction. When Congo gained its independence in 1960, the mine was officially closed. Managers poured concrete into the shafts and carted off the equipment. But the nuclear reactor acquired a year earlier from the U.S. company General Atomics remained open because Mobutu, a twenty-nine-year-old army officer who had come to power in a coup with American backing, loved the reactor as a source of national prestige. According to Zoellner, security at the plant has been a long-standing joke, and people still fear an accident or sabotage. In the 1970s, two uranium rods in the facility were stolen, with one of them turning up in Rome in the possession of "a Mafia family, who were offering it for sale to 'Middle Eastern buyers' who turned out to be undercover Italian police officers."[3]

After a rebel army overthrew Mobutu and the nation became the Democratic Republic of the Congo, Chinese companies entered the scene as major buyers of cobalt picked from the open pits. Meanwhile, a substantial amount of uranium had been smuggled out of Congo. Zoellner states, "A dossier from the government in Kinshasa reported that radioactive products, with no weights reported, have been sold in Katanga at prices ranging from $300 to $500 to a variety of traffickers from India, China, and Lebanon. [. . .] Uranium ore was now for sale."[4]

Zoellner also tells the story of Mount Brockman, a sacred Aboriginal site in northern Australia where, in 1969, the richest lode of uranium in the southern hemisphere was discovered. Soon Mount Brockman became the site of a mining colony, producing 8 percent of the world's uranium. The mine is located in the middle of Kakadu National Park. Since Australia is a nuclear-free country with no enrichment facilities, let alone nuclear weapons, the approximately nine thousand tons of uranium produced yearly are exported to nuclear reactors in Britain, South Korea, France, the United States, and Japan.

Not surprisingly, uranium mining has become a top domestic policy issue, deeply affecting "the white majority's long and rocky history with the dark-skinned native people who had occupied the island continent for forty thousand years. [. . .] The Aboriginals who wanted to save Mount Brockman [. . .] were seen as antediluvian whiners who needed to join the modern world or as noble martyrs to 'progress,' as embodied by all those uranium pyramids in the shadow of their holy site."[5] The estimated date of a petroglyph believed to represent the Rainbow Serpent is 4000 B.C., or the end of the last ice age. As in the nuclear borderlands of the American Southwest, the racism embedded in the nuclear colonialism directed at the Aboriginal people in Australia thus also entails deicide. The fated colonial encounter threatens an Indigenous history that encompasses the vast temporal expanse between Ice Age, Stone Age, and Atomic Age. The resulting disregard of Aboriginal land and violation of sacred sites, as well as the concomitant radioactive contamination, generation of nuclear waste, and threat of global destruction, have become the cause of massive antinuclear protest movements. Ancient Aboriginal stories warn that if the Rainbow Serpent would ever rise, she would create a flood so large that the world would end. Today a four-and-a-half-foot wooden fence separates the sacred mesa from the uranium pit. Yet, like in the Southwest nuclear borderlands, the Indigenous people have been made dependent on the uranium economy. Uranium has already changed their lives forever. And, to make matters worse, economic dependency threatens to generate a nuclear colonization of mind.

CRITIQUE OF NUCLEAR REASON

The examples of uranium mining in the Congo and at Mount Brockman in northern Australia demonstrate the entanglement of today's nuclear necropolitics with the legacies of colonialism and racism. In his introduction to *Critique of Black Reason*, Achille Mbembe provocatively uses the nuclear power plant as a trope for Blackness and race as the foundation of the modern project of knowledge: "Since the beginning of the eighteenth century, Blackness and race have constituted the [...] foundation, what we might call the nuclear power plant, from which the modern project of knowledge—and of governance—has been deployed."[6] The metaphor's suggestive force resides in its implied reference to a pervasive capitalist economy of extraction, be it the extraction of slave labor power from black bodies or the extraction of nuclear power from the earth. After the end of the Cold War, nuclear necropolitics took a new turn in the context of what Mbembe identifies as "neo- and paracolonial wars": "The forms of occupation have changed with torture, internment camps, and secret prisons, and with today's mix of militarism, counterinsurgency, and the pillage of resources from a distance."[7]

Both slave labor and nuclear power create energy, drive, and desire and herald the unlimited modification of genetic and biological structure. Mbembe speaks of the emergence of a "neuroeconomic subject" that is "a prisoner of desire."[8] Both slave labor and nuclear power pursue unlimited extraction of resources from bodies and the earth. Both are, however, haunted by the specter of death and annihilation. Thinking about nuclear power through Mbembe, we could say that it is "the spirit of death, the shadow of the dead."[9] What Mbembe says about the slave trade as "the world of raw extraction" applies, of course, to nuclear politics as well. Just as the victim of slavery, the victim of nuclear politics has to watch "the spectacle of his own doubling, acquiring along the way the capacity to separate from the self."[10] As I discuss in more detail in chapter 5, enslavement to nuclear politics generates the emergence of nuclear subjectivities whose psychic life is inevitably marked by splitting, doubling, and numbing. Robert J. Lifton speaks about the victims of nuclear violence as being haunted by a "double death," namely, the individual death and the death of extinction of the species.[11]

It is this haunting from a future of extinction that has led African and African American civil rights and peace activists from 1945 to this day to insist on an inextricable link between the struggle for civil rights and the antinuclear movement. In his preface to *Secure the Base,* Kenyan writer Ngũgĩ wa Thiong'o writes:

> The first explosion of a nuclear bomb in 1945 marks a clear historical ontological break with a past during which no human technology was capable of snuffing out life altogether and the beginning of a continuing present where such a technology reigns supreme. And yet this fact does not figure prominently in discussions of the constitution of the modern and postmodern, or its various posts. The human technology for the death of humanity is a more fundamental definition of our times than any linguistic musings or parsing of words.[12]

In his essay "Nuclear-Armed Tribesmen," he then asserts, "If one role of the intellectual is to use words in defense of human life, in our times this responsibility should translate into raising a hue and cry against the 'destroyers' of the world. Belief in stability built on mutual assured destruction is pure madness."[13] Ngũgĩ wa Thiong'o links the antinuclear struggle not only with the civil rights and social justice movements but with the struggle against "capitalist fundamentalism." Pointing to the well-known fact that it is the wealthy nations that use over 90 percent of global human and natural resources, he states, "This capitalist fundamentalism has generated other fundamentalisms in alliance with it, such as some elements of Christian fundamentalism popularly known as the Christian right or, in opposition to it, some elements of Islamic fundamentalism, popularly viewed as terrorism."[14] In this context, Thiong'o concludes, racism takes the extreme form of religious bigotry through the boast that "my race is the chosen race."[15]

In a similar vein, Arundhati Roy, in *The Ordinary Person's Guide to Empire,* declares, "In the twenty-first century the connection between religious fundamentalism, nuclear nationalism, and the pauperization of whole populations because of corporate globalization is becoming impossible to ignore."[16] For both Ngũgĩ wa Thiong'o and Arundhati Roy, the struggle for peace and nuclear disarmament is therefore inseparable from the struggle for social and economic justice and the struggle against racism and fundamentalism of any kind.

Considerations of race and its economic underpinnings under global capitalism are thus absolutely fundamental to the question of the nuclear. While a full discussion of the multiple ways in which race enters nuclear politics would require a book of its own, I will look at the history of African American nuclear resistance to outline the basic steps toward a critical nuclear race theory. The African American civil and human rights movements provide a robust foundation for such a theory. Since the immediate aftermath of Hiroshima and Nagasaki in 1945, these movements have established links with antinuclear and peace movements. In the late 1950s and 1960s, Martin Luther King Jr., one of the most forceful antinuclear activists, insisted that the struggle for civil rights cannot be divided from the struggle against nuclear weapons. Until the end of his life, he persistently linked the black freedom struggle in America with the need for nuclear disarmament. In a similar vein, black leaders were consistent in emphasizing the need to internationalize the fight against nuclear weapons as part of a global human rights movement.

Nuclear disarmament was also central to the platform of the Bandung Conference in 1955, a conference that in many ways inaugurated the civil and human rights movement at the international level. Black intellectuals like W. E. B. Du Bois and Paul Robeson shared Dr. King's commitment to linking the civil rights struggle with the antinuclear struggle. Tracing the roots of both racism and nuclearism back to colonialism and imperialism, they systematically refused to accept any attempt at separating these issues. Throughout the 1950s and 1960s, black women leaders, such as Coretta Scott King, Lorraine Hansberry, and Erna Harris, played a central role in organizations like the Women's International League for Peace and Freedom or Women Strike for Peace, traveling around the world and participating in disarmament conferences and rallies.

Black antinuclear activists were also at the forefront of a powerful critique of economic warfare, linking the prohibitive military budget required for the nuclear arms race to the elimination of funds for social services and programs, the increasing devastation of inner cities, the growing disenfranchisement of the poor, and the devastating effects of childhood poverty and hunger. In the 1980s, a strong contingent of prominent African American public figures, including Harry Belafonte and Toni Morrison, marched to demand an end to the nuclear arms race. Black politicians, clergy, athletes, activists, actors, writers, and entertainers joined the antinuclear activism at the time, insisting on the negative effects of Reagan's nuclear politics on African American communities and on global communities more generally.

This is a history that remains largely eclipsed from accounts that deal with the legacy of the Manhattan Project as well as accounts of the

African American civil rights movement. The tendency to focus almost exclusively on the contribution of African American political and activist leaders, scholars, and writers to the civil rights movement, while at the same time silencing their strong engagement with the antinuclear resistance, goes against their most radical political challenge, namely, to resist the categorical separation of the various struggles against racism, oppression, and war. They were the first to embrace a political ecology that saw and insisted on the inextricable entanglement of the fights against racism, colonialism, and imperialism and fights against the nuclear–military–industrial complex. They were the first to highlight racism at the heart of nuclear necropolitics.

How come so much of the African American antinuclear resistance, so many of the achievements, and so much of the intellectual labor of these times have remained eclipsed from current political debates? One of the tasks today, I insist, is to revive the memory of the powerful antinuclear movements of the decades from the late 1940s through the 1980s to fight the political and cultural amnesia around nuclear politics. This includes returning to African American antinuclear resistance as a basis for developing a critical nuclear race theory. Another task is to fight the compartmentalization of struggles to acknowledge how the fight against nuclear necropolitics is inextricable from all the other struggles against violence and oppression, including the everyday struggles against poverty and the increasing production of disposable populations, peoples, and lives. After all, the very premise of nuclear weapons is that, ultimately, life on earth is disposable.

In *African Americans against the Bomb: Nuclear Weapons, Colonialism, and the Black Freedom Movement*,[17] on which I will draw in the following, Vincent J. Intondi chronicles the history of African American antinuclear resistance. He particularly highlights the contributions of African Americans to thinking about the nuclear problem as part and parcel of the global anticolonial and human rights movements. Even before the invention of the atomic bomb, since the 1930s, Intondi reports, "black Popular Front groups had sought to connect the black freedom movement in America to peace, labor, anticolonial and antifascist movements around the world."[18] Insisting on the indivisible connection of Hiroshima and Nagasaki to colonialism and racism, Paul Robeson and W. E. B. Du Bois took a forceful antinuclear stance. "If power can be held through atomic bombs, colonial peoples may never be free,"[19] wrote Du Bois in a plea to outlaw the fabrication of nuclear weapons.

Moreover, in response to the atomic attack on Hiroshima and Nagasaki, Du Bois wrote in the *Chicago Defender* in September 1945, "We have seen [. . .] to our amazement and distress, a marriage between science and destruction. [. . .] We have always thought of science as the emancipator. We see it now as the enslaver of mankind."[20]

As early as 1946, at a rally organized by the Council on African Affairs, African American activist leaders condemned the radioactive colonization of African countries for uranium mining and the importation of uranium to the United States for the purpose of making atomic bombs. At this rally, Robeson spoke out against the continued colonization of African countries for resource extraction, including specifically the radioactive colonization of the Belgian Congo:

> Our government is getting uranium from the Belgian Congo for atomic bombs. American companies are prospecting for oil in Ethiopia and for minerals in Liberia. [. . .] We on the anti-imperialist side are handicapped by lack of money, lack of powerful organization, lack of influence in state and international affairs. [. . .] It is possible to win if the majority of the American people are brought to understand in the fullest sense the fact that the struggle in which we are engaged is not a matter of mere humanitarian sentiment, but of life and death. The only alternative to world freedom is world annihilation.[21]

In a similar vein, in 1950, Charlie Parker stated, "The power to decide whether humanity is destroyed or lives lies in the hands of the people—all of the people—not just the political few."[22] And in response to the 1950 Stockholm Peace Appeal, which 250 million people signed worldwide, Duke Ellington voiced his disbelief "that people should think of using the A-Bomb."[23]

It did not take long, however, before antinuclear activists were labeled Communist sympathizers, subversives, and enemies of the United States. Especially during McCarthy's anti-Communist persecution, any antinuclear activism was depicted as pro-Communism, and peace offensives were labeled Communist-inspired propaganda. Police maltreated and jailed activists who collected signatures. This political climate was deeply divisive, also affecting the African American antinuclear resistance. Du Bois in particular became a target of vicious criticism. George Schuyler, a spokesperson for the conservative wing, for example, accused him of totalitarianism and of "becoming a puppet of the Soviet Union."[24] In response to such charges, Du Bois retorted, "If we worked together with the Soviet Union against the menace of Hitler, can we not work with it again at a time when only faith can save us from utter atomic disaster?"[25]

Du Bois also linked nuclear militarism and war to economic warfare: "Big business wants to keep your mind off social reform; it would rather spend your taxes for atom bombs than for schools because in this way it makes more money; it would rather have your sons dying in Korea than studying in America and asking awkward questions. The system, which it advocates depends on war and more war."[26] However, according to Intondi, the Cold War and the McCarthyism of the 1950s, with its anti-Communist fervor and its systematic strategy of intimidation and criminalization of activists as alleged Communists, eventually led to a dramatic decline in the peace movement in the United States and destroyed most black leftist organizations.

At the international level, by contrast, especially with the Bandung Conference, at which twenty-nine Asian and African nations gathered in Indonesia, the antinuclear movement gained new momentum. The Bandung Conference linked the need to eliminate European colonialism and white supremacy with the need to eliminate nuclear weapons. The momentum gathered during this conference, which Richard Wright, among others, attended, also reignited the African American antinuclear resistance and contributed to the emergence of a new civil rights movement. Alarmed by the rise in nuclear weapons tests, writer Eugene Gordon sharply criticized what he perceived as the black community's complacency in the fight against nuclear war: "Don't our editors and publishers want us to know that a generation of Negro children with bone cancer and blood diseases would be less able to continue our fight for human rights? [. . .] Shouldn't we therefore pay some attention to less tangible but more sinister evils than those we meet daily face to face?"[27]

Gordon's plea highlights one of the most difficult challenges facing antinuclear resistance—a challenge that persists to this day—namely, the fact that it is much easier to mobilize political resistance in the face of daily discrimination and oppression than in the face of a threat that is looming in the perhaps distant future. This is a problem both of scale and of visceral experience. Violence that is experienced viscerally in the everyday or violence that is visible and tangible generates resistance much more easily than the threat of relatively intangible future violence or future wars. While this problem of scale, futurity, and the visceral shapes nuclear subjectivities more generally, it also presents itself as a conceptual problem for the development of a critical nuclear race theory. The insistence of thinkers like Du Bois, Robeson, and, later, Martin Luther King Jr. on the systemic entanglement of the nuclear threat with everyday racism and violation of civil rights goes to the heart of this problem. As these political leaders insist, neglecting to fight against a possible future nuclear war might render the fight for civil rights (or any other fight) in the here and now obsolete. To trace this entanglement in the way both everyday racism and the nuclear threat persist as slow and structural violence over and above their spectacular manifestations is one of the foremost functions of a critical nuclear race theory.

In 1959, France's declaration of its intent to perform nuclear tests in the Sahara marked a new phase in global radioactive colonization. People feared that the desert could become a base for nuclear war in North Africa and the Middle East. Protests erupted throughout Africa with the participation of international organizations as well as world leaders, including Egypt's president Nasser, Frantz Fanon, and activists from all over the world. With the spread of antinuclear resistance, the Algerian War intensified. The newly founded Committee for a Sane Nuclear Policy (SANE) helped to center the international peace movement. James Baldwin served on its advisory board, and prominent public intellectuals and leaders, including Albert Schweitzer, Bertrand Russell, Eleanor Roosevelt, and Martin Luther King Jr., supported its activities. The subgroup Hollywood for SANE included Nat King Cole, Sammy Davis Jr., Sidney Poitier, and Harry Belafonte.[28]

The start of the Vietnam War and the civil rights movement of the 1960s brought yet another turn in the struggle against nuclear war. Many African and African American intellectuals—for example, James Baldwin and Ngũgĩ wa Thiong'o—insist on seeing the arrival of nuclear weapons as an ontological break that forever changes the status of reality. In *The Fire Next Time*, James Baldwin writes, "The threat of universal extinction hanging over the world today [. . .] changes, totally and for ever, the nature of reality and brings into devastating question the true meaning of man's history. We human beings now have the power to exterminate ourselves; this seems to be the entire sum of our achievement."[29] In an address to the War Resisters League, King stated that we live in "an age of biological weapons, chemical warfare, atomic fallout and nuclear bombs. [. . .] Every man, woman, and child lives, not knowing if they shall see tomorrow's sunrise. [. . .] What will be the ultimate value of having established social justice in a context where all people, Negro and White, are merely free to face destruction by strontium 90 or atomic war?"[30] America had come to embody a "culture of fear,"[31] King insisted, dominated by the specter of nuclear weapons and racial annihilation.

Indeed, the notion that fear, according to King, could become the ultimate cause of nuclear war anticipates the conceptual framework that urban historian Mike Davis later developed in *Ecology of Fear*. King targets a politics of emotion and affect in which the very fear of nuclear weapons can paradoxically be co-opted to ignite nuclear war. In response to the Cuban Missile Crisis in 1962, King again linked nuclear disarmament to racial and economic justice, holding nation-states responsible for a "genocidal and suicidal" politics that threatens the very survival of mankind. King, in other words, already worked with a robust concept not only of nuclear necropolitics but also of a psychopolitical ecology of fear. According to such an ecological perspective, it is the political mobilization of fear that provides the grounding and rationale for the country's necropolitical nuclearism. In other words, fear is for King at the heart of the psychopolitical formation of nuclear subjectivities that are necessary to sustain nuclearism's work of death.

The 1960s also evolved into the decade that saw a flourishing movement of African American women against the Bomb, including, most prominently, Coretta King and Lorraine Hansberry, author of an antinuclear play titled *What Use Are Flowers?*[32] Both women linked the struggle for civil rights with anticolonialism and nuclear disarmament. Many of the black women activists at the time, including Angela Davis, joined the Women's International League for Peace and Freedom. Like Du Bois, Robeson, Martin Luther King, and others, these women activists stressed the political urgency of linking the civil rights movement and the antinuclear resistance movement. Dagmar Wilson, founder of Women Strike for Peace, states:

> The movement for civil rights is part of the movement for a world of peace, freedom, and justice. [. . .] It has been very tempting at times to drop everything and work for civil rights, except for the fact that we all realize that civil rights without nuclear disarmament won't do us any good. We realize that the two movements are different aspects of the same problem and that eventually the two will meet and merge.[33]

The next turn in antinuclear resistance emerged in tandem with the rise of the Black Power movement in the mid-1960s. One of its most radical proponents was Malcolm X, whose stance on nuclear war inspired the Black Panther Party, cofounded by Bobby Seale and Huey P. Newton. Like others before, the Black Panthers linked the struggle against racism and colonialism with the fight against nuclear weapons and war. Its Executive Mandate no. 1 stated:

> The enslavement of Black people at the very founding of this country, the genocide practiced on the American Indians and the confinement of the survivors on reservations, the savage lynching of thousands of Black men and women, the dropping of atomic bombs on Hiroshima and Nagasaki, and now the cowardly massacre in Vietnam all testify to the fact that toward people of color the racist power structure of America has but one policy: repression, genocide, terror, and the big stick.[34]

Kathleen Cleaver, one of the leaders of the Black Panther Party, was invited to travel to Japan to speak against nuclear weapons and the Vietnam War. Very much along the lines of Executive Mandate no. 1, she argues, "From its inception the Black Panther Party saw the condition of blacks within an international context."[35]

In the 1970s, as the development of nuclear weapons worldwide increased dramatically, the antinuclear movement once again stressed the links between nuclear militarism and economic inequality: "We are now turning out one nuclear bomb in the U.S. every eight hours, while every hour eight families die of starvation,"[36] Reverend James Orange stated. Vincent Intondi writes, "Many in the black community argued that poverty in the United States was linked to the government's nuclear policies. African Americans questioned why their children suffered from malnutrition as the administration continued to spend money on nuclear weapons."[37] The development of the neutron bomb under President Jimmy Carter led to a rise in black activism and antinuclear resistance worldwide. Eventually, in 1978, Carter had to cancel plans for the production of the neutron bomb. In the same year, the United Nations for the first time discussed universal disarmament.

While the antinuclear movement initially focused almost exclusively on nuclear war, the 1970s and 1980s increasingly expanded attention to include the dangers of nuclear energy. In the wake of President Eisenhower's Atoms for Peace Program (established in the late 1950s),

South Africa had obtained a cooperation agreement to create a nuclear infrastructure that provided the basis for the construction, in secret collaboration with Israel, of a nuclear weapon. This alerted people to the intricate connection between nuclear energy and nuclear weapons. Coretta King stated, "Thousands of nuclear missiles are aimed at our cities day and night. A hazardous nuclear energy technology readily lends itself to the proliferation of nuclear weapons. Together they threaten to bring the human venture to an end."[38] The year 1978 also saw an increase in demonstrations and protests organized by Mobilization for Survival, with the participation of prominent individuals and groups including Coretta King, Helen Caldicott, Daniel Ellsberg, Pete Seeger, and the activist musicians from Sweet Honey in the Rock.

Beginning with the election of Ronald Reagan, however, the 1980s saw a dramatic rise in the buildup of nuclear weapons. By 1984, the administration had cut $141 billion in social programs and increased military spending by $181 billion.[39] Needless to say, black and Indigenous communities suffered disproportionately. In response, black citizens, including politicians, athletes, and celebrities, joined the fight for peace and equality. Arguing that "the nuclear issue had not been addressed from a black perspective and the established peace groups did not make an effort to go into the black community," Greg Johnson, an African American librarian, together with his wife, founded Blacks Against Nukes (BAN). Consistent with the movement's commitment to internationalism, BAN established international relationships with the Green Party in Germany and peace organizations in Japan, South Africa, and India.

In 1982, approximately one million demonstrators, demanding the right to live free from nuclear terror, marched in New York City, with companion rallies held in Pasadena and San Francisco; 2.3 million signatures were collected. Prominent African American participants included Dick Gregory, Toni Morrison, Harry Belafonte, Coretta King, and Sweet Honey in the Rock. Speakers, including prominent members of the clergy, directly targeted the insatiable nuclear war machines. Revered Herbert Daughtry stated, "This is a nation with the mightiest military machine in the world and yet it cannot feed, clothe, shelter, educate, heal, and employ its people."[40] And Reverend William James, president of the Ministerial Interfaith Association of Harlem, proclaimed, "When you take a look at the military budget and then at our decaying cities, you can see that we are already victims of war. Not only would New York be a major target of any nuclear attack, it is already a target of the military budget."[41] Finally, the connection between racism, colonialism, and nuclear weapons was reiterated by Harlem Fight Back in an editorial for the *New York Amsterdam News* that could be read like a manifesto for the entire antinuclear movement:

> All sectors of society—Black, white, red, yellow, brown, young and old, male and female—are and will be affected by nuclear militarism. [. . .] The struggle over Native American lands and the building of one of the world's major nuclear arsenals in South Africa show that nuclear militarism and nuclear technology are clear expressions of racism. Recently there has been widespread theft of Indian lands where uranium has been discovered. [. . .] South Africa is one of the main sources in the world for uranium. It provides imperialism with uranium mined by Blacks. This bastion of racism poses a threat not only to Africa, but the world. Where in America do we hear the outcry? [. . .] There is no issue more overwhelming and all embracing than nuclear technology, militarism and power.[42]

Eventually, antinuclear activism forced President Reagan to change his nuclear policy. Reagan and then Soviet general secretary Mikhail Gorbachev signed the START treaty, to reduce each side's nuclear arsenal, and the Intermediate-Range Nuclear Forces Treaty, which banned medium-range nuclear-tipped ballistic missiles. In 1985, they issued a joint proclamation: "Nuclear war cannot be won and should never be fought."[43] In 1989, the fall of the Soviet Union marked the official end of the Cold War. It looked for a while as if the threat of nuclear war had been contained. However, the specter of limited nuclear war already loomed on the horizon, and September 11, 2001, brought the additional specter of nuclear terrorism.

Vincent Intondi ends his book with a chapter on President Obama's nuclear policy. It's a tortured chapter that struggles to address what Intondi perceives as Obama's schizoid split in his nuclear policy. While deeply critical of Obama's concrete political decisions, Intondi ends with what can almost be seen as an incantation of Obama's proclaimed vision of a world free of nuclear weapons. Yet, at the same time, he shows how the split he identifies left a devastating nuclear legacy, especially in light of Obama's consistently reiterated antinuclear vision. "The single most serious threat to American national security is nuclear terrorism," Obama said as a presidential candidate, only to assert unequivocally, "I think it would be a profound mistake for us to use nuclear weapons in any circumstance."[44] In 2009, during his presidency, Obama declared, "We'll work tirelessly to lessen the nuclear threat and roll back the specter of a warming planet."[45] This statement is significant, I think, because it reveals Obama's tacit awareness that the nuclear threat is indeed linked to global warming. Obama was not alone in his insistence at the time on the central role of nuclear politics in today's world. Secretary of State Hillary Clinton also affirmed that the number one threat in the world was nuclear weapons.[46]

After winning the Nobel Peace Prize, Obama submitted a proposal for a new START treaty. His *Nuclear Posture Review* stated that the United States would not design, produce, or test any new nuclear weapons and, most significantly, added, "The United States will not use or threaten to use nuclear weapons against non-nuclear weapons states that are party of the Nuclear Nonproliferation Treaty."[47] Obama's most important action happened in 2010, when he held a historic summit to discuss the locking down of all vulnerable nuclear materials. Forty-seven nations participated. Eventually, in response to what has been called Obama's "nuclear spring," Ukraine, Argentina, Chile, and Mexico committed to eliminating their nuclear materials, and Kazakhstan, Vietnam, and Canada agreed to dispose of their enriched uranium. The United States and Russia agreed to dispose of sixty-eight metric tons of plutonium.

Unfortunately, however, partly under heavy bipartisan pressure, as well as in response to tensions with Putin concerning his attempts to extend Russia's influence over former Soviet countries, Obama's policy on nuclear weapons began to shift. Despite his continued stated commitment to nuclear disarmament, the United States conducted its first nuclear test since 2006 under the Obama administration, albeit a subcritical one that did not create a nuclear explosion. Pressure from the Republicans mounted as they unified against the new START treaty. And while, in 2011, the United States destroyed its most powerful nuclear bomb, by 2012, Obama had agreed to invest an extra $85 billion over ten years to modernizing the nuclear weapons arsenal. In addition, he proposed spending $125 billion during the next decade for a new fleet of nuclear-armed submarines as well as new bombers and missiles. Needless to say, this deviation from his stated politics left Obama's supporters disappointed, if not betrayed. Nuclear weapons expert and president of the Ploughshares Fund Joseph Cirincione said in response, "I'm convinced the president wants to continue his efforts to reform U.S. nuclear policy, but the administration had a schizoid approach to the issue. They believe they have to buy off legislators with billions of dollars in expenditure in their states in order to get the votes for arms control later. The billions of dollars we are lavishing on the B61 is criminal."[48]

Cirincione's charge of a schizoid politics is right on target, especially given that in his 2013 speech in Berlin, Obama restated his conviction that "peace with justice means pursuing the security of a world without nuclear weapons."[49] In his conclusion to *African Americans against the Bomb,* Intondi states, "Obama, like Du Bois, Robeson, Rustin, King, and so many others before him, understands that stopping the process Harry Truman put into place is not only the most important thing he can do for African Americans, but for all human beings. The right to live without fear of nuclear war is not only a black issue but a human issue."[50] To act politically on the basis of this understanding, however, would have required avoiding the schizoid split about the nuclear weapons arsenal. This is where Obama clearly failed. But Intondi also qualifies this failure, reminding his readers that the implementation of Obama's vision of a nuclear-free world "may depend on how much concerned citizens are willing to fight for nuclear abolition."[51] This is a call to activism that echoes the many African American voices that have spoken out, since the dropping of the first atomic bombs, against complacency about the nuclear danger. It is a call for a new antinuclear movement. To fight for freedom from nuclear terror and its necropolitical work of death requires one to heed this call and revive the vision of this country's African American leaders in the antinuclear struggle (and, we may add, returning to the argument at the beginning of this chapter, the vision of its Indigenous leaders).

Such a revival is one of the goals of Paul Williams's *Race, Ethnicity, and Nuclear War.* Published in 2011, the book opens with a quote by Arundhati Roy, who insists that race is at the heart of what I have called *nuclear subjectivities*:

> It is such supreme folly to believe that nuclear weapons are deadly only when they are used. The fact that they exist at all, their very presence in our lives, will wreak more havoc than we can begin to fathom. Nuclear weapons pervade our thinking. Control our

behaviour. Administer our societies. Inform our dreams. They bury themselves like meat hooks deep in the base of our brains. They are purveyors of madness. They are the ultimate colonizer. Whiter than any white man who ever lived. The very heart of whiteness."[52]

This necropolitical shift from the "heart of darkness" to the "heart of whiteness" is reminiscent of Malcolm X's question "Can the white man be so naïve as to think the clear import of [the atomic bombings] ever will be lost upon the non-white two-thirds of the earth's population?"[53] Because of the intimate connection with colonialism, many people of color link the emergence of nuclear weapons to their collective memory of mass murder and race terror. In *Literary Aftershocks: American Writers, Readers, and the Bomb,* Albert Stone argues that "historical formulation can help Third World peoples, African-Americans, and others to empathize with the disintegrations of Hiroshima by analogizing them to such disasters as colonialism, slavery and the shipboard horrors of the Middle Passage, and the Civil War."[54] There is a new crucial element, though, to the traumatizing colonization of the mind by nuclear madness. While nuclear weapons facilitate a culmination of global processes of colonization, they do so by precipitating a "haunting from the future." Part of the reason why these weapons are "purveyors of madness" is that they generate a pervasive ecology of fear marked by a psychic state of hypervigilance, an anticipation of disaster that is always present, even if unconscious.

Another crucial new element that marks nuclear subjectivities is that they promote what Robert J. Lifton calls the "species self." Many African American antinuclear activists share the sentiment expressed by Hiroshima survivors that the atomic bomb forces humans to develop a "species self," that is, to think of themselves as a species in addition to their specific identification through race, class, gender, or nation. According to Paul Williams, Langston Hughes, for example, encourages his readers to look beyond individual safety toward the collective threat: "As a human species, we are all jeopardized by the threat of nuclear war, and unified as a consequence. [. . .] Only by accepting the interdependence of our lives and futures can this [complete annihilation] be avoided."[55] In "Antinuclear Politics and the Transcendence of Race," Paul Williams argues that what unites figures like Alice Walker, James Baldwin, and Martin Luther King Jr. is "the assertion that successful antinuclear politics must comprehend the divisiveness of thinking in terms of racial difference, and that campaigns against racism should be linked to calls for disarmament if they are to be meaningful movements for equality and human rights."[56]

The urge to overcome thinking in terms of racial difference in order to think in terms of the human species is, of course, generated by the specter of extinction. At the famous 1982 Anti-Nuke Rally, Alice Walker pushed the linkage between the specter of extinction and race to an extreme that was intended to shock her audience into recognition of the depth of the racialized nuclear imaginary. Arguing that the "hope for revenge" is "at the heart of People of Color's resistance to any anti-nuclear movement," she suggests that for some, the idea of nuclear apocalypse might appear as a just consequence of white racial chauvinism: "it would be good, perhaps, to put an end to the species in any case, rather than let white men continue to subjugate it."[57] Walker then turns around and affirms the need for social justice, or, as she puts it, the justice "for every living thing,"[58] as a precondition for averting extinction. Thus linking nuclear genocide with racial oppression, she affirms the need "to think outside of modernity's division of peoples into hierarchies of race."[59]

While Alice Walker's initial provocation is reminiscent of Jacques Derrida's equally provocative question of who can tell that we don't secretly desire a nuclear apocalypse, Walker's subsequent rejection of the fantasy of vengeance in favor of asserting social justice as a precondition for the antinuclear struggle anticipates the challenge posed by the very ending of Achille Mbembe's *Critique of Black Reason*: "But as we can see within certain strains of modern Black criticism, the proclamation of difference is only one facet of a larger project—the project of a world that is coming, a world before us, one whose destination is universal, a world freed from the burden of race, from resentment, and from the desire for vengeance that all racism calls into being."[60]

Alice Walker's stance resonates with the intersectional black feminism of the 1980s that linked civil rights and peace movements. In her introduction to *Home Girls: A Black Feminist Anthology*, Barbara Smith, for example, rejects the charge that black feminism relies on a narrow agenda by asserting that "a movement committed to fighting sexual, racial, economic, and heterosexual oppression [. . .] at the same time as it challenges militarism and imminent nuclear destruction is the very opposite of narrow."[61]

ENTANGLEMENTS AND ALLIANCES

Juxtaposing a theory of nuclear colonialism with a critical nuclear race theory should convey the urgency not only of integrating the two theoretical strands into an overall framework but also of linking the two antinuclear resistance movements. As many African American and African public intellectuals and activists insist, the struggle against nuclear weapons must be part and parcel of the struggle for civil rights. And, as Indigenous leaders insist, the struggle against nuclear colonialism is a necessary part of the larger struggle for Indigenous rights. Both Indigenous and African American activists maintain that antinuclear resistance must be at the very center of other political movements because civil and Indigenous rights lose their value if the world is destroyed by nuclear war.

This is also why leaders on both sides emphasize the importance of linking their antinuclear struggle to international movements. As they speak with survivors of Hiroshima and Nagasaki or take part in antinuclear protests in different parts of the world, they demonstrate that nuclear colonialism and racism are global issues. Indigenous and African American women leaders, including creative writers, musicians, and artists, further convey the pivotal role of gender and reproductive politics in the antinuclear fight. Finally, given colonial and racial histories, it goes without saying that class is the single most determining factor in the disproportionate impact of nuclearism on people's lives. Black and Indigenous public leaders are at the forefront of resistance against the economic warfare and its connection to nuclear warfare. They link the prohibitive costs of the nuclear arms race—which is now revived in the name of updating existing stockpiles—to the growing disenfranchisement of the poor, the elimination of social services, and the devastation of inner cities. Internationally, they relate the abject poverty across the globe and the radioactive colonization of African countries to the role nuclear politics plays in both militarism and energy politics.

The antinuclear resistance shares one conviction: tied to colonialism, racism, and classism, nuclear politics is necropolitics. It performs its work of death at the global scale, either through hitherto unimaginable mass killings, if not a nuclear holocaust, or through the slow violence of radioactive contamination that poisons air, water, soil, and food. This slow violence encompasses the entire earth, including the very bodies of those who inhabit it, albeit disproportionately—at least for the time being.

In conclusion, the most basic steps toward a critical nuclear race theory outlined in this historical survey can be summarized as follows: (1) critical nuclear race theory needs to anchor itself in the genealogy of nuclear colonialism; (2) movements for civil rights and for social, economic, and racial justice need to be linked to antinuclear resistance; (3) antinuclear resistance needs to build or become affiliated with international networks and address environmental racism across the globe; (4) critical nuclear race theory needs to operate as an intersectional movement, mindful of gender politics and the differential impacts of nuclear politics across lines of race and gender; (5) antinuclear resistance needs to mobilize psychological resistance against the formation of nuclear subjectivities through a nuclear politics and ecology of fear, denial, splitting, moral inversion, and negative hallucination; (6) antinuclear resistance needs to operate at both the communal level and the level of species and transspecies; and (7) antinuclear resistance needs to counter the nuclear colonization of mind that operates via the racially inflected creation of economic dependency. This is why the decolonization of nuclear subjectivities must be at the heart of a critical nuclear race theory, including attention to the racially inflected nuclear unconscious.

FOUR

THE GENDER OF NUCLEAR SUBJECTIVITIES

I don't remember the exact year when Alain Resnais's *Hiroshima, Mon Amour* was first screened in Germany. Since it came out in France in 1959, it probably hit German movie theaters in 1960. Years earlier, our high school did the mandatory screening of Resnais's *Night and Fog*, the single most traumatic film I have ever seen. That film changed my entire view of the world, of war and peace, of my country, my parents, and human nature. And it filled me with an unfathomable horror of war.

Hiroshima, Mon Amour only enforced this sense of horror. I had known about the atomic bomb and lived under its threat ever since I was a small child. But I had not seen images of bodies seared by atomic radiation, and I had not heard stories of the effect of the bomb on the people of Hiroshima. The atomic attack on Hiroshima had not been personalized by individual stories to which I could relate emotionally. Right at the opening of the film, I was deeply confused by the fact that I couldn't distinguish whether the bodies figured a couple making love or whether they were the bodies of injured Hiroshima victims. The proximity of sex and death was new to me, and deeply disturbing.

Of course, Resnais and Marguerite Duras, who wrote the screenplay, played with this ambiguity. Only much later did I find out that *Hiroshima, Mon Amour* was the only film at the time that contained actual footage of the nuclear attack. The stories about Hiroshima invoked in the film were horrifying. The Japanese man tells the woman that, while he was conscripted into the Imperial Japanese Army, his family was in Hiroshima and became victims of the atomic attack. The French actress told the story of her love affair with a German soldier who was shot on liberation day. I could relate to this young French girl, publicly shamed and locked up in a cellar, her hair shaven like that of Jewish victims of the Holocaust.

The film thus interweaves the two traumatic stories of World War II in Europe and Japan. The French actress relates to Hiroshima in a complicated play of transference, drawing the Japanese man in, even though he tries to resist by asserting, "You saw nothing at Hiroshima, nothing." For both of them, Hiroshima thus merges affectively with Nevers. It is the only way they can connect—by merging their stories through the highly subjective lens of personal transference. I think one of the most crucial achievements of *Hiroshima, Mon Amour* is that it positions the audience to enter this game of transference.

> As a woman I have no country. As a woman I want no country. As a woman my country is the whole world.
>
> —Virginia Woolf, *A Room of One's Own*

> They asked me what I thought of the atomic bomb. I said I had not been able to take any interest in it.
>
> —Gertrude Stein, "Reflection on the Atomic Bomb"

MODERNIST INFLECTIONS

If I open this chapter with two epigraphs by Virginia Woolf and Gertrude Stein, it is because, as two of the most prominent modernist women writers, they introduce a specific queering of perspectives on world politics at different crucial times in history. Virginia Woolf makes her antinationalist statement in *A Room of One's Own*, a seminal work of creative nonfiction that proposes a feminist argument for the economic independence of women. The book was published on October 24, 1929, the first day of the Wall Street crash that inaugurated the Great Depression, affecting all of the industrialized Western nations. The lack of economic and political cooperation in response to this economic crash fueled the growth of nationalisms across Europe, which in turn had a tremendous impact on the world economy and politics. Most fatefully, in Germany, it led to the instantaneous rise of the National Socialist Party that brought Adolf Hitler into power. In conjunction with the global economic crisis, Hitler's nationalist imperialism led to the outbreak of World War II in 1939, which ended with the bombing of Hiroshima and Nagasaki. Virginia Woolf's public declaration of her antinationalist stance can thus also be read as an early warning against the belligerent and destructive forces of nationalism that would eventually fuel the first atomic war.

Gertrude Stein's pronouncement on the atomic bomb was made seventeen years later in 1946, in the wake of this war. "Reflection on the Atomic Bomb," which might be Gertrude Stein's last published piece, develops a unique yet highly symptomatic expression of nuclear war as a psychological condition. "They asked me what I thought of the atomic bomb. I said I had not been able to take any interest in it," Stein opens her argument. She continues, "If they are really as destructive as all that, there is nothing left and if there is nothing there is nobody to be interested and nothing to be interested about." The very idea of "remainderless destruction" becomes, for Stein, a barrier to an engaged affective response: "what is the use of bothering to be scared, and if you are not scared the atomic bomb is not interesting," she concludes.

Stein's piece is symptomatic in many respects because it exhibits, in her characteristically formulaic and formalist way, a basic psychological defense against the fear of the atomic bomb. Since, according to Stein, any possible nuclear destruction is out of our control, the only viable reaction is to ignore the Bomb. This willful denial exhibits a remarkably detached psychological pragmatism: "really nobody else can do anything about it and so you have to just live along like always, so you see the atomic [bomb] is not at all interesting." Stein's disinterest constitutes, of course, a profound rhetorical provocation because it casually exposes what is in fact an inevitable splitting, a splitting embraced as the only possible condition of living with the atomic bomb. Psychological splitting is, according to Melanie Klein's theory of psychological development, a primitive defense mechanism developed during the so-called paranoid-schizoid position. What is intolerable or unfathomable becomes split off from psychic awareness and consciously felt emotions. But splitting is arguably also the most basic adaptive psychic mechanism in a dangerous, destructive, and persecutory world. One may wonder whether a pervasive politics of splitting is not an inevitable aspect of living in the nuclear age and in our increasingly toxic nuclear world.

At the level of the politics of emotion in Stein's piece, saying one has not been able to take any interest in the atomic bomb during the very year after it destroyed Hiroshima and Nagasaki—and, within four months, killed between 129,000 and 226,000 people—seems like the most callous dismissal of this monumental event that many claim had changed the world forever. If one tries to read Stein's statement as a queering of the atomic discourses at the time, and perhaps the gendered nuclear discourses today, one needs to look more closely at the provocation it might present. Short of dismissing the piece out of hand, what are Stein's rhetorical moves? To begin with, her style bears the familiar Steinian signature, such as bending of grammar, use of minor function words without inflection, characteristic rhetorical repetitions, and familiar rhythms. Critics have largely ignored the piece, most likely because they did not really know what to do with it. They might also have avoided it because it is admittedly a really shocking piece. In "The Politics of Politics; or, How the Atomic Bomb Didn't Interest Gertrude Stein and Emily Dickinson," Brenda Wineapple argues that, given Stein's exclusive concern with literary form and her systematic undermining of referentiality, her self-contained pieces mark aesthetic objects in and of themselves and treats everything else, like the atomic bomb, as extrinsic. However, she also argues that the piece is an invitation to reconceive the place of moral questions in art and aesthetics. What then could be a greater provocation to do so than claiming in 1946 that one was not able to take any interest in the atomic bomb? As Wineapple puts it, "not to be interested in the atomic bomb in 1946 is an inimitable, annoying, and clever rhetorical device drawing attention to itself."[1] What is it, then, that the piece is precisely drawing attention to, and how is its in-your-face aesthetics designed to provoke a particular response, not to say resistance, in its readers?

Stein opens with a quasi-confessional statement: despite the fact that she likes detective and mystery stories, she could never read any that dealt with "death rays and atomic bombs."[2] Once we take this as a possible resistance against closer confrontation with the nuclear work of death, we realize that Stein's entire piece is, in fact, less a "reflection on the atomic bomb," as the title suggests, than it is a reflection on the resistance against reflecting on the atomic bomb. This resistance is only enhanced by the systematic purging of affect from reflection that is a signature of Stein's writing more generally. The aesthetic strategy of purging affect from nuclear discourse showcases, I think, an important insight into the "politics of splitting"[3] by driving it to its extreme internal logics. Implicitly, Stein argues that nuclear war would only be interesting if it were an all-out nuclear war, in which case there would be nobody left to be interested. She thus targets the immediate postwar warnings against an all-out nuclear war, only to conclude that if "in spite of all destruction there are always lots left on this earth," then why even care about the issue?[4] This certainly doesn't attenuate the shock of her provocation. Stein then recommends to leave the issue of the atomic bomb to those who are inventing it or starting if off, because "really nobody else can do anything about it so you have to just live along like always."[5] This may appear like a formulaic shorthand rationalization for the very politics of splitting that leads to complete, if not cynical, depoliticization.

A politics of splitting is usually designed to ward off intolerable affect. Stein, of whom one could perhaps say that her entire writing is designed to ward off affect, nonetheless indirectly addresses the politics of fear at the center of nuclear necropolitics. Questioning the very motivation of those who reveal interest in the atomic bomb, she writes,

> Sure it will destroy and kill a lot, but it's the living that are interesting not the way of killing them. [. . .] They think they are interested about the atomic bomb but they really are not any more than I am. Really not. They may be a little scared, I am not so scared, there is so much to be scared of so what is the use of bothering to be scared, and if you are not scared the atomic bomb is not interesting.[6]

Interestingly, in its pseudo-logical abstraction, this passage goes to the core of how the politics of fear inevitably shapes nuclear subjectivities: we cannot but succumb to a certain amount of adaptive splitting if we want to continue leading our everyday lives. At the same time, in totalizing the politics of splitting by dismissing the interest in or concern with splitting off a terrifying extrinsic reality altogether, Stein displays an embrace of the very core of depoliticization. The effect of this rhetorical ruse is, almost paradoxically, a reverse psychology. The *pseudo-logical* reflection generates a *psycho-logical* one, designed to provoke resistance and, again paradoxically, enhance the interest in the atomic bomb.

It is important to note, however, that Stein's reflections position her on the opposite end of Derrida's reflections on the nuclear arms race analyzed in chapter 1, as he insists that every aspect of life—whether we know it or not—is marked by the atomic bomb. Like Derrida, however, she also insists on the fact that the real threat of the atomic bomb, namely, an all-out nuclear war, can only be apprehended as a rhetorical condition. While Derrida analyzes this rhetorical condition, Stein performs a rhetorical play on the psychological condition of the nuclear threat. Moreover, to the extent that splitting is successful, the fear of nuclear destruction is relegated to the nuclear unconscious. While we "just live along like always," as Stein suggests, our fears migrate to the unconscious. In this vein, I am tempted to read Stein's assertion that she could never read detective or mystery stories about "death rays and atomic bombs" as a manifestation not only of her lack of interest but also of a split-off unconscious fear of what she calls the "death rays" of atomic bombs. At the very least, her rhetorical choice seems to point in this direction. Why, for example, is her formulation "I never could read them," rather than, say, "I was not interested in reading them"?

Stein's rhetorical strategy belongs to a more general politics of queering at the heart of her use of language and rhetoric. Writing against the grain of familiar discourses, not only of the time but also of discourse in general, Stein works within the larger modernist trend of an antireferential experimental aesthetics. This also entails a particular queering of politics, namely, one that looks at the central issues of global politics, including gender politics, through the lens of aesthetic abstraction. As previously mentioned, "Reflection on the Atomic Bomb" was most likely the last piece Stein wrote. Written at the very inception of the so-called nuclear age, it also introduces a queering in the gendered politics of modernism that, I would argue, presents itself as a resistance against the early formation of *nuclear subjectivities*. While everyone else seems to say that after the invention of the Bomb the world will not be the same, and that the knowledge that we have acquired the power to destroy our planet will change us as a species, Stein defiantly asserts that since we cannot do anything about this, we "have to just live along like always."

But then Stein adds a crucial last sentence that has not caught much attention: "This is a nice story."[7] With this sentence, I submit, she mocks any attempt to read her story in referential or literal terms. Written at the very end of her last word on the atomic bomb, this too is a queering of (aesthetic) nuclear politics. One of the most interesting aspects of this queering is that Stein's resistance to the formation of gendered nuclear subjectivities comes at the very beginning of their earliest formation. To this day, Stein's piece remains unique and, as Brenda Wineapple says, an inimitable and annoying rhetorical device. Her attempt to think nuclear politics in nonreferential and nonrepresentational terms, however, is a challenge that has remained with nuclear aesthetics ever since.[8]

DEATH RAYS, ATOMIC GARDENS, AND SENTIENT BROCCOLI

Gertrude Stein's description of the atomic bomb's lethal radioactivity demonstrates how, from the very beginning, atomic light has generated a veritable iconography of death. "Like a dream, this form of light moved through objects, erased boundaries between objects, crossing their internal and external borders,"[9] writes Akira Lippit in *Atomic Light*. The mysterious power of this light elicits an entire range of highly gendered phantasmatic cathexes, most prominently generated by the awestruck experiences of nuclear explosions—what Joe Masco has referred to as the "nuclear sublime."[10] As a first instance, we should recall Oppenheimer's messianic awe after the Trinity explosion and his citation of the Baghavad Gita. However, after nuclear energy was promoted independently from militarism and warfare—mainly during the "Atoms for Peace" campaign—there instantly emerged more mundane forms of fascination that we may call "atomic surrealism," if not "nuclear gothic." Bound up with the early period of the commercialization of nuclear energy and commodification of nuclear products, such mundane forms include, for example, the flourishing X-ray fashions, like radium clothing and lingerie; radioactive water advertised as a healthy elixir; and radium toothpaste and cosmetics. Finally, it encompassed the cultivation of atomic gardens, including so-called gamma gardens, and the sale of mutant seeds. These mundane forms of fascination with atomic death rays reveal how even death can become an icon of consumer fetishism. As soon as the nuclear industry, in search of new markets, inaugurated the "Atoms for Peace" movement—mainly through the introduction of X-rays for medical and commercial purposes, and later through the advertising of nuclear power and the construction of nuclear power plants—atomic rays became objects of popular culture and consumption. Today, the commercialization extends into the burgeoning disaster tourism in and around Hiroshima, Chernobyl, and Fukushima.

Beginning in the 1950s, atomic gardens became coveted nuclear sites. Initially designed to test the effects of radiation on plants, they were soon used to grow mutant plants for consumption. In 1959, Muriel Howorth, a British pro-atomic activist, founded the Atomic Gardening Society and widely distributed irradiated plant seeds to its members. She collected over three and a half million seeds, mostly purchased from a Tennessee dentist who produced them in a backyard cinder-block bunker. Large-scale gamma gardens remained in use despite growing concerns about the danger of radioactivity and atomic energy, increasing particularly in the late 1960s.[11] Gamma gardens were organized with a radiation source in the middle, where for nearly twenty hours plants received an initial radiation bombardment.[12] Scientists in protective gear would then assess the results and found that, while

FIGURE 7. *Dilbert*, August 29, 1989. Copyright 1989 Scott Adams. Reprinted with permission of Andrews McMeel Syndication. All rights reserved.

plants nearest the center often died, there were other plants of interest further from the radiation source that featured a high range of mutations. Research into the potential benefits of atomic gardening has continued under the joint auspices of the International Energy Agency and the United Nations' Food and Agriculture Organization. Japan established a well-known Institute for Radiation Breeding to explore atomic gardening techniques. Gamma gardens were also established in laboratories in the United States, Europe, the former USSR, and India. At the height of the radiation breeding euphoria, atomic energy was expected to address worldwide problems, including famine and energy shortages. It also made its way into popular culture in a *Dilbert* comic strip and a play titled *The Effect of Gamma Rays on Man-in-the-Moon Marigolds* that both featured radioactive gardening, including marigolds and sentient broccoli.[13]

Among the atomic objects promoted during the "Atoms for Peace movement," X-ray machines became fashionable assets in shoe stores. Designed to show the toes through the leathery surface of a shoe, they were meant to give an infallibly accurate measure of a shoe's fit. In the small German border town where I grew up, they were all the rage. The first shoe store that prided itself with the acquisition of such a magical machine could demonstrate that it belonged to the cutting edge of the new fashion industry. The use of these machines was particularly praised to mothers who bought shoes for their children. As a child, I was absolutely mesmerized with this machine and tried on more and more shoes, just to see the skeletal bones of my feet again. They looked like ghostly photographs of my own future death. Little did I know that the very rays that generated my morbid fascination with the radioactive glow of my skeletal feet were really "death rays," depositing a toxic substance in my body that had the potential to kill.

The polymorphous perversity that fed into the thrill people all over the industrialized world experienced in their first contact with X-rays was widely exploited in an increasingly flourishing X-ray market. One of the most curious manifestations of the popular appeal with atomic death rays is the emergence of X-ray photographs and X-ray fashion for women. It started, as Akira Lippit accounts in *Atomic Light*, with Röntgen's publication of X-ray photographs of the skeletal structure of his wife, Berthe's, left hand.[14] In "Women, X-Rays, and the Public Culture of Prophylactic Imaging," Lisa Cartwright writes, "The frequently published image of a woman's hand gained enormous popularity, becoming an icon of female sexuality and death."[15] In her book *Screening the Body: Tracing Medicine's Visual Culture*, Cartwright further explores this icon and the surrounding fashion that turned the female hand X-ray into a veritable fetish object. She describes how New York women took X-ray photographs of their jewelry-covered hands, and married women began trading X-rays of their hands sporting the wedding band. The goal of illustrating that "beauty is of the bone and not altogether of the flesh"[16] testifies to the fact that the discovery of atomic rays and the invention of the X-ray machine figure prominently in refashioning the cultural perception and phantasmatic cathexis of the boundaries of female subjectivity, embodiment, and sexuality. What we might refer to as a "sexing of the bone" enforces the age-old cultural (often unconscious) equivocation between female sexuality and death in a new material concretization that displays decidedly necrophilic undertones. The new X-ray fashion thus generates a new fetish object for the male fascination with the exquisite corpse of the expiring heroine that proliferated in nineteenth-century culture. The combination of death and romance has, of course, long been a salient feature of gothic fiction. The latter constitutes an extreme form of Romanticism anchored in the threat of the heroine's mysterious death at a young age. Prone to spells of fainting, gothic fiction's female heroines become all the more attractive because they feed the subliminal link of male desire with female frailty and mortality.

The X-ray fashion that flourished in the 1950s retains, I argue, an element of this gothic necrophilia with its morbid lure of death. Safely contained in a mere image—an X-ray photograph—the nuclear gothic, however, no longer figures death as a constantly present threat. Rather, death appears as domesticated in a fetish image that provides a thrilling sanitized fashion of seeing death embodied in a seductive woman, so

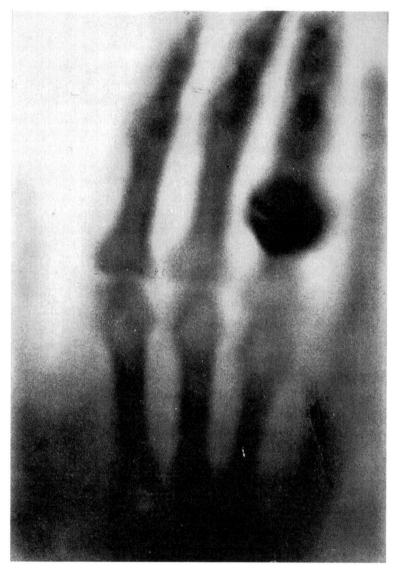

FIGURE 8. Wilhelm Conrad Röntgen, *The Hand of Mrs. Wilhelm Röntgen*, 1895.

to speak. The first wave of this fashion flourished at a time of relative ignorance about the real dangers of radioactive death rays. Even though Marie Curie, the pioneer in research on radioactivity, had already died in 1934 at age sixty-six of aplastic anemia caused by radiation exposure, this knowledge of the lethal power of X-rays had not yet become

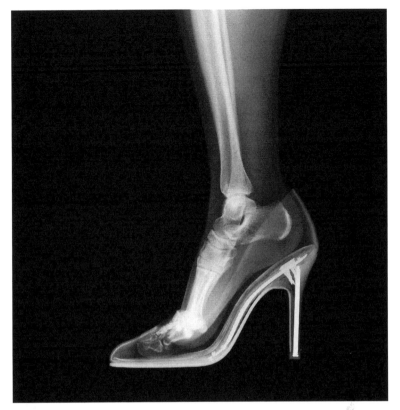

FIGURE 9. Nick Veasey, *Stiletto*, 2008.

part of public knowledge. Ironically, in 1956, at the time of this fashion boom, Curie's daughter Irene Joliot-Curie, a research assistant at the Radium Institute in Paris, died at age fifty-eight of leukemia, also because of radiation exposure. Her husband and lifelong collaborator died two years later.

In recent years, photographer Nick Veasey introduced a second wave of X-ray fashion that takes atomic surrealism and the nuclear gothic to a new level. To produce his highly aestheticized X-ray pictures, Veasey uses skeletons in rubber suits or cadavers donated to science instead of human subjects, for whom the risk of exposure would be too high. Veasey describes the goal of his photography as trying to find an antidote to our "obsession with appearance." The dark underside of this obsession with appearance has always been, especially in relation to the female body, an obsession with death, as it took an inordinately long time and tenacious official denial until the real threat to life of radioactivity was finally acknowledged.

In *The Radium Girls,* Kate Moore writes,"Radium has been known to be harmful since 1901. Every death since was unnecessary."[17] Moore's extensive study covers the lives and struggles of the women who worked in America's radium watch dial factories in the early twentieth century. The book opens with a prologue that describes the initial enchantment by this deadly toxic substance that Marie Curie had called "my beautiful radium." Highlighting radium's original emotional appeal, Curie writes, "These gleamings seemed suspended in the darkness [and] stirred us with ever new emotion and enchantment."[18] The pervasive cultural capture by this "almost supernatural power" thus precedes the later messianic glorification of the power of the atomic bomb. The U.S. general surgeon at the time said that radium "reminds one of a mythological super-being," and an English physician called radioactivity "the unknown god."

No wonder then that the young girls hired at the watch dial factories to paint watch dial numerals and hands with a luminous substance that glowed in the dark were mesmerized with the allegedly magical powers of the object of their work.[19] Magazines and newspapers at the time featured the new and wondrous element in advertisements that promoted new radium products. Selling for $120,000 per gram—$2.2 million in today's value—radium soon became the most valuable substance on earth. Before too long, radium clinics and spas opened for those who could afford them, offering enhanced vitality to the elderly. Pharmacists sold radioactive dressings and pills, and supermarkets offered radium-lined water bottles that made the water radioactive. Wealthy customers drank it as a tonic. Labeled "liquid sunshine," radium soon was used to light up hospitals, drawing rooms, theaters, music halls, grocery stores, libraries, and bookstores. Radium clothing and lingerie, radium butter and milk, radium toothpaste, and radium cosmetics became coveted commodities for those affluent enough to afford them.

The girls at the watch dial factory were overly excited to paint dials and hands with radium brushes. They even licked the brushes to moisten them and were told they could only benefit from the exposure. Working in darkrooms, they could see the glow of the luminous paint everywhere on the workers: "As some of them stood there, they fairly shone in the dark. They looked glorious, like otherworldly angels."[20] When the girls started to fall ill with sores and tumors in their mouths and with

FIGURE 10. "Radium Girls," *American Weekly*, February 28, 1926.

inexplicable diseases that were later diagnosed as radiation sickness or other radiation-related diseases, it was the beginning of a decades-long systematic cover-up and denial. Only many decades later did the Center for Human Radiobiology confirm the dangerous effects of the element with its half-life of sixteen hundred years and its decades-long infliction of serious damage on human bodies. Meanwhile the so-called radium girls suffered from a long series of ailments due to the lingering long-term effects of radium in their bodies: "the radium lived with them, a marriage from which there was no divorce."[21] These ailments included significant bone changes and fractures, osteoporosis, bone cancers, leukemia and anemia, swollen legs that turned black, amputations, heart disease, stroke, and infertility. In the late 1970s, family members of the diseased insisted on exhumations to prove the cause of death. One of the women had "19,500 microcuries of radium in her bones—one of the highest quantities found. It was more than 1,000 times the amounts scientists then considered safe."[22] In a postscript, Moore reports that a firm called Luminous Processes continued the practice of radium painting through to the late 1970s, until it was finally shut down in 1978 after inspectors found radiation levels 1,666 times higher than was considered safe.[23] Women had still been assured it was safe, and any connection to their increasing cancers was disputed. Radium was everywhere in the plant and outside on the sidewalk. Radioactive waste was emptied into the toilet. The supernatural shine was on women's hands and in their hair. After the shutdown, a graffito on the company's wall read "Dial Luminous for Death."

BACHELOR'S MACHINES: THE GENDER OF NUCLEAR FANTASIES

In relation to the use of death rays for warfare, the gendered fantasies focus, perhaps ironically so, less on death than on birth and a male-centered politics of reproduction. Nuclear weapons take the lethal power of radioactivity to an entirely different level that, at its very core, is a threat to life as such. Beginning with the scientists who invented and tested the first atomic bombs, people have reacted to this power with a mixture of awe and horror. The so-called nuclear sublime began to capture the cultural imaginary and continues to do so. It is no exaggeration to speak of a nuclear capture in the sense that, ever since the dawn of the nuclear age, people have been taken into possession, if not forcibly controlled by the nuclear. They have become prisoners of the nuclear age, and the capacity of nuclear power to captivate with sublime terror only enforces its hold. Nuclear capture, in other words, has become a central part of the collective unconscious. Michael Light's *027 OAK*, which depicts men gazing in awe at a spectral mushroom cloud, masterfully illustrates nuclear capture. Nuclear power's dark appeal is only enhanced by the fact that its long-range effects by far exceed the boundaries of the imagination. The very specter of a hitherto unimaginable annihilating blow against the enemy with what Winston Churchill dubbed "this almost supernatural weapon"[24] has from the very beginning inspired male fantasies of genocidal—not to mention suicidal—warfare. The cultural imaginary, however, associates the power of atomic rays not only with death but also with its opposite, namely, with the birth of an entirely new species, engendered exclusively by men without the help of women's reproductive power and inaugurated with the invention of the atomic bomb as the brainchild of the Manhattan Project.

In *Memoirs of the Second World War,* Winston Churchill writes, "On

July 17 world-shaking news arrived. In the afternoon Stimson called at my abode and laid before me a sheet of paper on which was written, 'Babies satisfactorily born.' [. . .] 'It means,' he said, 'that the experiment in the Mexican desert has come off. The atomic bomb is a reality.'"[25] This passage illustrates how, in masculinist discourses, the atomic bomb was from the very beginning cast in terms of what Michel Carrouges calls a "bachelor machine."[26] Embodying male fantasies of self-generation, bachelor machines reveal a tacit politics of reproduction in competition with women's reproductive powers. One could argue that what Freud and later feminist psychoanalyst Karen Horney have theorized as "womb envy" thus lies at the heart of militarist work of death. Seen in this way, bachelor machines also offer a manic defense against the envy of women's reproductive powers. The two first atomic bombs exploded at the Trinity Test Site are heralded as new babies—male babies, of course—brought into this world without the reproductive help of women. The perverse discursive logic that emerges from such male fantasies is emblematized by the cold cynicism of naming the first atomic bomb dropped over Hiroshima "Little Boy." Science writer William Lawrence, the official spokesman on matters of the early nuclear tests and journalistic eyewitness during the Nagasaki attack, described the Alamogordo test in a similar vein in terms that invoke phantasms of a bachelor's birth: "One felt as though he had been privileged to witness the Birth of the World" and "the first cry of a newborn world."[27] In reaction to these male fantasies, Bel Mooney, in *Over Our Dead Bodies: Women Against the Bomb,* speaks of "that monstrous bastard child of science and barbarism, of reason and ignorance—the nuclear bomb."[28]

Distinctly gendered fantasies of male reproduction inform the coded discourse exchanged among the scientists at Los Alamos. After the testing of the first uranium bomb, for example, George Harrison sent the following message: "Dr. Groves has just returned most enthusiastic and confident that the little boy is as husky as his big brother. The light in his eyes is discernible from here to Highold and I could hear his screams from here to my farm."[29] Decoded, Harrison's message affirms that the uranium bomb Little Boy is most likely as powerful as the plutonium bomb Fat Man that had been tested at Trinity. The offspring, in other words, is figured as a superhuman with atomic eyes whose light can be seen two hundred miles away. In the cultural imaginary, the nuclear war machine is thus figured as a bachelor's machine that has generated the most spectacular bachelor's birth the world has ever seen. "A bachelor's machine is a fantastic image which transforms love into a mechanism of death,"[30] writes Michel Carrouges. From the perspective of the perverse logic of bachelor machines, the explosion of the first atomic bomb at the Trinity Test Site is the culmination of new technological weapons that support the myth of the triumph of masculine technology over nature and the feminine. Taking the V2 Rocket as a precursor to the atomic bomb, Thomas Pynchon's *Gravity's Rainbow* explores the connection of this myth with fascist fantasies of the war machine as a sexualized reproductive technology: "Beyond simple steel erection, the Rocket was an entire system *won,* away from the feminine darkness, held against the entropies of lovable but scatterbrained Mother Nature. [. . .] He [Weissmann] was led to believe that by understanding the Rocket, he would come to understand truly his manhood."[31] While Pynchon describes the fantasies of a sexualized bachelor war machine that flourished under German and Italian fascism, the scientists involved in the Manhattan Project seamlessly reproduced them.

The Manhattan Project itself provides an almost orgiastic culmination of male fantasies of conquest. The scientists who worked in Los Alamos to prepare the testing and eventual use of the first nuclear weapons are carried away by a morbid fascination with the nuclear sublime that culminated in a veritable sacralization of the Bomb. This sacralization could indeed be compared to a "weak messianism" in the Benjaminian sense of a hope for future redemption. The fact that the scientists' redemptive fantasies about the Bomb, as it was supposed to end all wars, are based on a self-delusion that actually inverts the weapon's annihilating force, does not break its tenacious hold on the cultural imaginary. In this respect, Little Boy, born after his immaculate conception as the child of a sublime bachelor's birth, is a technological rebirth of the messiah who was destined to end all wars but instead becomes the destroyer of worlds.

These examples reveal how deeply nuclear necropolitics is marked not only by class but also by gender. While the nuclear world created by the Manhattan Project was a masculinist and militaristic war machine engendered by almost exclusively male scientists and engineers, the workers at the assembly lines that handled the uranium were commonly women, most of them lower class, who were sworn to absolute secrecy and left in the dark about their own work. In *The Girls of Atomic City,* Denise Kiernan tells the story of the women who were recruited

FIGURE 11. Michael Light, *072 OAK*, in *100 Suns*, 2003. Photograph courtesy of Michael Light.

at the height of World War II to work in Oak Ridge, a Tennessee town in the Appalachian Mountains that was literally refashioned as a secret atomic city, designed for the manufacture of plutonium. Without their knowledge, these women worked as factory workers and secretaries—a few of them even as chemists—in clandestine plutonium factories. The seventy-five thousand people of Oak Ridge were trained to guard absolute secrecy about what they did and the little they knew. Without their knowledge, these women were thus crucial in assisting the Manhattan Project and building the atomic bomb.[32] This example shows that, beyond gender—and, as discussed in chapter 2, beyond race—nuclear necropolitics operates predominately along the lines of class. Gender, race, and class, in fact, belong to the central aspects of nuclear cultures of secrecy and deception.

GENDERED ACTIVISMS

In 1977, during the months after my first son, Manuel, was born, I was suddenly seized by a rather inexplicable panic about a third world war. I was aware that this panic was partly related to particular postpartum vulnerabilities. But the anchoring of my fears in the threat of nuclear destruction was not only personal; it was also a symptom of the time. I was lying awake at night, trying to think where we could move so that I could protect my newborn from the horrors of atomic war. To be sure, it was the time of antinuclear activism in Europe, with massive demonstrations against the stationing of the Pershing rockets in Germany. But even this did not quite explain the intensity of my sudden fear. It had to do with the panic that there would be no livable world for the children of the future. I realized there no longer was a safe sanctuary on this earth.

During the Cold War era, the threat of a possible nuclear World War III was a tangible fear for most people, at least in Europe and the United States. In Germany, parents and teachers vividly described the horrors of World War II, including the air raids on German and Japanese cities and the atomic destruction of Hiroshima and Nagasaki. In the cultural imaginary, the Atomic Bomb became a mythical object of ultimate destruction. We heard of people burned alive, people running like living flares into the river to extinguish the flames, children whose eyeballs melted, infants abandoned in ruins next to their dead parents. And even though the Americans had dropped the first atomic bombs, the threat of nuclear war was always blamed on the Russians. In high school, we read books and saw films about nuclear destruction. Among those, I most vividly remember Günther Anders's *Die Antiquiertheit des Menschen (The Obsolescence of Man)* and the films *Dr. Strangelove* and *Hiroshima, Mon Amour*. We were truly interpellated by nuclear fear. A sense of responsibility and anger against the military machine propelled us into action, fueling a powerful antinuclear movement in which women played a crucial role. But it was only after my son's birth when I realized that the fear of nuclear destruction would forever be part of the shaping of my generation's psychic lives.

"The causes of recurrent warfare are not biological. Neither are they solely economic. They are also a result of patriarchal ways of thinking," writes Charlene Spretnak in "Naming the Cultural Forces that Push Us toward War."[33] Given the discursive gendering of nuclear necropolitics within a framework of reproductive politics, and especially the figuration of nuclear weapons as bachelor war machines, it is not surprising that, especially in their earlier phases, women's antinuclear movements have been transcoded with a rather traditional politics of reproduction that figured men as carriers of the work of death and women as carriers of the work of life. Rather than tracing the genealogy of this gendering of antinuclear politics, in what follows, I focus on a few crucial moments that have continued relevance for today's renewed concerns with a feminist antinuclear politics and movement.

Defining women's role as giving and sustaining life, of course, coincides with long-standing patriarchal norms that have also facilitated the oppression and marginalization of women. "The more widespread their mastery of the world," writes Simone de Beauvoir in 1947, two years after the atomic bombing of Hiroshima, "the more they find themselves crushed by uncontrollable forces. Though they are masters of the atomic bomb, yet it is created only to destroy them."[34] This fundamental ambivalence in the age-old patriarchal imaginary that casts women as bearers of life and men as warriors continues to haunt women's antinuclear politics. It has, in turn, generated a complex history of feminist philosophical reflection with a genealogy that reaches from its earliest inception in the late 1940s, with Simone de Beauvoir as the most prominent example, to more recent feminist theories of reproduction such as, for example, Michelle Murphy's theory of "distributed reproduction."[35]

Women have long been at the forefront of powerful movements of antinuclear resistance. Their antinuclear activism and antinuclear writings and other creative work continue to provide a productive ground for the construction of what Catherine Eschle calls "feminized subjectivities in oppositional relation to the masculinized nuclear state."[36] The history of women-led antinuclear politics goes all the way back to the dropping of the first atomic bombs on Hiroshima and Nagasaki and the emergent antinuclear movements in Japan and across the world. It peaked in the 1960s with the civil rights and women's movements and then again in the 1980s with the resurgence of the Cold War and the peace movement that emerged globally in response to it. The second wave of feminism generated a large-scale mobilization of women against nuclear weapons, including the foundation of Women's Action for Nuclear Disarmament (WAND) in the United States.

In the United States, the resistance of Indigenous women is central to the antinuclear movement. Internationally acclaimed Indigenous writers and activists Linda Hogan (Chickasaw) and Leslie Marmon Silko

(Laguna), for example, have both written about the devastating effects of nuclear war and the radioactive contamination and colonization of Indigenous lands. Linda Hogan wrote a sequence of powerful poems that voice her concern about sustaining life in the wake of destruction by nuclear arms and nuclear power:

> In her dark eyes
> The children of Hiroshima
> Are screaming
> [. . .]
> How quickly we could vanish.[37]

Seeing the children of Hiroshima screaming in her daughter's dark eyes, Hogan offers a politics of identification that crosses the boundaries between nations, intimating that nuclear weapons threaten the children of the entire world. The vanishing of the world's children is conjured as a haunting from both past and future. Uranium mining and milling on Indigenous lands as well as the long-range radioactive contamination of soil, water, and air from the fallout of nuclear testing have caused spikes in cancers, miscarriages, and genetic damage among the predominately Native population. Hogan, like many other Indigenous women writers and activists, sees this radioactive colonization as a violation of the spirit of the earth and of feminine energy. "When I write I keep in mind that it is a form of power and salvation that is for the planet,"[38] she asserts. Her poems are dedicated to Rosalie Bertell, who proclaimed at the Black Hills Alliance International Survival Gathering, "Everywhere I go, women are grieving the death of the species. You can either turn it around or help it to die."[39] In her poem "Black Hills Survival Gathering, 1980," Hogan writes,

> At ground zero
> in the center of light we stand.
> [. . .]
> We are waking in the expanding light
> the sulphur-colored grass.[40]

As the women stand to fight for the survival of the Black Hills, the image of sulfur-colored grass suggests that the expanding light illuminates the traces of radioactive contamination. They are aware of the nuclear dangers from below and above, from buried bombs and war planes: "Bombs are buried beneath us, destruction flies overhead."[41]

And yet the women are at a Survival Gathering, fighting against the destruction of the Black Hills.

Among these women, Charmaine White Face, Oglala Sioux from the Pine Ridge Reservation, is the most prominent Indigenous antinuclear woman activist and leader in the fight for the survival of the Black Hills. She is the coordinator of the Defenders of the Black Hills, a group that pressures the U.S. government to honor the Fort Laramie Treaties of 1851 and 1868. She also works at the international level for the recognition of human rights for Indigenous peoples at the United Nations in Geneva. Locally, she works on the monitoring of abandoned uranium mines and on the remediation of hazardous waste ponds. She participated in the Second Wounded Knee uprising and played a crucial role in the uprising at Standing Rock. Her work in the antinuclear power movement was recognized in Salzburg, Austria, with the 2007 Nuclear-Free Future Award.

In my reflections on a critical nuclear race theory, I have already discussed the role of prominent African American women, including Coretta King, Angela Davis, Toni Morrison, and the women in Sweet Honey in the Rock. Both Indigenous and African American women have stressed the importance of linking antinuclear resistance to international movements. Among the international antinuclear women activists and scholars, three women serve as paradigmatic examples that highlight different geopolitical locations of the struggle: Angie Zelter, cofounder of the Trident Ploughshares, an oppositional movement against British nuclear weapons; Helen Caldicott from Australia and the United States; and Arundati Roy from India and the United States.

Zelter was a leading activist in the global citizenship movement called Trident Ploughshares that issued an ultimatum to Prime Minister Tony Blair to comply with international law by disarming all British nuclear weapons. This happened in response to the historic declaration of the International Court of Justice in The Hague that the threat or use of nuclear weapons is contrary to the rules of international law applicable in armed conflict.[42] In 1996, Zelter was imprisoned for a peaceful act of civil resistance against violence. It was during her time in prison that she conceived the civil resistance campaign of people's disarmament that came to be known as Trident Ploughshares. Zelter wrote about this movement in her 2001 book *Trident on Trial: The Case for People's Disarmament*. More broadly, emphasizing transspecies connections and vulnerabilities, Zelter started her activism and writing to oppose the destruction of the planetary life support systems. Arguing that women and children are the primary victims of male-dominated weapons industries, war machines, and related human rights abuses, she sees the abolition of nuclear weapons and the renunciation of nuclear politics as crucial to the struggle for planetary survival.

Helen Caldicott, an Australian doctor and activist for Physicians for Social Responsibility (PSR) and International Physicians for the Prevention of Nuclear War (IPPN), is also the cofounder of WAND. She has published widely on nuclear politics from a feminist perspective. Among her twelve books on the topic, her early *Missile Envy* (1984) is directly addressing the gender of nuclear necropolitics from a psychoanalytic perspective. *Nuclear Power Is Not the Answer* (2006) addresses the dangers of nuclear energy and dispels the myth of nuclear power as a cleaner energy. With this book, Caldicott established herself as a crucial voice in the resistance toward the promotion of nuclear energy as a "safer alternative" to fossil fuels, able to mitigate the effects of climate change. In 2014, after the report by PSR and IPPN announced the expected ten thousand excess cancers as a result of the Fukushima disaster, Caldicott edited *Crisis Without End: The Medical and Ecological Consequences of the Fukushima Nuclear Catastrophe*.

While Caldicott's earlier work exhibited a certain biological determinism, equating male physiology and sexuality with the death drive that underlies violent aggression, and female physiology with women's life-affirming capacity to give birth and nurture children, her later work increasingly turns to a critique of male-dominated institutions, such as the military–industrial complex. She also targets the lack of accountability of the governments of nations with nuclear weapons.[43] Caldicott received numerous awards and twenty-one honorary doctorates for her work on nuclear necropolitics, and the Smithsonian Institution named her one of the most influential women of the twentieth century.

A crucial voice from the movement of non-Western feminism, Arundati Roy criticizes the ethnocentric bias of certain antinuclear discourses in the United Kingdom and United States from the perspective of gendered postcolonial nuclear subjectivities. She opens her 2003 impassioned antiwar and antinuclear manifesto *War Talk* by outlining the following dilemma of postcolonial nuclear politics:

> When India and Pakistan conducted their nuclear tests in 1998, even those of us who condemned them balked at the hypocrisy of

Western nuclear powers. Implicit in their denunciation of the tests was the notion that Blacks cannot be trusted with the Bomb. Now we are presented with the spectacle of our governments competing to confirm that belief.[44]

Roy further insists that India's and Pakistan's arrival on the scene of nuclear countries prepared the ground for fascism in India: "It breezed in after the Pokhran nuclear tests in 1998. [. . .] And now, one war and hundreds of dead later, more than a million soldiers from both armies are massed at the border, eyeball to eyeball, locked in a pointless nuclear standoff."[45] Class, of course, figures prominently in Roy's account, in which she views India's nuclear politics in the context of the "displacement and dispossession and the relentless everyday violence of abject poverty."[46] For most people who live under such conditions, she asserts, nuclear war is "completely outside the realm of most people's comprehension," and "no one knows what a nuclear bomb is."[47] Decrying India's and Pakistan's nuclear politics as a male politics that threatens planetary survival, she pointedly asks, "Why do we tolerate the men who use nuclear weapons to blackmail the entire human race?"[48] I would put one more twist on Roy's question by asking why we tolerate these men to use the threat of nuclear war to divert our attention from the relentless everyday violence of abject poverty? Nuclear madness, Roy declares, is threatening not only the human race but other species as well: "Rarely mentioned is the arrogance of the human race toward other living things with which it shares this planet. All these are forgotten in the fight for markets and ideologies. This arrogance will probably be the ultimate undoing of the human species."[49]

While Roy focuses on the nuclear standoff between India and Pakistan, she never forgets to mention that nuclear necropolitics has spread from the United States—the country with the largest nuclear arsenal and the only country that has ever used an atomic bomb in a war—to other countries around the globe. "The bombing of Hiroshima and Nagasaki was a cold, calculated experiment carried out to demonstrate America's power,"[50] she writes. As people around the world continue to live in the shadow of Hiroshima and Nagasaki, they are haunted not only by the future of a possible nuclear holocaust but also by the slow violence of the damage to cells and genes caused by internal radiation, that is, by so-called internal emitters that migrate to specific organs, where they emit high doses of radiation.

POLITICS OF REPRODUCTION

The long-term and transgenerational effects of radioactive contamination on reproductive functions, of course, affect women disproportionately. The Chernobyl and Fukushima disasters, for example, left the vicinity so toxic that pregnant women were directed to seek abortions and all women were advised not to become pregnant within the years following the disaster. Nuclear necropolitics has always also been gender politics. It is women who will become the bearers of damaged, stillborn, or mutant life. It is women who, in the aftermath of nuclear disasters, are asked to seek abortions and avoid pregnancies in the near future.

This is why, in the feminist antinuclear movement, women considered the overall impact of nuclear weapons on bodies and lives and contextualized the roots of nuclear violence within a larger cult of masculinity that systematically condoned, if not encouraged, violence by men and male-dominated institutions against women, racialized others, children, and nature. Eschle describes how, against the essentializing tendencies in some of these maternalist discourses, social constructionists emphasized the cultural construction of patriarchal, racist, and heterosexist forms of masculinity that, in turn, fueled the nuclear Cold War culture: "The abstractions of nuclear rationality, as pursued by a technocratic, Western, masculine subject, were thus confronted by the concrete, embodied mode of reasoning historically associated with feminine (and also non-white, non-Western) subjectivity."[51] The latter can, in fact, be productively mobilized for a global, transnational antinuclear solidarity among women under the assumption of a shared experience of patriarchal oppression of women worldwide, regardless of the different culture-specific manifestations. One of the shared values of this transnational women's movement was the commitment to oppose militarism and the stockpiling of nuclear weapons, if not nuclearism more generally. There was, as many non-Western feminists later pointed out, certainly a great deal of idealism in this conception of a global sisterhood. However, the movement's larger goal to transcend geopolitical, racial, ethnic, and religious differences in order to oppose the oppressive, violent, and ultimately suicidal nuclear necropolitics remains a challenge to this day.

However, the focus on reproductive politics, and the essentialism embraced by some proponents of the antinuclear movement, generated ideological divisions. The lack of racial diversity in some of the participating organizations was another source of ideological tension. While discourses on gender and nuclear weapons were highly diverse in the positions toward the larger struggle, most of them shared a tendency to oppose the life-affirming force of motherhood and a related ethics of transgenerational care to a patriarchal culture of domination, conquest, and warfare. The materialist underpinnings of antinuclear discourses on motherhood focused, of course, on the impact of radioactive contamination on the reproductive system as well as the damage to embryos in the uterus and to children, whose developing bodies are disproportionately affected by radioactive exposure. As Joseph Masco's interviews with women in the nuclear borderlands of the American Southwest have shown, the knowledge of nuclear contamination also creates what I call *phantasms of the mutant body*. A pregnant woman living at the end of the Cold War beside the nuclear facility, for example, expresses the terror of being the "potential mother of a mutant child." Masco writes, "As her womb is made foreign and dangerous to her, she is colonized by the psychosocial consequences of the nuclear security state. [. . .] The inability here to escape nuclear terror—in either the form of radioactive contamination or nuclear war—destabilizes a self that can no longer locate the boundaries between body and bomb."[52] Fears of mutation, indeed, phantasms of the mutant body,[53] have become a central part of the transgenerational ecopolitical legacy. Masco writes succinctly,

> A political ecology of the bomb that investigates the interaction between regimes of nature reveals the American nuclear project to have been ecologically transformative and multigenerationally productive: it has reinvented the biosphere as a nuclear space [. . .] and embedded the logic of mutation within both ecologies and cosmologies.[54]

In its darkest possible implications, this perspective anticipates a phantasmatic posthuman future in which humans, unable to adapt to the toxic environment, turn into mutants that inhabit zones of radioactive contamination. The same apocalyptic imaginary envisions the insects as the species whose superior adaptability enables them to survive humans on a posthuman earth. More recently, Michelle Murphy's work on distributed reproduction, which I analyze in more detail in chapter 8, opens up a new perspective that extends reproductive politics beyond the confines of the individual and even the species. Analyzing the effects of environmental damage from industrial chemicals, for example, Murphy opens up a theoretical perspective on the transgenerational reproductive damage of radioactive contamination that allows one to move beyond a narrow biologism to grasp the work of reproductive assemblages and transspecies entanglements in a more largely conceived reproductive politics.

It's not just people living in the aftermath of Hiroshima, Nagasaki, Chernobyl, or Fukushima who are affected by phantasms of the mutant body. Such phantasms have become deeply embedded in the popular cultural imaginary of the nuclear age more generally. I vividly remember an incident from my school years in Germany. A teacher told us the story of American women collecting the teeth of their babies and sending them to senators to find out if they were contaminated with radiation. We had heard about the atomic bomb and that it was killing people with radiation, that it was melting the eyeballs of children and burning their bodies. Now our teacher told us that when they tested the bomb, the Americans also contaminated their own country. Babies with radioactive teeth were proof. I was both horrified and fascinated by this story about baby teeth contaminated by the atomic bomb. Our teacher added that after the atomic bomb was dropped on Hiroshima, children were born with deformed bodies. Afterward, I had recurrent nightmares about disfigured babies. Perhaps memories like this are what made me so sensitive when I watched *Hiroshima, Mon Amour* and saw the opening shot with those naked bodies that one couldn't distinguish as being bodies of Hiroshima victims or bodies of people making love. Or was that just a projection of mine? In the shadow of Hiroshima, love and death became entangled.

Recently I tried to find out what could have been behind my teacher's story about children's radioactive teeth. To my surprise, I found an abundance of materials, among them an article by Andy Newman from the *New York Times*.[55] Newman reports about an antinuclear activist, Mr. Mangano, who runs Radiation and Public Health Project Inc. and has stored three thousand human baby teeth in his Brooklyn apartment that were collected more than half a century ago for a study of the effects of atom bomb tests in the United States called the Tooth Fairy Project. Since many teeth had elevated levels of the carcinogenic strontium-90, Mangano is trying to track down donors to find out if these levels correlate with cancer in later life. Mangano's new study is designed to show that the more than one hundred nuclear power reactors, even without any accident, are giving people cancer. If this sounds like a new instantiation of atomic surrealism, it also provides yet another example of the nuclear and its long-range radioactive dangers—real and imaginary—on our lives. My teacher's story of the radioactive baby teeth is bound up with a haunting from the future of our contaminated planet.

INTERLUDE

CHILDREN OF THE NUCLEAR AGE
with Simon J. Ortiz

In the sixth grade in the early 1950s at McCartys Day School, the federal government school on our Acoma Indian Pueblo reservation, I learned about X-rays, polio, and the iron lung. This was also the same time when I learned about uranium, a mineral newly discovered on the Laguna Indian Pueblo reservation land that was to the east, next to Acoma. The uranium was beginning to be mined at an open pit mine near the Pajuate village of Laguna Pueblo.

X-rays. Polio. The iron lung. And uranium. I didn't learn anything about uranium in school, but I learned about it in stories told in the Acoma community. All these—X-rays, polio, the iron lung, and uranium—were very new, and I didn't know a thing about any of them. In the 1950s, these were all part of new knowledge coming into my life as an Indigenous (or "Indian," as we had learned to call ourselves) student at the government reservation school.

New knowledge was the dictum of government schooling since it was intended to have wholesale impact and effect on Indigenous people. Merrieegaanah school could not be avoided. "Indians" were enrolled in school by U.S. federal law. We obeyed and lived by the law. There was no choice. It was simply a condition Indians lived with, a fact we had to go along with. Years later, I learned or realized all citizens were required to attain schooling—get an education—but I really felt it was applied differently to us. For us, going to school was a matter of obeying the law.

So it was at the U.S. Indian school on the Acoma Pueblo Indian reservation that I learned about X-rays, polio, and the iron lung. And I learned about uranium from oral stories I heard Acoma adults telling. "It is kcqueehskah," I heard haashtee'-tih-trah say. It is green. I could see the color of green, like the green color of a plastic cup. And they said, "It is yellow too, like sunflowers." So when the man telling the story moved his hands in front of him to show the height of sunflower plants, I could see those bright yellow sunflowers!

"Uranium is a hard stone," another said. "But some of it is crumbly and soft, and you can break it apart by hand." I could see the yellow-green mineral stone that was called uranium. And I could see it was mixed with the brown, gray, and reddish orange-brown landscape of mesas, canyons, and high desert lands we lived within and called our homeland.

X-ray machines hit our small town when I was still in primary school. They were all the rage. Everybody talked about this unbelievable new invention, the X-rays, that opened a window to the inside of our bodies. We kids were absolutely fascinated by this unfathomable power of sheer rays of light to reveal the secrets of our bodies' insides! We could look at our very bones, almost as if we were seeing ourselves as skeletons, seeing our own ghosts from the future! I thought I was incredibly lucky because a friend's parents owned a shoe store and, believe it or not, they had their own X-ray machine! The first time I got to see it was when my mother took me there to buy new shoes. The shoemaker made me stand on a pedestal and put my feet under the X-ray machine to see how far my toes reached. There they were, my feet translucent and my skeletal bones surrounded by a greenish, almost alien glow. Utterly mesmerized, I pressed the X-ray button again and again and again. I kept trying on new shoes, simply to be able to look at my bones as often as I possibly could.

My favorite time was when I got to play with my friend Bernd and his brother Peter, the shoemaker's sons. Whenever there were no clients in the store, we were allowed to play with the X-ray machine. We couldn't get enough of it. We even put our hands under the slot, but we could only see our friends' hands because, with our own hands in the slot, we couldn't stand up to look through the X-ray picture slot. There was an almost metaphysical thrill to this experience of X-rays. Seeing my bones made me think about death. "This is how I will look after I die," I thought.

A few years later, when construction workers stumbled upon an ancient Aleman burial ground, I spent many days there, watching archeologists dig up the graves. This was the first time I saw the skeletons of humans. One of the archeologists told me stories about the remains he found in the graves. "This here," he said, "was a young boy, not older than eighteen. He died in battle from a blow to his head. We can tell because of this fracture in his skull"—he showed me the fine line—"and because he was buried with his weapons." I looked at the rusty sword and felt a strange sorrow for this unknown boy who was killed in battle. Completely transfixed, I stared at the skeletons in the open graves, and they reminded me of my X-ray feet. I returned day after day, trying to explore the mystery of death. Why the skeletons of these distant ancestors had such a hold on my imagination was something I never fully understood. I was utterly mesmerized, spent literally all my free time with the skeletons and the archeologists on the hill and couldn't think of anything else.

Once in my late twenties, after I had moved to Constance, I returned to my hometown and wanted to pay a visit to my friend Bernd. "Didn't you know, both he and his brother died of cancer," my mother informed me. Nobody seemed to have made any connection with the magic X-ray machine.

X-rays, polio, and the iron lung also had to do with the March of Dimes crusade our school principal and teachers used to raise money from our Acoma reservation community. I have to admit at first I didn't know how these all fit together. I think I may have even believed the March of Dimes made them all fit together!

Like I said earlier, I did not know anything about X-rays, polio, and the iron lung. They could be anything since, in a sense, at the age I was then, I was beginning to think the modern world Indigenous people were part of and were to make sense of was sometimes puzzling, strange, not easily explainable, and dismaying.

But I was told by Acoma elders—our haashtee'-tih-trah—that school was the place to learn things you didn't know about. And it was the place where you went to understand what things were. At that age and time, I was learning and discovering a lot of things. And whether they were fact or fiction did not matter; it made no difference. I just wanted to learn and know, and I wanted to be fascinated.

Acoma haashtee'-tih-trah encouraged us to go to school and to learn. Firmly, they said, "Listen and learn, so you can know the way it is in the American world." In other words, we were told we were in school to prepare ourselves for life not as Acoma people but as American people.

I'll always remember hearing an elder say in the Acoma language, "Ehgoh sheh emee eh Merrleegaa-nah meh shtayaatih-tahno, tse-deegkow'-eh shraa-mee nuuwah-dyuumii-trah kuudruutsah." *Because you are becoming like the Americans, it is necessary to learn how to do it very carefully.*

Things were very different from the usual life of Acoma traditional community and culture. School, I figured, was the source of learning we were to partake of in order to prepare for our future lives in the American world. And likely I even presumed that what was at first unexplainable and incomprehensible would become sensible and clear once I was more informed and knowledgeable. I would comprehend and understand.

"Listen and learn," the Aacqumeh haashtee'-tih-trah said. Neh-chaa'-traa-shruu'. Now'-dyuu'mitrahsrou. *By listening, you will learn.* That's how you come to knowledge, they said.

For example, we learned about X-rays. What were X-rays? We were taught about X-rays in school by our American white teacher, Miss Colvert. "X-rays are invisible," she said. "You cannot see them," she repeated very firmly. And she added, "Invisible means X-rays cannot be seen." She spoke to us directly, looking straight into our eyes and faces. And then with chalk she drew squiggly lines on the blackboard and exclaimed, "But that's what they would look like if they could be seen."

We were learning about an X-ray machine, a new medical machinery used by American doctors to detect illness and disease in human bodies. The X-ray machine could see into the human body! "Can you imagine that?" Miss Colvert said to us with awe in her voice.

Looking at the teacher's face, I could see she was very excited about this medical machinery that could see things we human beings normally could not see. She explained the machine used X-rays that radiated from a central part of the machine and passed through a human body and showed the human body with all its parts on a screen. And it showed the parts that were diseased or had some illness inside the body. And it even showed bones that were broken!

I wondered: if X-rays were invisible, how could Miss Colvert know what they looked like in order to draw them as squiggly lines? No students raised their hands to ask about that or anything. I wanted to raise my hand to ask, but I did not.

I didn't ask even though school was where Indigenous peoples were to learn things they wanted and needed to know. That's what our parents had said to us anyway; even my grandfather Mah-yai said the same thing. The main thing I felt and thought was this: I was mystified by X-rays that saw into you and through you. What was the power that could do that? I didn't know. And that's what I wanted to know. And, yes, I even felt the teacher didn't know much or anything about X-rays.

I never trusted nuclear energy. The town began to talk about it when I was in high school. In my mind, atomic power plants were inextricably linked to the stories about the atomic bomb people used to tell when we were children. It was "the bomb of all bombs," we were told, "more terrible than anything humans had ever seen." It was a bomb, my parents said, that could destroy the entire world and kill all life on earth. They talked about the Americans dropping atomic bombs on Hiroshima and Nagasaki, killing more people in a day than ever before in any of all the terrible wars in world history. They talked about people burning alive, children whose eyeballs melted. The word "Hiroshima" was forever burned into our minds. The atomic bomb embodied the worst of terrors, far beyond the reach of imagination. And to think that, many decades later, the specter of Hiroshima and Nagasaki returned to haunt the victims of the Fukushima nuclear disaster!

Soon "the Bomb," as it was simply called, became a myth of sorts, a haunting from the future of World War III, and World War III in the stories told in our town was always connected to the specter of communism. "Wait until the Russians come!" was one of the most common threats leveled against children. We lived near Zurich airport, and when I was little, I would look at the airplanes flying over us. I was filled with terror that one day the Russians would drop an atomic bomb on us from one of those planes.

Then, in the sixties, Switzerland built its first nuclear power plant right across from my hometown. I had already moved away, but when I visited, people's fear and agitation were palpable. On these visits, my brother and I used to climb the watchtower high up in the forest to see the plant, lying right in front of our eyes, an ugly monster sitting across the border on the Rhine. Nuclear power plants were called *Atomkraftwerk* at the time, atomic power plant. But the very word raised people's fear of radioactive contamination because it became associated with the atomic bomb. Subsequently, the name was changed to *Kernkraftwerk*, that is, nuclear power plant. Sounds much less dangerous, doesn't it? At least, it doesn't as easily awaken unconscious fears of the atomic bomb.

It didn't take more than a few years after the opening of the first nuclear power plants in the area for rumors to start in my hometown.

People talked about the rise of childhood cancers, especially leukemia. I remember Klaus Brutsche, a classmate and childhood friend from my primary school times. He died of leukemia when we were in second grade, that is, before the advent of atomic power plants. When my mother took me to visit him in the hospital, his body was covered in large dark blue bruises. He was already too weak to talk. This terrifying image stayed with me and was mobilized again when people talked about the rise of childhood cancers caused by radioactive emissions from the power plants in the area. Some actually complained that the Swiss had deliberately built them near the border so that they would only have half of the fallout because the other would hit Germany.

When Stefanie, my younger sister, died in the early seventies of a uterus sarcoma at age seventeen, even her doctors wondered about a possible connection to the two power plants in the immediate vicinity of my hometown. But such suspicions are notoriously difficult to prove. Much later, when the radioactive dials on clocks and watches were taken off the market and the X-ray machines were forbidden in shoe stores, I remembered that as children we played with both. My father was a watchmaker and gave us broken watches to play with. Mesmerized, we looked at the radioactive dials glowing in the dark. Even our stuffed animals had glowing radioactive eyes. I had a little stuffed tiger and my mother said his eyes were made with the most powerful substance on earth. Just imagine!! But when I heard that radioactive dials and X-ray machines had to be removed, I began to wonder if they had contributed to causing my sister's—and later my father's—cancer. But I guess ultimately we will never know what caused the destruction of my sister's uterus at such a young age.

At the time of the opening of the first power plants, a widespread antinuclear power movement was beginning to form in Germany. The slogan "Atomkraft, nein danke!"—"Atomic power, no thanks!"—was spreading like wildfire. Icons of a yellow happy face that sported the slogan were soon to be found on walls, lampposts, park benches, cars, and strollers. My university had a park with small ponds, surrounded by tall blue postmodern sculptures. Their tops consisted of large round metal plates that looked like industrial treetops. One morning we found them all painted over with a glowing yellow happy face and the caption "Atomkraft, nein danke!" These antinuclear happy faces stayed there for many years; they were still there in the late seventies when my first son was born. But when I returned to Constance a few years ago as a scholar in residence, they had been painted over. The antinuclear movement was no longer at the center of people's attention.

Yet, in the meantime, more and more plants had been built everywhere, including in Germany. Even away from the limelight of the mass media, people kept protesting. They still do. After the Chernobyl and then the Fukushima nuclear disasters, the antinuclear movement regained momentum. Germany was one of the first countries that decided to phase out nuclear power altogether. Now, however, all over the world, corporations and governments have begun to promote nuclear energy again as an allegedly cleaner alternative to fossil fuels, in blatant disregard of scientific evidence to the contrary.

All of us Acoma children from our area of the Acoma reservation went to McCartys Day School. We had to. We were bound to it; it was bound to us. That was U.S. government law. We, as children, didn't really know what the law was or what it meant. We just knew it was a fact of life, and we were existent alongside of it. Whether or not we knew what the law was, it was fact. When I think about it, X-rays and X-ray machinery as fact used by American doctors were imposed and impressed on us in the same way. The elders said, "Tsee-chu hanoh shanaishteeyahshi skaiyah-ahtraaniih oosthumeh-shtahnih. Neewah namaah-te-kutruuwah drumah." The "big people father" built the school for us. So appreciate it. Yes, that's what the elders said. We were bound to it; it was bound to us.

So I learned about X-rays in school when we were learning about polio, a dreadful disease that caused crippling sickness. Miss Colvert showed us vivid and awful photographs in a book that came with the March of Dimes material. The dreadful photos and the teacher convinced us that children with polio could not breathe on their own; they had to be aided with a machine that breathed for them. The machine in the photos was called an iron lung. When I saw that the machine was mostly a large metal tube into which patients were installed, I was appalled.

We learned the disease of polio caused a person to be dilapidated, paralyzed, weakened, and absolutely helpless so that any chance for life could only be possible with the iron lung. A patient with polio had no chance for life, much less healthy recovery, unless the patient was aided by an iron lung! That's where the March of Dimes came in. With money collected—dimes and dimes and dimes—a child had a chance! In the 1950s, even in the dark ages that the 1950s era sometimes seemed to be, people stricken by polio, especially children, had a chance to live if they were aided by iron lungs. That's why even a very poor Indigenous community of Acoma Pueblo people was willing to help with the treatment of polio and to help people pay for iron lungs that would help them to breathe so they could live.

In 1984, the Chernobyl nuclear disaster happened. I had already moved to the United States and lived in Milwaukee at the time. Everybody was glued to the news. When we talked to our European friends on the phone, they told us that their kids had to stay indoors and that lists were handed out with prohibited foods. Even as far away as the United States, environmentally conscious people were concerned. We knew exactly when the radioactive cloud was supposed to pass over Milwaukee, but people didn't know how to react. Within a few hours, all the iodine supplements had disappeared from the shelves of health food stores, just like many years later in California, after the Fukushima nuclear disaster. Invisible and intangible dangers make people react in strange ways. My friend Heather asked her son Chenendoah and my son Manuel, who were both seven at the time, to hold books over their heads on their way back from school. This, she said, would possibly protect them from the radioactive Chernobyl cloud that was on its way across the United States and was scheduled to appear above Milwaukee that day.

Then, a few months after the Chernobyl accident, I attended a conference near Zurich. Just across the border, in Constance, I had gotten the list of prohibited foods: restaurants were not allowed to serve venison, wild mushrooms, or berries because the forest soil was the most contaminated. A few colleagues and I ate at a Swiss restaurant. The special menu of the day was venison, wild mushrooms, and berries. "Aren't restaurants prohibited from serving these contaminated foods?" I asked the waitress. "Oh, no," she quickly replied, "that's only in Germany, not here." "How did you get radioactive contamination to respect Switzerland's national borders?" I responded, less sarcastically than out of despair about people's capacity for denial.

"Chernobyl is like the war of all wars. There's nowhere to hide. Not underground, not underwater, not in the air," said one of the Chernobyl survivors in an interview with Svetlana Alexievich.[1] The area around Chernobyl was evacuated and designated a prohibited "zone of exception." People simply called it "the Zone," a term with a double meaning. For native Russian speakers, the widely used slang term "the Zone" also means "prison" or "labor camp." Quite a few people returned secretly to the Zone because they had nowhere else to go. For many it is the only place they can call home.

Sheer denial of its contamination and the related dangers is rampant: "We turned off the radio right away. We don't know any of the news, but life is peaceful."[2] Or "We're not going, period. We lived through the war. Now it's radiation. Even if we have to bury ourselves, we're not going!"[3] The contaminated Zone has become a deathworld, a zone of abject abandonment, of illness and death in life. Soon it begins to resemble an alien planet. Radiation causes plants to turn into a ghostly white and the cockscombs of chickens into a deadly black. Emaciated deer and wolves move back into the city, walking around in slow motion. The graves of those who die have to be covered with cement to prevent others from being exposed to the radioactive afterglow of their prematurely ended lives.

Photographer Victor Latun describes the myths that flourish in the Zone: "Some say that aliens knew about the catastrophe and helped us out; others that it was an experiment and soon kids with incredible talent will start to be born. Or maybe the Belarussians will disappear, like the Scythians. We're metaphysicians. We don't live on this earth, but in our dreams."[4]

Now, I have to tell about the uranium I started this story with. Like I said earlier, I didn't learn much about it in school, but I learned about it from stories told in the Acoma community. The stories connected uranium discovered on the Laguna Indian Pueblo land to the strange light one summer morning that suddenly appeared in the east over the far mountains. "It was not the dawn. Because it was in the wrong place," old man Shaahrrhow'kah said. The wrong place meant trouble for sure, and, yes, that's what it was from there on. Not long after that false dawn, the world saw the utter destruction, the "trouble" wrought in Japan when the United States dropped and detonated the atomic bombs that devastated Nagasaki and Hiroshima.

My memory of "the Bomb" is more imagination than anything. It's almost as if there's more of a sense of reality about what is imagined than what is actually experienced or seen firsthand or heard about as something of import taking place.

But I do recall when I heard of a light to the east that was seen by an elder who said it was the sun rising in the east but it was in the wrong place.

"I got up early," he said in the Aacqumeh dzeh-nee neeyah. Dyawaah-dyuu-stheepahtyuh. And he said the morning was somewhat dark still. "Skooweeshouw-uuh, sheh," he explained. Ehmee-eh heh yah. He said he needed to relieve himself, that's why he got up to go outside of his house.

I heard the telling of what he said from my mother or my father, who had been told by someone else, who had heard the elder speaking that morning. I was not yet of school age, so I heard about it from my parents I think. I pictured the elder, an old man, who I remembered in his garden near his home from time to time.

At four years of age, I was only minimally aware of events outside of the Acoma world that I was growing up in. I did know of a war taking place. And I knew Acoma people were involved with the war because of the young women and men soldiers in their military uniforms. And vaguely I knew—or perhaps, more correctly, I sensed—the tension that existed in an edgy way with regard to massive weapons the "Mericano" were building somewhere near our homeland that culminated in the first atomic bomb explosion in southeastern New Mexico.

Even that memory is almost more a dream memory than anything else. Not real, like it were an experience happening right then or an event that I had seen happen, but real like something that I believed. I believed because I was old enough then in the mid-1940s to know there was a war going on. A terrible turmoil of destruction somewhere. Yuunah buu teh-eh. Eh yuunah haah teh-eh. To the west far away. And to the east far away. I was not yet of school age. But I had heard of a terrible war taking place, and I knew oral stories of devastation afar yet close, severe injury, death, loss, sorrow. And I knew fear.

The elder walked to a juniper tree some yards from his home, and he stopped a short distance past where it grew from the ground. "Shruuweh sthee-shou-uh," he said in the Acoma language. And then I peed. "And I was looking eastward into the distance. Yuunah teh-eh haah. Far into the east distance. I saw this light then." The storyteller paused then, like the elder paused also. And then the elder went on. "'It is too far to the south,' I thought to myself. 'It's not the right place for Oo-shrah-tsah to be rising.'"

Knowledge in a cultural community that's dependent on oral tradition is strengthened and confirmed by the continuous use of this tradition. And, in a sense, it is sanctified by the nature of an imbued sacredness. Continuance or assurance of ongoing is, more or less, what sacred power is because of a motion that is always forward. To go forth is to go forward, not wavering aside with uncertainty. But always going forth directly with purpose, intention, commitment. Knowledge that is ongoing is secure and in place. And that is the direction that one seeks.

White Sands near Alamogordo, fewer than two hundred miles southeast from the Acoma Pueblo village of McCartys, where the elder lived, was the site of the U.S. experiment that led to the first explosion of the atomic bomb. "The Bomb" worked due to the design and technical-scientific know-how of American and European expertise that would culminate in the state of the world as we know it now. "The Bomb" also became part of the oral stories of devastation that told of injury, death, loss, sorrow, and fear.

The headline was on page four of the LA Times on March 30, 2012: "Fear Grows in O.C. Cities Near Nuclear Power Plant." Since Fukushima, the San Onofre plant has been on people's minds. It's a gigantic, white, dome-shaped monster near the ocean between San Diego and Laguna Beach, and adjacent to the Pechanga Reservation of the Luiseño people with its Vegas-style casino. Like Fukushima, the San Onofre plant was built near a major geological fault line, just five miles offshore. Yet, when the Fukushima nuclear disaster happened, a spokesman for Southern California Edison, the plant's operator, instantly assured the public that the generating station was built to withstand a magnitude 7.0 earthquake and that any tsunami would be deflected by the plant's twenty-five-foot-high tsunami wall. The only problem is that the Fukushima quake was a 9.0 quake, and the ferocious thirty-three-foot-high tsunami that followed swept easily over Fukushima's tsunami wall.

As everyone knows, in the foreseeable future, a major earthquake will inevitably hit California. And, as if this is not bad enough, there was a minor nuclear accident at the San Onofre plant just at the beginning of 2012, during which radioactivity was released into the air. The incident was covered up for a long time before it finally hit the news. Then the public received, of course, the all-too-familiar assurance that the levels of leaked radioactivity had been safe. However, during the mandatory inspections imposed on nuclear power plants in the United States in the aftermath of Fukushima, significant wear and tear was found at San Onofre on hundreds of tubes carrying radioactive water, and the plant was ordered to shut down. Cities in the ten-mile evacuation zone near the plant have issued potassium iodide tablets and conducted disaster drills. Irvine, where I live, is some twenty miles away, and nothing was done there. But some city officials, including the mayor, began to call for the decommissioning of the site.

On March 12, 2012, there was an anti-nuke rally at San Onofre to commemorate Fukushima, opened with a prayer led by a representative from one of the local Indigenous communities. While a few hundred people attended this rally, those with historical memory recalled another rally at San Onofre way back in 1980, at which fifteen thousand people voiced their concern about a potential release of radioactivity from the plant. We live in different times now. It has become exceedingly difficult to sustain a viable public sphere to protest environmental destruction. At the recent rally, some of the Indigenous people involved with the casino business voiced concern that fear of a radioactive leak might deter people from coming to the reservation to gamble. So people remain divided over the protests against Southern California Edison's design to reopen the plant, just as people in other Indigenous communities remain divided over corporate proposals to resume uranium mining or to use reservation lands for nuclear waste dumps. People remain divided over whether it is more important to alleviate excruciating poverty today or act in the interest of long-term safety for the community.

The boy—namely, me—who learned in school about X-rays, polio, and the iron lung grew up in that area of the southwestern United States where the world's most active uranium mining and refining took place. For a thirty-year period from the early 1950s to the early 1980s, there was no other area on planet earth where the uranium industry so utterly and absolutely devastated the land, culture, and community. After high school, he worked for a year at a uranium refinery that produced yellowcake, which is refined uranium ore, that was shipped to Oak Ridge, Tennessee, and Grand Junction, Colorado. There it was refined further and processed into nuclear fuel pellets and rods, used in nuclear reactors and nuclear weapons, as well as nuclear machinery designed for medical purposes, such as the X-ray machine.

The regions of the U.S. Southwest—namely, the area immediate to the Indigenous tribal communities of Acoma Pueblo and Laguna Pueblo, as well as the Navajo communities of Prewitt, Thoreau, and Crown Point to the west and northwest and Navajo and Ute tribal communities in the Four Corners area farther north—are all severely affected by radioactive nuclear contamination coming directly from the mining and refining of uranium ore bodies that are part of the natural landscape. Although the massive surface and underground mining and refining operations in the 1950s to the 1980s ceased for a while, a recent corporate push upon federal and state governments in the Four Corners states of Arizona, Colorado, New Mexico, and Utah have resulted in nuclear energy proponents getting ready to start mining and refining again.

Acoma and Laguna Pueblos and their citizens as well as those of the Navajo tribal peoples have the highest national rates of cancers caused by radioactivity. All of it is due to the close proximity of uranium mining and refining in their homelands, the principal sites for nuclear contamination! When Fukushima's nuclear reactor melted down due to earthquake and tsunami damage, the prediction of tens of thousands of nuclear contamination-caused cancers hit the Japanese people hard. They have experienced and endured such disasters since the 1940s, when the first atomic bombs were detonated at Hiroshima and Nagasaki.

Indigenous peoples in New Mexico have tried to stop uranium mining starting up again in the Mount Taylor area, Kaweshtima in the Aacqumeh language, which has one of the largest underground bodies of uranium ore in the world. But New Mexico's legislature and its governor have pretty much allowed the uranium process to begin again. And in Arizona, on the south rim of the world-renowned Grand Canyon, the Havasupai and Hualapai peoples have also protested reopening of uranium mining on their homelands. But the federal decision makers in the Department of the Interior waylaid their efforts. They were lobbied by corporate energy developers wanting uranium ore for profitable energy production. Too soon, mining will begin again. And refining will follow shortly after.

"Such irony, such irony, such irony," that boy who is now a haatrudzai—who is also me—murmurs on occasion. When I think about it, this situation is fraught with irony upon irony. School is important for the acquisition and development of knowledge because, theoretically, knowledge benefits society. However, when Indigenous peoples were by government policy provided knowledge in school, the knowledge replaced or pushed aside Indigenous peoples' own traditional knowledge. School knowledge was imposed by "the law" of federal policy by which Indigenous peoples had become bound against their will. Indigenous peoples, however, are also conceptually bound by traditional law that governs their bond or tie to the land. They are conceptually bound by an ageless traditional obligation to take care of the land because the land—Mother Earth—provides for them. They are part of the earth that provides for them; they have to take care of it because it takes care of them. Irony upon irony, he murmurs once again.

In the meantime, driven by economic concerns about the prohibitive costs of securing the plant and the accumulated nuclear waste, Southern California Edison has agreed to keep the plant shut. In April 2017, the trial over the legality of a beachfront nuclear waste dump at San Onofre has been postponed. Settlement talks are initiated to discuss the removal of the 3.6 million pounds of nuclear waste from the bluff overlooking the Pacific. The construction of a huge concrete monolith—reminiscent of the famous Chernobyl nuclear sarcophagus—is already under way, costing hundreds of millions of dollars. Southern California Edison has agreed to remove the nuclear waste if an appropriate storage site is found. Where could this possibly be, and at what cost to that region and its inhabitants?[5] Yucca Mountain is the proposed site, but Nevada, a state without nuclear power plants, has voiced opposition against the proposal. Negotiations are continuing.

Recently, in a yearlong workshop on ecopolitics, I taught Ward Churchill's "Radioactive Colonization" alongside Simon Ortiz's poems on uranium mining from *Woven Stone*. Churchill exposes the devastating statistics on cancers among the Indigenous peoples who live on reservations near uranium mines. None of my students knew about the extent of the devastation. Several years ago, Simon and I visited his cousin Jimmy at Acoma. Jimmy was in the last stages of dying from lung cancer. To give Simon some private time with his cousin, I went outside with Jimmy's son and grandchildren. The son told me family stories and showed me the stunningly beautiful pottery of Simon's mother, who was a well-known Acoma potter. Eventually he talked about his father's illness. He had no doubt, he said, that the cancer came from his father's work in the uranium mines. Like many cancers among the Acoma people, he thought it evolved as an effect of radioactive contamination.

Simon had already told me that his mother and grandmother most likely also died of cancer. Nobody can be absolutely sure about this because neither of them agreed to see a Western doctor and therefore never received a conclusive diagnosis. But the symptoms were undoubtedly indicating that they suffered from cancer. Not only the men who worked in the uranium mines and refineries but the Acoma people more generally are afflicted with disproportionally high cancer rates. One of the reasons Simon can think of is that, after the Kerr McGee Corporation simply abandoned the mines without any proper procedure of decontamination, people at Acoma went underground to take the wooden boards from inside the mines. They made wonderful floorboards. But, as I said earlier, it is almost impossible to provide conclusive and legally actionable proof of a connection between the drastic increase in cancer rates and uranium mining on reservations. This remains true despite the fact that the story that can be gleaned from statistics unequivocally points to such a connection. Slow nuclear violence thus continues with impunity.

On our way home from saying farewell to Jimmy, Simon told me about his own work in the uranium refinery near Acoma. He came right out of high school and, like other Indigenous people working in the mines, had only the faintest idea about the dangers involved. He said that workers went into the mines without putting on the cumbersome protective gear. Simon remembers that during the showers after work, the water was full of yellowcake. He was lucky to survive. Many of his people have died or are continuing to die of cancers related to radioactive contamination. As I am reading the testimonies of survivors from Chernobyl and Fukushima, I wonder what it will take to change extractive energy politics on this earth. How many Chernobyls or Fukushimas does it take to convey that we depend on clean water, air, and soil for our survival?

Part II

HAUNTING FROM THE FUTURE

THE AFTERLIFE OF NUCLEAR CATASTROPHES

THE MANHATTAN PROJECT, TRINITY, AND THE NUCLEAR BORDERLANDS

> Trinity Site, New Mexico
> 5:30 A.M., July 16, 1945
>
> *"Let there be light."*
> *And there was light.*
>
> —Benjamin Alire Saenz, "Creation"

Benjamin Saenz's poem "Creation" opens by locating the dawn of the nuclear world in time and place: Trinity Site, New Mexico, 5:30 A.M., July 16, 1945. He then adds an epigraph that draws an arc to the biblical myth of creation: "'Let there be light.' / And there was light."[1] This opening resonates with many descriptions of how the scientists who had run the Manhattan Project stood motionless and in awe at this first explosion of a nuclear bomb at the Trinity Test Site, the birthplace of the nuclear age and of the first experience of the nuclear sublime. Saenz's poem evokes a field of associations that range from the biblical creation myth to apocalyptic visions of the destruction of earth by atomic light. The biblical God as the creator of the world is juxtaposed with the destroyer of worlds Oppenheimer invoked after he witnessed the first atomic explosion at the Trinity Test Site. The successful detonation of the first nuclear weapon marks a rupture in the order of things and of being: man—and I emphasize masculinity here—has for the first time invented a tool that has the potential to propel the destruction of the world. Man is playing God, challenging the very creation of Earth. Let there be light. And there was atomic light, brighter than a thousand suns. The most stunning artistic figuration of atomic light can be found in Michael Light's series *100 Suns*. This artist perfectly captures

FIGURE 12. Michael Light, *053 GEORGE*, in *100 Suns*, 2003. Photograph courtesy of Michael Light.

the uncanny convergence of terror and beauty that underlies the experience of the nuclear sublime.

In *Nuclear Borderlands,* Joseph Masco writes, "The purple fireball and glassified green earth created in the deserts of New Mexico at exactly 5:29:45 a.m. on July 16, 1945 can only be narrated as a moment of historical rupture and transformation."[2] *Nuclear Borderlands* presents an interrogation of "the repressed spaces within nuclear modernism," namely, the construction of a global nuclear economy rendered invisible by the national fixation on an imaginary of extinction during the Cold War. Masco writes, "For while we all still live in a world quite capable of nuclear war, the cumulative effects of the nuclear complex are already both more subtle and more ever-present than (post) Cold War culture has allowed, affecting some lives more than others, and impacting local ecologies and cultural cosmologies in ways that we have yet to recognize fully."[3] Apocalyptic visions of an all-out nuclear war can thus, according to Masco, also function as a screen to divert attention from the world's everyday involvement in a nuclear economy that disproportionately affects poor, mostly Indigenous, communities in the United States and poverty-stricken populations—disproportionally Indigenous too—across the world whose territories are systematically targeted for resource extraction, nuclear tests, or nuclear waste disposal. This entanglement of the ecological and the economic is also a defining feature in the formation of nuclear subjectivities.

If I open this chapter with a focus on the shaping of nuclear subjectivities in atomic survivors, it is because, in highlighting the deadly force of nuclear weapons and power in extreme manifestations, their subjectivities are paradigmatic of the socializing processes in a nuclear world more generally. One could argue that the socialization of atomic survivors is part of the slow violence that adapts humans to the conditions of living in the nuclear age. In what follows, I trace some of the cumulative effects of the nuclear complex in the ever-present psychic afterlife of nuclear attacks and disasters. I pinpoint, in other words, the reshaping of the subjectivity of victims of nuclear disaster and radioactive colonization. Victims of nuclearism display different vulnerabilities: those of nuclear catastrophes are the most vulnerable to apocalyptic visions, while those of nuclear colonialism are most vulnerable to economic exploitation and coercion.

I see the combined impact of nuclear disasters and radioactive colonialism as symptomatic of the larger nuclear trauma that potentially affects everyone within the nuclear–military–industrial complex. Given the nuclear culture of secrecy and deceit, the impact of nuclearism often remains under the surface of concrete lifeworlds. However, it will continue to shape the nuclear unconscious even of those who are only indirectly affected by nuclear catastrophes or colonization. Referring to director of Los Alamos National Laboratory Sig Hecker's *Reflections on Hiroshima and Nagasaki*, Masco argues that, according to Hecker, the

Bomb's primary power is cultural, not technological, because "nuclear weapons affect how people think."[4] Nuclear realities also affect knowledge regimes, epistemologies, and the boundaries of imagination and thought. They affect how people feel, shaping everything from psychosocial realities, ways of being in the world, communal lives, and relationalities to the very boundaries of subjectivity, including conscious and unconscious psychic life.

The Bomb creates a colonization of the mind and the future, a psychic toxicity, and a particular form of transgenerational nuclear trauma. In New Mexico, where the Trinity Test Site is located, the effort to normalize nuclear nature has, according to Masco, been a multigenerational process, "one affecting concepts of social order, ecology, health, and security."[5] Masco further states that New Mexico's citizens, especially its Indigenous populations, experience the nuclear colonization and contamination of their lands also as a psychic intrusion, if not as "a quotidian experience of nuclear terror."[6] One of the activists he interviews speaks of a proliferating anxiety and inability to escape the nuclear terror generated by the knowledge of both radioactive contamination and nuclear war. Masco argues that this terror "destabilizes a self that can no longer locate the boundaries between the body and the bomb,"[7] creating "a new kind of trauma, one that corrupts the possibility of an everyday life lived outside the plutonium economy."[8] Masco argues that, from the perspective of New Mexico's colonization as a nuclear borderland, New Mexicans are indeed nuclear survivors, but, he asks, "survivors of what nuclear trauma?"[9]

Nuclear terror reaches far beyond the local level at which populations are directly affected in their everyday lives. The psychosocial legacies of living within a nuclear ecology are all-pervasive at the global level as well, albeit with a radically unequal distribution. The formation of nuclear subjectivities under the impact of nuclear trauma is, of course, most pronounced in victims of nuclear catastrophes such as Hiroshima, Nagasaki, Three Mile Island, Chernobyl, and Fukushima. In the following, I will therefore trace major features of the psychic life and emergent nuclear subjectivities of survivors of nuclear catastrophes, focusing on oral histories collected by R. J. Lifton, Svetlana Alexievich, Lucy Birmingham, and David McNeill in the aftermath of Hiroshima, Chernobyl, and Fukushima. The subjectivities of survivors can also be read as symptomatic of the effects of nuclear culture on psychic life more generally. When she interviewed the survivors of Chernobyl, Alexievich felt she was recording the future. Similarly, we could say that by tracing the formation of the nuclear subjectivities of atomic survivors, we are also drawing a map of a much more pervasive threat that looms over the nuclear world, if not a future anterior of nuclear subjectivities and psychic lives to come.

HIBAKUSHA: POST-NUCLEAR WAR SUBJECTIVITIES

Invoking the white light from an atomic explosion, Eleanor Wilner's "High Noon at Los Alamos" suggests a cycle of fateful repetitions: "As if compelled to repetition / and to unearth again / white fire at the heart of matter."[10] These lines confront readers with the provocative suggestion that an evolutionary repetition compulsion propels the human species to repeat, again and again, the violence of humans upon humans that burns bodies and city walls "from Troy to Nagasaki."[11] Freud, and later Lacan, linked the compulsion to repeat with aggression and the death drive. Wilner's title, "High Noon," of course recalls the film with that name, evocative of the legendary showdown between two mortal enemies in a New Mexico desertscape. The poem thus suggests that the compulsion to kill is also bound up with fantasies of western-style masculinity, fantasies that have fueled the colonization of New Mexico's Indigenous territories and the conquest of land, resources, and human energy that culminates in the splitting of the atom and the release of the energy of the sun's white fire.

But Nagasaki introduces a caesura into the cycle of repetition. For the first time, it is broken by "a pause to signal peace, or a rehearsal for the silence." The poem insinuates that there is no alternative to the choice between peace and extinction. Nagasaki stands for both a "prologue for the murders yet to come" and the "signal fire" that announces the (final) silence. "High Noon at Los Alamos" was from its very beginning a deadly endgame. The opening of another poem, "A Liturgy for Trinity" by Barbara La Morticella, draws out the implications of this choice:

Our fathers of the atomic industry
thought there was a chance
New Mexico might be destroyed
[...]
They took the chance.[12]

Ever since they took the chance, humans have either lived under the shadow of the white atomic light or *become* this shadow—like the incinerated humans whose shadows were engraved in the stones of Hiroshima. Nothing humans have ever done since or will ever do can escape this shadow. It has become their double, their *anima* or atomic soul. Atomic energy and light have reshaped their bodies and minds, their selves and their unconscious. Atomic rays have penetrated their skin and bones, the walls of their cells, the structure of their genes, and the boundaries of their subjectivity. Atomic rays have remade the boundaries of earth and stone, of communities and nation, of selves and species. This is why we can learn from atomic survivors. This is why we need to heed their warnings.

The knowledge of past nuclear destruction, present and future nuclear danger, and the burden of guilt from the responsibility we, the generations who were born into the nuclear age, have for the survival of life on earth, including that of future generations, irrevocably shapes the formation of nuclear subjectivities. Designed to eclipse an overly painful awareness, even strategies such as denial and splitting are based on the knowledge that atomic war fashions our subjectivities as nuclear. So does our fear of radioactive contamination or nuclear destruction, even if it remains unconscious. The nuclear age marks the boundaries of subjectivity at both a conscious and an unconscious level.

In 1968, American psychiatrist Robert Jay Lifton published *Death in Life: Survivors of Hiroshima,* an extensive psychoanalytically informed study of the psychological effects of Hiroshima on survivors. Drawing on interviews and oral histories, *Death in Life* theorizes the impact of the first nuclear trauma on the formation of subjectivity. Fourteen years later, in 1982, Lifton cowrote with Richard Falk *Indefensible Weapons: The Political and Psychological Case against Nuclearism,* and another thirteen years later, in 1995, he cowrote with Greg Mitchell *Hiroshima in America: Fifty Years of Denial.* With his work spanning over half a century, Lifton has become one of the most important voices in antinuclear politics and is certainly the foremost expert in theorizing what I call *nuclear subjectivities.* While Lifton focuses on the psychological effect of nuclear violence on survivors, ultimately, his study also bears upon the formation of subjectivity in the nuclear age more generally.

Perhaps not surprisingly, Lifton's interviews with Hiroshima survivors, the *hibakusha,* show that the atomic attack and its aftermath profoundly affected survivors' entire sense of what it means to be human. In

FIGURE 13. Yamamoto Keisuke, *Hiroshima*, 1948. Oil on canvas, 180 × 224.2 cm. Courtesy of Hyogo Prefectural Museum of Art, Kobe, Japan.

a flash, the atomic bomb undermined any ontological security or basic trust in the world. As survivors struggled to remake their shattered senses of self, apocalyptic fantasies of the end of the world abounded. Many of the victims of the bomb felt unmitigated anger and rage that translated into apocalyptic fantasies. One of the surviving women confesses to Lifton: "I sometimes wish that all of the earth would be annihilated."[13] We may recall Derrida's statement: "The breaking of the mirror would be, finally, through an act of language, the very occurrence of nuclear war. Who can swear that our unconscious is not expecting this? Dreaming of it, desiring it?"[14] Lifton links the woman's "end-of-the-world wish" or fantasy of total nuclear destruction to a common hostility many *hibakusha* feel in the wake of the nuclear attack, a hostility that feeds into a wish for cosmic retaliation.[15] Even beyond the culture of *hibakusha*, such conflicted feelings are deeply embedded in the early psychohistory of the bomb and are therefore central as a particular formation of nuclear subjectivities.

Two opposite poles of apocalyptic nuclear fantasies thus emerge: at one extreme end, we find fears marked by the horror of total nuclear destruction; at the other, we find the secret, if not unconscious, wish for an annihilation of cosmic proportions. These poles suggest a deep ambivalence at the core of the nuclear imaginary, an ambivalence for which Lifton finds confirmation in many of his interviews. Highlighting the "general human capacity for complex and contradictory inner imagery,"[16] Lifton argues that the *hibakusha*'s attempt at "psychohistorical mastery" of the catastrophic event mobilizes contending symbols, both apocalyptic and life affirming. While *hibakusha* experience a yearning for reintegration into the continuity of human existence, many also remain deeply suspicious of the postbomb care they receive, especially when it comes from the American perpetrators who now serve as the occupational forces in the country.[17]

This suspicion of what Lifton calls a "counterfeit nurturance or care" was especially strong in the stray children who were picked up in front of Hiroshima Station during the early postbomb months: "Sensitivities about counterfeit nurturance were extremely strong in all children forced to depend upon special care, particularly care coming from city or government agencies."[18] Lifton observes that atomic bomb orphans share the ontological crisis experienced by all atomic bomb victims: "a vast breakdown of faith in the larger human matrix supporting each individual life, and therefore a loss of faith (or trust) in the structure of human existence."[19]

Psychic survival under these conditions depended largely on the ability to tap into one's own ambivalence and mobilize life-affirming counterimages. For A-bomb orphans, the experience of abandonment, vulnerability, and impaired nurturance generates an ontological insecurity that shapes their entire subject-formation. "Japanese sociologists have described a profoundly disaffected prototype of the A-bomb orphan as a young adult: working irregularly at low-status jobs, moving about frequently and having no permanent address, diffusely anxious and in poor health, and living generally on the fringe of society."[20] Lifton concludes that, for all *hibakusha*, the "A-bomb's original disruption of psychological and social bonds becomes perpetuated, and inextricably bound up with the general dislocations of postwar Japanese experience."[21]

Lifton also emphasizes how strongly gender marks the formation of the nuclear subjectivities of *hibakusha*. Women are disproportionally affected by the effects of radioactive contamination, especially in respect to reproductive damage, but also in respect to disfiguring keloids formed at the site of burn scars. In post–World War II Japan's sexist patriarchal system, the social stigmatization of *hibakusha* women was much stronger than that of men. Proportionally to their disfigurement, their chances of finding a marriage partner dropped drastically. This disadvantage was compounded by fears of genetic damage, especially after information became publicly available about the horrific fate of children born in the wake of Hiroshima and Nagasaki: "a two-headed baby born to a *hibakusha* in 1950, another born without a brain in 1951, a picture of a one-eyed baby, [. . .] grotesque shots of children, living and dead, who had been born with tiny heads, without hearts or other organs, and with other kinds of malformation."[22] As a result of this widespread fear of bearing mutant children, women tried to hide their *hibakusha* status much more frequently than men, even though this meant that they would become excluded from free medical treatment for survivors.[23]

In addition, if a married woman did want to claim her right to acknowledge her status as a *hibakusha* socially, she could do so only with her husband's approval and confirmation. Often husband and wife colluded in a willful denial of the woman's status to ward off their shared fears of genetically damaged offspring. Lifton describes situations in which "husband and wife indulge in a shared fiction that the wife is not a *hibakusha* in order to still both their fears about offspring; [. . .] they live out this fiction *as if* it were true, perhaps even half believing it, until either bodily fears or increased awareness of medical advantages induce them to give it up."[24] Not surprisingly, these examples demonstrate how social stigma colludes with and feeds into denial.

Psychologically, this means that women, more so than men, lived in a state of denial about their health condition and their status as *hibakusha*. One of the women told Lifton, "I have never felt myself to be a *hibakusha*. [. . .] I refuse to carry on my back all this misery. [. . .] So I always have the feeling that I wish to deny *[hitei shiyo]* all of this."[25] By contrast, it is the more politicized women who refused to live in denial or in submission to patriarchal norms, often joining antinuclear protest movements. A young woman leader in the Burakumin (Outcast) Liberation Movement, for example, insisted that equality for women is more important than the status as a *hibakusha* and defiantly asserted, "I oppose the kind of marriage in which I must 'shrink myself down in wretchedness.'"[26]

Lifton attributes part of the psychobiological differences between men and women to strong roots in the Japanese cultural tradition, specifically the restrictive norms that defined acceptable "feminine" behavior in the Japanese culture at the time:

> A Japanese woman demonstrating incisive theoretical gifts runs the risk of being considered (by herself as well as others) "unfeminine." These attitudes have contributed to longstanding discrimination in educational opportunity, and to stress upon woman as nurturer and seductress.[27]

Yet, under the surface of a performative adherence to feminine rhetorical conventions, Lifton detects a "strong feminine commitment to the perpetuation of organic life and a related propensity for 'organic knowledge.'"[28] He links the prominence of women in certain forms of A-bomb literature and art to their embrace of organic life forces: "women are expressing their close identification with organic life and its perpetuation as an antidote to nuclear severance."[29] These women writers, artists, and critics thus generate a countermovement to the work of death performed by nuclear necropolitics by emphasizing the work of (organic) life, albeit often tied—as it will later be in the worldwide feminist antinuclear movement—to traditional politics of reproduction.

What Lifton describes as women's commitment to organic life also informs the gendering of affective politics. The imposition of restraint and denial on Japanese women, for example, leads to the repression of allegedly unfeminine affects, especially anger and rage. Women artists and writers, however, find a mode of indirection to express such repressed emotions by using the traditional Japanese figure of the angry female ghost. A muralist told Lifton, "There are many ghost stories in [. . .] Japan [. . .] stories of women ghosts who lift their arms halfway and whose hands are burning with anger. [. . .] Japanese women could not [at the time of the A-bomb] express their human anger as anger. [. . .] But where resentment cannot be expressed for a long, long time, malignant and incomprehensible spirits [. . .] leave their traces."[30] Thus compounded by centuries of patriarchal oppression, the haunting legacy of Hiroshima mobilizes traditional ghost stories to create the figure of an angry female radioactive ghost.

Finally, there is also a rhetorical gendering at work in discourses about the American nuclear attack and the subsequent occupation of Japan. From the perspective of male fantasies, the United States is seen as having "raped" the Japanese nation and "its cultural heritage—especially the feminine-maternal substrate of that heritage."[31] The widespread postwar conspiracy of silence and "inevitable collusion between groups of occupiers and occupied in prostitution, narcotics and petty crime,"[32] and the GIs' corruption and abuse of the Japanese population, ranging from humiliation and physical violence to rape and murder, generated widespread resentment, nourished by the sense that the Americans despoiled the purity of Japanese culture and its women.[33]

Behind this specific image, a more pervasive sense lingers that the atomic bomb has forever despoiled the world and that the radioactive contamination of environments, bodies, and genes has also produced a psychic toxicity, thus radically changing human psychology and the sense of being in the world. At a time when the Holocaust had already shaken up the very foundations of ontological security, the existence and use of a weapon with the potential to destroy planetary life reverberated around the globe. Meanwhile, the American military lauded the use of the atomic bomb as part of a "war to end all wars." This may well become true one day. Yet, the sentence's very rhetorical ambiguity reveals the problem: the end of all wars can mean either peace or annihilation.

THE AFTERLIFE OF NUCLEAR DISASTER:
VOICES FROM CHERNOBYL

"Fear's harder to retain than hope or indifference," writes Mary Joe Salter in a poem titled "Chernobyl." While there are undoubtedly certain symptomatic historical and cultural differences, the nuclear subjectivities created in the aftermath of nuclear disasters share significant features with those of survivors of nuclear war, among them the warding off of fear and the emotional numbing, psychic toxicity, and, most prominently, splitting and denial that come with it. In the testimonies of survivors from Hiroshima, Chernobyl, and other sites of nuclear disasters, we witness the clinging to hope against all odds or the psychic numbing that may easily turn into indifference. Anything is better than living in the throes of quotidian fear or free-floating anxieties about the effects of radioactive contamination. In *Accident: A Day's News,* her memoir about the Chernobyl disaster, Christa Wolf writes, "How strange that a-tom in Greek means the same as in-di-viduum in Latin: indivisible. Those who invented these words knew neither nuclear fission nor schizophrenia."[34] Wolf, in other words, suggests that there is a family likeness between nuclear fission and schizophrenia: they both divide something that should be indivisible—a rock or a self. Initially constituting a desperate attempt to adapt to the aftermath of disaster, the psychopolitics of splitting may, at its extreme, result in a schizoid division of the self.

In the following close readings of literary texts, oral histories, and historical essays, I foreground post-Chernobyl subjectivities as specific examples of postnuclear subject-formations more generally, formations whose basic features have, for example, also been observed in the aftermath of Fukushima. The structural similarities of subjectivities formed after nuclear accidents to those formed after nuclear war show that it is possible to describe certain features that justify an overall conceptualization of *nuclear subjectivities*.

In many ways, these features also resemble subjectivities formed after other traumatic events, such as colonial subjugation, war, or the Holocaust. While major trauma is the common denominator, the analysis of nuclear subjectivities will also show that there are certain features that mark nuclear trauma specifically. Among those are, to name just a few, obsession with illnesses developing in radioactively contaminated bodies; fears of reproductive damage and related phantasms of the mutant body; the phantasmatic refashioning of the disaster zone into an idyllic space of freedom; and finally, the often apocalyptic haunting from the future, linked to the vision of planetary extinction.

After the Chernobyl nuclear disaster in 1986, the town Pripyat in the reactor's vicinity was evacuated and declared a contaminated "zone of exclusion." Secretly, however, many of its citizens returned and resettled there illegally. In the early 1990s, journalist Svetlana Alexievich gathered the oral histories of Chernobyl survivors. She ends her book with the words I referred to earlier: "These people had already seen what for everyone else is still unknown. I felt like I was recording the future."[35] In a similar vein, anthropologist Adriana Petryna in *Life Exposed* speaks of the lives in Chernobyl's "zone of exclusion" as "machines for designing the future."[36] If the testimonies of Chernobyl survivors can indeed be read as allegories of a haunting from the future, we may ask how psychoanalysis theorizes the unconscious impact of pending, yet predictable, catastrophes.

I will read the emergent subjectivities of Chernobyl survivors as hallmarks of a posthuman future determined by a "political economy of emotions"[37] based on "expendability,"[38] "sacrifice zones,"[39] and the global production of disposable people.[40] Nuclear subjectivities are marked by certain features that include a pervasive epistemology of deceit and denial, a fascination with the nuclear sublime, a devastating awareness of the psychic toxicity of living in a nuclear zone, and a haunting from the future. People also share a sense of living perpetually in the shadow of death and madness[41] in a world in which "the order of things was shaken."[42] In his discussion of the nuclear sublime, Joseph Masco highlights a fascination with nuclear power that generates a particular philosophical sense of the increasing precarity of life on our contaminated planet. In a similar vein, one of the survivors of the Chernobyl nuclear disaster says, "Chernobyl [. . .] happened so that philosophers could be made."[43] "It's [. . .] a philosophical dilemma," says another. "A perestroika of our feelings is happening here."[44]

In *Die ausradierte Stadt* (The erased city), a study of Chernobyl's catastrophes, Francesco Cataluccio portrays "the Zone" as an area of "extreme emotions,"[45] replete with the strange attraction and freedom that come when all familiar orientations are rendered obsolete. The forms of life that flourish in the Zone are endowed with intensities that provoke a philosophical attitude to life, a radical contemplation of the human condition and confrontation of mortality or its inverse, a willful embrace of the lures of the nuclear sublime. One of the survivors says,

> Sometimes I turn on the radio. They scare us [. . .] with the radiation. But our lives have gotten better since the radiation came. I swear! Look around: they brought oranges, three kinds of salami. [. . .] What's it like, radiation? Some people say it has no color and no smell. [. . .] But if it's colorless, then it's like God. God is everywhere, but you can't see Him. They scare us! The apples are hanging in the garden, the leaves are on the trees, the potatoes are in the fields. [. . .] I don't think there was any Chernobyl. They made it up.[46]

The invisible danger that emanates from radiation has an element of the uncanny. It creates a paradoxical feeling of hypervigilance, while at the same time maintaining the lure of deniability. Radiation as invisible matter is a material force in the world that possesses vibrancy, albeit one that cannot be experienced, except in its deadly impact on all things living. Survivors apprehend radiation as "vibrant matter"[47] only via indirection through mass media warnings and coverage of dangers; through the circulating rumors in the community; and finally, through the radioactive contamination that affects their or others' bodies. The comparison of radiation with a godlike substance highlights not only the fundamental ambivalence of the nuclear sublime but also its inevitable entanglement with willful denial and self-deception. All of these features operate within a larger epistemology of deceit. Transformed into a godlike omnipresence, the invisible danger of radiation is neutralized and contained in a familiar structure of quasi-religious belief. Ultimately, nothing is new in the nuclear Garden of Eden.

At the same time, however, people are keenly aware of the fact that they live in a world where, as one of the survivors says, the order of things was shaken. After the nuclear disaster, nothing will ever be as it was before. More than ambivalence, this is actually a paradox of nuclear sovereignty, reminiscent of imaginary transitional spaces that suspend the laws of the real. The zone of exclusion outside Chernobyl is, literally speaking, a space beyond the law. The people who returned to live there did so illegally and clandestinely. Unmoored from their former lives and social worlds, they enjoy a kind of paradoxical freedom. Shared by both soldiers and civilians, tropes of freedom are among the most common rhetorical invocations of a nuclear imaginary. A returnee to Pripyat says:

> I was running away from the world. [. . .] Then I came here. Freedom is here. [. . .] I fell in love with contemplation. [. . .] I go to the cemeteries. People leave food for the dead. But the dead don't need it. They don't mind. In the fields there is wild grain, and in the forest there are mushrooms and berries. Freedom is here.[48]

This "freedom" also generates a new conviviality with animals and, almost paradoxically, a new connection with the natural world. Survivor Kovalenko says, "A strange thing happened to me. I became closer to animals. [. . .] I want to make a film to see everything through the eyes of an animal."[49] Human subjectivity can no longer be neatly separated from its entanglement with that of other species. The surviving animals are a sign of life in a zone of catastrophic loneliness, bare survival and living death. In nightmares about being evacuated, Kovalenko finds herself in an unknown place that's "not even Earth."[50] Her testimony about her lonely companionship with animals and plants expresses the core of nuclear subjectivities that emerged in the wake of the Chernobyl disaster: the disbelief about the uncanny invisible power of radiation; the clinging to life in the wake of catastrophe; the symbiotic bond of survival with animals who, unlike humans, can sense radiation; and the precarious denial that creates a simulated return to normality. "What radiation? There's a butterfly flying, and bees are buzzing,"[51] Kovalenko says, and starts crying.

With their superior sensory organs for the registration of radiation, animals also function like nature's own dosimeter. Sensing the nuclear explosion, bees stayed in their nests for three days and wasps only came back six years later.[52] Similarly, the vanishing of May bugs, maggots, and worms is an indicator of radioactive contamination. After the disaster, people find mutated fish, especially pike, in the rivers around Pripyat. Phantasms of the mutant body signal a return of the dark underside of the idyll, thus highlighting what is repressed in the nuclear sublime. These phantasms can be seen as a radicalized version of Lacan's phantasms of the fragmented body. While the latter signal the fragility of the ego, phantasms of the mutant body signal the precarity of life in the nuclear age as well as the fear of transgenerational genetic damage. They function as hallmarks of nuclear subjectivities and the nuclear unconscious, haunting survivors of Hiroshima, Chernobyl, and Fukushima alike. They even haunt women living in the nuclear borderland.

The zone of exclusion has become a mutant transitional space of the living dead, a deathworld that has radically changed the nature and status of the human, other living species, and technologies. The soldiers who are brought in to patrol the evacuated zones encounter Pripyat and the surrounding villages as ghost towns, deathworlds marked off-limits, with sealed-up houses and abandoned farm machinery. Animals have become dangerous carriers of radioactive contamination, destined for extermination. A commander of the guard units who calls himself "the director of the apocalypse" tells of "empty villages where the pigs had gone crazy and were running around"[53] and where native plants—burdock, stinging nettle, and goosefoot—were taking over the untended communal graves of radiation victims.

Life in the zone of exclusion has created new types of assemblages between humans, animals, plants, and technology that reveal beyond any doubt that it has become impossible to define the boundaries of the human in isolation from either other living species or human technologies. To begin with, Chernobyl was a technologically induced disaster, but it also turned out that radiation destroys the technological tools humans have created to domesticate nature. A helicopter pilot describes the scene near the Chernobyl reactor: "thin roes and wild boars move in slow motion eating contaminated grass. Next to them, a ruined building and a field of debris with an assemblage of dead machinery and dead robots, their wiring destroyed by the radiation."[54] One of the soldiers laments the death of robots: "The robots died. Our robots, designed by Academic Lukachev for the exploration of Mars."[55]

Characterized by the logic of deathworlds, new makeshift assemblages between humans, animals, and technological objects manage survival in the exclusion zone. These assemblages exist in a transitional mode of being between life and death. Together with the effects of radiation on their bodies, grief and catastrophic loneliness turn humans into walking dead, their ambition of exploring Mars with robots shattered before their very eyes. Emaciated by contaminated plants, radioactive animals pass by like ghosts in a slow-motion film scene. Erosion breaks technological objects, turning them into obsolete debris, ruins that testify to a force stronger than any hard material. Genetic mutations affect living species, either immediately or transgenerationally. Epidemic cancers cast a shadow of death over the Zone's citizens.

"You can't understand anything without the shadow of death,"[56] says Chernobyl photographer Victor Latun, who then concludes with a forceful recourse to the nuclear sublime:

> Some say that aliens knew about the catastrophe and helped us out; others that it was an experiment, and soon kids with incredible talent will start to be born. Or maybe the Belarussians will disappear, like the Scythians. We're metaphysicians. We don't live on this earth, but in our dreams, in our conversations. Because you need to add something to this ordinary life, in order to understand it. Even when you're near death.[57]

These invocations of a nuclear sublime, if not nuclear surrealism, testify to the fascination with nuclear power as something beyond comprehension, something unfathomable, surreal, alien. "We heard rumors that the flame at Chernobyl was unearthly, it wasn't even a flame. It was a light, a glow."[58] The collapse of all categories of measuring and judging one's world may well feel like an artificially induced madness *(versania)*. It is no longer possible to distinguish between reality and fantasy, between real danger and freely floating fear. Not only can radiation block the function of certain organs; it can also block certain functions of the mind and induce something akin to a specific nuclear repression at the level of nature as unconscious life. Rumor reigns supreme; a new "life of public secrets"[59] emerges along with "informal economies of knowledge."[60] When people find pike without heads or tails in the lakes and rivers, rumors are spreading that something similar is going to happen to humans: "The Belarussians will turn into humanoids."[61] A teacher says, "The fear is in our feelings, on a subconscious level."[62] An ever-present pervasive unconscious fear generates the psychic toxicity of radioactive ecologies. "It's not just the land that's contaminated, but our minds,"[63] says another teacher from Pripyat.

Psychic toxicity has many facets beyond the mere internalization of fear. It also translates into various forms of denial necessary to continue with everyday life. The very fact that the danger of radioactive toxins is invisible, while at the surface everything seems normal, enhances deniability. Combined with the official cover-up, a collusive willful denial facilitates living on borrowed time. The pervasive psychopolitics of splitting thus works both at the individual and collective levels. One of the reasons why governmental cover-up works so thoroughly is the collusion by individuals who do not want to know, especially when it comes to the threat of slow nuclear violence that manifests in long-term cancers and reproductive damage.

Chernobyl thus created a new form of nuclear subjectivity, one that Christa Wolf in *Accident* links to a collective "compulsion to split,"[64] a *"Zwang zu Spaltungen."*[65] The latter manifests in a fission at the core of the self, a nuclear schizophrenia of sorts that affects not only survivors but also humans living in the aftermath of Chernobyl's nuclear disaster more generally. The historical rupture caused by this disaster—which Wolf describes as "once again [. . .] our age had created a Before and After for itself"—resonates with this fissure within the self that Wolf equates with the isolation and encapsulation of toxic emotions. Wolf suggests that unbearable "radioactive feelings"[66]—she uses the metaphor of *"radioactive Gefühle"*[67]—need to be split off and stored like nuclear waste in an isolated waste disposal vault within the self. This image of a crypt of sorts that harbors the radioactive ghosts of nuclear subjectivities is suggestive of the haunting quality of this fission within the self.

It is this very fission that also causes a nuclear explosion within poetic language. Old poetic metaphors like the "radiating sky"[68] or the "white cloud"[69] become, as Wolf states, unusable because they now resonate with toxic meaning. Recalling the line *"Marvellous Nature Shining on Me!"* she cannot but wonder "what to do with the libraries full of nature poems."[70] Radioactive contamination is contagious, affecting not only the material world and its organisms but also the ecology of mind and nature, generating both a linguistic and psychic toxicity that transforms our being in the world. Language itself has been affected by nuclear fallout, and survivors are at a loss for words to describe this radically new experience. Wolf's text is permeated by reflections on this challenge to the boundaries of language and writing.

People in the wake of Chernobyl cannot but oscillate between two modes of being. On one hand, they live under traumatic shock and a haunting from the future. Fears of another nuclear disaster, if not war, augment fears of the slow radioactive violence that causes deadly illnesses after a period of latency. On the other hand, people are forced to continue living in a mode of *as if*—as if the disaster had not happened—a temporary denial in the service of adapting to the necessities of everyday survival. Splitting is a painfully ambivalent mode of defense that protects the self from traumatic assault, while also tearing it apart.

In her analysis of psychological responses to the trauma of Partition in India, Veena Das argues that women had to become masters in deploying this form of splitting because they had to continue to care for surviving family members, especially children and the elderly. While facing similarly daunting tasks, women in the wake of the Chernobyl disaster had the added burden of coping with the slow effects of radioactive contamination. In addition to fearing for their own health, they also had to care for husbands dying from radiation sickness and for children born with birth defects or radiation-induced illnesses. They also had to face social isolation and, indeed, social death from being ousted by relatives who feared them as carriers of toxic and contagious radiation.

By contrast, the gendering of nuclear subjectivities interpellates men to perform the role of a sacrificial hero. Alexievich includes an interview with a soldier who volunteered for a helicopter mission above the radiating nuclear reactor. This interview can be read as a testimony not only to the afterlife of the Chernobyl disaster but also to the gendered politics that structured the cleanup efforts and the management of survival. The soldier admits that he volunteered for the helicopter mission because he "felt this desire to be a hero,"[71] a desire initially common among the volunteering men. The experience, according to the soldier, "appealed to our sense of masculinity: Manly men were going off to do this important thing. And everyone else? They can hide under women's skirts, if they want. There were guys with pregnant wives, others had little babies, a third had burns. They all cursed to themselves and went anyway."[72]

Having historically always sustained war cultures, masculinity and heroism and the pressure to conform to its norms are becoming even more pervasive in the increasing militarization of life more generally. At the end of their mission, the soldiers were ordered by a KGB man not to talk to anyone, anywhere, about what they had seen. The number of Roentgen measured is declared a military secret.[73] When the soldier returns from his mission, he gives the cap he wore to his little son. Two years later, the boy is diagnosed with a tumor in his brain. The soldier fears for his own life too: "When I made it back from Afghanistan, I knew that I'd live. Here it was the opposite: it'd kill you only after you got home."[74]

Masculinity and heroism—it's the same old story, the same cliché of manhood. We see it with the men who worked for the Manhattan Project, the men who fight the new wars in the aftermath of World War II, the men who volunteer for the cleanup efforts at Chernobyl, Fukushima, and other toxic industrial sites around the world. Yet, upon their return from nuclear missions, many of the volunteers who were shamed or bribed into working at Chernobyl became outcasts, feared by neighbors, families, and wives. Their heroism shattered, many of them became bitter, and some took their own lives.

Since radioactive contamination affects these men's sex lives and reproductive futures, they often turn their frustration into sexual aggression, resorting to what now passes under the label of locker room banter. One of the soldiers describes how, upon his return, he goes dancing and meets a girl he wants to date but is turned away: "You're a Chernobylite now. I'd be scared to have your kids."[75] The disaster thus directly impacts the boundaries of subjectivity and community and the relationships among survivors, including familial and sexual ones. The commander of the guard units who calls himself "director of the apocalypse" expresses his resentment against his wife, who took their child and left. "That bitch! But I'm not going to hang myself like Vanya Kotov. And I'm not going to throw myself out a seventh-floor window. That bitch lived with me fine. She wasn't afraid." And he begins to sing:

Even one thousand gamma rays
Can't keep the Russian cock from having its days.

"Nice song. [. . .] That bitch. She's afraid of me. She took the kid."[76]

What this complex mixture of denial, aggression, and sexual prowess desperately tries to cover up is a deeper disavowed layer of affect:

mourning the loss of his loved ones, fear about his own health and survival, and the acknowledgment that, instead of being celebrated as a hero, he has been made a sacrificial victim by a government that swore him to secrecy, only to abandon him like his other comrades—contaminated, disposable, with nowhere to go.

"I'm not afraid of death anymore. Of death itself. But I don't know how I'm going to die."[77] Like so many others, he was, as he describes with a healthy dose of sarcasm, interpellated by the age-old military code of masculinity: "the court of manhood, the court of honor! That was part of the attraction—he didn't go, so I will. Now I look at it differently. After nine operations and two heart attacks. [. . .] But I would have gone anyway. That's definite. He couldn't, I will. That was manhood."[78] He would have gone anyway, but now he realizes that he remains behind, a sacrificial victim of the nuclear–military–industrial complex, condemned to living with the knowledge of radioactive poison in his body that will bring him a slow death.

As I described earlier, the situation was different for women because they were socialized to follow an ethics of care rather than heroism. Women living near the reactor were left coping on their own in a zone of contamination and abject abandonment: "in every house, someone's died. [. . .] All the women are without men, there aren't any men, all the men are dead. [. . .] And all our women are empty. Not all of them managed to give birth in time. What else will I say? You have to live. That's all."[79]

You have to live. That's all. In *Life Exposed,* anthropologist Adriana Petryna analyzes how, in the wake of Chernobyl, a new civic culture developed in which Chernobyl survivors, depending on the severity of exposure and symptoms, acquired a new status as biological citizens. Biological citizenship redefines the parameters of selfhood and interpersonal relationship. It is the ticket to becoming admitted into the Chernobyl "community of sufferers." In the process of negotiating their status as biological citizens to access medical and financial support, people become "medicalized selves."[80]

Petryna also traces the gendering of slow daily violence in Chernobyl's afterlife. In her collection of oral histories from survivors, she registers an increase in domestic violence among the disempowered and traumatized men. She also describes how the women become the carriers of the burdens of reproductive and transgenerational damage. The deformed children of Chernobyl become emblematic of a haunting from the future in which "radiation is pulverizing the gene pool."[81] A doctor describes to Petryna the infants who are at her hospital's critical unit in German-donated Plexiglass incubators: "One born premature, another survived the death of his twin; another born with a dysfunctional esophagus; another with signs of prenatal asphyxiation. One born to a mother who, at age nine, was evacuated from the Chernobyl zones; her infant has half a lung. Another was born to a Chernobyl worker: there are six fingers on his left hand. He's missing a trachea. His gut lay on the outside of his body. His left outer ear is gnarled and deformed."[82] Women, as the oral histories of *Voices from Chernobyl* show, are doubly haunted, both by the reality of mutant children and fears of future transgenerational mutations and by the manifestation of such fears in phantasms of the mutant body. Women do give birth to mutant children and need to take care of them if they survive. Alexievich felt as if she was recording the future. What else can we say? You have to live. That's all.

Wolves Eat Dogs
Apart from being treated in oral histories, the subjectivity of Chernobyl survivors has also been the subject of a wide range of poetry, fiction, and film. In what follows, I focus on Martin Cruz Smith's *Wolves Eat Dogs*, a detective novel set in post-Chernobyl Ukraine and Russia in 2004. My selection of this particular text is motivated by the fact that Cruz Smith highlights a dimension of the psychopolitical afterlife of Chernobyl that is less central in oral histories, namely, the culture of corruption and crime that flourishes in the zone of exception and spreads from there to the post-Soviet underworld and its entanglement with illegal global shadow markets. With his two novels, *Stallion Gate* (which I deal with in chapter 2) and *Wolves Eat Dogs,* Cruz Smith establishes himself as one of the predominate Indigenous authors dealing with nuclear necropolitics.

Official cover-up, corruption, denial, self-deception, and all kinds of violence, crime, and murder flourish in the wake of Chernobyl's nuclear disaster. They are the stuff of detective fiction. Martin Cruz Smith published *Wolves Eat Dogs* eighteen years after telling the story of the Manhattan Project in *Stallion Gate*. *Wolves Eat Dogs* is set in Chernobyl's zone of exclusion and post-Soviet Moscow. Russia has transitioned to a capitalist state, and Ukraine has seceded from the former Soviet Union. Investigator Arkady Renko tries to solve the mystery of two deaths: Pasha Ivanov, a leading figure among Russia's new billionaire class, was poisoned with cesium-137, a lethal radioactive isotope, and his business partner Timofeyev was also poisoned with cesium before he was found with his throat cut.

During his investigation, Renko encounters the people who have returned illegally to live emergent forms of life in the Zone: peasant squatters, the elderly, scientists, a medical doctor and a radiobiologist, local poachers, scavengers, and profiteers. Their subjectivities are marked by the Zone's new biopolitical regime, by an economics of sacrifice and self-sacrifice, and by the psychic toxicity that inevitably accompanies their catastrophic endangerment. The crime novel deals with the cultures of secrecy and corruption that emerge after the disaster in the vicinity of Pripyat, the Zone's remaining ghost town. Arcady Renko, a rogue cop of sorts, often continues his crime investigations after being officially taken off the case for political reasons. Cruz Smith designs his character partly to exhibit what Jean and John Comaroff call the "con/fusion of politics and crime."[83] Trying to solve the mystery of the death of millionaire Pavel Ivanov, Renko realizes that Ivanov's entire apartment is contaminated with cesium chloride and finds evidence that Ivanov, realizing he was poisoned, committed suicide.

The subsequent murder of Ivanov's business partner Timofeyev leads Renko from Moscow to Pripyat, where he discovers a dense network of crime and corruption, culpability and cover-up. Alex Gerasinov, leader of the radiobiology team and ex-husband of Renko's lover, admits to planting grains of cesium on Ivanov and Timofeyev. His motif was revenge. While working under his own father, Felix Gerasinov—the Soviet Union's leading authority on nuclear accidents—Ivanov and Timofeyev were responsible for the official cover-up that allowed millions of people to be exposed to the fallout. Renko then finds out that an elderly man, unaware of the cesium poisoning, murdered Timofeyev by cutting his throat. This murder too was committed as an act of revenge. The old man holds Timofeyev responsible for his grandchildren's death from radiation poisoning. Renko, who had already been taken off the case by his boss, realizes that in the Zone, the order of things has been disrupted so radically that the boundaries between law and criminality no longer obtain. The actual culprits who are responsible for poisoning millions of people with radioactive toxins go free unless people commit acts of revenge that take justice into their own hands. Deciding to follow his own ethics and sense of justice, Renko therefore keeps the murders under cover and remains silent.

The confusion of politics and crime, and hence of victims and perpetrators, that underlies the world of *Wolves Eat Dogs* is part of a larger, indeed, global trend toward transforming the proportionality of crime and punishment. In Cruz Smith's crime fiction, moral ambiguities abound, even though Renko, the rogue detective, is representative of a new moral code, often in defiance of the law. His portrayal as a caring and vulnerable man, devoted to his lover and an abandoned, traumatized boy he is taking care of, generates a strong transference that enhances the inclination of readers to accept the moral ambiguities of his actions and the blurring of boundaries between politics, crime, and justice.

Defying the stereotypes of conventional crime fiction, Cruz Smith portrays a moral universe in shades of gray, attuned to the scary zones of nuclear necropolitics. Jean and John Comaroff write, "Some of the most profound existential explorations of economy and society, citizenship and social being, humanity and its sensibilities are to be found, these days, in forensic fiction."[84] Through Renko's silence and his decision to value social justice more highly than abstract law enforcement, Cruz Smith exposes the Zone's contradictory social realities where law and order have long ceased to function. In showcasing a precarious (counter)balance between the large-scale corporate and governmental crime of the cover-up of Chernobyl's nuclear disaster and the small-scale, often petty crimes of the community of people who try to survive in the Zone, Cruz Smith's nuclear crime fiction shows how crime inevitably saturates everyday life in the zone and has become "the new normal."[85]

Following Alexievich's sense that her interviews with Chernobyl survivors were recording the future, one may also read Cruz Smith's nuclear crime fiction as an imaginary ethnography of the future. Cruz Smith presents a haunting from the future of a rising interdependence of corrupt, if not criminal, nuclear corporations and their big business, on one hand, and the small, everyday criminality this economy generates in a contaminated nuclear world. Nuclear necropolitics depends on this "tight interweaving of criminality, legality and commerce."[86] Cruz Smith exhibits how, in this necropolitical zone of exclusion, the "interior working of economy and society in the global age of the market"[87] is almost seamlessly taken over by a national and international black market. The latter flourishes both in the streets of Moscow and in illegal international trade that facilitates the sale of radioactively contaminated goods, including household items, fur coats, old cars, and salvaged parts, as well as fruit and vegetables, meat, fish, and milk from Pripyat's vicinity. Corporate and governmental crimes, as well as the petty crimes of illegal settlers in the Zone and their survival on the black market with radioactive goods, become signifiers of a toxic future world in which crime has become the order of the day, the "new normal" in zones of exclusion, exemption, and abandonment.

Cruz Smith thus highlights something that exceeds oral histories and ethnographies that focus exclusively on survivors: the psychic toxicity bred in Chernobyl's orbit has radiated outward and gone global. Global corporate crime and illegal transactions with radioactive materials are entangled with the petty crimes of scavengers and poachers who barely survive in the Zone as peddlers of radioactive food, consumer goods, or salvaged cars. The political economics of expendability, the creation of disposable people, and the death from radioactive poisoning have become systemic, including even murders of protagonists at the top of corporate and financial power. If we read ethnographies and crime fictions of Chernobyl's zone of radioactive contamination as ethnographies of the future, then Cruz Smith's *Wolves Eat Dogs* insists on the fact that, in the precarious balance of a nuclear ecology, virtually everybody becomes a potential victim of the global production of human expandability in toxic sacrifice zones.

Arcady Renko, the "picaresque outlaw cop,"[88] thus reveals both the vulnerability and impotence of the people he investigates and his own vulnerability in a world of necropolitical sovereignty where everyone— rich and poor, cops and criminals, scientists and government officials— has become disposable and where the very radioactive substance that has affected the lives of millions of people can now also be used as an invisible murder weapon. Regarding the use of radioactive poisoning in murders more specifically, Cruz Smith's crime fiction about a Russian millionaire who was involved in the cover-up of the Chernobyl disaster and poisoned with cesium-137 can thus also be read as an allegorical portrayal of a new type of covert and potentially invisible murder that includes extrajudicial assassination with radioactive substances.

Published in 2004, the novel, in a sinister instance of life imitating art, anticipates a real extrajudicial assassination in the spectacular case of the radioactive poisoning of Alexander Litvinenko. Litvinenko was a former officer of the Russian Federal Security Service (FSB) and the Committee for State Security (KGB) and an outspoken critic of Vladimir

Putin, whose rise to power he described as a coup d'état organized by the FSB. After accusing Russian secret services of having arranged the famous Moscow theater hostage crisis and the 1999 Armenian parliament shooting, as well as the assassination of forty-eight-year-old journalist Anna Politkovskaya, Litvinenko had to flee Russia and received political asylum in the United Kingdom, where he was assassinated by radioactive polonium-210 in 2006. Ten years later, in 2016, a U.K. public inquiry found that Andrey Lugovoy and Dmitry Kovtun were responsible for the poisoning, with a strong probability that they were acting under the direction of the FSB with approval by FSB director Nicolai Patrushev and President Putin. The Litvinenko case is so spectacular that Fredrick Forsyth and Andy McNab, well-established writers of detective thrillers, claimed that, if they offered a Litvinenko-style story to a publisher, they would be fighting a losing battle. This is precisely the blurring of the boundaries between fiction and reality that Jean and John Comaroff describe as a feature that defines the global transformation of criminality and the socioeconomic and political order in today's world.

As I mentioned in the introduction, one of the investigators of Alexander Litvinenko's radioactive poisoning was none other than the ex-spy Christopher Steele, who recently leaked the files about the connection between Trump and Putin.[89] *Los Angeles Times* reporter Kurtis Lee identified Steele as the author of the controversial dossier, according to which "Russian officials had gathered compromising information about President-elect Donald Trump that could be used to blackmail him." As a spy for the British intelligence agency MI6, Steele was a Russia specialist and worked, among other things, on the investigation of Litvinenko's murder. Following the publication of his dossier, Steele has reportedly gone into hiding. After telling *NBC News* "he's James Bond," intelligence historian Nigel West made the following statement to the British TV station ITV News: "If it is validated, Chris will be confirmed as one of the great intelligence officers of the decade. If not, I fear the worst."

I mention Litvinenko's case to demonstrate that, to understand the full scope of nuclear politics in light of "the truth about crime," one needs to include these covert operations designed to silence dissent with targeted assassinations by radioactive poisoning. Nuclear scientist Nick Priest called the choice of polonium-210 a "stroke of genius" because this particular radioactive material can be carried in a vial in water through airport screening devices without setting off alarms and is hard to detect when ingested.

Radioactive poisoning marks a qualitative leap in the use of covert assassinations by poison in yet another sense: it can spread to other victims and involve potentially a large number of people. Following the polonium trail in Litvinenko's case, investigators found polonium in all the hotel rooms where the assassins had stayed, in several hotel bars and restaurants, on a fax machine, and on everything Litvinenko had touched during the three days before he was hospitalized. The car that brought him to his home was rendered unusable because of radioactive contamination. His wife tested positive for polonium poisoning, and his family was unable to return to their house for more than half a year. Finally, traces were found in Hamburg, Germany, where one of the assassins stayed on his way to London, as well as in the passenger jets from Moscow to Heathrow used by the killers on different occasions, suggesting that there had been previous failed attempts to poison Litvinenko. A team of scientists concluded that the trail involved hundreds of people and dozens of locations. In addition, British Airways published a list of 221 flights of the contaminated aircraft, involving the potential exposure of thirty-three thousand passengers to dangerous levels of polonium-210. The passengers were advised to contact the U.K. Department of Health for help. These details expose the fact that, in addition to the culture of secrecy, cover-up, and corruption that defines nuclear politics, there is the absolutely lethal invisible danger even of relatively minuscule radioactive substances. They operate as ghostly lively matter, spreading like viruses undetected through material objects and bodies and leaving an invisible deadly trail whose half-life extends over time.

If, in our day and age, politics, life, and, indeed, the politics of life itself sound more like crime fiction than actual detective stories and crime novels do, it is also, as Jean and John Comaroff have shown, because crime is, more than ever, permeated and inspired by fiction. In a political world of alternative facts and fake news, crimes are haunted by a paradox: they are no longer entirely or necessarily confined to a culture of secrecy and cover-up. Often they are, like Poe's purloined letter, hidden in plain sight. Given the excess information about small and large crimes we receive in the daily news, we may no longer be able or willing to see what lies right before our eyes. Facts seem to have lost their force in the age of their technological reproduction as fakes. Moreover, they no longer seem to be enough to move people politically and emotionally. "Why repeat the facts—they cover up our feelings," writes Svetlana Alexievich at the end of *Voices from Chernobyl*.[90] Many of her interviewees decry the criminal cover-up of the disaster and its consequences. To confront the truth about these crimes, Alexievich suggests, we need more than information and the chatter of daily news: we need fiction, oral histories, and ethnographies of the future able to open the heart of crime.

CHERNOBYL'S AFTERMATH

In the aftermath of Chernobyl, Soviet officials did everything possible to silence the knowledge that massive clouds of radiation were pouring over Europe and bound to reach the United States ten days later. The United States, in turn, did nothing to warn the public about negative effects of either Chernobyl or Fukushima. In 2010, the most credible death toll of the Chernobyl disaster, according to Wassermann, was 985,000. The construction of a massive movable sarcophagus that is supposed to cover the continuing release of radiation is yet to be completed. Fires around Chernobyl continue to generate the release of massive quantities of radiation. Fifteen Soviet-era reactors remain operable in a de facto war zone in Ukraine, creating dangerous uncertainties.

In 1986, after the partial collapse of the blasted Chernobyl nuclear reactor, a two-thousand-ton radioactive blob of uranium, concrete, steel, and assorted junk was created that remains there to this day.[91] The sarcophagus is supposed to contain the blob and is expected to last one hundred years, which is a far cry from the one hundred thousand years the Onkalo experts had estimated as the necessary time period to safeguard against a new disaster. According to experts who studied Chernobyl, a nuclear waste dump like Chernobyl Reactor No. 4 must last at least three thousand years. That means the area surrounding Chernobyl will be safe for people to once again inhabit in the year 4986. "Detlef Appel, a geologist who runs PanGeo, a Hamburg, Germany, company that consults on such nuclear storage issues, notes that 3,000 years probably isn't long enough. He suggests that truly safe radioactive waste storage needs to extend a million years into the future. Think back to when man's earliest relative began to walk the Earth."[92]

Cancer remains one of the foremost health problems in Ukraine more than thirty years after the Chernobyl disaster. The number of cancer-caused deaths is disputed but is believed to be in the thousands. So far there is no viable solution for the cleanup. Verbytska, one of the spokespeople for the cleanup, emphasizes that "the mass of uranium debris inside Reactor Number 4 is now a mess that goes beyond human ability to clean up. [. . .] Undoubtedly, the solutions for our Chernobyl problems are very much 'seal it for now.' We will have smart children and smart grandchildren who in 100 years or so will figure out what to do."[93]

Sirota, who was a child in 1986, chose to stay in Pripyat. "Obviously, I'm drawn to Chernobyl," he explains. "It's the source of the greatest sadness of my life, but that's also because it was the source of my greatest joy. I feel that the accident at the plant stole a perfect childhood, a perfect life, from me. I know this isn't rational, but I stay here, hoping that someday I might get it back."[94]

In this context, I should also mention the spectacular side of Chernobyl's aftermath that is widely covered in the news and especially on social media, namely, the fact that wildlife and vegetation are seemingly thriving, mainly due to the lack of human interference. How well they are really doing remains highly controversial among scientists as there is no conclusive study yet about their health and longevity. It also remains an open question whether the mutations in animal and plant species that have been observed in the aftermath of the nuclear disaster are transmitted transgenerationally. Undoubtedly, however, the increase of wildlife in the area has fed the flourishing disaster tourism.

Meanwhile, people are also moving back to the contaminated areas to settle in the formerly abandoned villages.[95] While it was until recently illegal to live inside the exclusion zone, the poorest of the poor are moving back due to a lack of opportunities elsewhere. Some are also political refugees from eastern Ukraine, where an estimated ten thousand people have been killed and about two million displaced. Houses in the exclusion zone are dilapidated, and for some, the only water is from a polluted well and needs to be boiled before use. Residents are keeping livestock and growing food in the contaminated soil. Professor Valery Kashparov, director of the Ukrainian Institute of Agricultural Radiology, reported dangerous levels of cesium-137 in cow's milk. Ingested in large quantities, it can damage human cells and cause thyroid cancer. One of the residents says, "Radiation may kill us slowly, but it doesn't shoot or bomb us. It's better to live with radiation than with war."[96]

FUKUSHIMA'S DEATHWORLDS

In *Strong in the Rain,* their commemorative book about Fukushima, Lucy Birmingham and David McNeill reflect on the persistence of transgenerational trauma. "How do people with millennia of horrific collective memories manage to repress them and get on with life? One answer is that they don't—at least not completely."[97] This is a reflection on the *longue durée* of nuclear trauma. The following are glimpses of the here and now. "We're isolated. The government does not tell us anything. They're leaving us to die."[98] These are the desperate words of Katsunobu Sakurai, mayor of Minamisoma, a coastal city located in the Fukushima prefecture fifteen miles south of the Fukushima Daiichi nuclear power plant. He made this statement in an interview with BBC during the first week of the nuclear crisis at the Fukushima Daiichi plant. The citizens of Minamisoma were left in the dark for twenty-two days with no word from the responsible Tokyo Electric Power Company (TEPCO). Finally, in his desperation, Sakurai made an eleven-minute video with English subtitles that was uploaded to YouTube. After the video's release, Minamisoma became overnight one of the most sought-after disaster sites in the world. The global interest in the stories of people who stayed at Minamisoma after the mandatory evacuation of seventy thousand to eighty thousand people was also fueled by the memory of the Chernobyl nuclear disaster a quarter of a century earlier.

The parallels between Chernobyl and Fukushima were astounding, ranging from the ghostly sites of nuclear towns and villages with deserted homes, stray pets, helpless nuclear workers, and people who stayed because they had nowhere to go to the criminal official cover-up of the extent of the disaster that cost the lives of thousands of people. A freelance journalist who went to the zone of exclusion near the disaster site with his own camera and dosimeters complained about the official news coverage: "All they did was quote experts, TEPCO and others from the 'nuclear village.' So that meant that everything they showed was wrong."[99]

Fearing panic, the Nuclear and Industrial Safety Agency withheld data from the public that showed the direction of the radioactive plume heading toward the town of Namie twenty-five miles northwest of the Fukushima Daiichi power plant. At the same time, they released it to the U.S. military stationed in Japan. The mayor of Namie called the withholding of the data "akin to murder."[100] We know the rest of the story. People remembered stories about the end of World War II, the firebombing of Tokyo by U.S. bomber planes that incinerated one hundred thousand people, left the city in ruins, and created five million war refugees. Rumors spread that the rain was contaminated with radioactive toxins, and people referred to the "black rain" of Hiroshima.[101]

Behind the scenes, officials tried desperately to prevent the worst case scenario, namely, a complete meltdown of the power plant, whose fallout would affect more than thirty-five million people. They even feared and discussed what Yukio Edano, the government's top spokesman, later called a "demonic chain reaction," meaning that Fukushima Daiichi could trigger meltdowns elsewhere. On March 15, Prime Minister Naoto Kan received the news that TEPCO officials and seven hundred workers were preparing to abandon the plant. In this case, six reactors and seven nuclear fuel pools would be left to spiral out of control, and most likely the nearby Daini plant would have to be abandoned too. "The most apocalyptic scenario suddenly looked very real. A serious radioactive fire could send cesium and other toxins to greater Tokyo, forcing the evacuation of 35 million people."[102] Chairman Katsumata alerted the company's top executives to the fact that abandoning the plant would create a disaster three to four times worse than Chernobyl. He requested the officials to stay in a *kamikaze*-like mission.

Finally, the workers were able to prevent the worst case scenario by a hair. Workers managed to get water into the reactors and clean up the debris. In April, the Japanese government officially raised the Fukushima crisis to an International Nuclear and Radiation Event (INES) scale level 7—the same as the Chernobyl disaster. Fallout from the Fukushima Daiichi plant contaminated the city of Minamisoma and required the evacuation of its citizens. A year later, one-third of the population—twenty-seven thousand residents—remained scattered across Japan, Europe, and the United States, unable to return to their homes. Dosimeters outside hospitals and schools kept "showing airborne radiation in blinking red figures."[103]

In the wake of the Fukushima nuclear disaster, Prime Minister Kan turned against nuclear power. As a reason, he stated the cumulative experience of dealing with Fukushima and prospective nations pursuing plans to double the world's nuclear reactors within two decades. It took but a few months before the nuclear industry, with the help of hostile conservative media, hounded him out of office, accusing him of mishandling the crisis. This was the onset of a pervasive discrimination against antinuclear citizens and activists. Mothers against nuclear power, who tried to prevent schools from handing out to the children milk from the vicinity of the Fukushima disaster site, were ostracized and accused of being unpatriotic.

Meanwhile, "many observers have begun referring to another generation of Fukushima *hibakusha*, who must also endure a lifetime of worry, state support or the lack thereof, and even discrimination."[104] The impact of the disaster was "replicated along the northeast coast, where 19,000 people are dead or missing. The deluge left behind gaping landscapes reminiscent of the atomic aftermath in Hiroshima and Nagasaki."[105]

Buddhist writer and social activist Kenji Miyazawa (1896–1933)—whose signature poem "Strong in the Rain" inspired the book on the Fukushima nuclear disaster with the same title by Birmingham and McNeill—believed that the Japanese would "die in spirit" if they did not learn to coexist with nature. Miyazawa died in 1933 and never knew of the nuclear attacks on Hiroshima and Nagasaki and the nuclear disaster at Fukushima Daiichi. Yet, his words are truer than ever, not only in Japan but also everywhere in today's world, whose very survival is threatened by nuclear necropolitics and climate change. Unless humans resist this global work of death, they will die in spirit long before planetary life will die. They will die in spirit if they do not face the possible worst case scenario: human-induced planetary annihilation with no one left to witness the traces of the human species with its amazing achievements, destroyed by nuclear madness and its spectacular and slow violence.

The major reason for the Fukushima Daiichi nuclear disaster was that the plant was built on a fault line, despite warnings about the dangers of putting reactors in a tsunami zone. Experts were dismissed as alarmists. To this day, the whereabouts of the melted cores remain unknown. The four reactors that blew up at Fukushima were from General Electric. The reactors exploded despite fifty years of assurances that American reactors could not explode. Thirty times more cesium-137 was released at Fukushima than during the bombing of Hiroshima. "Some 300 tons of radioactive water continues to pour into the Pacific Ocean from Fukushima every day. Thousands of highly radioactive spent fuel rods remain scattered around the Fukushima site; thousands are also still suspended in damaged spent fuel pools 100 feet in the air atop weakened buildings above shattered, melted reactors."[106]

Fukushima is still owned by TEPCO, which manages the cleanup for profit with "a labor force thoroughly infiltrated by organized crime."[107]

In early 2017, the headlines of newspapers around the world reported the dying of Fukushima robots from radioactivity and the need to replace them with humans, that is, with so-called bio-robots. This sounds like a dark replay of the scene of dying robots and their replacement by humans who sacrificed themselves as bio-robots in the aftermath of the Chernobyl disaster. In response to the crisis at Fukushima, Alexander Kluge, German filmmaker and author of *Der Sarkophag* (The sarcophagus), said in an interview with *Welt Online*[108] that the handling of radioactive materials with a half-life of three hundred thousand years by far exceeds the capacity of communities and governments. Under these conditions, the atom turns into an enemy. Addressing the dangerous appeal of radioactive power, he warns against the initial nuclear euphoria that emerged from its mobilization of all sensory organs. The sheer scale of the nuclear and its effects, which have been described in terms of the "nuclear sublime," have led people to override the knowledge of its dangers. The complexity of such denial led Kluge to conclude that events like the lingering nuclear crisis in Fukushima open up an "entrance to the tunnel for the study of all questions that move us"[109] as human beings. Kluge concludes, however, that this does not mean that we are already able to manage nuclear power. And, he adds, as long as we are not able to manage it, we should suspend its use.

THE YEAR 2017: THE RUINOUS LIFE OF NUCLEAR REACTORS IN THE UNITED STATES—HANFORD, THREE MILE ISLAND, DIABLO CANYON, SAN ONOFRE

In the meantime, the slow violence of relatively "small" nuclear threats that develop over long stretches of time continues. On May 10, 2017, the *Los Angeles Times* reported an accident at the Hanford nuclear reactor site in Washington State. A tunnel containing radioactive materials caved in after a twenty-by-twenty-foot section of soil collapsed over the tunnel. Established in 1943, the so-called Hanford Nuclear Reservation was part of the Manhattan Project and contained the world's first full-scale plutonium production reactor. The plutonium manufactured at the Hanford site was used for the first nuclear bomb tested at the Trinity Test Site as well as for Fat Man, the bomb detonated over Nagasaki. During the Cold War, it produced plutonium for more than sixty thousand nuclear weapons under conditions of grossly inadequate safety and waste disposal procedures. As a result, significant amounts of radioactive toxins have been released into the air and the Columbia River. After the Cold War, the plant was decommissioned, but fifty-three million gallons of highly radioactive nuclear waste remain in storage tanks, and twenty-five million cubic feet of solid radioactive waste remain buried underground. While already contaminating the ground water, hundreds of billions of gallons of liquid waste was poured or buried in the ground. All twelve double-shelled tanks have been discovered with serious flaws, leaking radioactive waste into the ground and water. Hanford, which also hosts a commercial nuclear power plant, is the most contaminated nuclear waste site in the United States. So far, no solution for the cleanup and storage of its immense amount of nuclear waste has been found. Together with Oak Ridge and Los Alamos, it was in 2015 designated to become part of the Manhattan Project National Historical Park.

During the recent accident, no radioactivity was reported as released into the air, but more than forty-seven hundred workers were ordered to take shelter, some were evacuated, and federal officials instituted a five-mile no-fly zone around the site. Nationwide, aging facilities pose a continued and escalating risk. "The longer you wait to deal with this problem, the more dangerous it becomes,"[110] said Robert Alvarez, a former policy advisor at the U.S. Department of Energy. And Frank Wolak, head of Stanford University's Program on Energy and Sustainable Development, insists that the nationwide part of the risk comes from having to maintain and safeguard so many sites with different types of nuclear waste: "You're asking for trouble with the fact that you've got it spread all over the country. [. . .] The right answer is to consolidate the stuff that is highly contaminated and apply the best technology to it."[111]

Almost four decades ago, in 1979, the nuclear accident at Three Mile Island sent warnings about the dangers of nuclear energy across the globe. The official response followed the familiar pattern of pervasive deceit and denial. As Harvey Wasserman, coauthor of *Killing Our Own: The Disaster of America's Experience with Atomic Radiation*,[112] reports, the lies that were spread in the wake of the Three Mile Island disaster have been repeated at Chernobyl, Fukushima, and Diablo Canyon in the United States.[113] Wasserman lists some of the major legacies of denial about nuclear power's destructive effects, claiming that we are seeing mainly the tip of the iceberg. Among them are, most prominently, the systematic denial of the harmful effects of disastrous amounts of radioactive materials released by the Three Mile Island accident into the atmosphere, of mass mutations and death among animals in the vicinity of the plant, of major outbreaks of cancer in the downwind areas of the plant, of children born with Down syndrome and other mutations, and of adults dying from the effects of radiation. (The industry paid at least $15 million in out-of-court settlements on condition the victims did not speak about it in public.)

The Diablo Canyon reactors in California were, like Fukushima and, for that matter, San Onofre, built in a tsunami zone surrounded by earthquake faults. Diablo owner Pacific Gas and Electric has violated regulatory requirements and colluded illegally with the Nuclear Regulatory Commission and the California Public Utilities Commission. Violating state and federal water regulations, Diablo Canyon's cooling system is "dumping huge quantities of hot, radioactive liquid into the Pacific, killing billions of marine creatures while unbalancing the ocean ecology and contributing to climate chaos."[114] Diablo Canyon and the other old nuclear reactors in the United States cannot compete in the electricity markets with renewable energy sources and can only continue to exist with massive public subsidies. Astronomically prohibitive costs of maintaining nuclear power plants and storing nuclear waste are the rule. They have led several U.S. plants to the brink of bankruptcy. In March 2017, Westinghouse Electric Company filed for bankruptcy, a move that puts the completion of two nuclear power plants in the Southeast, if not the "nuclear renaissance" heralded by nuclear energy corporations, in jeopardy.[115] Could it be that for once, the economy is aligned with the protection of the planetary ecology against nuclear madness?

Meanwhile, close to my current home in Orange County, California, Southern California Edison (SCE), major owner of the San Onofre nuclear power plant, struggles with the vexed problem of storing its nuclear waste. "Perhaps no plant in the country spotlights the waste issue more than the San Onofre Nuclear Generating Station. Even though the San Onofre Plant has not produced any electricity and is in the process of getting decommissioned, some 3.6 million pounds of spent nuclear fuel sit on the beach, within 50 miles of 8.4 million people,"[116] wrote journalist Rob Nikolewski in the *Los Angeles Times* on April 17, 2017. To avoid a spectacular court hearing, SCE agreed to begin negotiations to relocate the tons of nuclear waste. There is so far no solution about where to store it. Possible locations include a permanent long-planned national

FIGURE 14. Anne Lund, *Nuclear Power? No Thanks*, 1975. Copyright OOA Fonden. http://smilingsun.org/.

repository, the so-called Yucca Mountain project in Nevada. However, this repository faces strong opposition by Nevada residents and needs yet to be approved by the federal government. Nevada, a state that doesn't have a single nuclear power plant, is opposed to accepting the waste at a site only one hundred miles from Las Vegas and vulnerable to earthquakes. The dilemma is not unlike the one faced by the group of interdisciplinary scientists and experts responsible for exploring the Onkalo nuclear waste deposit in Finland described in Michael Madsen's *Into Eternity*. They were charged with figuring out how to secure the site for one hundred thousand years.[117] In San Onofre, federal regulators had certified the storage devices SCE was planning to use for twenty years. Who can guarantee that the storage at Yucca Mountain—or anywhere else—would be safe for one hundred thousand years?

HIROSHIMA'S GHOSTLY SHADOWS

A few years ago, my son Leon and his girlfriend Lucia gave me a pendant for Christmas with a beautiful four-hundred-million-year-old Moroccan fossilized orthoceras. As this little creature began to speak to me across the distance of hundreds of millions of years, I formed a curious attachment to it. Once I misplaced it and grieved as if I had lost a living creature I felt close to. Some would call this fossil "vibrant matter," and I agree about the vibrancy, as long as we recognize that it is not innate to the orthoceras, not part of its ontology, but emerges from a complex transference between humans and objects, that is, from the ways we as human beings relate to the world. I am also aware that the object of my attachment is not the nautiloid cephalopod it was when it lived in the Sahara Desert in Morocco during the lower Ordovician to Triassic ages, at the time the Sahara was still an ocean. My little orthoceras, in other words, is not the creature it was when it became stone and left its permanent imprint, its trace and testimony to its extinct existence, for hundreds of millions of years to come.

The orthoceras intrigues me because it seems to hold not only the secret of life and death but also the secret of extinction and its remainder, its persistent trace. It invites me to "imagine extinction,"[1] even to grieve for the beauty of life that once was. Engraved in stone, its elegant shape remains intact. Rather than the relative immediacy of an encounter with a living being of a different species, the orthoceras offers an encounter with the remainder of an extinction that happened millions and millions of years ago. The vibrant fossil thus seems like a portrait designed by nature in the process of recording its own history. I like to think of it as an ancient precursor of the photograph. And, like the photograph, it speaks of life and death, facilitating a paradoxical witnessing of impermanence through a permanent trace. It exhibits the permanence of a stone that contains the cumulative recordings of the ages in their wear and tear, their catastrophes and extinctions.

I imagine that the orthoceras's mesmerizing attraction lies in its ability to present an image of survival that seems to speak to us from across the ages. While it does not let us witness the survival of life, the sheer scale of time memorialized in this fossilized rock is testimony to the survival of a trace of former life that helps us imagine a creature and its extinction. The trace speaks of a history of the earth that survives as fossil, reminding us that whatever happened to the earth, no matter how long ago, is still with us in some form and leaves its imprint on the present.

> The words are spoken
> of those who survived for a while.
> living shadowgraphs, eyes fixed forever
> on witnessed horror
> —Denise Levertov, "Gathered at the River"

THE ATOMIC TRACE

Strangely enough, for me the orthoceras bears a certain kinship with the ghostly imprints of a human body left after the nuclear attack on the stone steps leading to the Sumitomo Bank in Hiroshima. These "shadowgraphs" are the enduring remainders of a human incinerated on the stone steps by the flash of atomic heat rays of temperatures well over one thousand and possibly two thousand degrees centigrade.

The image of this ghostly human shadow left by thermal rays on stone has haunted me ever since I first saw it in high school. It was the images of *Night and Fog,* Alain Resnais's documentary about the concentration camps, and this shadow image of an incinerated human that embodied for me the twin horrors of World War II: the camps and the bomb. As the continuing history of its reception in the cultural imaginary demonstrates, the Hiroshima shadow image is haunting in its very iconic value. It is haunting because this trace of a human incinerated and burned into stone turns viewers into witnesses of a trauma that extends from the past into the distant future. "Burning, another world enters through the shadows of bodies flashed on walls,"[2] writes Linda Hogan. Evoked by the past trauma of an individual life that was annihilated by the first atomic bomb, this "other world" mobilizes the knowledge of a possible future annihilation, a world of "bodies flashed on walls" that heralds extinction of life. The latter causes a permanent trauma, that is, a hitherto unknown anticipatory haunting from the future.

We cannot resist imagining this man's life as it was snatched away from him in a second, consumed by a murderous nuclear force whose

FIGURE 15. Shadowgraph left on the stone steps leading to the Sumitomo Bank: an enduring remainder of a human incinerated on the steps by the flash of atomic heat rays after the nuclear attack on Hiroshima during World War II. Universal History Archive/Getty Images.

radiation left nothing but his shadow image, a stain on the stair, an icon of atomic death. And yet, as Stephanie Strickland's powerful poetic image reminds us, the stain erases the individual human in the very moment that monumentalizes his trace as "a grey stain fused in concrete, a shadow cast on three steps in Hiroshima":

> [. . .] Not a man
> Not a woman. An effigy: human
> by deduction,
> like a cloak.[3]

Perhaps it is the very erasure of the human, its presence by mere deduction, that turns this shadow image into a prime icon of Hiroshima, an empty graph on which viewers project the affects that fuel their nuclear imaginary. Yet Strickland's poem also likens the shadowgraph to an effigy, that is, a model of a particular person originally designed to be damaged or destroyed in protest or expression of anger. The image of the effigy thus invokes both a haunting from the past nuclear attack on Hiroshima as an act of retaliation and a haunting from the future of an all-out nuclear annihilation that leaves nothing behind but a shadow world of incinerated humans, reminiscent of the one evoked in Toge Sankichi's ghostly image:

> Burned onto the step, cracked and watery red,
> the mark of the blood that flowed as intestines melted to mush:
> a shadow.[4]

Decades after I first saw the Hiroshima shadowgraph, I was reminded again of its power when I read Arundhati Roy's *War Talk*, her manifesto against nuclear madness and global wars. Composed of a sequence of speeches, this short book has itself a haunting force. Roy describes how, during the nuclear standoff between India and Pakistan, the Hiroshima shadow image comes back to her:

> My friends and I discuss *Prophesy*, the documentary about the bombing of Hiroshima and Nagasaki. The fireball. The dead bodies choking the river. The living stripped of skin and hair. The singed, bald children, still alive, their clothes burned into their bodies. The thick, black, toxic water. The scorched, burning air. The cancers, implanted genetically, a malignant letter to the unborn. We remember especially the man who just melted into the steps of a building. We imagine ourselves like that. As stains on staircases. I imagine future generations of hushed schoolchildren pointing at my stain. [. . .] That was a writer. Not she or he. *That*.[5]

In her personalization of the shadow's haunting from the future, Roy imagines her own annihilation, including the way future generations will see her as a depersonalized trace, a stain on the staircase. This powerful projection invites readers to acknowledge that one day they might disappear like this, their traces left as stains on a stone.

The Hiroshima trace, however, does not have the sturdy permanence of fossils. Unlike the orthoceras, the imprint of this human victim of the first nuclear bomb is vulnerable to the wear and tear of time. Ten years after the bombing, it began to erode and had to be moved to the Hiroshima Peace Memorial Museum. Yet, like the fossilized orthoceras, this Hiroshima shadow image invites us to imagine extinction, albeit of a different kind, one induced by humans with a weapon that has the power to extinguish planetary life. The shadow image thus embodies a haunting from the anticipated future of our own species' suicide. Will the last remaining humans, animals, and plants on earth be incinerated in an all-out nuclear war, leaving nothing behind but their shadows engraved on stone? The image thus serves as a memento mori of an entirely new kind, not one that recalls mortality and the impermanence of life but one that memorializes the work of death and annihilation humans have created. Anticipating our own extinction as a species, it mirrors our necropower—suicidal, driven by an embrace of death over life.

This haunting fantasy, not to say phantasm, of shadow images left by the last living beings on the stones and ruins of a dead planet reaches beyond Derrida's fantasy of a remainderless destruction of the human archive in an all-out nuclear war. Together with boulders that have been on the earth for millions of years, the stones and ruins of our civilization might retain a nuclear shadow archive of our lives, albeit without anyone left to witness. Will we be literally buried in an archive, the shadows of our bodies inscribed on stone tablets like the original Ten Commandments? Will we be entirely and forever forgotten, or will an alien civilization arrive on earth in time before the erosion of stone has erased our shadows? Will they read our remaining traces like hieroglyphs of an alien language? And is this apocalyptic vision the only consoling fantasy once we imagine planetary extinction in a nuclear war?

Shadows have not been given ontological status in Western metaphysics, Alfonso Lingis asserts: "We do not have concepts for all their motley forms; they are not a text. They exist in the free spaces of the world of weighty things. [. . .] They are glories and menaces that emanate of things."[6] Burned into stone, the menacing shadows of irradiated humans, however, also become archival. Remainders of catastrophic light or, as Lippit calls it, atomic light, these images merge the weightlessness of shadows with the weight of stone. The strong worldwide reactions to these images are testimony to a transference in which the depicted shadow humans assume the quality of dream images. They recall the two competing forces toward differentiation and dedifferentiation at work in dreams and artistic compositions. In *Atomic Light*,

Lippit describes them as follows: "one brings the image closer, by pushing deeper and further into the body, toward greater clarity, figuration, and materiality; the other follows the same route toward dissolution, disappearance, and formlessness."[7] While the movement toward bringing the image closer marks the transference of viewers who know the story of its formation by atomic rays, the route toward dissolution, disappearance, and formlessness is marked by the gradual effacement of the remaining bodily trace over time. Paradoxically, the human "buried in this archive" comes alive, returning to viewers as living dead, a radioactive ghost.

Exhibiting the bodily trace of a human killed by the heat and light of an exploding nuclear weapon, the shadow figure on the steps in Hiroshima, and now in the Hiroshima Historical Peace Museum, constitutes a material archive of destruction. Formed by a force that preserves a visible trace of the bomb's annihilating flash, what remains is a spectral shadow archive of atomic writing. It is this implicit allusion to a "phantom world of total destruction"[8] that has generated the image's intense transference. According to Lippit, this destruction violated the very boundaries that marked the place of humans in the world:

> The atomic radiation that ended the war in Japan unleashed an excess visuality that threatened the material and conceptual dimensions of human interiority and exteriority. It assailed the bodies it touched, seared and penetrated them, annihilating the limits that established human existence in the world. The destruction of Hiroshima and Nagasaki in 1945 exposed the fragility of the human surface, the capacity of catastrophic light and lethal radiation to penetrate the human figure at its limit.[9]

The first use of the atomic bomb inaugurates, as Lippit argues, the age of "invisible warfare," that is, a warfare that extends beyond immediate damage into the distant future. The waves of invisible radiation that had infiltrated the survivors' bodies continue the warfare indefinitely and out of sight, so to speak. Beyond its immediate annihilating destruction, the atomic work of death continues to operate as a form of slow violence inside the bodies of victims, thus extending into the aftermath of the official end of the war. While many of the victims suffer and die from radiation sickness, and later from cancers, this invisible warfare also operates transgenerationally, potentially inflicting genetic damage on subsequent generations of children of victims and their children.

While previous wars had left a psychic transgenerational legacy of war trauma, this invisible warfare is the first that leaves a transgenerational physical legacy of genetic damage.

Paradoxically, this warfare's invisibility goes hand in hand with what Lippit calls the "excess visibility" generated by "catastrophic light." The witnesses of the first atomic explosion at the Trinity Test Site suddenly saw their bones shining through their bodies, just as the young women who later painted the dials of watches with radium saw their bodies glow in the dark. This excess visibility that opened the interior of bodies to sight or made them glow in the dark, however, came at the high cost of posing a potentially lethal threat to these very hypervisible bodies. Paradoxically, the lethal substance itself is invisible. A highly dangerous invisible substance thus produces a "destructive visuality, a visibility born from annihilation."[10] This is the threatening paradox of atomic light: it creates excess visibility at the same time as it operates as "violent invisibility."[11] This is also the ghostly play of radiant light and dark shadows that Michael Light's photos capture so perfectly. It is as if these images themselves affect their viewers like spectral hauntings from both past and future. While they capture the past of a nuclear explosion, they also cast a shadow forward toward a threating future annihilation.

Before the end of World War II and the atomic destruction of Hiroshima and Nagasaki, Adorno and Horkheimer warned, "The fully enlightened earth radiates disaster triumphant."[12] Inevitably, this radically destructive and annihilating visuality also transforms the visual regime of representation. Abstract painter Willem de Kooning, Lippit reminds us, reads this transformation with unabashed messianic enthusiasm: "Today, some people think that the light of the atom bomb will change the concept of painting once and for all. The eyes that actually saw the light melted out of sheer ecstasy. For one instant, everybody was the same color. It made angels out of everybody."[13]

Lippit argues that de Kooning's vision of "redemptive ecstasy" pertains to the "sadistic metaphysics" inherent in a "sacrificial logic."[14] This reading aptly captures the core of a logic that drives nuclear necropolitics more generally, beginning with the establishment during the Manhattan Project of so-called sacrifice zones[15] in the American Southwest. Similarly, what Lippit identifies as the redemptive ecstasy of a sadistic metaphysics had already been inaugurated by the scientists who worked on the Manhattan Project as they fell back on messianic

FIGURE 16. Michael Light, *025 DIABLO,* in *100 Suns,* 2003. Photograph courtesy of Michael Light.

discourses to translate their awe as witnesses of the first atomic bomb's explosion at the Trinity Test Site.

It was during the Manhattan Project that the powerful, and I would argue, masculinist and phallic notion of "the nuclear sublime"[16] was born, and it continues to hold sway over those who embrace the shock and awe of nuclear weapons today. J. Robert Oppenheimer's famous recitation, after witnessing the first atomic blast, of a Vishnu quote from the Bhagavad Gita best captures this spirit of the nuclear sublime: "If the radiance of a thousand suns were to burst at once into the sky that would be like the splendor of the mighty one. [. . .] Now I am become Death, the Destroyer of Worlds." Oppenheimer then added his proclamation: "We knew the world would not be the same." And indeed, it never was.

Generated by the violence of splitting the atom, the "radiance of a thousand suns" functions as an icon that further illustrates the relationship of nuclear warfare and light. Paul Virilio describes its effect as the inauguration of the age of "light-weapons": "the bombs dropped on Hiroshima and Nagasaki were *light-weapons* that prefigured the enhanced-radiation neutron bomb, the direct-beam laser weapons, and the charged-particle guns."[17] Virilio then traces the imprints left by atomic rays on walls and human bodies:

> The first bomb [. . .] produced a nuclear flash which lasted one fifteenth-millionth of a second, and whose brightness penetrated every building down to the cellars. It left its imprints on stone walls, changing their apparent color through the fusion of certain minerals. [. . .] The same was the case with clothing and bodies, where kimono patterns were tattooed on the victims' flesh.[18]

It took Hiroshima and Nagasaki to expose the destructive effects of invisible radiation and generate a first wave of public awareness. Expanding on Virilio, Lippit describes these effects in their resemblance to photographic negatives:

> Nothing remains, except the radiation. At Hiroshima and Nagasaki, two views of invisibility—absolute visibility and total transparency—unfolded under the brilliant force of the atomic blasts. Instantly penetrated by the massive force of radiation, the *hibakusha* were seared into the environment with the photographic certainty of having been there. In the aftermath of the bombings, the remaining bodies absorbed and *were absorbed by* the invisible radiation. These bodies vanished slowly until there was nothing left but their negatives.[19]

This vanishing of bodies into their lonely inscriptions on walls creates an archive of nuclear destruction that becomes emblematic of a possible future to come, a future when the living species on this planet might have ceased to exist, leaving nothing but their traces on walls and other solid objects. If this archive is material rather than remainderless, as Derrida imagined it to be, it has nonetheless become obsolete because there is no one left to see or read, an archive whose posthumous existence we can only envision in an imaginary mode. While the Hiroshima shadow figure offers us concrete material evidence, exemplary of the only traces that may remain after an all-out nuclear war, we need fiction or poetry to tell a fuller story of this haunting from a future that outlives us.

NUCLEAR SURREALISM: SCALE AND THE BOUNDARIES OF IMAGINATION

Five years after Hiroshima, Ray Bradbury published his short story "August 2016: There Will Come Soft Rains." Set in the aftermath of nuclear war, it is a story without humans. All that remains is a house that stands alone in a city of rubble and ashes, enveloped in radioactive glow. On the black west face of the house, there is another shadow archive of destruction:

> The silhouette in paint, of a man mowing a lawn. Here, as in a photograph, a woman bent to pick flowers. Still farther over, their images burned on wood in one titanic instant, a small boy, hands flung into the air; higher up, the image of a thrown ball, and opposite of him a girl, hands raised to catch a ball which never came down.[20]

A "still life" of total annihilation, the scene depicts a world in which time is frozen into an image of life halted in a flash, its only witness the imaginary narrator who must have come upon this archive of destruction from elsewhere, because otherwise she would not have lived to see. Is she a returnee, a stranger, an alien? Reminiscent of the scenes of everyday life in Roman civilization left in the excavated city of Pompeii after its destruction by the devastating volcanic eruption of Vesuvius in the year A.D. 79, Bradbury's scene depicts life in permanent standstill. Like the orthoceras, the citizens of Pompeii had become fossilized, so to speak, by volcanic lava, solidified by the extreme heat into hard stone. Yet, while the bodies of the orthoceras and the citizens of Pompeii become spectral sculptures—remaining intact in density, form, and shape and retaining clarity, figuration, and materiality—the "still lifes" of the victims of nuclear destruction become two-dimensional, photographic, spectral images.

We need to be mindful, however, about the ambiguity inherent in these spectral remainders of life. While we may read them as testimonies of death and destruction, they also bear witness to the tenacity of life and its traces in fossils or imprints in stone. These remainders or traces thus evoke a paradoxical coincidence of impermanence and persistence, precariousness and tenacity. In *After Finitude*, Quentin Meillassoux develops a concept of ancestrality or the arche-fossil, that is, of the manifestation of the world anterior to any human form. According to Meillassoux, the problem of the arche-fossil "concerns every discourse whose meaning includes a *temporal discrepancy* between thinking and being—thus, not only statements about events occurring prior to the emergence of humans but also statements about possible events that are *ulterior* to the extinction of the human species."[21] Meillassoux, in other words, raises the question of how we can think and speak about times beyond the life-span of the human species.

While this "*before* and *after* the human" is accessible to scientific speculation, it transcends the boundaries of human experience and imagination. Since this problem of temporality and scale imposes itself on any form of imagining extinction, we may say that it is constitutive of the nuclear age. The threat of nuclear extinction, however, pushes the arche-fossil's challenge to human imagination beyond the "mathematicization of nature" on which Meillassoux focuses. If one wishes to grasp the philosophical and ethical implications of thinking pre- and posthuman temporalities, the challenge of ancestrality or the arche-fossil cannot be reduced to a scientific problem. Imagining ancestrality, I argue, needs to include the politics of emotion and affect and the necessary rearrangement of desire required to expand imagination beyond the "terrestrial-relation-to-the-world."[22]

Thinking along the trajectory of the arche-fossil also bears upon the question of the archive and its quasi-symbiotic relationship to witnessing. Meillassoux addresses the "sense of desolation and abandonment which modern science instills in humanity's conception of itself and of the cosmos," a desolation tied to the knowledge of "thought's contingency for the world [. . .] a world that is essentially unaffected by whether or not anyone thinks it."[23] In "The Climate of History," Dipesh Chakrabarty revisits the traditional separation of human from natural history. The question of the "existence" of rocks, for example, has generated categorical confusion because of a long philosophical tradition according to which existence is a human concept. So while rocks are undoubtedly material things in the world regardless of whether humans think them or not, they do not exist for humans in any meaningful sense.[24] This separation of humans from natural history—which is arguably an overly narrow Western division and legacy that ignores even the history of alchemy—generates the sense of a divided world in which humans belong to a different order than the natural world. This division spawns both a crisis of meaning and a crisis of belonging.

In the past decades, especially with the debates about climate change and the Anthropocene, the separation of human and natural history has been profoundly challenged. Humans are no longer seen merely as biological agents but as geological agents who radically interfere with the course of natural history. This entanglement, however, is not experienced as a blissful one. Humans are for the first time in history forced to recognize themselves as agents of radical extinction, potentially perhaps of all planetary life, a recognition that weighs heavily and tinges the belonging to the natural world with a deep sense of guilt.

For Meillassoux, the challenge of ancestrality also generates a crisis in belonging. While humans may know that they belong to the infinity of the cosmological order, their belonging is not meaningful in any metaphysical sense. On the contrary, it is suddenly seen as utterly contingent. The world does not *care* about the human species or human thought, hence the sense of desolation and abandonment. Meillassoux, however, does not ask why and how do we as humans care about our belonging, and why do we feel a responsibility when human-induced forces propel extinction? This question, I think, needs to be at the center of theorizing the human species and its political responsibility today.

Significantly, Meillassoux links both science's insistence on thought's contingency and the human sense of desolation and abandonment to the nuclear:

> Science's dia-chronic statements assume that the 'question of the witness' has become irrelevant to knowledge of the event. In other words, the decay of the radioactive material, or the nature of the stellar emission, are described in such a way that they must be assumed to be adequate to what we manage to think about them, while the question as to whether or not they were witnessed becomes irrelevant to the adequacy of this description. Or again: both this decay and this emission are conceived in such a way that they would have been identical to what we think about them even if human thought had never existed to think them.[25]

Again, Meillassoux does not address the one distinct fact that considerably enhances the sense of desolation and abandonment generated by the nuclear threat of extinction, namely, the knowledge that this threat, like other current forms of environmental destruction, is generated by humans. While it is true that radioactivity is part of stellar and solar emission, without human thought and its generation of the sciences that invented the technologies for nuclear destruction, radioactive contamination would not reach the dangerous proportions that pose the threat of extinction today. The impact of radioactive material and the monumental time-span of its decay would, in other words, not reach a level that forces humans to imagine a human-induced extinction of planetary life.

It is this very knowledge that magnifies the sense of desolation and abandonment with a sense of (conscious or unconscious) guilt. The latter also bears upon the question of the witness Meillassoux raises. While it is true that the concrete events of a nuclear destruction of planetary life would be unaffected by the lack of a (remaining) witness, the disappearance of the last human witness itself would be a human-induced event. This knowledge inevitably tinges the sense of desolation and abandonment with a sense of mortifying guilt. It is this anticipation of a human-induced extinction that generates a haunting from the future of an archive without witness. And it is this very haunting that pushes the human imagination beyond the boundaries of what Meillassoux calls the "terrestrial-relation-to-the-world." I would further argue that this is also one of the reasons why the Anthropocene has emerged with such force in current theoretical debates. Posing the question of the archive henceforth poses the scalar challenge of thinking the arche-fossil and the anticipated traces of the posthuman. Under these conditions, desolation, abandonment, guilt, and a crushing responsibility define the human condition in the age of nuclear necropolitics. Perhaps this is why human imagination has become so enmeshed, if not obsessed, with a new kind of archive fever in which visions of an archive without a witness have assumed iconic, if not allegorical, value. And it is these archives without a witness that generate the sense of catastrophic abandonment both Meillassoux and, long before him, Ray Bradbury invoked:

Not one would mind, neither bird nor tree,
If mankind perished utterly;

And Spring herself, when she woke at dawn
Would scarcely know that we were gone.[26]

Finally, Jorge Luis Borges's "Library of Babel," too, presents a paradigmatic example of a ghost archive in a world without humans: "I suspect that the human species—the unique species—is about to be extinguished, but the Library will endure: illuminated, solitary, infinite, perfectly motionless [. . .] useless, incorruptible, secret."[27] These spectral shadow archives, we might say, will forever seal the culture of secrecy and deception at the heart of nuclear necropolitics—solitary, motionless, useless, incorruptible, and secret—into eternity. Imagining human extinction through the lens of its remaining archive of books confronts us with an image of the remainder of accumulated thought without a witness.

We can, however, also imagine possible nonhuman witnesses after the extinction of the human species. How would they encounter the remainders of our lives and cultures, our objects and artifacts, our buildings and burial sites, our bones and teeth? This is the question posed by the work of Argentinian artist Adrián Villar Rojas. In "Today We Reboot the Planet," he places his viewers in the position of an alien observing the remainders of the human world long after its demise. Like Borges in *The Aleph*, Villar Rojas envisions a holonomic space that contains everything that has ever existed or even been imagined. It is a space suggestive of a scale beyond human time, of deep history and a geological time that includes prehistoric millennia as well as future ones that emerge beyond the lifetime of the human species on earth. Allegorically depicting the entirety of human worlds in fossilized ancient ruins or fragile clay replicas of humans and their object world, Villar Rojas challenges his viewers to think and imagine a scale larger than human, larger even than the planetary life of species. The mood of this world is mournful, replete with reminders of humans' guilt, of their complicity in their own extinction, their footprint in the Anthropocene. While the fossilized orthoceras are reminiscent of the tenacious traces of life across millennia, Villar Rojas's fossilized worlds with their fragile clay replicas generate an artificial archive of the pending extinction of the human world.

In principle, the long duration of the existence of fossils within rocks predisposes them to become emblems of both extinction and survival. We could see them as solid embodiments of the indestructible trace of life left after death, if not extinction. In "Trilobytes," a Hiroshima poem dedicated to the potter Sakutaro Ishihara, who died in 1947 at age fifty as a victim of the atomic attack on Japan, Kent Johnson describes how, in one of their last encounters, Ishihara placed a concave stone with fossils of trilobytes in the space between them. Johnson cradles the stone

> through the ruins, past the shadows of bodies
> and bowing to his memory,
> placed it, soundlessly,
> at the epicenter.[28]

With its juxtapositional logic, the poem contrasts the fragility of human bodies and the threat of their annihilation without a trace—lest it be a shadowgraph that fades over time—with the fossilized survival of the trilobytes that are among the most ancient species on the planet. Have they become, perhaps like the orthoceras, consoling objects that affirm our belief in the perennial persistence of the trace of all life? Is this the secret of Ishihara's fascination with the trilobite? Do we hope or fear that one day, in the distant future, as Beryle Williams suggests in "Strategies for Survival," the "post-nuclear children" will find our "fossilized bones"?[29] This deep ambivalence about atomic destruction and the trace persists at the very heart of imagining nuclear extinction. Do we want to leave a trace to postnuclear children? Will there even be postnuclear children, or will nuclear annihilation indeed be "remainderless"? How do we inhabit the rhetorical and phantasmatic condition of imagining the end of planetary life?

GHOSTLY BURIALS: ARCHIVES OF RADIOACTIVE WASTE

We could argue that, among other toxic substances, the residues of radioactive contamination will most likely propel this extinction at an accelerated rate. And indeed, there will be another remainder and material archive of the nuclear age that will outlast the human species as we know it today: the nuclear waste humans have accumulated and buried underground. Living in subterranean crypts, nuclear waste is a deadly form of vibrant matter with a half-life of up to 4.5 billion years. *Into Eternity*, a speculative documentary film by Danish director Michael Madsen released in 2010, tells the story of this vibrant matter and its possible encounter with descendants of the human species thousands, if not millions, of years from now. The film deals with the construction of the Onkalo waste repository at the Olkiluoto Nuclear Power Plant in Finland, the world's first permanent nuclear waste repository.

Into Eternity's speculative addressee is an audience in the distant future that encounters the waste repository like an alien site. Since the Onkalo waste repository is designed to remain undisturbed for one hundred thousand years, that is, the time the nuclear waste deposited there remains hazardous, the imaginary addressee comes from such a distant time that no one can know today how the human species might have evolved by then. From this perspective, the film explores crucial existential questions at the core of nuclear necropolitics. It is an entirely speculative perspective that can only operate under the conditions of an "experimental system." I borrow this concept from science historian Hans-Jörg Rheinberger, who used the notion of "playing in the dark" to define experimental systems as "spaces of emergence that invent structures in order to grasp what cannot yet be thought." Experimental systems, according to Rheinberger, function as generators of surprise and machines for the production of the future and, we might add with Michael Fischer, new forms of life.[30]

Into Eternity is a radical imaginary ethnography of the future, designed to pose the hard and often unanswerable questions that usually remain under the radar of nuclear politics. These are questions posed under conditions of an experimental system. What could a possible ethics of nuclear politics, and specifically the construction of long-term nuclear waste repositories, look like? Assuming that, at the time when some of our distant descendants might come upon the repository, human languages and forms of communication might have changed so dramatically that they would be unable to read the warning instructions at its entrance, what is our responsibility today? And even if they understood, would they heed the warnings? How do we prevent them from thinking they found a buried treasure or an ancient burial ground like the Giza pyramids? Posed by the team of scientists, researchers, and experts affiliated with the Onkalo waste repository, these and similar questions form the core concerns of Madsen's film.

As the title suggests, *Into Eternity* also addresses the vexed problem of scale. The half-life of radioactive materials is so long that it by far surpasses the scale of human imagination and comprehension. The human mind cannot adequately grasp the multimillennial timescales of nuclear waste risk, except in the experimental mode of speculative fiction. Even a documentary film needs to rely on speculative experimentalism to grasp this enormous scale of distant futures. Ethnographies of the "deep" timescales required to assess the risk of nuclear waste must ultimately include elements of imaginary ethnographies.[31]

In "When Deep Time Becomes Shallow: Knowing Nuclear Waste Risk Ethnographically," Vincent F. Ialenti describes his experience of doing fieldwork at the Onkalo nuclear waste repository. He reveals that, before starting his fieldwork, he watched *Into Eternity* to understand how nuclear risk that is calculated over hundreds of thousands of years is communicated to the public. While the Finnish waste management company that was to build the Olkiluoto repository submitted multi-millennial geological, ecological, and climatological forecasts, Ialenti's fieldwork with the community of experts involved in the project shows that the deep timescales and futures were soon displaced by practical concerns with the here and now:

> I have come to see nuclear waste risk's deep timescales as less and less enchanted with the auras of mystery, terror, or sublimity common in popular depictions. Instead, I have come to see them increasingly as sites of busy technical calculation, of banal documentation requirements, of frustrating uncertainties, of difficult-to-manage office predicaments, and of specialized labors of analysis and re-analysis.[32]

This is a perfect description of the epistemological, mental, and practical dilemma of the deep time of nuclear waste repositories. The fact that the very scale of nuclear waste's continued toxic vibrancy explodes the boundaries of human knowledge and imagination throws those in charge of dealing with the risk and its management back onto the mundane and practical tasks of the here and now. Ialenti's ethnographic project is therefore transformed from a study of the deep futures of nuclear waste (his initial idea) into a study of the mundane work of experts involved in nuclear waste risk management in the here and now. The problem is, however, that we would need both, a quotidian perspective of the practical tasks at hand and a deep history and philosophical ethics that address the large-scale implications of storing nuclear waste. Only a combination of these two perspectives that operate at radically different levels would allow one to relate to the problem of nuclear waste in a way that at least tries to grasp—albeit inevitably in a very limited approximate and necessarily experimental way—the existential consequences nuclear waste posits for today's humans as well as future generations over millennia. It is precisely the function of films like *Into Eternity* and other speculative fictions to do this work of an experimental future-oriented imagination. We cannot do without it if we want to deal responsibly with the environmental problems we have caused at a scale that by far surpasses our mental capacities.

Ialenti addresses the dark appeal of Madsen's speculative imagination when he discusses the film's aesthetics. Its depiction of the nuclear waste repository shows "a place where dark souls tended to the world's most lethal waste in a lifeless cave [. . .], a place of gloom and gravity, stillness and darkness."[33] Ialenti speculates that it is the dark moods, the ambiances, and the cadence of the film and its engrossing story that captivated the audience's imagination across the world. Interestingly, in my own reading of the film, I was most struck by something else, namely, the incredible optimism at the heart of its dark aesthetics—the assumption that, given the risks of the nuclear economy and necropolitics, including the risks of an all-out nuclear war, there will still be descendants of humans alive millions of years from now.

In *Climate Trauma*, E. Ann Kaplan describes the dark mood of *Into Eternity* in terms of a "pretraumatic scenario, a trauma waiting to happen."[34] Kaplan's concept of "pretrauma" bears certain affinities with my concept of "haunting from the future." The main difference between the two concepts lies in the fact that I work with the premise that a "haunting from the future" already generates trauma in the present, while the term *pretrauma* suggests a time before trauma. If Madsen's film interpellates us, as Kaplan suggests, into the position of a witness to a catastrophe in an unfathomably distant future, it also invites us, I argue, to enter into an experimental apprehension of scale that is almost impossible to imagine.

It was the fascination with this problem, Madsen says, that motivated him to make *Into Eternity*. Thinking about the problem of scale opened up by the film, we could in fact argue that, apart from the irresolvable problem of toxic waste, it is scale itself that haunts the film as well as its viewers. This haunting by scale bears upon the responsibilities humans today assume when they leave this deadly crypt for future generations. "How far into the future will your way of life have consequences?"[35] Madsen, as the film's narrator, asks.

Kaplan argues that the viewer is put in the position of "the ghostlike human"[36] who is the film's imaginary addressee. And it is indeed this spectral addressee that haunts viewers of *Into Eternity* from a distance of one hundred thousand, if not millions of, years. Madsen also anchors the scale of this haunting in the sheer unlimited capacity of radioactive substances to cause damage. He defines atomic light as "a fire that cannot be extinguished" because it has already penetrated everything, soil, crops, and bodies, human and animal. And assuming that this catastrophic "fire" has already irreversibly damaged the human gene pool (along with those of other species), the film's imaginary addressee is literally a radioactive human ghost.

But how do we communicate about the dangers of the nuclear waste repository to such a ghostly being who is supposed to discover the site one hundred thousand years from now? Since the evolution of languages will presumably have made current languages incomprehensible, the scientists and philosophers Madsen interviews debate whether it is better to leave the site completely unmarked or to try to imagine iconic markers that will remain readable and translatable across millennia. Among these are, for example, a monolith with layered messages about the dangers of radiation, cartoon-like warnings, and a forbidding surrounding wall of thorns and rocks. Someone suggested including a copy of Norwegian artist Edvard Munch's *The Scream* as universally terrifying.[37] The German title Munch gave the painting was actually *Der Schrei der Natur,* that is, the "scream of nature," and in 1895, he made a lithograph stone with the painting that could easily be imagined as a pictorial version of the warnings on a monolith the scientists and philosophers had suggested.

Munch's painting belongs to another traumatic archive, featuring a ghost from a past traumatic memory, presumably of an explosion—not a nuclear one, of course, but a volcanic one. At least according to the controversial claim of some art critics, Munch's painting was inspired by his memory of the volcanic eruption of Krakatoa in the years 1883–84. The idea to use Munch's painting as a warning about the danger of radioactive materials is, of course, based on the remarkable hope of a transgenerational and indeed transmillennial iconic communication between ghosts that would save our distant descendants from the lethal danger we have left them as our haunting legacy.

As a material archive, the Onkalo waste repository also has a dimension of psychic haunting by radioactive ghosts. The "archive fever" that afflicts the scientists and philosophers who work at the plant comes from the heat of radical uncertainty. Just as we cannot know anything about an all-out nuclear war, we cannot know anything about the future of this archive. Following Derrida, we are therefore restricted to apprehending it in the mode of a rhetorical condition. The spectral dimension of the archive as that which remains and as that about which we speak in common language games as "buried in the archive," however, takes on a more sinister dimension in the case of a "nuclear archive." If this archive is ever opened, the ghosts buried there will haunt the distant descendants of humans as radioactive ghosts, inflicting damage and death, if not annihilation. It is as if they were vengeful ghosts, taking retribution for a violation of the earth in a far-distant past. The archive thus becomes a crypt, a burial ground for radioactive ghosts. If, psychically, a crypt houses what haunts humans because they do not want to let it die, the crypt of the waste repository, rather, houses what haunts the descendants of humans because it *cannot* die. Madsen's title *Into Eternity* resonates with this haunting temporality of radioactive ghosts.

And indeed, one of the scientists raises the issue that within one hundred thousand years, the human species will have changed so radically that we, or, more precisely, any remainder of our culture, will be completely alien to them. Somewhat oddly, Madsen wonders if, under these conditions, we can trust future generations. It does not seem that he grasps the irony behind this question of trust. Is our generation one even to raise the question of trust? Aren't we the ones who are leaving a legacy of dangers capable of destroying the entire planet? And is there an element of cruel optimism in our very assumption that any of our descendants—or, for that matter, any living being—will still be around in one hundred thousand years?

The film ends with a scene in which our imaginary descendant has opened the repository. Madsen enunciates a hauntingly melancholic epilogue:

> You have now come deep into the repository; radiation is everywhere; you do not know it, but something is happening to your body; something beyond your senses. You cannot feel it or see it or smell it, but a light is in your body, it is shining through you. It is the last glow of the powers we have harvested from the universe.[38]

Ending on this melancholic note, the film also performs and draws its viewers into a deep mourning of the future, that is, of a suffering at a distance that spans thousands, if not millions, of years. It raises the question how we relate with our sensual and affective being to catastrophic events that we may predict but that have not yet happened, yet of which we know that, if they happen, it is because of the footprints our generation left on the planet. We are, in other words, responsible even if the catastrophe will occur at a distance that our imagination will never be able to grasp. Many of those with ecological literacy already mourn the extinction of species, the destruction of planetary resources, and the global production of disposable people and lives, but how do we mourn the possible annihilation of those who come thousands of years from now? How do we mourn the possible extinction of all life on our planet? To learn to think and to feel in those terms is the challenge we face in developing a responsible (anti-)nuclear politics.

Kaplan aptly links the aesthetics of *Into Eternity* with its appeal to the unconscious, and with affect more generally, proposing a reading of the film within a genre that we could call, with James Clifford, "ethnographic surrealism":[39] "As a kind of dreamscape, the film suggests a visual correlative of the unconscious. The stark, gray, foggy landscapes denuded of vegetation and viewed through a slow-tracking camera seem ghostly, surreal, fantasmatic."[40] The film, I would add, is thus also an imaginary ethnography about one of the most fundamental conditions that marks nuclear subjectivities: a haunting from the future, that is, a haunting by a scale of time, danger, and destruction that neither our senses nor our minds are able to grasp. It is because the very material of the film transcends the boundaries of what could be represented within the genre of realist documentary, I suggest, that Madsen resorts to ethnographic surrealism.

FICTIONS OF THE UNTHINKABLE

In *The Great Derangement: Climate Change and the Unthinkable,* Amitav Ghosh ascribes to literature and other cultural objects the function to facilitate an imagination across scale that would allow one to grasp and mourn suffering and extinction in the distant future. It is the experimental arts, he suggests, that enable one to experience, at least in a mediated and inevitably limited way, what such processes would feel like and what imagining their possibility could mean for humans today in terms of a politics of both action and emotion. Unless ecological politics addresses the psychic life of witnessing the accelerating process of planetary destruction and imagining extinction, he suggests, it will be doomed to fail. To attain even a minimal sense of the looming threat to planetary survival, however, requires, according to Ghosh, the invention of new forms of imagination, communication, and creative expression.

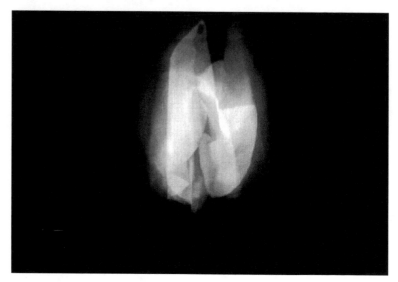

FIGURE 17. Pierre Huyghe, *Dance of Radium,* for his season at The Artist's Institute, 2015. Photograph by Mae Fatto. Courtesy of The Artist's Institute.

Since realist genres are too bound to a presentist imagination, thinking in terms of long-range ecological futures necessitates, for Ghosh, the invention of new experimental literary and artistic genres.

One of the most stunning experimental artworks on radium that plays with the unconscious appeal of radioluminescence is Pierre Huyghe's *Dance for Radium,* an image created from the glow-in-the-dark costume he created for The Artist's Institute in New York in 2014 in homage to Loie Fuller's "Radium Dance" and "Serpentine Dance."[41] Huyghe's suggestive piece invokes radioluminescence as vibrant matter, what people in the early times of the discovery of radium perceived as an almost futuristic light of the future.

Such experimental works also entail, we could add, mobilizing literature's and art's potential to function as "experimental systems" designed to explore what we cannot yet know. Only if one creates and uses literature, and the arts more generally, as "ethnographies of the future"[42] can one approximate thinking and feeling across distant futures. Learning this skill is imperative to countering the nuclear "work of death" with "work of survival."

Pushing the pressure on communication even further, Ghosh raises the issue of communication not only with descendants of humans across millions of generations but also with nonhuman interlocutors. Climate change and other environmental disasters, he argues, force humans to become aware that the earth and its objects are speaking back to them, and that "nonhuman forces have the ability to intervene directly in human thought."[43] Ghosh asks why we commonly don't think of these processes as communicative acts: "Is it perhaps because the shadow of language interposes itself, preventing us from doing so?"[44] He then wonders if the catastrophic long-term environmental changes that have become nonhuman interlocutors will not force humans to expand the boundaries of language, relinquishing their logocentric fixations and shifting more emphasis toward thinking in images. This would entail a sea change in communicative practice, since, as Ghosh asserts, "the Anthropocene resists literary fiction."[45] It resists fiction because of the scale at which the Anthropocene happens. Ghosh speculates that, to make these shifts and processes an object of literature, one would have to rely on hybrid literary forms that bring text and image together, forms that will, in turn, change cultural practices of reading.

Yet, while the earth undoubtedly "responds" to human actions, Ghosh's reflection on the communication with nonhuman interlocutors is, in fact, a communication not *with* but *about* nonhuman interlocutors. It is a communication designed to enhance awareness and guide actions toward *inter*-actions with these nonhuman interlocutors. Given the entanglement between humans and planetary environments, acknowledging responsibility for the survival of future generations of living beings on earth will require a profound rearrangement of current ways of life, including, most importantly, economy and politics, but also communicative action as well as the entangled ecologies of mind and desire.

HYPEROBJECTS AND ANIMACIES

Some of Ghosh's reflections on nonhuman interlocutors are inspired by Timothy Morton's concept of "hyperobjects," a concept designed for a new mode of thinking across vast scales. The latter is necessary, for example, to grasp vibrant matter like plutonium. "The future of plutonium exerts a causal influence on the present, casting its shadow backward through time. All kinds of options are no longer thinkable without a deliberate concealment of the reality of radioactive objects,"[46] writes Timothy Morton in *Hyperobjects*. In the so-called Atomic Age, however, deliberate concealment, compounded by denial, has been the order of the day. The nuclear culture of secrecy thus pursues these unthinkable options at great risk in a mode of *as if*—as if the nuclear threat and, for that matter, the threat of climate change and other environmental disasters did not exist.

Inspired by Madsen's *Into Eternity,* Morton claims that humans are becoming, in Heideggerian terms, "guardians of futurality."[47] Morton links this notion with the Nuclear Guardianship movement, cofounded by Buddhist scholar and systems analyst Joanna Macy. Designed to deal with the safe storage of nuclear waste, the Rocky Flats Nuclear Guardianship is a transgenerational project that aims at securing a citizen commitment to present and future generations to keep radioactive materials out of the biosphere. Intrigued by the Nuclear Guardianship's suggestion to encase plutonium in gold (which can absorb gamma rays), Morton states, "Nuclear Guardianship sees nuclear materials as a unit: a hyperobject."[48] Hyperobjects, such as radioactive materials or climate, affect, according to Morton, "core ideas of what it means to exist, what Earth is, what society is."[49] They also force humans to acknowledge that, as Morton says, "nuclear materials are already occupying social space."[50] We might add that the challenge to think across unimaginable scales and spans of time also affects the boundaries of subjectivity and intersubjectivity as well as the appropriate modes of communication.

In this context, a brief reflection on the challenge of nuclear materials to notions of time and space, and especially the notion of the "spacing of time,"[51] seems to be in order. "The spacing of time is the condition not only for everything that can be cognized and experienced, but also for everything that can be thought and desired. On the other hand, the spacing of time has an ultra-transcendental status because it is the condition for everything *all the way down* to the minimal forms of life," writes Martin Hägglund in "Chronolibidinal Reading: Deconstruction and Psychoanalysis."[52] The half-life of nuclear materials presents a formidable challenge to rethinking this spacing of time from the perspective of scaling. The difficulties arise from the limitations the boundaries of visceral knowledge and experience impose on imagining the timescale of this half-life. For Kant, time and space were the a priori conditions of human sensibility. Hägglund argues that the ultratranscendental status of the spacing of time is not limited to sensibility. Time can transcend the limits of the knowable. In his critique of Hägglund, William Egginton foregrounds Kant's concern with the "limits of the knowable," insisting that while we require the structure of spacing "to sense, imagine, think, or desire [. . .] we can certainly posit [. . .] unimaginable notions like eternal simultaneity."[53] Egginton then proposes a thought experiment that directly raises the issue of scaling, suggesting that we imagine "a world in which beings like ourselves who can only cognize in spatial and temporal terms are moved in their limited selves across a vast, eternal, and permanent sort of landscape." In our attempts "to imagine such a world," Egginton states, "words and images fail."[54]

The reason why words and images fail in the face of such an unthinkable referent is, I would argue, because of a crisis of scaling. This crisis of scaling is precisely the challenge we face in trying to grasp the half-life and the long-range effects of nuclear materials. Transcending experiential abilities of spacing and scaling, nuclear materials strain the limits of what we can know about the world. Yet, the very threat of long-range radioactive contamination also makes it imperative to imagine the impossible and to extend the scale of thinking about the world. In other words, as Egginton's thought experiment suggests, we move our "limited selves across a vast, eternal, and permanent sort of landscape." This challenge also affects how we think about the boundaries of human subjectivity and communication. At stake is nothing less than the reach of affect and emotion, moral thought and action, across vast scales.

As we recall, Ghosh makes a case for extending the boundaries of communication toward the figural and the iconic. Ghosh's thoughts on the shadow of language and the urgency of remobilizing the ability to think in images bear a certain resonance with the visionary reflections of André Leroi-Gourhan on figurative representation in *Gesture and Speech*. First published in French in 1964, this monumental work on the history of human communication maintains an astounding actuality in light of today's debates about environmental politics in the Anthropocene. "Figurative representation," Leroi-Gourhan writes, "is the language of visible forms. Like the language of words it holds humanity by the root, and the human solution has to be based on the construction of historical trajectories that support the creative urge in the long ascent followed by a fall and by other, new trajectories. The search for the figurative is therefore written into the future of humankind."[55]

Unparalleled in his attunement to thinking across scale, Leroi-Gourhan thinks in terms of gigantic waves of communicative leaps with long ascents and falls throughout the history of humans, dating all the way back to the early humanoids. The final chapter of *Gesture and Speech*, "Imaginary Freedom and the Fate of *Homo sapiens*," asks where *Homo sapiens* as a thinking animal is going. Interestingly, Leroi-Gourhan traces the great derangement, so to speak, back to the time when, with the formation of large cities, the relationship between the psychic and the physical has lost its balance. This lack of equilibrium culminates, according to Leroi-Gourhan, in such vastly diverse phenomena as today's increasing dominance of electronic media, dispersed forms of traditional warfare, the atomic bomb, and the environmental crisis. Speculating about the future of *Homo sapiens,* Leroi-Gourhan wonders if one of the "silent controllers of atomic launching towers [. . .] will perhaps one day pull the handle which will automatically release the bomb at the precise starting point of a trajectory selected by an electronic computer."[56]

Leroi-Gourhan imagines "several possible solutions for human planetarization," the first being that "atomic processes will bring the human adventure to a full stop."[57] As the last and only hopeful solution, he envisions a new balance with the planet:

> We can imagine the human of the near future as being determined by a new awareness and the will to remain *sapiens*. In such an event the problem of the individual's relationship with society will have to be completely rethought [. . .] unless we decide that humankind has really run its course. Our species is still too closely bound to its origins not to strive spontaneously for the balance that made it human in the first place.[58]

Striving for balance in today's threatened planetary ecology, however, means also—and some say first and foremost—to deal with the nuclear danger. Nuclear materials are, once released, essentially uncontainable vibrant matter.[59] They are invisible, yet immensely mobile, able to penetrate walls, bodies, and cells. They can change cell structures and genetic makeup. They can melt eyeballs, burn up humans, and leave their shadow imprints on walls and solid objects. They have the potential to annihilate life on earth. Or, in Morton's terms, they are hyperobjects, unique beings not limited in time and space. "Hyperobjects are *futural*."[60] Nuclear hyperobjects are futural in the sense that they have become part of all living bodies, changed the boundaries of subjectivity, and marked humans as nuclear subjects. In addition to the natural radioactivity they receive from the sun and the earth, all humans today have traces of human-generated radioactivity in their bones, blood, and genes. Nuclear materials are uncontainable. This is the paradoxical task of nuclear waste repositories: to contain the uncontainable. As fascinating as it is in its nuclear aesthetics, the idea of the Onkalo scientists to encase plutonium in gold also testifies to the essential helplessness of all attempts to recontain the most destructive force humans have ever released.

Yet, even the necessity to think across deep time, distant futures, and unfathomable scales is not enough. We also need to learn to think at smaller scales, including the minute scale of the atom. If we were to consider nuclear materials with Morton as "unique beings," we would need simultaneously to think at a scale of millennia and at the small scale of what we could call, with Deleuze and Guattari, the molecular. Interestingly, Morton's sense of nuclear materials as unique beings bears certain resonances with Mel Chen's concept of "animacies" and her related thoughts on molecularity. Originating in linguistics, where the term *animacy* "generally refers to the grammatical effects of the sentience of liveness of nouns,"[61] Chen expands the concept of "animacy," drawing on queer of color scholarship, critical animal studies, biopolitics, disability theory, and critical theory more generally, with the goal of using animacy as a supplement to concepts such as "life" or "liveliness." In performing such diverse tasks as rewriting conditions of intimacy, engendering different communalisms, and revisiting biopolitical spheres, the concept helps Chen "to theorize current anxieties about the production of humanness in contemporary times."[62]

One of Chen's interests lies in analyzing the agency or animacy of objects, and especially substances that do not belong to living organisms, yet enter into relationships or even fusions with them that lead to what she calls "the marriage of bodies and chemicals."[63] Considering the animacy of toxic substances, such as lead, Chen states, "Animacy becomes the property of lead, a highly mobile and poisonous substance that feeds anxieties about transgressors of permeable borders, whether of skin or country."[64] In addition, the term *animacy* assumes a mobile, molecular form in the study of "the biopolitical impact of environmental toxins on human bodies in the context of present-day emergent illnesses."[65]

Chen's study of animacies makes a crucial intervention, urging us to "rethink the significance of molecular, cellular, animal, vegetable, or nonhuman life."[66] Moreover, Chen's work demonstrates that mobile toxic and molecular animacies deeply affect the boundaries of the human and other species:

> In a scene of human intoxication, for toxins and their human hosts, the animacy criteria of liveliness, subjectivity, and humanness (where the human wins) come up short against mobility and sentience (where the toxin wins). [. . .] Toxicity becomes us, we become the toxin. [. . .] There is, indeed, something "unworlding" that might be said to take place in the cultural production of toxic notions. A "normal" world's order is lost when, for instance, things that can harm you permanently are not even visible to the naked eye.[67]

I have discussed Chen's work in such detail because her analysis provides an astute description of a similar "unworlding" that happens as an effect of the splitting of the atom and the unleashing of its lethal power, its work of death. The *invisibility* of the danger radioactive substances present to living organisms paradoxically contrasts sharply with the *hypervisibility* of its blinding light and its instantaneous destruction, its annihilating force that leaves nothing but a shadow trace on stone. Yet, there is also the afterlife of this spectacular work of death, namely, the slow violence and damage the lethal substance deposits in the bodies of survivors, the damage it imposes on the cellular, molecular, and genetic levels. And since all human beings have absorbed and now "host" some of the radioactive fallout of nuclear explosions in their bodies, we can say with Chen that they have become not only nuclear subjects but nuclear bodies as well.

In *The Politics of Life Itself*, Nicolas Rose argues that contemporary biopolitics must now be considered *molecular*: "It is now at the molecular level that human life is understood, at the molecular level that its processes can be anatomized, and at the molecular level that life can now be engineered."[68] In the move from biopolitics to necropolitics, this engineering of life at the molecular level performs the "slow violence" of a "work of toxic death."[69] In Deleuze and Guattari's terms, we could speak of a nuclear micropolitics that operates at the molecular level of the body.[70] As we have seen, nuclear necropolitics demands both a macropolitics that extends the imagination to span millions of years and a micropolitics that accounts for the transgenerational effects of the engineering of life at the molecular level.

Paul Virilio, Akira Lippit, and others have argued that atomic light challenges the very boundaries of vision. Like others before him, including Lippit and Schell, Amitav Ghosh argues that nuclear and other environmental catastrophes challenge the boundaries of thought, emotion, and language. Moreover, the arc from "hyperobjects" to "animacies" I traced above shows how nuclear forces challenge the boundaries of life itself. The fact that we deal simultaneously with a monumental hyperobject and with molecular animacies allows us to understand why it is so hard to grasp the terrifying scope and scale of nuclear necropolitics, let alone to tell its stories. But this very predicament also compels us to understand why we can't stop doing so. "It's all of us," writes Arundhati Roy. "That's what nuclear bombs do. Whether they're used or not, they violate everything that is humane. They alter the meaning of life itself."[71]

SEVEN

POSTNUCLEAR MADNESS AND NUCLEAR CRYPTS

> You may well ask why people with a kind heart and humanist feelings would go and work on weapons of mass destruction.
> —Hans Bethe, *Hiroshima in America*

> There are no longer problems of the spirit. There is only the question: When will I be blown up?
> —William Faulkner, Nobel Prize Acceptance Speech, 1950

In 1946, James Agee, author of the *Time* magazine article on Hiroshima, published his highly satirical "Dedication Day: Rough Sketch for a Moving Picture." "Dedication Day" deals with an elderly scientist who is haunted by guilt over having participated in the construction of the atomic bomb. The story revolves around the dedication of the so-called Arch, a monument in Washington, D.C., designed by Frank Lloyd Wright to commemorate Hiroshima and the American victory over Japan. Allegedly, the Arch is not made of stone but of fused uranium that creates a "glistering more subtly than most jewels."[1] The satirical title "Dedication Day" invokes the Christian tradition of presenting a child to the congregation with a vow to raise him or her in the Christian faith. We may thus assume that the dedication of the Arch entails a tacit allusion to the presentation of the two atomic children, Little Boy and Fat Man, to the American congregation. In a festive celebration with invited guests and tourists, an Eternal Fuse is to be lit, chemically calculated to consume itself at the rate of one inch per second. Like the Olympic flame, it was to be lit in an opening ceremony and then kept burning eternally by so-called Keepers of the Flame, mostly disabled war veterans and Japanese collaborators who survived the "experiments at Hiroshima and Nagasaki."[2]

This is when the guilt-ridden scientist interferes, requesting to be employed to work underground with the Keepers of the Flame, a work he considers as symbolic atonement. When he engages in loud speeches of self-vilification, tears his hair, and beats his face, he is diagnosed as "a psychoneurotic," fired from his job, and offered "lifelong residence and treatment, gratis, in whatever sanitarium in the nation he might prefer."[3] He agrees but asks to be allowed to throw the switch in the underground vault that would light the Eternal Fuse. The authorities indulge the former hero by granting him his wish. A few minutes after the climactic dedication, he is found dead next to the eternal flame. In a suicide note, he declares his death to be an "ethical sacrifice" for the sake of atonement. Officially, however, the cause of his suicide is ascribed to a failure of nerves due to "exaggerated scrupulousness."[4] "Dedication Day" ends with the celebratory announcement that his body will be interred in New Mexico where he "first saw the light of the New Age."[5]

Agee's darkly sarcastic story targets the emergence in post-Hiroshima of a symptomatic attitude that R. J. Lifton and Greg Mitchell call "moral inversion." Evolving to shape America's nuclear unconscious, this attitude fosters a pervasive denial by condemning or pathologizing any "negative" feeling about Hiroshima. America's official postwar spirit was celebratory glee, and the rhetorical construction of the first nuclear attacks in human history swiftly inverted the calculus of mass slaughter into one of saving American lives. Accordingly, those who participated in the construction of the bomb or in the military action that led to its catastrophic use were celebrated as war heroes. Someone who, like the scientist in "Dedication Day," disagreed with this official narrative because he is guilt-ridden over having participated in the excessive slaughter of the civilian population was declared unpatriotic at best and insane at worst. Any counternarrative to the official celebration of the Bomb was considered a threat to the celebratory nationalist rhetoric and spirit. Accordingly, the only viable place for the scientist was considered to be an insane asylum. After his suicide, those in charge come to the conclusion that the cause was a "piteous derangement of a man of former genius" and a "grievous error of exaggerated scrupulousness."[6]

Under the impact of the American post-Hiroshima "moral inversion," anybody who declared the dropping of the atomic bomb to be an act of undue violence against Hiroshima's or Nagasaki's civilian populations is instantly denounced, if not punished. As the case of Nobel Peace Prize winner Linus Pauling shows, for example, antinuclear peace activism is repudiated and linked, in the emergent flourishing Cold War rhetoric, to the so-called Communist peace offensive. In response to his antinuclear stance and membership in Einstein's Emergency Committee of Atomic Scientists, Pauling was temporarily denied a passport to speak at a scientific conference in London and later ordered to appear before the Senate Internal Security Subcommittee.

The most famous case to illustrate this moral inversion is that of Claude Eatherly, the pilot who flew the reconnaissance aircraft over Hiroshima that gave the go-ahead signal to the Enola Gay to drop the first atomic bomb. In the year in which President Truman announced the construction of the hydrogen bomb, Eatherly, consumed by guilt over his responsibility in the mass slaughter of civilians, tried to commit suicide but survived and was committed to the psychiatric hospital for veterans in Waco, Texas. During his institutional confinement, this man, who had been publicly celebrated as a war hero, became a fervent peace activist. An article about him in *Newsweek* caught the attention of Günther Anders, the prominent German philosopher and antinuclear activist who had been forced into exile by the Nazis and spent thirteen years in the United States before returning to settle in Vienna in 1950. Anders's book *Die Antiquiertheit des Menschen (The Obsolescence of Man)* is one of the German classic works that inspired the antinuclear activist movement. After Anders contacted Eatherly at the psychiatric hospital, a years-long correspondence ensued that was published in Germany in 1961 (*Off-Limits für das Gewissen*) and in an English translation, *Burning Conscience*,[7] in 1962, with a preface by Bertrand Russell and a foreword by renowned Viennese antinuclear critic Robert Jungk.

Once Eatherly was released from the psychiatric hospital, his desperate attempts to appease his bad conscience with public confessions and antinuclear speeches were seen as nothing but mental confusion. His complete failure to convince the authorities of his guilt in tandem with his psychological need for punishment eventually pushed him over the edge again. This time, instead of trying to take his own life, he set out to prove his guilt by committing various illegal acts. Now indeed mentally unstable, he performed a hold-up with a gun after which he left without taking the money. On a different occasion, he forged a check and paid the money into a fund for the assistance of Hiroshima war children. Designed to prove that he deserved punishment, these acts led to a brief incarceration, which he, in one of his letters to Anders, described as a temporary relief from his unbearable pangs of conscience and nightmares about the victims of Hiroshima and Nagasaki.

Interestingly, the history of Eatherly's mental illness can itself be read as a symptom of America's official attempts to confine antinuclear resistance. When Eatherly was first hospitalized in Waco, he was diagnosed with a mental disability attributable to war service, that is, with what we would today call post-traumatic stress disorder. Yet, once his writings against the dangers of nuclear weapons and war increasingly caught public attention, the Air Force considered him to be a threat and tried to have him committed permanently as mentally insane, defying the diagnosis of his doctor, who deemed him fit for release. In his foreword to *Burning Conscience,* Jungk writes,

> The torments of his conscience were brushed aside as pathological, the sensibility [. . .] was interpreted as a "lack of emotional stability." [. . .] He, the morally more healthy, could not come to terms with the sick society [. . .] because, after his experience in 1945, he had failed to develop that protective pachyderm, which allowed his contemporaries to accept, more or less complacently, the horrors of Hiroshima and Auschwitz and all the fresh war crimes with which wars of the future threatened them.[8]

This is not to contest that Eatherly had developed a mental illness. All signs point to the fact that his war experience and his ensuing crushing sense of guilt induced a genuine mental break. Rather, it is to point out that it is the healthiest aspects of Eatherly's changed personality that are pathologized when his antinuclear activism is deemed as mental insanity and his feelings of guilt are labeled a guilt complex. Like the senior scientist in "Dedication Day," Eatherly is faulted for the "grievous error of exaggerated scrupulousness."

Jungk analyzes this pathologization as a consequence of the radical shift the beginning Cold War years generated in American attitudes toward nuclear war. Jungk writes that, before the Cold War,

> consternation over the horrors of Hiroshima had not yet come to be regarded as a sign of weakness, or condemnation of the use of the atomic bomb as grounds for suspicion. [. . .] Public opinion was all but unanimous in demanding the outlawing of nuclear instruments of war.[9]

This dramatic turn in attitude is a manifestation of what Lifton calls "moral inversion" at a national scale, an inversion that goes hand in hand with a concomitant politics of emotion. Negative emotions about the nuclear attack on Hiroshima and Nagasaki, such as guilt or shame or fear or horror, are considered misguided, a sign of weakness, if not an un-American sentiment. Implicit is a pathologization of humane reactions such as compassion, love for peace, protectiveness, and the acknowledgment of the fragility of human life.

In a remarkable letter to President Kennedy from January 13, 1961, Anders invokes the notion of *Seelenblindheit*, or "soul blindness," a classical technical term in psychology to designate an overly weak reaction to a major disaster or trauma. In light of the pathologization of negative emotions in response to the atomic attacks on Japan, the absence of a proportionate reaction to the use of atomic weapons has become the norm. Soul blindness, in other words, is a symptom of the nuclear age. In the United States, it has become a national pathology. Admittedly, this is in part an adaptive reaction to the fact that it would be virtually impossible to go on living in our nuclear world if one were, at all times, feeling reactions proportionate to the nuclear horrors of the past, their persistent threat in the present, and their haunting from the future. A certain amount of splitting is, as I argued earlier, unavoidable to function in today's world. However, splitting can easily shade over into traumatic numbing, and beyond a certain point, traumatic numbing is a psychosocial pathology that affects individuals, communities, and nations in the aftermath of violent histories. The longer this psychic numbing persists, the more it becomes vulnerable to a repetition of the very violence it is designed to repress.

Perhaps Eatherly's case is so important because his illness is a symptom of his time. Incapable of the adaptive splitting that would have allowed him to function in the post-Hiroshima world, he at all times feels proportionate reactions to the nuclear horrors and the urgency toward antinuclear work that comes with them. He, who is healthier in the sense that his emotions are more proportionate to the events, breaks down because such emotions are no longer tolerable. This is why those whose souls are blinded by the inhumane powers of atomic light consider the man who is free from soul blindness a threat to their selves and their nation. Eatherly needs to be confined to an insane asylum because he threatens to puncture the nation's emotional defenses, its psychic numbing to the horrors of Hiroshima.

While Eatherly's might be the most spectacular case in exposing the official attempts at pathologizing concerns about nuclear weaponry, it is by far not unique. Susan Griffin, for example, mentions a much earlier attempt to silence antinuclear sentiment in the story of a navy ensign posted to the factories at Oak Ridge. The production at Oak Ridge of fissionable material for the first atomic weapons operated in almost exclusive secrecy. When the navy ensign suffered a mental breakdown and began to rave about a terrible weapon that will soon bring the end of the world, the navy built a special wing for him at the Oak Ridge hospital, staffed with psychiatrists and physicians sworn to secrecy. "The ensign is given continual sedation. Whenever he begins to speak, he receives another injection. His family is told that he is on a long mission at sea."[10] This case thus reveals that the moral inversion in America's nuclear culture is emerging even before the manufacturing of the first nuclear weapons is completed. At least the military perceives the concern with nuclear weapons from the very beginning as a threat.

In *Hiroshima in America,* Lifton and Mitchell write:

> Since Hiroshima, we have become captives of nuclear weapons. [. . .] We rely on them and flaunt them, but psychologically and politically they have imprisoned us. [. . .] Ever since, we have struggled to overcome our own terror [. . .] by means of embracing the objects of that terror and attaching ourselves to their ultimate power, their omnipotence.[11]

Moral inversion, if not an Orwellian reversal, is, according to Lifton and Mitchell, part of this embrace of the objects of terror: "From the time of Hiroshima, Americans have assigned themselves the task of finding virtue in the first use of the most murderous device ever created. We have felt the need to avoid at any cost the sense of moral culpability for this act."[12] On the basis of such moral inversion, Eatherly's insistence on guilt and responsibility must of course be perceived as a threat.

In ever-new iterations of the confabulatory assertion that the atomic bomb is "a *preserver* rather than a *destroyer* of life," the American nuclear imaginary can maintain its celebratory stance and denounce antinuclear sentiments as morally wrong. Emotions proportionate to the "sense of radical evil, of having crossed a terrible boundary into an unprecedented realm of mass killing,"[13] are seen as the exaggerated scrupulousness of a weak mind. The reluctance to embrace the notion of an all-out nuclear war is pathologized as an "Armageddon syndrome."[14]

Lifton and Mitchell counter this pathologization with the argument that we might as well speak, on the contrary, of a "'Hiroshima syndrome' that prevents us from taking on a truly moral stand on the weaponry."[15] One of the emotionally devastating effects of this inversion of moral imagination, the authors conclude, is the creation of a counterfeit psychopolitical universe. The collective memory and unconscious of Hiroshima have for so long been systematically distorted and misinterpreted that it has become a universe of confabulation in relation to which any countermemory is, paradoxically, censored as a threat to national security. Moral inversion, in other words, is part and parcel of the larger epistemology and psychopolitics of deception and self-deception that mark the nuclear imaginary at large. The predominately unconscious psychic logic underlying this confabulation and moral inversion is a manifestation of what Freud calls *Verkehrung ins Gegenteil*, that is, a perception that renders events psychically as their opposite. As such, moral inversion facilitates and enhances psychic numbing as a more general defense against confronting atrocities.

Entirely consistent with this moral inversion, Eatherly is also perceived as a threat because he is not only incapable but also morally and emotionally opposed to psychic numbing. In the immediate aftermath of the nuclear attack, Hiroshima survivors described how a sudden paralysis of emotions seized them in the middle of witnessing the most horrendous human suffering and carnage. They simply could not feel what was happening. Closing off psychically was at the time a survival mechanism that prevented them from being emotionally destroyed by the violence they witnessed. While serving long-term survival in the aftermath of disaster, psychic deadening, once it persists to the extent that it becomes part of the survivor's identity, constitutes a form of death-in-life. As I discuss in more detail in the following pages, Lifton and Mitchell see psychic numbing as a psychopolitical symptom that characterizes American society since Hiroshima.

DENIAL AND DEATH-IN-LIFE:
REFLECTIONS ON NUCLEAR SUBJECTIVITIES

In his conversation with Bruno Latour, Michel Serres emphatically asserts, "Hiroshima remains the sole object of my philosophy."[16] We could argue that, together with Günther Anders, Michel Serres is one of the prime philosophers of nuclear/antinuclear politics. In response to the dropping of the atomic bomb on Hiroshima and Nagasaki, Serres resigned from the Naval Academy (in 1949) and, abdicating his earlier scientific optimism, shifted his career from the sciences to the humanities. His famous statement that "Hiroshima remains the sole object of my philosophy" presents a profoundly challenging invitation not only to think of nuclear/antinuclear politics as a philosophical object but also to explore the specific role of the humanities in these politics. Serres made his statement in an interview with Bruno Latour in 1990, asserting that for him, the legacy of the Manhattan Project "involves morality, sociopolitics, philosophy."[17] In addition, this legacy of course also involves psychology, including trauma theory, affect theory, and psychohistory.

I have discussed Robert Jay Lifton's pathbreaking *Death in Life: Survivors of Hiroshima* earlier in chapter 5. Here I want to shift the perspective away from the focus on victims to emphasize the role of the sciences as well as the official denial and moral inversion in the United States. As Lifton's interviews reveal, Serres's questioning of the implication and responsibility of scientists and the sciences in the unparalleled destructive power of nuclear weapons also resonates with statements made by nuclear physicists in Hiroshima. One of them openly declared, "I felt that science had a lot to do with this enormous destruction."[18] He also emphasized the "unique significance of Hiroshima, a belief that 'there is a special historic destiny which Hiroshima had been given in relationship to atomic energy, and that atomic energy has a special role to play in changing or converting mankind and influencing human culture.'"[19] In a similar vein, Hiroshima's mayor Shinzo Hamai stressed the predominant role of the sciences, while at the same time shifting the perspective toward the destructive desires unleashed by warring nations. Exposing the mistake of "the use of the fruits of science for killing, maiming, and destroying," he argues that, although the United States is to blame for the first use of the atomic bomb, "all belligerents had a desire to possess such formidable weapons, [. . .] everyone, as part of mankind, must bear his portion of the responsibility."[20]

The invocation of Hiroshima's "special historic destiny" can be extended far beyond nuclear politics and the actual use of nuclear weapons. After the dropping of the first atomic bomb, there was no return. The knowledge of the Bomb's unequaled power of destruction has an irreversible impact on social, mental, and psychic ecologies, profoundly affecting all thinking of the future. Radioactive contamination constitutes the most devastating qualitative leap in the footprint human beings leave on their planet, irreparably altering its ecologies of mind and matter.

It is not surprising that the psychohistory of the atomic bomb opened with an apocalyptic imaginary that left deep imprints, not only on the survivors of the attacks on Hiroshima and Nagasaki, but also on the world at large. The very knowledge of the first weapon that could literally destroy planet Earth was received with unfathomable horror, fear, and guilt. Lifton speaks of "a vast breakdown of faith in the human matrix supporting each individual life, and therefore a loss of faith (or trust) in the structure of human existence."[21] One of the interviewees, a social worker, expresses this ontological insecurity in terms of the impossibility to "believe in tomorrow" and a general lack of an "adequate philosophy or disciplined point of view about life."[22]

It was twenty-eight years after the publication of *Death in Life* that Robert J. Lifton and Greg Mitchell published *Hiroshima in America: Fifty Years of Denial*.[23] In this immensely provocative psychopolitical intervention, Lifton and Mitchell suggest that, because of America's refusal to confront the violent legacy of Hiroshima, psychic numbing has come to shape America's politics of emotion toward Hiroshima and become formative of the American psyche. This is not to say that Americans have refused to study the effects of the atomic bomb on Japanese civilians in Hiroshima and Nagasaki. Scientists have widely studied its physical and environmental impacts, including the long-term effects of radiation. Lifton points out, however, that, since the time when he first went to Hiroshima sixteen years after the end of the war, there had been no study on the Bomb's broadly human consequences.

A comparable attempt to eclipse the emotional effects of mass violence and genocide also marked German reactions to the Holocaust. As I argued in *Haunting Legacies: Violent Histories and Transgenerational Trauma*, when I grew up in postwar West Germany, there was an abundance of information available on the Holocaust but no culture to process the information psychically. The psychic numbing of Germans and their inability to mourn resulted, according to Frankfurt School psychoanalysts Alexander and Margarete Mitscherlich, in a cultural and emotional paralysis. The latter is reminiscent of the American numbing toward Hiroshima that Lifton and Mitchell describe:

> While the tendency toward numbing in relation to Hiroshima is universal, it is bound to be greatest in Americans, where numbing serves the additional purpose of warding off potential feelings of guilt. As in the very different case of German attitudes toward Auschwitz, we have not wished to permit Hiroshima to enter our psyches in ways that could affect our feelings. And we are greatly aided in our nonfeeling by the distancing technology of the Hiroshima attack.[24]

Claude Eatherly's refusal to participate in this foreclosure of guilt must have felt like an unacceptable provocation because it went entirely against the grain of the official post-Hiroshima politics of emotion. "One was supposed to be numbed to Hiroshima," argue Lifton and Mitchell. "It became [. . .] politically suspect if one was troubled or inclined to make a fuss about it."[25] It is this psychic numbing that generates a pervasive psychic ecology of fear and haunting from the future. Any repression, denial, or refusal to confront violent histories comes back to haunt, both individually and collectively. People are haunted by the fear of the atomic bomb. According to polls, until the late 1980s, half of all Americans expected to die in a nuclear war during their lifetime. Even when the country tries to banish this sense of doom with the manic defense of omnipotent posturing, it continues to live within an ecology of nuclear fear.

At the same time, the psychic numbing toward the suffering of others, and perhaps even one's own, can, as Lifton and Mitchell maintain, spread to other areas until it becomes all-pervasive:

> By closing ourselves off from the human costs of our devastating weapon, we are more able to do the same in relation to other experiences of collective suffering—for example, the 1990s genocides in Bosnia and Rwanda. [. . .] As the numbing spreads, we can become increasingly insensitive to violence and suffering around us, to killing in general, but also to poverty and homelessness.[26]

This larger context of nuclear necropolitics has prepared the psychological ground for the United States to become a country where common goods, such as Social Security, health care for all, subsidized housing, and affordable education, are vilified as socialist goods. The numbing toward violence at a mass scale has gradually seeped into a numbing toward the slow structural violence that targets quotidian lives.

Under the surface of more tangible fears about everyday subsistence and survival, however, nuclear fear persists in the form of a nameless dread that pervades everything, even if only unconsciously. In the wake of nuclear trauma and increasing ecological imbalance, a young generation is growing up without any sense of a viable future. The two massive threats to planetary survival—nuclear war and climate change—are looming over them, infusing them with a veritable terror of futurelessness. Without adaptive splitting and psychic numbing, they will no longer be able to carve out a life for themselves, have children, engage in creative work or art, or experience a sense of even temporary happiness. This is why Lifton and Mitchell say that, if we can speak of an age of numbing, it begins with Hiroshima.[27]

Nuclear subjectivities in this age of psychic numbing are shaped by the entwinement of and interaction between three basic psychic operations: splitting, doubling, and numbing. While splitting and numbing are intimately tied to the psychic closing off of overwhelmingly terrifying or painful aspects of experience, doubling—a term coined by Lifton and Mitchell—deserves some further consideration because it addresses a more active agency and participation in, if not collusion with, nuclear violence. Lifton and Mitchell speak of "an inner division so extreme as to constitute a form of *doubling*, of the formation of separate, relatively autonomous selves."[28]

This concept of doubling also helps to understand how people can entirely split off their humane and compassionate selves when they perform tasks in the service of mass violence and genocide. While the Nazi doctors are prime examples of such psychic doubling, Lifton and Mitchell argue that it is also present in people involved with the production and use of nuclear weapons. More generally, doubling helps to understand one of the most troubling psychological mechanisms that facilitate atrocious acts like murder, torture, and mass violence. Lifton and Mitchell put this in painfully succinct terms in relation to the implication of doubling for nuclear culture: "The most decent and loving person could be capable, under certain circumstances, of forming a relatively autonomous second self drawn to and joining in with the immortalizing appeal of nuclear desecration and transgression."[29]

Finally, Lifton and Mitchell argue that doubling also supports the nuclear phantasms of an "apocalyptic self" related to death and immortality. The authors consider a certain doubling of the self in relation to death—a division between a "measured self" and an "apocalyptic self"—to be ubiquitous. While people are usually trying to make their way through the natural life cycle in measured ways, Lifton and Mitchell argue, certain traumatic events or psychic states reactivate the "apocalyptic self" that is preoccupied with premature or violent death, such as death through catastrophic illnesses, mass killings, genocide, or nuclear holocaust. All ecologies of fear, we can surmise, mobilize phantasms of the apocalyptic self. We have seen, however, that Hiroshima has forever disrupted the expectation of a natural life cycle and therefore released the dangerous energies of the apocalyptic self. In a ubiquitous ecology of nuclear fear, the apocalyptic self becomes part of the cultural unconscious.

Lifton and Mitchell analyze the dangers of the apocalyptic self in relation to nuclear fundamentalism, a term Lifton had already coined in the early 1980s, defining it as "the embrace of the bomb as a new 'fundamental,' as a source of 'salvation.'"[30] In *Hiroshima in America*, Lifton and Mitchell specify how the apocalyptic self fuels nuclear fundamentalism:

> The apocalyptic self has grave dangers. It may press toward totalistic behavior—toward destroying or killing—in order to head off a perceived death event. Expressions of the apocalyptic self invite extremes of ethnic passions and even genocide.[31]

The psychological patterns of post-Hiroshima apocalypticism also took hold in the American ecology of fear. Lewis Mumford once commented that in the late 1960s and 1970s, young people were acting as if the bomb had already been dropped. Lifton and Mitchell wonder if "unconsciously such young people were preparing for an American Hiroshima."[32] The dark side of such apocalypticism is the rise of fundamentalism:

> There is a connection between nuclear threat and the worldwide epidemic of fundamentalism. Fundamentalism in general, including its political forms, stems from the loss, fear of loss, of fundamentals—of principles and capacities basic to creed, community and collective life.[33]

Nuclear fundamentalism is intimately tied to the experience of a nuclear sublime. The first nuclear tests' unprecedented scale of destruction inspired a cosmic fear that was phantasmatically transformed into a sublime encounter with an almost godlike force. Lifton sees the connection to fundamentalism in the resemblance of this experience of the nuclear sublime with a religious conversion. Psychologically, this association requires an acrobatics of moral inversion during which destruction is equated with salvation, some would say perversely so. In 1956, William Lawrence, official journalistic witness to nuclear tests, reported that the test explosion of a hydrogen bomb in the northern Pacific evoked for him an image reminiscent of H. G. Wells's vision in *A World Set Free*. He imagined "what the fireball and mushroom I was then watching would do to any of the world's great cities—New York, Washington, Chicago, Paris, London, Rome, Moscow." He then instantly inverted this image by asserting that with this dawn of the nuclear age, "any sizable war had become impossible." From there he proceeded by envisioning the mushroom cloud as a "world-covering, protective umbrella [. . .] shielding us everywhere" and heralding "an era of prosperity such as the world has never dared dream about."[34]

This shockingly extreme example of a psychological inversion of horror and fear into salvation and awe also prepares the ground for the moral inversions that followed and continue to form, as the case of Claude Eatherly demonstrates, a powerful trend in the national nuclear imaginary. Lifton refers to the example of Edward Teller, the physicist in the inner circle of scientists working on the Manhattan Project, who was later called the "father of the hydrogen bomb." Asserting that there should not be any restrictions on nuclear weapons, Teller equated advocacy for restraint on work on the hydrogen bomb with being unfaithful to the tradition of Western civilization. Fears of nuclear annihilation were for Teller nothing but monstrous anxieties that eclipsed the American Dream.

"Nuclear fundamentalism," writes Lifton, "is the ultimate fundamentalism of our time. The 'fundamentals' sacralized are perverse products of technicism and scientism—the worship of technique and science in ways that preclude their human use and block their true intellectual reach."[35] I would add to these sacralized fundamentals the entire range of masculinist phantasmagoria of the bomb as a sublime object of desire. In merging psychologically with the bomb, nuclearists endow themselves with a godlike technological power that fills them with a sense of omnipotence and, paradoxically, immortality. Lifton argues that, in its phantasmatic lure of omnipotence and immortality, the bomb becomes a replacement object for a lack in true spiritual fundamentals and values. "In what may be the ultimate human irony, we seek in a technology of annihilation a source of vitality, of sustained human connectedness or symbolic immortality."[36] Nuclear fundamentalism is thus also a symptom of the psychological fundamentalism of our time.

Ultimately, one could argue that what the nuclear phantasms of immortality cover up is the imagination of extinction. Extinction needs to be thought of not only in terms of what Derrida calls the "remainderless destruction" of an all-out nuclear war but also in terms of what Lifton calls "death in life," that is, the psychic condition in which massive trauma has literally extinguished the capacity to feel. Lifton's interviews reveal that, in the immediate aftermath of a nuclear attack, psychic numbing is a protection against the terror of mass death. Someone unable to feel alive does not need to fear death. However, survivors continue to live a form of death-in-life. Lifton also analyzes the equivalent feeling in the perpetrators of nuclear attacks:

> Patterns of psychic numbing have surrounded the overall creation, testing, and military use (actual or planned) of nuclear weapons: a combination of technical-professional focus and perceived ideological imperative which excludes emotional perceptions of what these weapons do. It is no exaggeration to say that psychic numbing is one of the great problems of our age.[37]

We thus encounter psychic numbing and death-in-life as manifestations of an isomorphic psychic damage that affects both victims and perpetrators, albeit in different ways and to different degrees.

SCALE, SPECIES-LIFE, AND NUCLEAR CRYPTS

In "Reflections on the H-Bomb," Günther Anders writes, "Although we are unchanged anatomically, our completely changed relation to the cosmos and to ourselves has transformed us into a new species." This transformation, however, operates largely at an unconscious level. To trace it and give it a voice is one of the cultural functions of literature and philosophy. In *Hiroshima in America,* Lifton cites a critic who "has observed that the 'usual place' for Hiroshima in Western literature is 'the unconscious.'"[38] We could extend this observation to argue that Hiroshima is part of the political and cultural unconscious of American culture, if not, to a certain extent, of global culture, literature, and the arts more generally. One of the most central functions of literary and artistic works is finding ways to penetrate the protective shell of psychic numbing and to mobilize responses that reconnect recipients with the repressed emotional depth of nuclear destruction. Another is to incite the development of the moral imagination necessary to envision a new ethics for the nuclear age. In "Reflections on the H-Bomb," Anders writes,

> We must strive to increase the capacity and elasticity of our intellectual and emotional faculties, to match the incalculable increase of our productive and destructive powers. Only where these two aspects of human nature are properly balanced can there be responsibility, and moral action and counter-action.[39]

To promote such balancing is also a foremost political task for philosophies, psychologies, and theoretical writings on nuclearism more generally. Moreover, it is the foremost task of literature and the arts to break through the shield of psychic numbing. It is no longer enough to provide empirical data about nuclear necropolitics; its full existential impact on the human species needs to be conveyed in ways that elicit emotional response and moral responsibility without mobilizing defense mechanisms. In the formation of nuclear subjectivities, moral imagination and emotional connectivity are inextricably intertwined and sustain each other. Both of these psychic qualities face three fundamental challenges that interact with each other: overwhelming fear, defensive numbing, and the incommensurability of scale. The sheer scale of nuclear disasters generates overwhelming fear, which, in turn, generates psychic numbing as well as the other previously mentioned psychological defenses, including splitting, denial, doubling, and inversion. Such overwhelming fear is not only generated by the spectacular violence of nuclear catastrophes; it is also triggered by slow nuclear violence. Traci Voyles links this upscaling of emotions to nuclearism's multiscalarity:

> Because it is impossible to see, feel, or taste your exposure to radiation, nuclearism triggers human anxiety to an almost incomparable extent. Nuclearism's affective multiscalarity has produced gut-wrenching fear in communities downwind of nuclear test shots, defiant rage in environmental activists, and apocalyptic bravado in the culprits behind the Cold War's mad doctrine of mutually assured destruction. These multiscalar natures of nuclearism—environmental, spatial, temporal, and affective—make it a particularly apt site for exploring wastelanding as a racial and spatial process of signification.[40]

One of the most crucial challenges presented by scale is how to imagine the possibility, if not the likelihood, of our own extinction as a species and to react in proportionate ways to that imagination. "Because we are the first generation with the power to unleash a world cataclysm, we are also the first to live continually under its threat," writes Anders, thus describing one of the most basic conditions of nuclear subjectivities. "Imagining extinction"[41] at the large scale of nuclear annihilation challenges the boundaries of emotional capability. Imagining extinction at the smaller scale of slow transgenerational nuclear violence, by contrast, poses the temporal difficulty of a visceral comprehension of the uncertain futurity concerning one's children and the generations of children to come after them. It also poses the difficulty of relating emotionally to suffering at such a large temporal distance.

Oral histories of survivors from Hiroshima to Chernobyl and Fukushima—and even of victims of radioactive colonization in the nuclear borderlands—testify to deep-seated reproductive fears. These are, in a sense, anticipatory imaginary manifestations of corporeal transgenerational trauma. Rampant phantasms of the mutant body, particularly among women survivors of nuclear disasters who are or want to become pregnant, reveal a deep transgenerational anxiety in what Lifton calls our "species self." He defines the latter as the recognition of "our *shared fate* as fellow members of a single species in trouble [. . .] a sense of being part of humankind."[42] The nuclear threat, Lifton argues, paradoxically enhances this recognition of a common humanity because of the knowledge that all human beings on earth could be wiped out.

In the next chapter, I propose a more encompassing concept of a transspecies self to extend the anthropocentric focus of Lifton's definition to other species with which humans share the same fate, albeit as the only species with full knowledge of and responsibility for this threat. One could even go further and think of today's challenge as the task to develop a "planetary self," that is, a self that acknowledges the permeable boundaries between the self and its multiple environments. Regarding the latter, Indigenous conceptions of personhood could serve as a model for developing a more encompassing ecology of mind and psyche. Seen from this perspective of a psychic ecology, phantasms of the mutant body emerge as symptoms signaling an ecological disturbance that threatens species-life in its very reproductive capacities.

In their final vision of the aftermath of an all-out nuclear war at the end of *Indefensible Weapons,* Lifton and Erikson write, "For those who manage to stay alive, the effects of radiation may interfere with their capacity to reproduce at all or their capacity to give birth to anything other than grossly deformed infants. But few indeed would have to face that prospect."[43] Unconsciously, however, we are facing that prospect. As the phantasms of the mutant body show, the fear of irreversible genetic and reproductive damage is already firmly rooted in the cultural unconscious.

Indefensible Weapons ends with an appendix written by Lifton and Kai Erikson. Designed to break through psychic numbing, the appendix offers an exercise in imagining extinction after a nuclear disaster. The authors pose the question "Would the survivors envy the dead?" to which they give the following answer: "No, they would be incapable of such feelings. They would not so much envy as, inwardly and outwardly, resemble the dead."[44]

How would survivors mourn their contaminated lives and lands? How would they mourn the lives lost to nuclear madness, theirs and those of other species? How would they mourn their forfeited futures and the extinctions they imagine? There is a simple answer. It is impossible properly to mourn these losses. Nuclear entrapment has also fostered a profound inability to mourn. This is not to say that survivors wouldn't feel pain and grief and sadness about the damage humans have brought to the planet. Rather, it is to say that their grief, just like ours today, will never be proportionate to that damage.

A profound inability to mourn is, as Lifton and Erikson show, already among us, inevitably paralyzing some of our most compassionate emotions. The very range of emotions has been narrowed to a scale that allows people to live their daily lives until the bitter end. But this curtailing of emotions comes in the form of an injurious psychic splitting and collective denial. It is a schizoid splitting that creates an internal crypt that houses the shadow lives of everything that cannot be grieved, the shadow lives of foreclosed futures, of contaminated land, water, air, and bodies. The shadow lives of radioactive ghosts poison us from inside. This is what Herman Agoyo, the Indigenous activist from the nuclear borderlands, identified as psychic toxicity. In *Death in Life*, Lifton describes such a toxicity of the mind in the case of a Hiroshima survivor: "The embittered world-view becomes his total vision of the way things were and the way things are. Not having been able to 'vomit' his 'bitter water,' such a survivor finds his entire psychic life poisoned by it."[45]

The "nuclear crypt"[46] forms a space of haunting, a haunting that comes from both past and future, from outside as well as inside. The legacy of nuclear violence haunts not only its actual victims but, knowingly or unknowingly, everyone on the planet, including future generations. In *The Shell and the Kernel*,[47] Abraham and Torok envision a crypt in which people bury unspeakable events or unbearable, if not disavowed, losses or injuries incurred during violent histories. In the twentieth century, Auschwitz and Hiroshima are the names that designate such unspeakable histories of violence. Both also stand for the first instances of technologically induced mass extermination. "In the extermination camps natural death was completely eliminated," writes Anders, and he concludes that, as a consequence, "all men are exterminable." The crucial step from Auschwitz to Hiroshima, he argues, lies in the fact that "what is exterminable today is not 'merely' all men, but mankind as a whole."[48] It is this shift that inaugurates the nuclear age.

Abraham and Torok argue that any form of unnatural death creates ghosts that come to haunt the living. The complete elimination of natural death in Auschwitz and the fear of nuclear annihilation, a manmade unnatural event, create a collective haunting from both past and future. Formed in response to a refusal or inability to mourn, nuclear crypts harbor radioactive ghosts like an undead vibrant matter.[49] Just like the material half-life of radioactive matter, the psychic half-life of nuclear trauma approximates notions of an immortal force. Nuclear trauma resists integration into the psychic fabric. It is virtually impossible appropriately to mourn the loss of a prenuclear world that provided humans with a sense of permanence and transgenerational continuity. Yet, while we may disavow the loss of such a world, we keep its memory psychically alive, if only unconsciously. Nuclear crypts are collective crypts, formed by the silences and secrets of nuclear necropolitics. They emerge in the wake of disavowed nuclear violence, blurring the boundaries between psychic and social life and voiding the world and its forms of expression of their vital force. Those who encapsulate silences and secrets in collective crypts psychically merge with the ghosts they harbor. In a complex process of identification, crypts subject those who harbor them to a psychic state that increasingly resembles the living dead.

Finally, we could say that the crypt prevents us from facing the Angelus Novus of our time, the Angel of Nuclear History. Is the angel staring at, yet moving away from, the world's nuclear contamination, his face turned toward the past? Does he, as Benjamin suggests, see one single catastrophe, which keeps piling wreckage upon wreckage and hurls it in front of his feet? Would the angel like to awaken the dead and make whole what has been smashed? And is it a nuclear storm that is blowing from Paradise, getting caught in his wings with such violence that he can no longer close them? Benjamin writes, "The storm irresistibly propels him into the future to which his back is turned, while the pile of debris before him grows skyward. This storm is what we call progress."[50] Can we find a better image for the nuclear storm that pushes life toward its final extinction, while the Angel of History looks at the pile of radioactive waste that is growing skyward?

TRANSSPECIES SELVES

Intimacies, Extimacies, Animacies

In the early 1970s, I volunteered as a therapist in the Psychiatric Hospital at Arezzo, Italy, under the direction of Agostino Pirella. The hospital participated in the famous anti-institutional psychiatric movement, initiated by Franco Basaglia. One of my patients there was a.middle-aged psychotic man whom I will call Guiliano. Always highly agitated, this man communicated with me about his persecutory inner world in a manic style and a hybrid mix of European languages. Sometimes he handed me coded messages in a multilingual private language, designed to warn me of imminent attacks by constantly mutating alien forces. One of his most prominent recurring doomsday scenarios was the invasion of Italy and our hospital by a gigantic insect army, which he pictured as the last survivors of a nuclear war. These larger-than-life insects—giant ants, cicadas, dragonflies, and toxic mosquitoes—were now bent on eradicating the few remaining humans on the planet. Guiliano awaited this army in a state of panic, throwing himself on the ground or trying to pull me aside to hide in the bushes, all the while shouting his alarming messages to the doctors, staff, and other patients. In his calmer states, he would draw the insects with black pencil on huge sheets of white paper. Sometimes they had humanoid faces, staring at their viewers with cold eyes. Often there were tiny humans writhing on the ground, crushed by their insect legs or poisoned by their stingers. Only the dragonflies seemed to hover above the scene, serenely, as if from a position of distant observers. Guiliano believed that his purpose on earth was to save the surviving humans from the extinction of the species.

TRANSSPECIES ENCOUNTERS AND PHANTASMS OF METAMORPHOSIS

Phantasms of metamorphosis and transspecies selves are as old as human storytelling. They abound in the cultural unconscious of the most diverse cultures around the world, challenging the stable boundaries of the human as a species. Modernist literature and art generate a flourishing resurgence of this fascination, inventing transspecies characters and artistic bodies. Mobilizing unconscious phantasms of a biological, mental, and emotional traffic across species boundaries, they invite us to expand the imaginary boundaries of the human toward other species in ever-new experimental ways.

Taking readers through the nightmare of "becoming insect," Kafka's Gregor Samsa, the human who metamorphosed into a gigantic insect, has become an iconic figure in the cultural imaginary. Importantly, Kafka interpellates his readers to take this metamorphosis literally: "As Gregor Samsa awoke one morning from uneasy dreams he found himself transformed in his bed into a gigantic insect. [. . .] It was no dream."[1]

Julio Cortázar's short story "Axolotl" explores a man's fascination with this tiny amphibian creature, pushing his growing obsession to the point of a phantasmatic merger in which the human protagonist is becoming axolotl: "There was a time when I thought a great deal about the axolotls. I went to see them in the aquarium at the Jardin des Plantes and stayed for hours watching them, observing their immobility, their faint movements. Now I am an axolotl."[2]

Liu Sola, in her short story "The Last Spider," features an arachnid protagonist endowed with a transspecies consciousness and voice who feels disgust upon realizing that, when he annihilates his fellow spiders, he has become part human: "When I'd annihilated my opponents, I'd look at their carcasses apologetically, feeling disgusted with myself because I was no longer a spider of fine pedigree but one infected with a human disease who had overcome his opponents with sixty percent spider force and forty percent human force."[3]

Other works are about transspecies reproduction. In "Confessions of a Bioterrorist,"[4] Charis Cussins relates the adventure of a fictional anthropologist working in a frozen zoo, designed like a high-tech posthuman ark, in which specimens of endangered animal species are kept in a frozen state, awaiting revival in the distant future. When the anthropologist's work awakens her desire for transspecies procreation, she impregnates herself with a bonobo embryo and records the auto-ethnography of the first transspecies birth. Finally, Cuban artist Roberto Fabelo makes larger-than-life sculptures of gigantic cockroaches, some of them with human heads, that he displays on the sidewalk and the walls of the Museo de Bellas Artes in Havana.[5] Titling his art installation *Survival*, he ironically invokes scientific research about the higher resilience of insects against radioactivity and the related urban legend that it is the cockroaches that will survive humans in a nuclear war.

All of these works highlight the prominence of phantasms of the mutant body and transspecies visions in the cultural and particularly nuclear imaginary. Perhaps they reveal a cultural fantasy, if not desire, that something of our species would survive a while longer in the form of mutant humanoids. These images and stories belong to the expanding phantasmagoria of the mutant body that recalls the fragile and permeable boundaries of species and their embodiment. Mutant figures like Fabelo's life-size humanoid insects are also reminders of the fear that certain insects might be the species that survive humans in a nuclear holocaust. With their human faces, Fabelo's giant cockroaches emerge as imaginary companion species in the nuclear ecology of mind. Are these our consoling phantasies?

With the exception of Donna Haraway's "Camille 5," to which I return later, the stories and artworks of transspecies bodies I analyze are intimately linked to reproductive anxieties, especially those concerned with genetic damage and mutations as well as related fears about the survival of the species. In a chapter titled "A Republic of Insects and Grass," Jonathan Schell discusses the possible survival of the insect class after an imagined ten-thousand-megaton attack:

> Most of the mammals of the United States would be killed off. The lethal doses for birds are in roughly the same range as those for mammals, and birds, too, would be killed off. [. . .] The one class of animals containing a number of species quite likely to survive, at least in the short run, is the insect class.[6]

Schell's speculative fiction of "a republic of insects and grass" presents a dystopian postapocalyptic scene in which millions of corpses litter the landscape, water and food are polluted, and the surviving population is suffering from radiation sickness, open wounds, and compromised immune systems that make them vulnerable to epidemics. "The corpses would also feed a fast-growing population of insects, and insects happen to be the prime vector of disease."[7] And yet, even insects are not invulnerable to nuclear or other ecological disasters. Scientists have argued that ecological degradation, particularly ozone depletion, "might bring about the blinding of the world's animals. [. . .] The disorientation of insects would be fateful not only for them but for plant life."[8]

Jonathan Schell's speculative republic of insects as well as the flourishing of transspecies selves in modernist and postmodern literature and art testify to the nuclear age's pervasive preoccupation with extinction and phantasmatic survival. At the heart of this imaginary that features a deathworld of corpses taken over by a "republic of insects," and the flourishing literature and art scene populated by transspecies bodies and selves, is an awareness of the entanglement of species in relation to threats of extinction and the concomitant struggle for survival. The concern with transspecies relationships and survival, however, affects the cultural imaginary more generally, including science studies. In this context, the nuclear imaginary plays a crucial role because of its preoccupation with both genetic mutations and the survival of species, if not planetary life. One of the most prominent examples is the work of famous Swiss science artist Cornelia Hesse-Honegger, whose insect paintings straddle the boundaries between art and science.

"The first time she saw a deformed leaf bug, so tiny, so damaged, so irrelevant, she lost her mental balance, her perspective, her sense of scale and proportion. For a moment, she was unsure if she was looking at herself or the animal."[9] This is how anthropologist Hugh Raffles, in *Insectopedia*, relates an exchange he had with Hesse-Honegger, whose concrete art depicts mutant insects in radioactively contaminated areas. We may read this artist's reaction to her first encounter with a mutant insect as exemplary of the challenges of transspecies encounters in nuclear territories, challenges that impact the very boundaries of nuclear subjectivities.

The fact that Hesse-Honegger lost her "sense of scale and proportion" reveals that the challenge scale presents to the boundaries of human imagination operates not only at the level of large-scale annihilating events, such as nuclear war or destruction caused by radioactive substances whose half-lives extend over millions of years. We need to add the almost immeasurable long-term slow violence as a result of radioactive emissions from uranium mines, nuclear power plants, and the storage of nuclear waste. Finally, scale presents a challenge to attempts to measure, let alone imagine, the damage inflicted at the molecular level to cells and reproductive systems. In more tangible ways, scale also operates at the level of what humans might see (from their perspectival bias) as a minor form of nuclear violence done to one of the smallest living species, the insects. However, what humans might perceive as a small-scale nuclear violence affecting tiny insects appears

FIGURE 18. Cornelia Hesse-Honegger, *Harlequin Bug from Three Mile Island, Pennsylvania,* 1991.

magnanimous in terms of its impact on their bodies. Accordingly, their deformations elicit a seemingly disproportionate response, causing the human witness, as Hesse-Honegger describes, to lose her mental balance, her sense of scale and proportion.

We learn, however, that the artist's singularly intense transference is linked to a traumatic encounter with deformity after the birth of her son. At the time, the doctor came into the room and made a drawing for her to show that her child had a clubfoot.[10] Many years later, Hesse-Honegger saw the first deformed leaf bug that had a crippled foot, and it provoked a delayed reaction to her earlier experience. Hesse-Honegger's own experience of having given birth to a child with a disability elicits such an intense identification with the leaf bug that a veritable sense of merging causes her to be "unsure if she was looking at herself or the animal."[11]

From a psychoanalytic perspective, this extreme reaction appears as a belated response to the trauma of learning about her child's disability. Seen in this way, the leaf bug presumably triggered an incidence of "deferred action" (*Nachträglichkeit*), that is, a delayed reaction to an original trauma so intense that at the time the proportionate emotion could not be consciously registered. However, the unconscious memory trace of such a traumatic dissociation can be mobilized at a later time, often triggered via association by a comparable smaller-scale trauma. Freud's example for such a deferred action is the case of a man who could not shed a tear after his father's death but fell completely apart at the later funeral of a distant neighbor. In a similar vein, after her son's birth, Hesse-Honegger might have had to contain her pain and shock over his clubfoot, only to see it released much later in the encounter with the leaf bug.

Hesse-Honegger's unsettling encounter with this first deformed insect leads to her lifelong interest in insect mutation, which she channels into a veritable passion for developing a unique art form to record their existence. Once she realized that the mutations were connected with radioactivity, she began to visit areas in the vicinity of nuclear reactors in Europe and the United States, including Leibstadt and Aargau in Switzerland, Chernobyl in Ukraine, Cap de la Hague in Normandy, Sellafield in England, Hanford in Washington, and Three Mile Island in Pennsylvania. While her antinuclear commitment grew with the progression of her work, she wanted to leave her paintings as free as possible from her subjective transference and political views. This was her way of aiming at an aesthetic recording capable of grasping these insects on their own terms. As a result, she leaves her paintings open for a multiplicity of reactions by viewers, who inevitably bring their own nuclear subjectivities to bear upon the artistic engagement.

In my own response, one of Hesse-Honegger's paintings carried me straight back to the advent of nuclear power at the time I was growing up in a small German border town near Switzerland. It is the painting of a deformed scorpion fly found in Küssaburg, in Germany, close to the Leibstadt nuclear power plant in Aargau, Switzerland, right across

FIGURE 19. Cornelia Hesse-Honegger, *Scorpion Fly near Nuclear Power Plant Leibstadt, Switzerland,* 1988.

the border from Germany. This is where I grew up and where, during my high school years, I witnessed the beginning construction of a giant towering plant and the controversies it triggered among the people living in the vicinity. One can see the power plant from the Vitibuck, a hill in the forest behind my parents' house. People talked about plans for the new Leibstadt nuclear power plant with high anxiety, worrying about radioactivity and safety.

Preparations for the construction began in the early 1960s with a concept of river water cooling, using water from the Rhine. During my high school years, we used to swim right in the plant's vicinity. In 1971, however, after new safety regulations prohibited river water cooling, a cooling tower was built instead. Then the Three Mile Island nuclear accident happened in 1979. In response, Switzerland increased its safety regulations, and the plant's completion was delayed even further. After eleven years of construction, it finally started full operation in 1984.

As far as I can remember, the debates about the Leibstadt plant overshadowed debates about another plant, namely, the nearby Beznau nuclear power plant, which, in fact, began its energy production in 1969 as the first nuclear power plant in the area and, as I learned much later, is the world's oldest nuclear power plant in commercial operation. The Leibstadt plant, however, generated considerably more concern in nearby communities, partly because it was supposed to be much larger than the Beznau one and partly because the degree of information about nuclear dangers was growing with the antinuclear movement. Eventually, both plants' final operation was negatively impacted by the Chernobyl nuclear disaster.

I found Cornelia Hesse-Honegger's painting a few years ago. It depicts a rather beautiful, if deformed, garden bug from the Küssaburg, a popular tourist site on a hill with the ruins of a medieval castle. Küssaburg was the very place where my family used to go on our Sunday excursions. Hesse-Honegger started collecting her bugs in 1987, a few years after the plant was in full operation. Just like in the vicinity of the other power plants she visited, she found mutant bugs near Leibstadt, which is not too far from Beznau. The vicinity of the two plants may well have compounded the mutations. The painting of the mutant insect Hesse-Honegger found in Küssaburg shows a tumor-like growth on its left side with a black dot at its center. In addition, the bug's entire neck plate seems deformed. I thought about the rumors in our town concerning increased rates of cancer and deformations in children born after the operation of power plants. People were carried away by high anxiety, and sometimes their legitimate fears grew to irrational proportions. They felt helpless in the face of what they saw as an inevitable development. I was also thinking of the artist's son again. There are many hypotheses about what causes a clubfoot to develop. Most assume that it involves environmental or genetic factors, or a combination of both. While studying and painting her leaf bugs, Hesse-Honegger must have wondered about the genetic damage radioactivity causes in humans, especially since it is known that mutations in genes involved in muscle development are risk factors for clubfoot.

Hugh Raffles dedicates an entire chapter of *Insectopedia* to Chernobyl, focusing on Hesse-Honegger's work. He identifies another traumatic origin for her encounter with the leaf bug. Twenty years earlier, she had worked as a scientific illustrator at the Institute of Zoology in Zurich and was asked to draw the so-called Quasimodo mutants, that is, insects that had been fed contaminated food to induce mutations for research purposes. This work had come to haunt Hesse-Honegger ever since, making her particularly sensitive to the encounter with the mutant insects in the vicinity of nuclear reactors and disaster sites. These haunting connections from her past thus triggered a special care for insects, that is, victims from another species usually not high on the list of human attention.

The ethics of care that becomes visible in Hesse-Honegger's work illustrates a crucial dimension of transspecies responsibility rarely found in nuclear politics. Earlier I argued that the sheer magnitude of the nuclear potential for destruction pushes the limits of human imagination. A perhaps even more insurmountable limit is reached in relation to care and compassion. If psychic numbing already paralyzes the care for human suffering at a distance—including the suffering of generations to come—it does so even more radically when it comes to the care of other species. This became evident, for example, when Astrid Schrader taught Hugh Raffles's chapter on Hesse-Honegger and her students asked how one could possibly care about deformed leaf bugs in light of the immensity of human suffering after the Chernobyl nuclear disaster.[12] But Hesse-Honegger's exceptional extension of the limits of concern, care, and responsibility is precisely why her work makes a crucial intervention about the scale of nuclear necropolitics.

Moreover, her work with the damaged insect populations generates an extreme form of closeness and intimacy. The latter is indispensable for conveying the stakes of care for other species in terms that make knowledge and emotion inseparable. Hesse-Honegger vividly describes what this process looks like for her:

> Although I was theoretically convinced that radioactivity affects nature, I still could not imagine what it would look like. Now these poor creatures were lying under my microscope. I was shocked. It

was as if someone had drawn back the curtain. Every day I discovered more damaged plants and bugs. [. . .] The horror of what I had found tortured me in my sleep and gave me nightmares. I began to collect and paint feverishly.[13]

To react in this emotionally involved and compassionate way, one needs to "draw back the curtain," that is, the defensive screen built to protect oneself from the horror of what one would otherwise have to confront. Penetrating the screen of defenses requires a rare intimate connection, not only with humans, but also with other species that suffer at a distance. While we would not be able to function on a daily basis at the level of such intimate connection, Hesse-Honegger's intervention suggests that we need to practice breaking this screen temporarily and at regular intervals so that what we see behind it can become the basis of ethical consciousness and political action. Once again, we encounter in Hesse-Honegger's work a crucial function of the arts, namely, to break the defensive screen of psychic numbing, including the defenses that facilitate trauma fatigue, even if only temporarily.

To reverse the deadening effect of psychic numbing, Hesse-Honegger's work further suggests, we need a particular aesthetic practice that is transformational to how we see and read. Hesse-Honegger is foremost an artist when she paints her mutant insects, but she cannot be the artist she is without reaching across the boundaries of disciplinary screens. She thus also becomes a scientist, integrating both her artistic and scientific practice in a particular aesthetics of care.

The groundbreaking nature of Hesse-Honegger's aesthetic practice lies in its delicate balance between proximity and distance. To attain the precision so crucial to her work, she goes to great lengths to reduce the traces of her subjectivity, transference, emotional involvement, and passion. One of her ultimate goals is to see without prejudice, including not only the prejudice of her political convictions as an antinuclear science activist but also the prejudice of conventional forms of seeing.

Aesthetically, Hesse-Honegger's strongest influence is the concrete art movement, especially Kazimir Malevich's nonobjective art, known for its attempt to break with the conservatism of representational art. This art pursues and refines the goal of concrete art to let the work speak of nothing but itself, thus leaving the viewer complete interpretive freedom. The nonobjective art movement informs Hesse-Honegger's almost exclusive emphasis on formal aesthetics, including color, geomet-

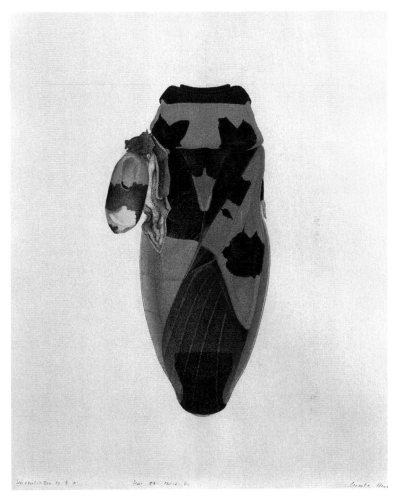

FIGURE 20. Cornelia Hesse-Honegger, *Scentless Plant Bug Environs, Paul Scherrer Institute, Switzerland,* 1989.

ric form, angle, and a quasi-cubist composition that de- and recomposes the insect bodies for the sake of making the mutations visible to the untrained eye. Following this modernist antirepresentationalism, Hesse-Honegger practices an aesthetics of defamiliarization to train herself to see as if for the first time.

Yet, as Raffles reports, "subjectivity proved to be a stubborn presence."[14] Despite the artist's technical efforts to free her paintings from subjective involvement and presence, including environmental politics, personal care, and passion, traces of subjectivity inevitably inscribe themselves in particular choices of objects and artistic form. It is as if these choices inform Hesse-Honegger's modernist portraiture in a way that invites, if not trains, viewers to see insects otherwise, as if for the first time.

Hugh Raffles describes this aesthetic practice in terms of a dance on the tightrope of shifting intimacies. Almost paradoxically, Hesse-Honegger's most intimate connection to the insects emerges when she effaces her intimate engagement with individual leaf bugs, thus discarding her personal attachment in the process of artistic production. Raffles writes,

> Yet somehow the portraits also achieve a doubling, a breaching of the line between human and animal. [. . .] Her portraits [. . .] transcend species difference by recognizing a conjoined fate, a common witnessing, a shared victimhood. It is quite unsettling: the eye of the painter and the viewer suspended between the clinical and the empathetic, a loss of stable distinction between subjects and objects, between humans and insects, between intimacy and distance.[15]

Just as Hesse-Honegger's aesthetics transcends the boundaries of representational art, this particular intimacy transcends the boundaries of identification. The portraits do not simply elicit a conventional empathy with the mutant insects as suffering a similar fate as humans, a form of empathy that would ultimately remain confined within the boundaries of an anthropocentric perspective. Rather, the portraits elicit a unique form of care for the radically incommensurate other. We will never know what these insects feel or whether they know pain and suffering as we do. But we experience pain in witnessing the violation done to their bodies and the human-induced deformations that affect both their individual existence and their species-being.

If we follow Marx in assuming that species-being is always determined by specific social and historical conditions, we might wonder whether we have reached a stage at which the massive intervention into the natural order of things forces us to recognize the entanglement of the fate of humans with that of other species and therefore compels us to extend our sense of species-being to include all living species. Analyzing Robert J. Lifton's notion of "species self" as an extension of the individual and communal self, I argue that we must extend the notion of species self to include other species as well as humans. This would mean facing the challenge of thinking of humans as transspecies beings—not in

FIGURE 21. Cornelia Hesse-Honegger, *Damsel Bugs from within Paul Scherrer Institute, Switzerland*, 1990–91.

the sense of a posthuman transspecies reproduction but in the sense of the human entanglement with other species. As corporeal, sensuous beings, humans share vulnerability and mortality with other species and are dependent on sustainable environments for their well-being. The extent to which humans have threatened the life of a sustainable planet by exploiting its resources generates a particular responsibility and obligation to care. We are, in other words, at a historical conjuncture where our ethics of care needs to include transspecies care.

Hesse-Honegger's art can be seen as practicing a concrete form of such care. The radical alterity of her portraits creates an almost paradoxical intimacy that places viewers in an experimental subject position by opening the boundaries of subjectivity toward a genuine transspecies self that includes human and nonhuman species. In "Abyssal Intimacies and Temporalities of Care: How (Not) to Care about Deformed Leaf Bugs in the Aftermath of Chernobyl," Astrid Schrader draws on Derrida's notion of "abyssal intimacy" to analyze Hesse-Honegger's particular form of nonanthropocentric intimacy and care. Abyssal intimacy requires a radical passivity, an active withdrawal of the self in encounters with the incommensurable alterity of other beings with whom we nonetheless share a fundamental vulnerability and mortality.

The radical passivity in abyssal intimacy allows for human–insect relations to be both intimate and wholly other[16] and is therefore central to an experience of compassion. It is linked to a nonanthropocentric form of *curiositas*[17] based on the desire to know insects (or other species) differently, that is, to approach them—as much as humanly possible—on their own terms. According to Schrader, abyssal intimacy thus stands for "a mode of engagement and a new kind of relationship between humans and other animals that is neither continuous nor discontinuous. [. . .] Abyssal intimacy describes a creative engagement that relies on the withdrawal of the self, a passivity that enables an active listening, an opening to surprises"[18]—or, as Schrader states in her conclusion, "an active listening requires a withdrawal of the self, an exercise in passivity and engagement at the same time."[19]

Interestingly, what Schrader describes here is very close to the familiar psychoanalytic mode of attention. According to Winfred Bion, for example, "the purest form of listening is to listen without *memory* or *desire*."[20] This form of listening is designed to practice an attunement to the unconscious of the analysand to facilitate an encounter on his or her own terms, that is, as if for the first time—without memory or desire. The radical passivity required in the analyst's encounter with an analysand thus suspends judgment and prejudice, including the prejudice of preconceived psychoanalytic categories. The encounter involves, in other words, a particular ethics of care that is attuned to what we do not yet know and what we therefore encounter as radically other. In this context, becoming affected entails first and foremost becoming attuned to difference. In artistic or scientific encounters, it also entails encountering the other as if from within an experimental system.

On the other hand, becoming thus affected may feel like temporarily losing oneself in the other, to the extent that one is becoming other.

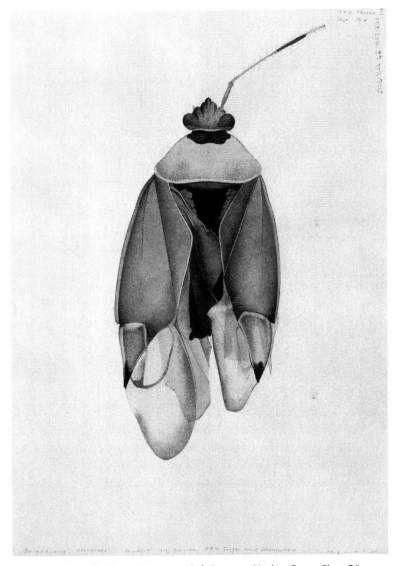

FIGURE 22. Cornelia Hesse-Honegger, *Soft Bug near Nuclear Power Plant Gösgen, Switzerland*, 1988.

Hesse-Honegger describes the process of losing herself in the insect as feeling extremely connected, feeling a bond so deep that it appears as if "she herself had once been such a creature—a leaf bug—'and had a body remembering.'"[21] This extreme and intimate connection in an experience of the radical other also recalls the Lacanian notion of "extimacy" that insists on the presence of exteriority in every intimate encounter. In the deepest recesses of the subject's sense of interiority, Lacan insists, there is always an element of exteriority and radical otherness. There is no intimacy without extimacy. Learning to become attuned to the radical difference of a leaf bug may thus also attune us with more openness and curiosity to difference more generally. In terms of such a transspecies ethics, we could argue that this nonanthropocentric form of intimate encounter also works toward decolonizing transspecies relationships. It is a step toward an ecology of the transspecies self.

In *The Imperative,* Alphonso Lingis describes transspecies relationships in terms of a summons by what appears as alien to us. Modern technologies, he argues, may help us in our extimate encounters with other species:

> We go forth to outlying regions of the alien with the prostheses our sciences have devised to enable us to see with the eyes of eagles and wasps, the sonar echolocation of bats and the sixth sense of fish, the magnetic or cosmic sense of migratory birds and insects, the sensitivity of single cells or single molecules in those bats and fish. The millimeter-wide gardens in which protozoa range and for which technology has devised for us microscopes summon us; the great orbits of the planets and the comets for which technology has devised for us detached honeycomb eyes in space capsules summon us, as they had the Babylonians, the Nasca, and the Aztecs.[22]

For Lingis, transspecies encounters require a heightened sensitivity for both small-scale and large-scale beings and hyperobjects. Tracing encounters with the alien and the human fascination with other planets and the cosmos back to the Babylonians, the Nasca, and the Aztecs, Lingis sees the summoning by the underlying *curiositas* as an intimation that human transspecies selves might be as old as human history. Some of the necessary sensitivity and connection to other species might have been lost in the wake of industrialization, urban living, and the concomitant increasing alienation from nature. But, as Lingis suggests, this connection can be remobilized, even with the help of technologies. Lingis's notion of perceiving "with the sensitivity of single cells or single molecules," moreover, suggests that our molar modes of perception are not enough for encounters at the molecular scale.

This also holds for the perception of (nuclear) time. In "Troubling Time/s and Ecologies of Nothingness," Karen Barad writes, "What is the scale of time? When the cascading energies of the nuclei that were split in an atomic bomb explosion live on in the interior and exterior of collective and individual bodies, how can anything like a fixed, singular, and external notion of time retain its relevance or even its meaning? In a flash, bodies near Ground Zero 'become molecular'—nay, particulate, vaporized—while *hibakusha,* in the immediate vicinity and downwind, ingest radioactive isotopes that indefinitely rework body molecules all the while manufacturing future cancers, like little time bombs waiting to go off."[23] Considering the scale of matter, Barad then adds, "The indeterminacy of space, time, and matter at the core of quantum field theory troubles the scalar distinction between the world of subatomic particles and that of colonialism, war, nuclear physics research, and environmental destruction."[24] Lingis's notion of learning to perceive with the sensitivity of single molecules highlights that "becoming molecular" might also help to attune perception to the scale of time and matter that Barad invokes. Moreover, it might enhance attunement to the entanglement between species that calls for a notion of "transspecies selves." Suggesting a "relational-ontology sensibility to questions of time, memory, and history,"[25] Barad asserts that the nuclear story needs to trace "a journey across spacetime, nation states, species being, and questions of being/nonbeing."[26]

ANIMACIES

At the molecular scale, the notion of a transspecies self includes the awareness that humans are transspecies selves not only through their relationships to other species but also because they already harbor other species in their bodies, including the bacteria without which they would not be able to live. While molecular perception and thinking heighten transspecies sensitivity and ethics, they might also increase awareness of dangers that occur at the molecular scale, including the dangers of the "alien" toxins humans introduce into the environment, among them the radioactive substances that affect the bodies of humans, animals, and plants at the molecular level.

Drawing an arc from intimacy and extimacy to animacy will help to convey a clearer picture of radioactivity as vibrant matter. "Animal and science studies have offered tools through which we can rethink the significance of molecular, cellular, animal, vegetable, or nonhuman life," writes Mel Chen in *Animacies.*[27]

Chen's notion of animacy allows one to foreground the particular dimension of Hesse-Honegger's artistic work that concerns the transformative affection of bodies by this alien vibrant matter. We may see the portraits of leaf bugs as prime examples revealing the type of embodiment that Chen describes in terms of a "marriage of bodies and chemicals."[28] Mutations are an extreme manifestation of such a "marriage," inscribed at the molecular level of cells. They are concrete embodiments of what Jasbir Puar calls the "bio-necro political"[29] aspect of contemporary life. From the perspective of animacy, radioactive substances as vibrant matter that mutates bodies and minds appear as a force that compels one to envision entirely new forms of entanglement. Chen describes the challenge in terms of a new ecology of mind, body, and affect:

> Environmental toxicity and environmental degradation are figured as slow and dreadful threats to flesh, mind, home, and state. Myths of immunity are challenged, and sometimes dismantled, by transnationally figured communicable diseases, some of them apparently borne by nonhuman animals.[30]

All of these threats are magnified by radioactive contamination since it operates at such a large scale that it includes the threat of planetary survival. Thinking in terms of animacy thus adds a new facet to the problem of scale that is so central to the nuclear imaginary.

The concept of animacy is particularly attuned to dealing with nuclear issues because it enables a vision that encompasses both large- and small-scale effects. Or, to put it differently, animacy is concerned not only with the large-scale nuclear challenges mentioned earlier but also with small-scale molecular ones. "The concept of 'animacy' can be regarded as some kind of assumed cognitive scale extending from human through animal to inanimate,"[31] writes cognitive linguist Mutsumi Yamamoto. Informed by "philosophical considerations of life, care, and molecularity,"[32] the concept of animacy is implicated in political questions of the distribution of power and the recognition of different forms of life, challenging one to "rethink the significance of molecular, cellular, animal, vegetable, or nonhuman life."[33]

In relation to the nuclear threat to human, animal, or plant bodies, animacy addresses the biopolitical impact of radioactive pollutants on bodily integrity and health as well as the emergent illnesses induced by them, including mutations. It also addresses ways of relating to such illnesses and forms of (nonanthropocentric) care. Chen's notion of "molecular intimacies,"[34] for example, allows one to envision how people enter intimate relationships with the alien, inimical, and sometimes lethal toxic substances and forces they host inside their bodies. It is as if they carry a silent killer inside. These forces form a material manifestation of death-in-life that affects bodies and minds alike.

Finally, Chen also uses the concept of animacy to address the abjection and stigmatization usually associated with mutant bodies, their deformities and illnesses, and their toxicity, or, as Chen calls it, "toxic queerness": "I reside in this so-called negative zone, one of abjection, racial marking, toxic queerness, and illness, to think about the epistemic riches of possibility within."[35] Hesse-Honegger explores such riches in the mode of a unique form of artistic knowledge and creation. Unlike most nuclear aesthetics, hers belongs to the genealogy of an aesthetics of the beautiful rather than an aesthetics of the sublime. Instead of exploring the limits of human imagination, she finds and creates beauty that exhibits mutant bodies without the judgmental gaze of their social abjection. She thus refuses to submit to animacy hierarchies that establish which things can or cannot affect or be affected. Her portraits show the concrete affection of insect bodies by radioactive fallout, and she, in turn, lets herself (and induces her viewers to) become affected by them. She insists on including mutant bodies as a new norm in a world in which the very order of things has been violated. "A 'normal' world's order is lost when, for instance, things that can harm you permanently are not even visible to the naked eye,"[36] says Chen. Hesse-Honegger's portraits make the invisible visible through its dramatic effects, its production of mutant bodies.

In *The Politics of Life Itself,* Nicolas Rose argues that contemporary biopolitics must now be considered *molecular* in character. This view is confirmed by the fact that radioactivity has become part of our bodies, our earth, water, and air. It has become part of what Michelle Murphy has described as "chemical infrastructures."[37] Murphy defines chemical infrastructures as "the spatial and temporal distributions of industrially produced chemicals as they are produced and consumed, and as they become mobile in the atmosphere, settle into landscapes, travel in water ways, leach from commodities, are regulated (or not) by states, monitored by experts, engineered by industries, absorbed by bodies, metabolized physiologically, and as they bioaccumulate in food changes, break down over time, or persist." Needless to say, radioactivity is a prime agent in the makeup of chemical infrastructures, partaking in all the processes Murphy identifies. Its spatial and temporal extension and persistence open up the haunting scale of radioactive half-lives. It may cause immediate responses in the aftermath of nuclear attacks or disasters and/or long-term effects that take decades and, through reproductive damage, generations to manifest. Radioactivity is a form of slow violence that injures human and other organisms, ecologies, and the planet's atmosphere. And, as I argued earlier, contrary to claims by nuclear industries, it also contributes to climate change. Analyzing the temporal aspect of chemical infrastructures, Murphy emphasizes latency in addition to slowness and persistence. Latency refers to the time lag between radioactive exposure and the manifestation of symptoms, a lag that can extend over generations. This transgenerational nuclear legacy is part of what Murphy's concept of "distributed reproduction" is able to grasp. The very politics of reproduction is thus entangled with the radioactive infrastructures generated by nuclear necropolitics.

Apart from the persistent fears of another nuclear war or catastrophe, it is this time lag and the role radioactivity plays in distributed reproduction that contributes to what I have called a *nuclear haunting from the future*. "Through latency, the future is already altered," Murphy argues. Moreover, the myriad sites of nuclear tests, accidents, leaks, and waste—or even, as Hesse-Honegger demonstrates, the vicinities of nuclear power plants and, we could add, the radioactive substances in bodies and organisms—become material archives of the planet's pervasive radioactive contamination.

Radioactivity as part of our chemical infrastructure has thus become part of our minds, our affects, our nuclear subjectivities. Seen in this way, we could say that Hesse-Honegger makes an intervention in contemporary molecular biopolitics by rendering visible otherwise invisible xenobiotic substances, that is, substances that are improper, inherently alien, and damaging to living bodies. Seen through Hesse-Honegger's portraits, Chen's notion of "molecular intimacies" becomes permeated by molecular extimacies. We already harbor this xenobiotic substance, radioactivity, inside us. The radically incommensurable other lives within us like a radioactive ghost that changes us from inside. Whether we know it or not, it is transforming us into mutant selves. Perhaps one day this form of extimacy will become truly unlivable.

The increasing importance of the molecular in scientific and theoretical discourses, including Rose's insistence that contemporary biopolitics itself has become molecular, has led critics to argue that we are witnessing a molecular turn in the life sciences that inaugurates a new episteme more generally. Interestingly, the molecular turn—just like the invention of the atomic bomb—was already prefigured in science fiction. As early as 1961, Robert Moore Williams published *The Day They H-Bombed Los Angeles,* figuring a malignant mutation of protein molecules that came into existence as a consequence of the radioactive contamination left behind after the American H-bomb testing in the South Pacific. Giant mutant protein molecules figure as characters in William's novel, arriving on the surface of ocean waves to invade Southern California and turn its population into cannibalistic zombies.

At the time Williams's novel appeared, phantasms of the mutant body flourished in the popular imaginary in response to the pervasive anxieties and ontological insecurity generated by the knowledge of the bomb's ability to mutate DNA molecules. In this context, Williams's mutant molecules allegorize not only the phantasms of the mutant body that have come to haunt humans in the nuclear age but also the unintended consequences, the blowback so to speak, of nuclear necropolitics, including involuntary and uncontrollable genetic engineering. Williams envisions the molecular turn as a revenge story, a molecular warfare with an alien species. The aliens, however, do not come from another planet but are a species of our own creation, invading human bodies so that mutations spread like uncontrollable viral infections. In a necropolitical revenge of the genes, humans are to pay the price for messing with the transgenerational genetic heritage.

During the melodramatic showdown between the patriotic survivalists and the once-human mutant zombies who are led by howling wolf women, a dying zombie reminds his adversaries that the new mutants still harbor a human part in a crypt inside their selves. In this respect, Williams's phantasms of the mutant body also serve as allegories of an extreme anxiety at the core of nuclear subjectivities, namely, that the nuclear age might already have generated mutant human selves that act in a deterritorialized molecular world of ontological insecurity, a world beyond good and evil in which the parameters of familiar human ontologies are forever destroyed. Williams's story of molecular warfare is, of course, consistent with the imperialist and survivalist imaginary that fuels so much science fiction of alien invasions. Beyond this generic convention, however, the fact that his characters are mutant protein molecules suggests, in anticipation of the molecular turn, that in the cultural imaginary, anxieties about alien invasion have migrated to the molecular level, unsettling both corporeal ontologies and ecologies of mind.

In response to current discourses of the molecular turn, Jordy

Rosenberg, moreover, traces the resurfacing of a familiar colonial imaginary as a supplement to imperialist phantasies of invasion. Developing a sustained critique of the specific use of the molecular in object-oriented ontology (OOO), he argues that in certain discourses, the molecular turn promotes a new primitivism that has its genealogical roots in neoliberal settler colonialism, thus occluding the turn's potentially problematic sociopolitical implications. In "The Molecularization of Sexuality: On Some Primitivisms of the Present," Rosenberg writes, "The ontological turn [. . .] reshapes an old paradigm, a primitivist fantasy that hinges on the violent erasure of the social."[38] Generated by a combination of ancestrality (Meillassoux), (apocalyptic) futurity, and queerness, this fantasy locates queerness in the molecular and links subject-formation and the production of desire to the biopolitical optimization of life. Rosenberg argues that texts such as Timothy Morton's "Queer Ecology" misread Deleuze and Guattari's concept of the molar and the molecular to perform a "flight into an ontological queerness" that severs ontology from the social and political underpinnings that are central in *Mille Plateaux*.

Rose maintains, for example, that molecular material may generate a "new frontier of primitive accumulation and resource extraction." In a similar vein, Eugene Thacker and Beatriz Preciado insist that the body itself becomes a new ground for capitalist resource extraction and dispossession. Rosenberg concludes that we thus find "the collusion of primitivism and productivism lodged in the molecular" and recalls Deleuze and Guattari's assertion that, while desiring machines constitute a microphysics of the unconscious, they never exist independently of the historical molar aggregates and macroscopic social formations. Desires and fantasies, in other words, are inevitably entangled with the social.

Rosenberg's critique of OOO's particular use of the molecular turn as the basis for a queer and ultimately apocalyptic ontology is relevant for considerations of the molecular in nuclear necropolitics, because the latter inevitably faces questions related to imagining extinction, if not the apocalyptic imaginary. Apocalyptic fantasies emerge in and are shaped by the macrosocial and political formations that create nuclear necropolitics. If, as I have argued throughout *Radioactive Ghosts*, the nuclear age is haunted by the specter of extinction, the challenge is to imagine extinction within its sociopolitical parameters without succumbing to the lures of the apocalypse or what Rosenberg calls the "apocalyptic aphrodisiacs." Denying the specter of extinction, in other words, would be as detrimental to understanding the nuclear challenge of our time as embracing its phantasmatic lure. Only an irreducibly social conception of ontology can avoid this double trap.

Recent ontological work, Rosenberg writes, "has reterritorialized desire within the molecular as if the molecular itself constitutes a kind of productive, autonomous realm." A final warning emphasizes the embeddedness of the molecular in the (extractive) sociopolitics of capitalism. "Let it never be said of us that our consciousness was sheerly molecular, that we truly believed that all the baleful historical foreclosures of capitalism were ontologically true." Resisting apocalypse, Rosenberg embraces a consoling fantasy, envisioning a collective within "which, at the end, we are not extinct but transformed."

Nuclear haunting has always and perhaps inevitably generated an entire range of consoling fantasies. Cortazar's axolotl protagonist, for example, who cannot quite decide whether he harbors a radically incommensurable human inside or whether his incommensurable axolotl self inhabits the human, thinks of a time before the existence of the human species, "a remote dominion destroyed, an age of liberty when the world had been that of axolotls."[39] His story ends with a consoling fantasy about the human, who, after becoming axolotl, has outgrown his obsession: "I console myself by thinking that perhaps he is going to write a story about us."[40] Perhaps this is one of the secrets of Hesse-Honegger's strangely moving, beautiful, and melancholic paintings of mutant insects. By recording their story, she is opposing the nuclear work of death that has damaged their bodies and rendered them extraordinary biological indicators of the threat radioactive contamination poses to bodies and lives. To become visible to the human species, that is, to those who perform this work of extinction, these insects need a story. Hesse-Honegger paints portraits that enfold the tale of their mutant bodies. She paints portraits that illuminate the agent of their fate, the permanent corporeal inscription of vibrant matter, frighteningly invisible, radioactivity. She tells their story in order not to let them die in silence.

THE DAY OUR ROBOTS DIED

There is, finally, yet another sphere in which radioactivity manifests as toxic vibrant matter. It is the technological sphere of robots, mechanized humanoids designed to perform the work of nuclear decontamination that is too lethal for humans. But it did not take long before it became clear that, just like humans, robots are vulnerable to radioactive contamination. "Our robots died," said one of Alexivich's interviewees, a soldier sent to the zone of exclusion after the Chernobyl nuclear disaster. "But there were soldiers in their rubber suits, their rubber gloves, running around."[41] Vibrant matter killing vibrant matter. The story of dying robots sounds almost allegorical in its evocation of a strange posthuman world. Once the robots that were supposed to clean up the radioactive contamination at the disaster site "died," humans were called upon again to continue the work. They are used as sacrifice humans, their bodies exposed to lethal doses of radioactivity. They become the victims of slow nuclear violence. Ironically, they are officially called "bio-robots" or "green robots." In his interview with Alexievich, Sergei Sobolev tells her,

> The radiocontrolled machines they used often failed [. . .] because their electronics were disrupted by the high radiation. The most reliable "robots" were the soldiers. They were christened the "green robots." [. . .] Three thousand six hundred soldiers worked on the roof of the ruined reactor. [. . .] They were young guys. They're dying now. [. . .] They were a sacrifice.[42]

In *Die Wächter des Sarkophags: 10 Jahre Tschernobyl* (The guardians of the sarcophagus: 10 years of Chernobyl), prominent German philosopher and film director Alexander Kluge describes how, after the mechanical robots failed in their cleanup work at Chernobyl, soldiers were used as so-called bio-robots.[43] Kluge interviews a reporter, Kostin, who tells him that before these bio-robots were called upon, there were two mechanical robots working on the roof of the reactor, a German and a Japanese one.[44] One of them, he says, was a "killer-robot" (*Killer-Roboter*), that is, a robot whose sensorium is capable of aggregating important things and who goes into the Zone. But once in the Zone, this robot could no longer steer itself and fell down. A helicopter had to "rescue" it because there was a desire by the government to cover up the failure and loss of robots. Kostin reports that humans had to clean the robots that "died" from radioactive contamination.

Technological tools and images are as vulnerable to radioactive destruction as human bodies. Kostin took hundreds of photos of the disaster, but only two remained. Destroyed by radioactivity, the rest of the film came out black. Yet, the two salvaged images show "human robots" (*Menschenroboter*) who cleaned up the contaminated materials and nuclear rods with their hands.[45] After the two robots that worked on the roof were destroyed by radioactivity, they were replaced by two humans. People jokingly called them "Robot Peter" and "Robot Wassilij." These bio-robots look like cyborgs with lead plates covering their heads and mouths.[46] In addition to soldiers, scientists using improvised search equipment were employed as bio-robots to look for the substance that had disappeared from the reactor.[47]

Dying robots were not unique to Chernobyl. "Experts Baffled as Robots Sent to Clean Up Fukushima Nuclear Site Keep Dying"[48] is the headline of a more recent article about the Fukushima nuclear disaster in the *Independent*. The Japanese, whose robots were used after the Chernobyl disaster, are now using purposely built "scorpion" robots with attached cameras to survey the scale of damage at the Fukushima plant because the radiation levels are far higher than any human could survive. The robots were supposed to be able to cope with 73 sieverts of radiation, but the radiation level inside the reactor reached 530 sieverts. In early February 2017, one of the scorpion crawlers stalled after its radiation exposure reached its limit after just two hours.

Outside the plant, mutant daisies grow. Inside, the robots are dying. A sarcastic commentator posts, "At least we know what sort of weapons to use when the robots eventually rise up against us." Even the alien species of robots, created to measure or clean up the sites of radioactive contamination, cannot survive the lethal force the human species has unleashed upon the world.

PRECARIOUS SURVIVAL IN THE RUINS OF A RADIOACTIVE WORLD

However, ever since humans have begun to imagine extinction in apocalyptic visions and stories, they have also supplemented them with stories of precarious survival. One could even argue that the entire genre of science fiction thrives on supplementing apocalyptic visions with survival narratives. With a few final remarks on the "Camille Stories" from *Staying with the Trouble*, I want to highlight Donna Haraway's crucial intervention into the transspecies imaginary. Choosing a science fiction that is utopian, irreverent, audacious, and hopeful, Haraway frees herself from the generic convention of transspecies anxieties to embrace a positive vision of transspecies reproduction as a creative mode of survival in a world threatened by the so-called sixth extinction. The protagonists in Haraway's "Camille Stories" are so-called symbiont children, that is, human children who are genetically engineered with genes from endangered animal or plant species to give them "a chance to have a future in a time of mass extinctions."[49] Human parents use animals or plants to contribute cellular and molecular materials for modifying their transspecies offspring. For example, Camille 1 receives genes that allow her to taste chemical signals in the wind like monarch butterflies, and her skin is tattooed with the beautiful colors and patterns of butterfly wings. Symbiont children may acquire visible traits, such as the androgynous appearance inherited from the sexually dimorphic monarch adults, or they may become endowed with more subtle sensory similarities. In Haraway's futuristic vision, symbiont children develop "a complex subjectivity composed of loneliness, intense sociality, intimacy with nonhuman others, specialness, lack of choice, fullness of meaning, and sureness of future purpose."[50]

Most importantly, perhaps, Haraway emphasizes a radically new ethics of care designed to enhance survival by healing planetary destruction, an ethics that Haraway describes as a difficult process of learning "to live collectively in intimate and worldly care-taking symbiosis with another animal as a practice of repairing damaged places and making flourishing multispecies futures."[51] While Hesse-Honegger's ethics of care focuses on recording the genetic damage that induces deforming and dysfunctional mutations, Haraway's ethics of care thus focuses on genetic enhancement and multispecies world-making, embracing environmental justice and survival to accompany the ongoing wave of mass extinctions. Instead of the pervasive ecology of fear that imagines extinction within the boundaries of an apocalyptic imaginary, Haraway offers us the consoling fantasy of imagining extinction in a transformational survival within "a potent network of refugia and foci of resurgent naturalcultural diversity."[52]

And yet, imagining survival requires a "practice of vital memory," that is, an ongoing process of mourning that keeps the lost ways of life and species alive in the present. To fulfill this task, Camille 5 is designed to perform the "work of the Speakers for the Dead":[53]

> The Speakers for the Dead are also tasked with bringing into mind and heart [. . .] the emerging kinds of beings and ways of life of an always evolving home world. The Speakers for the Dead seek and release the energies of the past, present, and future Chthulucene, with its myriad tentacles of opportunistic, dangerous, and generative sympoiesis.[54]

It is the central role the work of mourning plays in Haraway's "Camille Stories" that saves them from being a purely lighthearted utopian defense, if not negative hallucination. Instead, they morph into emblematic stories visualizing what it could mean to survive in the ruins of our damaged world. This includes conveying the immense suffering and mourning caused by the double death of individuals and species, of ways of life and ways of dying. Beyond false hope and despair, Haraway invites us to actively participate in rebuilding our damaged planet and supplement her "Camille Stories" with our own. Writing such stories, for Haraway, is both a practice of mourning the dead and an imaginative act of rebirthing.

Here, then, is my own transspecies story: my symbiont child, Camille X, is genetically engineered with the gene of *Deinococcus radiodurans*,[55] a bacterium that, belonging to the species of extremophiles, can live through radiation so intense that it could survive a thousand times the amount of radiation released in the atomic attacks on Hiroshima and Nagasaki. A small number of *Deinococcus radiodurans* would even be able to survive three thousand times this amount. The secret of this superbug is its extraordinary ability to repair broken DNA with special molecular techniques still unknown to humans. *Deinococcus radiodurans* are, in Edward O. Wilson's poetic formulation, "Earth's outcast nomads, looking for life in all the worst places."[56] They are also prime candidates for space travel, potentially able to drift away from Earth, riding on stratospheric winds, and settle alive on Mars. And, resonant with the molecular turn in the life sciences, their use of molecular self-healing practices qualifies them as masters of molecular species-being. Harboring radiodurant genes, we could say that my symbiont child embodies a radically new molecular turn in genetic engineering.

I imagine symbiont children endowed with *Deinococcus radiodurans* genes as lone survivors of a nuclear catastrophe, living in the atomic land- and cityscapes of a bygone world. I imagine the generation of parents who engineered them as visionaries who, anticipating the extinction of their world, built a transgenic ark of sorts, creating genetically engineered transspecies symbionts of human, animal, and plant species, all endowed with the miracle gene of *Deinococcus radiodurans* and its power to repair broken DNA. In this way, they populated the earth with a virtual ark well before the cataclysmic extinction of most living species. The symbiont species look like a perfect simulacrum of the original host species because, unlike the genetic material, let's say, of a bear or a monarch butterfly, that of a bacterium does not manifest in outer corporal changes. And yet, internally, they were profoundly changed in their species-being.

In their spirit of survival, the visionary parents of radiodurans children taught them with meticulous history lessons to avoid their human ancestors' violent and destructive ways of life. This included lessons that taught them of the sinister times during the eugenics movement in the twentieth century, when people with damaged genes were murdered. They were made to read Jon Beckwith's *Making Genes, Making Waves*. Beckwith was a geneticist and scholar activist at the turn of the twentieth century who wrote about the murderous eugenics movement, calling it "Our Own Atomic History."[57] In contrast to this destructive use of genetics, radiodurans children were taught that genetic engineering is a precarious practice to be used solely for purposes of repair. Their very radiodurans gene served, after all, like an internal genetic police that instantly repaired genes. Transspecies engineering by design, however, was subject to strict rules and regulations in the service of survival; the practice was only allowed to save species from extinction. Moreover, the parents trained their offspring to use the genetic disposition of extremophiles to think in larger than human spatiotemporal scales, which enabled them mentally not only to navigate the vast expanse between deep time and the minute scale of molecular being but also to feel compassion for suffering at extreme distances, including that of radically different species.

Finally, the parents initiated their symbiont children in the supreme arts of M: memory, mourning, migration, metamorphosis, mutation, and metempsychosis. They are trained to use *memory*, including body memory, to remain mindful of the inscriptions of the past in the present and the future. Knowing that no memory ever disappears without a trace, they refine their mnemonic practices to include evolutionary memories. Given their history as survivors of mass extinctions, memory is for them inextricably tied to *mourning*. I imagine symbiont children performing mourning rituals in the ruins of ancient cities, consumed by an intense yearning for the extinct human species. Mourning is not only a way to pay tribute to ancestral legacies; it is also a safeguard against the repetition of haunting legacies of destruction. *Migration* is a passion bequeathed to them by "Earth's outcast nomads," the *Deinococcus radiodurans*. Their inherited genetic disposition endows them with a yearning for space travel to other planets. Imprinted by past histories of human lives, their selves also extend into distant space-times. Nomads of the future, they want to explore Mars, Venus, and the moon. Some would eventually settle there and build civilizations informed by a completely new transspecies ethics, a self-sustaining agricultural lifestyle and an economic system of exchange without possession. But their yearning for the beyond drives many on to other shores. Unable to fly like the radiodurans superbug on stratospheric winds, they satisfy their migratory urge by becoming master designers of interstellar spaceships. While some of them settle temporarily in remote abodes, most of them enjoy planet-hopping and many return, at least temporarily and with a tinge of nostalgia, to a newly terraformed Earth.

Like their parents, these children enjoy the art of genetic engineering, creating ever-new symbiont species. Employing their surviving passion for ancient texts, they draw on Ovid's *Metamorphoses* as well as Indigenous stories of shapeshifters to inspire their proliferating transspecies designs. *Metamorphosis* is a trickster art, reminding them at every turn of the entanglement of species. *Mutation* has lost its terrifying legacy. While, for their parents, phantasms of the mutant body incarnated the threat of transgenerational radiation-induced reproductive damage, the skill inherited from the *Deinococcus radiodurans* to repair and manipulate compromised DNA enables them to use mutations creatively, often enhancing species survival in the process.

Metempsychosis is a mystic art for symbiont children. From the time of their first embodiment, they were mystified by the secrets of the soul. How did soul-making happen? What was the imprint of the radiodurant gene on their soul? What exactly is the relationship between gene and soul? Is the soul trying to survive in all the worst places by turning into a migrant nomad, traveling from one embodiment to the next, just like the symbiont children themselves travel from one planet to the next? Is this the secret of reincarnation and immortality? Are genes and souls immortal because they know the art of transmigration? And if so, is this a consoling fantasy? While it may be consoling when imagining extinction, symbiont children are all too aware that it doesn't spare them grief and mourning. They still mourn each species that has become a victim of extinction, just as they mourn each individual death in the here and now. Isn't it their very soul that mourns? they ask themselves. Grieving deeply, then, they nonetheless hold out the hope that by transmigrating to other bodies, their souls carry the traces of former lives. For them, the mystery of metempsychosis is the mystery of an eternal trace. They are cosmic mystics, then, disseminating the traces of their unique being to farther and farther reaches of the universe.

POSTNUCLEAR ECOLOGIES

Language, Body, and Affect in Beckett's *Happy Days*

> Asking for the moon.
> —Winnie in Samuel Beckett, *Happy Days*

Imagine an expanse of scorched grass in a wilderness where nothing grows, a hellish sun creating a heat so intense that objects and bodies are expanding and spontaneously burst into flames. Or, conversely, imagine an earth that has lost its atmosphere and persists motionless in an everlasting perishing cold. Imagine an eternal dark, a black night without end. Now imagine two human beings, a woman and a man, in this otherwise lifeless world, the woman buried to her waist in a sandy hill and the man living in a decrepit state in a hole behind it. By now, you will have recognized that I am evoking the apocalyptic scenery of Samuel Beckett's *Happy Days*.

Performing an experimental abstraction of human adaptability to extreme conditions in the aftermath of catastrophe, *Happy Days* plays with a large referential horizon. An array of intertextual allusions and citations from works that deal with the loss of paradise, the decay of empires and dynasties, or the sinking of human characters into madness and despair are woven together to evoke a psychohistorical imaginary of possible end-time scenarios. The play's allusion to disasters of apocalyptic proportions is thus doubled by references to literary figurations of world endings, mostly from a Western canon. But rather than citing these texts as genealogies, Winnie, the main character, invokes them as remnants of a ruinous language that no longer fits her current world. Detached from their original meaning, her quotations of "wonderful lines" assume a life of their own, producing a proliferation of meaning. They are running on empty, hollowing metaphoric images out from within. The latter belong to Winnie's mnemonic arsenal of speaking in the "old style." It is as if the remainders of a wasted language proliferate endlessly, almost comparable to the proliferation of nuclear waste. In this respect, Winnie's monologues resemble a frantic effort to ward off the effects of the disaster of nuclear language. And yet, over and over again, throughout the play, she reiterates its core refrain: "another happy day."

In *Civilization and Its Discontents,* Freud poses the question of the purpose and intention of human lives. What, he asks, do humans "demand of life and wish to achieve in it?" The answer to this question, he continues, "can hardly be in doubt. They strive after happiness; they want to become happy and remain so."[1] While Freud's answer provides the foundation for his concept of the pleasure principle, he hastens to argue for the necessity to moderate claims to happiness by substituting the pleasure principle with the reality principle.[2] Beckett's *Happy Days* leaves these choices behind. In Winnie's world, any recourse to something resembling a reality principle seems obsolete. At the level of the play's imaginary lifeworld, the entire sphere of *bios* has been reduced to the conditions of a dying planet. The environment is a hostile place, threatened by a merciless sun that extinguishes all life. Within this framework, Winnie seems to have no choice but to perform the role of one clinging to the pleasure principle and its hallucinatory suggestion that this will have been yet another happy day.

The end-time scenario of *Happy Days* is, however, doubled by self-reflexive exhibitions of the play's own theatricality. Winnie productively occupies a transitional space where the binary oppositions between life and theater, the real and the imaginary, language and meaning, being and nonbeing, life and death, happiness and despair, have been undermined. Life and theater have merged to the point that life is theater and theater is life. Almost as if language becomes, as in Burroughs, a "virus from outer space,"[3] Winnie is infected by the unavoidability of obsolete metaphors, condemned to speak in the "old style," in a mode of *as if.* As old metaphors proliferate along positive feedback loops, any attempt to adapt them to Winnie's current world becomes a trap, for both Winnie and the audience. Just as her body is trapped in a heap of sand, her mind is trapped in a heap of metaphors. As audience, we witness a unique ecology of mind and language. Operating like a totalized catachresis, language infects the mind with the proliferating waste of literary and philosophical remainders of a bygone civilization.

From the outset, *Happy Days* defies conventions of theatrical realism. The play opens with a scene in which the spectators see Winnie buried to her waist in a mound of sand, and as they realize in the course of the play, she is gradually sinking deeper into the ground. In the second act, Winnie is buried up to her neck, deprived of any mobility except the movement of her eyes. How did she get there? Who buried her? Why did Willie, her husband who lives in a hole behind Winnie's mound, not dig her out? Why is he himself not sinking into the ground? And, most strikingly, how can both characters live day by day without food and water in a searing heat that has, as Winnie suggests, destroyed life on the planet? Such questions remain, of course, bound to the conventions of theatrical realism. And yet, it is impossible not to ask them, because Beckett teases his audience with those very conventions, inviting interpretive projections only to introduce new elements and twists into his language games that expose their inadequacy.

Questions of the real, including affects and thoughts of existential depth, are impossible to suspend completely, if only because the play abounds with existential metaphors and displays an astounding adaptability to a wide range of possible life scenarios. In Beckett's "endgames," the real is always there, looming darkly, albeit as an absent cause. Any effort to mobilize theatrical conventions and existential habits of thought to glean the play's meaning is doomed to fail. Just like Winnie, the audience thus becomes trapped in a condition of impossibility to which the only mode of adaptation is an adaptation to inevitable failure.[4] Through Winnie's speech performances, Beckett challenges the audience to see that in language, among the many proliferating (nuclear) options, only failure seems worth pursuing.

This is significant because Winnie explicitly addresses human evolution and adaptation to changing environmental conditions. Moreover, beyond invoking evolutionary biology, adaptability is also a central strategy of communication in Beckett's play. *Happy Days* offers itself as a projective screen onto which Beckett invites us to transfer our own concerns, phantasms, desires, and philosophical/theoretical legacies, albeit only to have them unsettled and defamiliarized. Adaptability thus becomes first and foremost adaptability to failure and catachresis. Beckett uses the projective screen, in other words, as the site of a "theater of cruelty" designed to entrap the audience in a double bind, that is, a productive impasse that exposes the partial and constricting nature of every single referential attribution. To "speak in the old style" by invoking the proliferating waste of "wonderful lines" that are imposed on Winnie is the only way of speaking, albeit one in which failure and catachresis are inherent. Ultimately, speaking in the old style throws us back onto the basic existential questions and presuppositions that mark and delimit our being in the world. At the theatrical level, on the other hand, we have been trained to take things as they are on stage without challenging them. In the transitional space of the theater, the boundaries between the real and the imaginary are so plastic that we are invited to cross and redraw them as a matter of course. Winnie herself oscillates between her imagined lifeworld, where she is buried on a hill and exposed to a merciless sun, and her life as an actress, happily playing her role day after day in endless repetitions. While in her lifeworld, she constantly pulls herself from the edge of despair and her fear of being left alone as the last human in the wilderness, as an actress, she imagines a timeless space of eternal repetitions, a "world without end"[5] and a life without death.

Winnie's almost seamless oscillation between the play's two levels suggests that, for her, there is no longer any difference between being in the world and being on stage. For those acting as Winnie in Beckett's play, however, the dynamic plays out differently. In 2013, I played the role of Winnie at the Studiobühne in Constance, Germany. We did an experimental trilingual staging of the play with three actresses who weaved Beckett's three languages together: English, French, and German. Often the days of rehearsal were anything but happy days. Each of the actresses emphasized a different aspect of Winnie's personality, and we composed our trilingual collage of the play accordingly. The Irish Winnie was the humorous one, alluding to or inventing an entire range of funny lines. The French Winnie was the seductive one, always preoccupied with her appearance and her cosmetic objects. But she was also the one clinging to the consoling objects in her bag that help her to get through the day. I played the German Winnie, who was the philosophical and literary one, and the one most bent to the dark side of her existence.

What we all shared, regardless of these differences, was the pain and suffering that came with acting this particular role. We had to get through the hours of sitting buried to the waist, and in the second act completely immobile, with the exception of the motion of our eyes and facial expressions. We had to learn to do the entire acting with modulations of our facial expressions and with the movements of our eyes. By the time I had to cry out "My neck is hurting me!" on most nights my neck *did* really hurt. For me, the hardest part was to keep my hands still under the canvas used to simulate the mound of sand, since I tend to use my hands for emphasis while speaking. During the rehearsals, the stage director kept calling, "Your hands are moving the hill!" Yet, whenever I concentrated on keeping my hands from moving, it became extremely difficult to focus simultaneously on remembering the lines.

Embodying Winnie in her tortured position made us merge with her discomfort at a corporeal level. The more intense our physical strains and tensions grew, the more we gained a sense of "becoming Winnie." Beckett's "theater of cruelty" thus doubles the cruelty of language with the cruelty of the body. Actors have no choice but to embody Winnie's condition of being trapped in an impossible world and a language that is always already doomed to distort it. Inhabiting language under these conditions generates an intimate link of language to the body, a somatic form of language, a *biolingua*.

As actresses, we also shared Winnie's terror of no longer remembering "those wonderful lines." As many of the actresses who played Winnie had complained, this is an excruciatingly hard role to memorize, especially because of the many repetitions and concomitant lack of a continuously evolving narrative. Moreover, affected by Winnie's mental state, we sensed the terrors of aging, of losing mobility, of losing one's mind. And yet, after many weeks of rehearsals, we also began to feel the comfort of knowing that the next day we would be there again on our hill, with our objects and with Willie behind us in his hole. The more we attuned ourselves to Beckett's unique poetic language and Winnie's mode of being in a catastrophic world, the more we felt a sense of comfort and, indeed, bouts of happiness.

By the end, I believe, we had all internalized the rhythms and moods of Beckett's play, and with these came a rare form of hitherto unknown paradoxical happiness. It was the happiness of merging with a theatrical experience both utterly alien and utterly familiar. It was the paradox where inhabiting failure becomes the only possible success. Or, to put it differently, adaptability under these conditions implies adaptation to catachresis or, more precisely, a mobilization of catachresis that becomes transformational within a new ecology of mind. From this perspective, the only viable, if always already inadequate, answer to the crisis of representation provoked by the two major catastrophes of human destructiveness that mark our time—the Holocaust and Hiroshima—unfolds along Beckett's "wonderful lines": There is nothing to say; we'll say it. We can't go on; we'll go on.

This is also the sentiment we shared during the often very painful rehearsals of *Happy Days*. The persistent anxiety of drawing a blank and not remembering the lines—lines, that is, that simply could not be securely embedded in a chronological narrative—was accompanied and indeed aggravated by the physical discomfort that kept demanding attention and threatened to distract us from the rehearsed sequence of monologues. How often we thought we couldn't go on, and yet we kept going, day after day. As much as we suffered through times of pain, frustration, fear, and doubt, when I look back at our rehearsals and performances, I feel like affirming, yes, they were happy days—if this notion can be maintained. Perhaps we finally learned to inhabit the notion of "happy days" in the mode of a catachresis.

The oscillation between two levels of theatricality also affects the audience, albeit in less visceral corporeal affectations. Initially, the strongest pull comes from the intense atmosphere of Beckett's setting, which is suggestive of disaster: a merciless light shining on an arid desert world and a lone woman buried to her waste in the sand. There is no way to escape this pull that is existential and aesthetic in one. Moreover, *Happy Days*' first publication in 1961 by Grove Press inevitably engaged a cultural imaginary deeply informed by the nuclear age and the threat of a nuclear apocalypse. Many directors have staged the play with allusions to a postnuclear world. In an earlier version, Beckett himself had made references to a nuclear holocaust to explain Winnie's condition. He later took them out to remove the concreteness of a particular historical event and thus increase the play's horizon of possible references and thereby its timelessness in confronting always proliferating unpredictable catastrophes. In other words, if the play is timeless, it is so in the radical sense that it operates—like the nuclear—outside the scale of human time or outside chronology. To put it differently, it operates at a scale of radical unpredictability or, more specifically, the unpredictability of the final catastrophe. The latter, as Derrida reminds us, can only be apprehended as a rhetorical (or theatrical) condition and, as Beckett compels us to add, in a mode of catachresis.

At the time when *Happy Days* first appeared on stage, images of Hiroshima, Nagasaki, and their aftermath were at the very core of the cultural imaginary. So were stories of humans exposed to the hellish light of the atomic bomb that melted skin and eyeballs and damaged genetic material for generations to come. In this context, Beckett's "hellish sun" recalls the "radiance of a thousand suns"[6] Robert Oppenheimer quoted from the Hindu Bhagavad Gita after the Trinity explosion. Given

FIGURE 23. Poster for *Glückliche Tage/Happy Days/Oh les beaux jours* by Samuel Beckett, directed by Tessa Theodorakopoulos, staged at Universitätstheater Konstanz, 2013. Poster design by Tessa Theodorakopoulos. Courtesy of the artist.

the prominence of global warming in the cultural imaginary of the past decades, one might further read Beckett's vision of a dying world as the performative figuration not only of a nuclear wasteland but also of a world destroyed by climate change.

More generally, *Happy Days* could stand for any world in the aftermath of catastrophe. It is a deathworld where human beings linger in a state between life and death. Eventually, the play suggests, Winnie will be quite literally buried alive. For today's audience, her gradual sinking deeper and deeper into the ground may appear as an uncanny literal figuration of the "downward mobility" that comes with the environmental, political, social, and psychic precarity caused by late capitalism's catastrophic fallout. Winnie's burial in the sand is further suggestive of a form of "existential immobility," as Ghassan Hage describes it in *Alter-Politics*.[7] Hage analyzes how what he calls "existential stuckedness" undermines any sense of a viable life. In today's neoliberal state of permanent crisis, he argues, this existential immobility does not provoke resistance but is rather "transformed into an endurance test."[8]

In this vein, Winnie can be read as a literal figuration of existential immobility. Moreover, her attitude is beyond endurance as she mobilizes psychic defenses to define her state of being as a happy one that protects her from the "curse of mobility." Almost paradoxically, Winnie's corporeal confinement and immobility mobilize psychic space. She becomes a master of emotional inversion, performing a generative balancing act on the tightrope that spans above the transitional space between happiness and despair. In fact, Winnie's habitual emotional inversion is reminiscent of Lifton's reflections on "moral inversion." As we recall, Lifton describes how, in the aftermath of nuclear catastrophe, survivors tend to take recourse to moral inversion to avoid the abyss of unfathomable moral outrage.[9] In a world like Winnie's that is beyond good and evil, generative defenses are mobilized less against moral outrage than against the abyss of unlivable despair.

And yet, as we witness between the first and the second acts, Winnie is slowly moving farther down into the ground. Her downward mobility forms an entropic system of sorts that includes her material, social, and mental being. Buried before her time, Winnie does not seem to die but rather to go on endlessly, repeating the same routine day after day, except with a degree of entropy that makes her world, her life, and her body literally go downhill. Within the ruinous life of a dying planet, biological life or *bios* has become an anachronism, if not a threatening occurrence to be apprehended with disgust. "Yes, life," says Winnie, "I suppose there is no other word."[10] Any movement toward life always happens in recoil. One of the play's most salient moments is the emergence in front of Winnie's eyes of an ant, or as she calls it, an "emmet." "'Oh I say, what have we here? [. . .] Looks like life of some kind. [. . .] An emmet!' *Recoils. Shrill.*"[11] Just as Winnie recoils at the sight of animal life, she also balks at the idea that something could still be growing on earth. With her assertion "What a blessing nothing grows, imagine if all this stuff were to start growing. [. . .] Imagine. [. . .] Ah yes, great mercies,"[12] she echoes Clov's famous pained words in *Endgame*, "imagine if life would start all over again!" *Happy Days* is yet another one of Beckett's endgames, in which the end of life on earth is performed in the mode of an inversion of expectable affect, an inversion that transforms the endgame into a consoling fantasy.

Winnie's relentlessly affirming iterations of "happy days" and "great mercies" in the midst of all her woes begs the question of happiness. Given the play's dire setting in a merciless deathworld, how does Winnie manufacture happiness? How are we to read the fact that, seemingly unfazed by her miserable condition, Winnie holds on to what appears at the surface to be an unreconstructed optimism, declaring every day another happy day? The fact that she manages to see even the dead earth and the absence of life as a blessing makes her, as one of the critics suggested, a veritable "comedian of misery."[13] From the perspective of such emotional inversion, every day can indeed be thankfully welcomed with her "happy expression" and perennial mantra "This is going to be another happy day."

One might be tempted to see this as an instantiation of a particular form of optimism about adverse life-negating conditions, that is, yet another inversion that Lauren Berlant calls "cruel optimism."[14] Or one might think of the findings in the brain sciences that humans are genetically hard-wired toward an "optimism bias" that makes them adjust their beliefs "more in response to information that was better than expected than to information that was worse."[15] Would this neurobiological bias predispose humans toward an incurable, if not cruel, optimism, even at the cost of emotional inversion, if not an all-out denial of catastrophe? Placed at the cutting edge of a self-manufactured pursuit of happiness, Winnie not only seems to be endowed with a high level of the "optimism gene"; she is also a master of self-modulation and, as I stated earlier, of emotional inversion. She opens the play with the line "Another heavenly day." Like a refrain, she repeats with "happy expression" her ever slightly altered mantra: "This is going to be a happy day" or "This is a happy day! This will have been another happy day." Whenever her thoughts are drawn to darker matter, she instantly shrugs them off by mobilizing phrases like "This is what I find so wonderful!" or "Oh the happy memories!" Could we then read Winnie as the embodiment of a human condition fully adapted to catastrophe and endowed with a psychic disposition of survival, a proclivity toward optimism that never settles for bare life? Could this be Winnie's secret appeal? Could it be why she continues to speak, even if no longer to us?

In "What Does Fiction Know?," Richard Powers asserts, "It won't be our capacity for despair that does the race in; we are damned by how easily we shrug the darkness off."[16] "Shrugging darkness off" is exactly Winnie's forte. And yet, in her self-modulation, darkness and happiness belong as inseparably together as the two sides of a Möbius strip. For her, any "happy," that is, accurate, expression merges with the feedback loop of all expressions she borrows from the ruinous wonderful lines. Whatever disaster might have caused the dire conditions of her current situation—be it a nuclear holocaust, climate change, or simply the dying earth at the end of times—Winnie does not take it as the signature of a threatening future but as a given reality to which she has adapted with her particular manner of speaking, seemingly forever.

Reading Winnie as a biased, if not cruel, optimist thus turns out to be just another Beckettian trap. From Winnie's perspective, the invocation of "happy days" and "old mercies" belongs, like all the other eternally reiterated "wonderful lines," to the "old style" of catachrestic remainders.[17] Adaptability can no longer be grounded in false hope or cruel optimism. Rather, it would, if it were possible, reside in finding congruence between worlds and words. In this respect, it could emerge from a specific adaptability, albeit not to a dying environment but to the simple persistence of objects and words within the cataclysms of environmental catastrophe. Whatever happens to them, Winnie's objects—the sunshade, the mirror, the bag full of stuff—will always be there for the next performance. And however inadequate, her words and wonderful lines will always be there, functioning against all odds as testimonies to the simple persistence of language. In Beckett's play, they, too, seem to be moved outside of chronological or historical human time.

The sense of timelessness and eternal recurrence is, of course, also related to the paradox of theatrical time. When Winnie's sunshade goes on fire, she muses, "Ah earth you old extinguisher. [. . .] I presume this has occurred before though I cannot recall it,"[18] only to conclude, "The sunshade will be there again tomorrow, beside me on the mound, to help me through the day."[19] And, of course, so it will be on stage for the next performance. Winnie thus playfully uses the paradox of theatrical reality systematically to mitigate the existential conditions invoked by her role in the play. This paradoxical fusion of the play's two layers generates a figuration of affect that oscillates between the psyche of Winnie as protagonist and her psyche as actress. This explains why the prospect of an apocalyptic ending does not generate fear and trembling but a self-soothing state of waiting "for the day to come—[. . .] happy day to come when flesh melts at so many degrees and the night of the moon has so many hundred hours."[20]

Here Winnie appropriates Hamlet's "Oh that this too, too solid flesh would melt"[21] as an apt metaphor for imagining the material effects of a burning planet on the human body. As if she were the last witch on earth who shares the fate of her medieval sisters, Winnie's sense of an ending is bound to the fantasy of being burned alive, igniting spontaneously like her sunshade, her flesh melting or being charred like a piece of coal: "With the sun blazing, so much fiercer down, and hourly fiercer, is it not natural things should go on fire never known to do so? [. . .] Shall I myself not melt perhaps in the end, or burn, oh I do not mean necessarily burst into flames, no, just little by little be charred to a black cinder, all this [. . .] visible flesh?"[22] But before this fearful vision can congeal into an affective state, Winnie's mind rushes to Shakespeare's sonnet "Fear no more the heat o' the sun," which she cites for Willie with exalted bravado. And while she stops short of Shakespeare's next line, "Nor the furious winter's rages," she wonders later whether gravity is still what it used to be or whether the earth has lost its atmosphere. "It might be the eternal cold [. . .] everlasting perishing cold,"[23] she speculates.

It is the peculiar condensation of the play's dire lifeworld with its theatrical reality that generates a paradoxical space in-between, a transitional space, that is, in which life is cast as theater and theater as life. Seen in this light, whatever is destroyed today will be there again tomorrow. The temperate times and torrid times Winnie speaks of are but empty words.[24] Winnie has an entire archive of "empty words" and "wonderful lines" that belong to the objects that help her through the day (or the play). She clearly has a literary education in a predominately Western classical canon—ranging from the Bible and Dante, Shakespeare, Milton, Keats, and Yeats to a range of popular music and literature. Yet, within this archive, echoes and citations function as sources polluted by an endlessly distorting proliferation. Quoted in the end times of a dying earth, her archive—which is of course also Beckett's archive—exhibits the ruins of Western culture and is, to speak with Derrida, in the throes of an "archive fever" that puts the future into question.

As Derrida argues, traditional notions of the archive are turned toward the past, presupposing a closed heritage and faithfulness to tradition.[25] A more dynamic notion of the archive should, according to Derrida, "*call into question* the coming of the future."[26] It would, he concludes, have to attend to psychoanalysis and to "everything that can happen to the economy of memory and to its substrates, traces, documents, in their supposedly psychical or techno-prosthetic forms."[27] While Derrida certainly thought of very different uses of the archive than Beckett, Winnie performs a paradoxical use in which the archive puts the future into question: she hallucinates a ritualized endless reiteration of Western archives' "wonderful lines," a reiteration that moves the archive out of human time into a timelessness that is always out of sync. In this dis-located archive, the future is *now* and *never*; it is a future in which the dying earth already belongs to an entire archive of endlessly imagined extinctions.

Winnie's archive of "wonderful lines" from her classics,[28] however, just as her empty words and the objects in her bag, all become "consoling objects" that she shores up against the ruins of what she remembers of her former life. This I see as the true secret of Winnie's modulation of the self. Consoling objects facilitate her peculiar manufacture of happiness. They allow her with a supremely performative and mediated "cruel optimism" to continue and, in whatever minimal sense, to survive. Lauren Berlant links the term *cruel optimism* to optimistic attachments that hold on to "that moral-intimate-economic thing called 'the good life.'"[29] These attachments, she argues, are a fantasy that covers up the "dramas of adjustment" in the increasingly precarious conditions of life and life building.[30] For Berlant, cruel optimism is an affective response to the crises and impasses of precarious lives. In Beckett, by contrast, cruel optimism—if the notion can be maintained—is an affective response to catastrophe and immobility in a state between life and nonlife. Optimistic attachments emerge from desperate attempts to stay attached to life, even if life is barely livable. If Berlant calls such optimism cruel, it is because under certain conditions, optimistic attachments seem no longer to make sense even as they remain powerful. If life is cruel and we nonetheless sustain an optimistic attachment to it, Berlant seems to say, then the very optimism that sustains this life becomes cruel. "Even those whom you would think of as defeated are living beings figuring out how to stay attached to life from within it, and to protect what optimism they have for that, at least."[31]

Cruel optimism, in other words, appears as nothing but a defense against seeing the world in its brutal and cruel state. We might call it—with Christopher Bollas and Ackbar Abbas—a "negative hallucination,"[32] that is, the ability not to see what is in front of your very eyes or the refusal to see the existence of an object or an other. Winnie is a master of negative hallucination, using even language as hallucination. She invokes Shakespeare's Ophelia to allude to the dangers of seeing what you rather would not want to see: "woe woe is me [. . .] to see what I see."[33] Her immediate transition to the "blaze of hellish light"[34] suggests that the problem is one of overexposure. Ophelia utters her "woe is me to see what I see" when she realizes that Hamlet has gone mad. One of Winnie's recurrent fears is that she might lose her mind. Yet, instead of letting these "woes" emerge, Winnie begins in slapstick fashion to polish her spectacles. To the extent that her optimism might seem cruel in relation to the cruelty and madness of her surrounding world, it is also life affirming and self-sustaining in her use of language as a form of bilingual hallucination. And if optimism has always been first and foremost a psychic technology supposed to enable happiness and the "feeling good" that belong to a good life, then consoling objects function to protect and facilitate such optimism.

In this context, Winnie's manufactured shifts in mood deserve closer attention. There is method in her madness. Her last remaining routine preoccupation is the handling of the defunct objects from her bag, mostly of a cosmetic nature: a mirror, a nail file, a comb and hairbrush, her spectacles and a magnifying glass, a toothbrush, the last bit of toothpaste, and, above all, Brownie, the revolver and prized fetish object that reminds her of a time when it would still have been possible to end life voluntarily. Facilitating a futile routine, these consoling objects prevent Winnie from sinking into despair. They are the material tools of her ritualized "manufacture of happiness."

My concept of "consoling objects" draws on W. D. Winnicott's theory of transitional objects. The latter are, according to Winnicott, the first objects an infant uses to create a sense of self and world. They are paradoxical objects, located in a transitional space in which the distinction between I and not I is not yet established. According to Winnicott, the cultural objects of later life are derivatives of these early transitional objects. In the transitional space of cultural objects, the boundaries between discourse, self, and world are temporarily suspended. Consoling objects, I argue, are objects generated when a subject's environment has become a "landscape of risk," if not of devastation, personal or communal. It can be a nuclear landscape or a planet in the throes of climate change, as suggested in *Happy Days*, but it can also be a war zone or a camp.

In a contemporary setting, discursive figurations of environment can also evoke the proliferating sites of waste, disposable lives, and global deathworlds. Its theatrical doubling as a comedy of misery notwithstanding, Beckett's *Happy Days*, I argue, can be read as a multiply mediated metaphor of the struggle for psychic survival in such landscapes of devastation, catastrophe, and death, albeit a metaphor that operates within Beckett's (psycho)logics of an always already failing arsenal of imposed rhetorical tools and figurations. In fact, the comic and absurd elements of Beckett's staging of a minimalist deathworld make its impact all the more intense. "That is what I find so wonderful [. . .] the way man adapts himself [. . .] to changing conditions," says Winnie about her body's adaptation to the "hellish heat."

Exploring ways humans survive catastrophe, Beckett exhibits Winnie's psychic "splitting," that is, her strategy to ward off what Melanie Klein calls the "depressive position," by holding on to the fantasy of the "good life." Winnie uses her consoling objects to populate the space of her "good-enough life," to fill the unbearable void and to hold despair at bay. Her self-consoling techniques have become a psychic automatism, always at hand, yet always brittle and short-lived. She supplements her consoling material objects with consoling mental objects, composed of the literary remains and remainders of Western culture. Her consoling objects are therefore always objects of language, mediated by philosophical, poetic, and theatrical discourse. Borrowed from Thomas Gray's "Ode on a Distant Prospect of Eton College," for example, one of her consoling "wonderful lines" is "laughing wildly amid severest woe."[35] In his ode, Gray calls this condition a "moody Madness."[36]

Moody madness is indeed an apt depiction of Winnie's persistent flight from moods of despair into a happiness that she has learned to manufacture with her arsenal of consoling objects.

Winnie's "woes" of course also echo Milton's *Paradise Lost*: "Oh fleeting joys / Of Paradise, dear bought with lasting woes." But whenever a nostalgic sense of "paradise lost" enters Winnie's mind, she instantly transforms it into "paradise regained." Or she creatively counters allusions to *Paradise Lost* with the romantic hedonistic ideal "Paradise enow" remembered from FitzGerald's translation of *The Rubaiyat of Omar Khayyam*.[37] Winnie's "moody madness" has the consistency of a psychic automatism. Removed from their function within a lived culture, her consoling mental objects—the "wonderful lines" from cherished classics to sentimental poems and songs—have become frozen bits of memory, reminiscent of Dali's frozen liquid clock, that she can nonetheless mobilize to modulate and transform moods of despair.

Consoling objects thus function primarily as "transformational objects."[38] As they modulate Winnie's sense of self, they also change her sense of being. Far beyond their initial use-value as consumer objects, they assume the form of vibrant matter.[39] As if the detritus of capitalist consumer culture has lost its functionality in the imagined far-distant postconsumer culture, it assumes a life of its own. "Things have their life, that is what I always say, *things* have a life,"[40] says Winnie as she handles the miscellaneous objects in her bag. And yet, for Winnie, things do not have a life in the sense of vibrant matter, a sense she would abhor as much as she abhors the sense of life itself. Things have a life for her because she animates them as hallucinatory stand-ins or props for a life that no longer is. Winnie is, in other words, not a speculative realist or a proponent of object-oriented ontology; rather, she invokes the sense of vibrant matter as a performative ruse, a comic enactment, such as when the sunshade assumes a life of its own and spontaneously ignites. One of the ironies of this scene is, of course, that the very object that is supposed to give shade and protection from the searing heat is itself going up in flames.

I have focused my reading on the peculiar doubling of the play's imagined lifeworld and its theatrical self-reflection. In this context, I have highlighted how the quasi-referential linkages to a setting that features the diminished life of two humans in the aftermath of catastrophe are systematically disrupted by references to the play's theatrical reality. Beckett's removal of the explicit references to a nuclear holocaust from an earlier version of the play is symptomatic of his overall strategy to unsettle referentiality. How are we to take his warning "no symbols where none intended," given the fact that it constitutes a kind of double bind? Mustn't we realize that we are caught in this unavoidable double bind because it is not up to Beckett, the author, to resolve it? Rather, he posits it as foundational for the available (theatrical) modes of being and relating.

Highly suggestive of a world at the brink of extinction, Beckett's play is thus replete with what we could call symbolic traps. Its very setting virtually begs for allegorical readings. More precisely, these traps call for allegories in the Benjaminian sense. For Beckett, as for Benjamin, allegories are reliant both on symbols or metaphors and the distortions they produce. I also see the ways in which Beckett draws the audience into a double bind as a particular form of what his analyst Bion calls "attacks on linking."[41] Bion defines the latter as "destructive attacks on anything which is felt to have the function of linking one object to another."[42] A veritable signature of Beckett's entire work, his attacks on linking are directed against language itself as the primary human tool of linking. In his theater, Beckett attacks possible referential linkages because he mistrusts the easy equivalence of language and world. And yet, language is all we have as a link to the world. We must inhabit catachresis or remain silent. And remaining silent is, for Beckett as well as his characters, an always elusive and ultimately unattainable goal.[43]

Happy Days, I have argued, performs this unsettling of referential horizons by doubling its quasi-material apocalyptic scenario with the self-reflexively staged theatrical reality. While Beckett evokes an entire range of possible extratheatrical references as hooks to solicit an existential engagement of the audience, he mocks these references by insisting on confinement to the theatrical frame. This is what creates the double bind for an audience forced constantly to oscillate between shifting perspectives and moods. According to Bion, attacks on linking are directed against too-powerful emotions and, by extension, the external reality that stimulates them.[44] Beckett's attack on the linking function of referential realism and of language as "the medium of symbolic and cognitive linking"[45] entails a paradoxical process of dis-identification with the existential, cultural, and political implications of his theatrical world. Commonly, the referential horizon of a play helps the audience grasp its specific interventions that complicate or unsettle familiar conventions of either lifeworlds or theatrical worlds. Beckett, by contrast, lures the audience into a game of projection, only to have them undermined, rejected as inadequate, or mocked by his characters. Thus questioning familiar expectations, habitus itself appears as a toxic residue from a bygone world. It can no longer provide a reliable orientation or sense of adequacy, let alone belonging. By helping the audience to viscerally experience these residues as a waste of old cultural baggage, it is as if Beckett's work itself turns into a screen or detoxifying repository of the terrors and horrors that are expelled from the world and the self in a creative act of self-preservation.[46]

Once the linkage between the world on stage and the world outside is challenged, this creative disidentification leaves the audience with an experimental poetic abstraction of psychic worlds and affects. This abstraction, however, has a rare affective intensity. Rather than representing the terrors of world and self, it absorbs and transforms them into a poetic alchemy according to the conditions of theatrical space-time. Thus pushed beyond its referential function, language emerges in its very materiality as vibrant matter, as a biolingua that becomes itself the locus of an ecology with the power to affect through its formal and theatrical quality. The theatrical, in this context, is always entangled with a process of deaesthetisization that pushes language itself to the liminal space of failure. While the attacks on language as a medium of symbolic and cognitive linking modulate intolerable emotions, Beckett's dreamlike images and theatrical spaces release affects that were formerly encapsulated in ordinary language as well as conventional literary language. Together with other theatrical elements—light, sound, spatial organization, imagery, pace—language itself becomes a transformational bilingual object that generates a secondary aesthetic effect at the very threshold of its failure.

Seen in this light, *Happy Days* is also about intolerable, if not unsustainable, emotions and affects. Casting Winnie as a character who modulates intolerable emotions to manufacture happiness, Beckett attacks the manufacture of conventional emotions through theatrical realism as well as manufactured emotions encapsulated in the prison house of ordinary language. In breaking familiar referential ties to catastrophic worlds, he seems to suggest that habitual references have themselves become complicit with the vast expanse of negative hallucinations. Or, to put it even more radically, for Beckett, ordinary language itself is complicit in helping us not to see what we do not want to see.

With his strategy of unsettling theatrical realism and its quasi-referential techniques, Beckett performs a unique intervention in the cultural imaginary that focuses on apocalyptic writings of disaster, including the proliferating environmental imaginary of destroyed ecologies, such as globally spread toxicity, environmental devastation, depletion of resources, climate change, the dying of species, and the threat of a nuclear holocaust. Beckett's tragicomic minimalist experimentalism undermines the lures of an apocalyptic imaginary as well as the trauma fatigue that creates a protective shield against realist depictions of zones of disaster and deathworlds. By defamiliarizing the audience's gaze on the dying (stage) world in *Happy Days,* Beckett reaches toward a deeper level of affect, lodged in an apocalyptic unconscious. Rather than allowing us to "shrug darkness off" like Winnie, Beckett's strategy makes us laugh from within the heart of darkness. It is a guilty laughter, reminiscent of the carnivalesque laughter at death that holds grief at arm's length. If we find ourselves "laughing wildly amid severest woe," it is the scary laughter of a human on the verge of a cataclysmic breakdown of self and world. It is a laughter that returns us to the most fundamental questions of life and death. "Nothing is funnier than unhappiness."

If Winnie would give up her negative hallucinations and truly "see what she sees," would she be able to bear witness to the madness of her world, or would she, like Ophelia, end her life in order not to see? If this is the alternative, is her optimism really so cruel? Is it cruel because it is an optimism of postpolitics? Or does Beckett give us Winnie to show that we are, as Richard Powers asserts, damned because of how easily we shrug off darkness?[47] But even these questions do not reach far enough. We need to remember that, in Beckett's theatrical world, they are no longer formulating viable alternatives: darkness and perishing cold belong together with hellish light and merciless sun, and cruel optimism is but the mirror image of despair. In this world, happiness is but a more bearable form of suffering. The choice is only between different forms of suffering. As we have seen, in this theater of cruelty where choice is always, as Conrad puts it in *Heart of Darkness,* a choice between nightmares. Perhaps Winnie's clinging to a fake happiness explains why this might well be the darkest of Beckett's plays. Ultimately, we (the audience) don't "laugh wildly amid severest woe." We laugh the "stifled laughter"[48] of those witnessing an ingenious performance of the ecological imbalance of a mind spiraled out of control among the remainders and ruins of the "wonderful lines" left behind by an entirely disinherited language.

ACKNOWLEDGMENTS

Radioactive Ghosts emerged as a project when I spent the 2012–2013 academic year as an International Fellow at the Center for Excellence at the University of Constance, my alma mater. I was part of a collaborative research group on "Knowledge and Social Integration" and had submitted a proposal on ecological violence of which *Radioactive Ghosts* was supposed to be a chapter. My colleagues' engaged responses soon made it clear that the topic would demand a book-length study. I am deeply grateful for the generous financial support provided by the University of Constance, without which *Radioactive Ghosts* would never have taken the shape it has now. Above all, I thank Kirsten Mahlke, whose unfailing support over many years has been unparalleled. Our weekly discussions belong to the most inspiring in my academic career. At Constance, I also gained from discussion with a collaborative research group on "Disappearances," and I particularly thank Silvana Mandolessi for translating and publishing my work in Spanish. Other colleagues at Constance helped me deepen my initial framing of the topic: Aleida and Jan Assmann, Irene Albers, Astrid Bochow, Heike Drotbohm, Thomas Flierl, Eva Johach, Thomas Kirsch, Ernst Köhler, Renate Lachmann, and Mike Roth. Most surprising was the role my longtime friend Tessa Theodorakopoulos played in refining my thinking about *Radioactive Ghosts*. My stay coincided with her last years as director of the University Theater Group, the Konstanzer Theatergruppe, to which I had belonged during my assistant professorship. During my research year, Tessa recruited me to play the role of Winnie in Samuel Beckett's *Happy Days*. We had a stunning trilingual performance of the play (with three Winnies!) that inspired my Coda on *Happy Days*. It seems almost uncanny that *Radioactive Ghosts* was conceived in my beloved German hometown, where I had initially become an antinuclear activist in the 1970s and 1980s and where I had written my dissertation on Beckett's *Endgame,* a play also replete with resonances to an environmental, if not nuclear, catastrophe.

Many other institutions gave me a chance to present from my work in progress. These engagements shaped my book, often opening up new perspectives and trajectories. At the last IAPL in Singapore in

2013, the late Hugh Silverman featured a Close Encounter with panels around my work, and I presented on *Radioactive Ghosts* in my response. Thanks also to Achille Mbembe, Sarah Nuttall, and David Goldberg, whose invitation to the International Wiser/HRI Summer Seminar on "Happiness" in Johannesburg in 2015 helped me shape my reading of Beckett's *Happy Days*. In 2017, Esther Pereen and Ann Rigney organized an event in honor of my work at the ACLA in Utrecht, at which I presented on "Haunting Legacies of Nuclear Necropolitics." My heartfelt thanks also go to them for the deeply engaging responses to my work they presented. Special thanks go to Stef Craps, who invited me to present a keynote on "Hiroshima's Ghostly Shadows" at the International Summer School "Mnemonic 2018: Ecologies of Memory" in Leuven, Belgium, in 2018. I thank the participants for their inspirational engagement, particularly Andrew Hoskins for the ensuing exchanges about nuclear politics. One of the highlights in sharing this work was my Distinguished Lecture Series in Women and Gender Studies at Johns Hopkins University. I particularly thank my generous and caring host Katrin Pahl as well as Bill Egginton, Bernadette Wegenstein, Sophie von Redecker, Alphonso Lingis, Bill Connolly, and Clara Han for galvanizing exchanges and supportive friendship.

Special thanks go to Gregg Lambert and Cary Wolfe for sponsoring me through the Society for Biopolitical Futures at various SLSA meetings in Italy, the United States, and Canada. My collaboration with them over the past years has helped me frame my theory of nuclearism at the intersection of the biopolitical, the psychopolitical, and the necropolitical. I also thank my colleagues and friends at the Heinrich Heine University in Düsseldorf who brought me back over several years to talk about *Radioactive Ghosts*: Vittoria Borso, Rheinhold Görling, Susan Winnett, and Soelve Curdts. Similarly, I was excited that Kaushik Sunder Rajan invited me to speak about my project at the 2016 celebration of Ten Years of Theory at the University of Chicago. In addition to Kaushik, who has supported my work for many years, I thank Joseph Masco, Michael Fischer, and Lisa Wedeen for invaluable exchanges. I also thank Catrin Gersdorf for her unfailing support and for inviting me to present "Nuclear Borderlands and the Ghosts of the Future" at the University of Würzburg. I thank E. Ann Kaplan for years of exchanges and for inviting me to speak on Chernobyl's Aftermath at a conference at SUNY Stony Brook in her honor. I developed my theory of the nuclear unconscious for Alan Bass's conference "The Undecidable

Unconscious." Its first incarnation, titled "Haunting from the Future: Psychic Life in the Wake of Nuclear Necropolitics," was published in *The Undecidable Unconscious: A Journal of Deconstruction and Psychoanalysis* 1 (2014). I warmly thank my friend Ilse El Badawi for accompanying me to the archives of Hiroshima and Nagasaki and her sister Gisela Doi for sending me informational materials on Fukushima and for hosting me on my trip to Japan.

I am grateful for multiple opportunities to present from *Radioactive Ghosts* at my home university: Jason Willwerscheid's conference "Ecocritical Theories"; Kristen Monroe's Ethics and Politics lecture series; Julia Elyachar's workshop on Nuclear Legacies with Joseph Masco; and Stergios Skaperdas's speaker series at the Center for Global Peace and Conflict Studies (CGPACS) and then his remarkable Conference on the Nuclear Threat in the Twenty-First Century. I also thank Kamal Sadiq for inviting me back to speak at CGPACS 2020. Jessica Pratt invited me to present on *Radioactive Ghosts* for the Research Group on Ecology and Evolutionary Biology. Finally, I owe thanks to the colleagues who engaged with my work in more informal ways: Ackbar Abbas, Aijaz Ahmad, Luis Aviles, Ngũgĩ wa Thiong'o, Catherine Malabou, David Goldberg, Adriana Johnson, Jane Newman, John Smith, Ketu Katrak, George Marcus, Kris Peterson, Eleana Kim, Margherita Long, and John Whitely at UCI as well as many colleagues dispersed across continents, including John Cash, Donna Haraway (for whom I wrote my Camille X story), Achille Mbembe (who inspired my theory of nuclear necropolitics), Sarah Nuttall, Richard Powers, Gayatri Spivak, Marianne Hirsch, Maria Whiteman, Elisabeth Weber, Hugh Raffles, Michael Levine, Judith Casper, Irene Albers, Anselm Franke, Renate Lachmann, Ulla Haselstein, Florian Sedlmeier, Bettine Mehnke, Ulrike Ottinger, Nicole Sütterlin, Arlene Avakian, Ayse Gül Altinay, and Nayat Karaköse.

Most important, I thank the people who helped to put this book together. James Goebel and Lucia Cash, my research assistants, provided immeasurable help with careful readings, with formatting and technological production, and with securing the copyrights for the illustrations. Robert Barrett kept finding real treasures, such as antinuclear protest songs and stickers from the 1960s and 1970s. Tamara Beauchamp, Aijaz Ahmad, Ackbar Abbas, Michael Berlin, Alicia Cox, Anirban Gupta-Nigam, Liron Mor, Nima Yolmo, Martin Schwab, Leon Schwab, and Lucia Cash all read sections of *Radioactive Ghosts* and provided important feedback and encouragement. I also thank the students in my graduate and undergraduate seminars for exciting discussions and ideas on nuclear politics.

I thank indigenous poet, writer, and activist Simon Ortiz for co-writing the interlude "Children of the Nuclear Age" with me. This interlude is one of many interwoven memory pieces from our different cultures we co-wrote over a period of thirteen years and have published in different venues. It adds a more creative and personal dimension to my reflections on this deeply existential topic. I also express my deepest gratitude to two artists, Cornelia Hesse-Honegger and Michael Light, who granted me permission to reprint their work free of charge. I am very excited about their art and moved by their generosity in support of critical scholarly writing. Their art deepens the way I have come to think about nuclearism with an irreplaceable creative dimension. I am also most grateful to Roberta Baj for granting me permission to reprint her late husband Enrico Baj's *Figura atómica*. And I thank Petuuche Gilbert for sending me information on indigenous antinuclear activism as well as a personal photograph to use in my book. I thank UCI's Humanities Commons, whose modest grant helped me defray the cost for the remaining illustrations.

I thank the people at the University of Minnesota Press for supporting and helping with the production of *Radioactive Ghosts*. Doug Armato was a careful, experienced, and encouraging reader whose feedback certainly made it a better book. Cary Wolfe, the series editor, was one of my most astute readers. Not only did his feedback address the project's most salient intervention in current debates but he also lucidly grasped the nonlinear structure of the chapters with their resonances, recursivity, and feedback loops. Cary's support and encouragement were truly invaluable. I also thank editorial assistant Zenyse Miller, assistant managing editor Mike Stoffel, copy editor Holly Monteith, and production editor Ana Bichanich for their editorial help with the manuscript, as well as Doug Easton for preparing the index. Their care for detail was essential. I am grateful for their patience and persistence in assuring that I attended to the tedious last tasks that emerge in the final stages of preparing a manuscript for production.

I dedicate *Radioactive Ghosts* to Leon and Lucia. Their unfailing emotional support kept me from falling into a black hole when I lost several loved ones while working on this book. They offered me the gift of joy and love of life, no matter what, as an antidote to grief.

NOTES

PREFACE

1. I am grateful to Robert Barrett, who reminded me of this episode when we discussed my argument about "phantasms of the mutant body."
2. Important to note is that Blinky is not the effect of a postcatastrophe nuclear plant. In a poignant instance of life imitating art, twenty-one years after "Two Cars in Every Garage and Three Eyes on Every Fish" first aired, fishermen in Córdoba, Argentina, caught a three-eyed wolffish in a reservoir fed by a local nuclear power plant. And, indeed, mutations in the flora and fauna observed near operating nuclear plants have been widely and thoroughly documented.
3. The Manhattan Project, for example, divided Indigenous communities in the vicinity of Los Alamos. On one hand, the project provided work and a minimal livelihood for these communities. On the other hand, it destroyed communal infrastructures and contaminated the land (and, unbeknownst to the local residents, their bodies). The same double bind later marked the impossible choice between supporting and opposing uranium mining in the nuclear borderlands of the Southwest.
4. Finally, the episode's title, "Two Cars in Every Garage and Three Eyes on Every Fish," alludes to the consumer culture of postwar America while also demonstrating how this culture is implicated in the destructive impacts of extractive economies that depend on fossil fuel and nuclear power. I recall that, at the time *The Simpsons* aired on television, it was a law in Orange County that every house had to have a two-car garage.
5. See Gregory Bateson, *Steps to an Ecology of Mind: Collected Essays in Anthropology, Psychiatry, Evolution, and Epistemology* (Northvale, N.J.: Jason Aronson, 1987).
6. For one notable exception, see Helen Caldicott, *Nuclear Power Is Not the Answer* (New York: The New Press, 2006).
7. Karen Barad, "Troubling Time/s and Ecologies of Nothingness: Re-turning, Re-membering, and Facing the Incalculable," in *Eco-Deconstruction: Derrida and Environmental Philosophy*, ed. Matthias Fritsch, Philippe Lynes, and David Wood (New York: Fordham University Press, 2018), 215.
8. See Achille Mbembe, "Necropolitics," trans. Libby Meintjes, *Public Culture* 15, no. 1 (2003): 11–40.
9. See Jeffrey A. Larsen and Kerry M. Kartchner, eds., *On Limited Nuclear War in the 21st Century*, 1st ed. (Stanford, Calif.: Stanford University Press, 2014).
10. Dahr Jamail, "California Wildfire Likely Spread Nuclear Contamination from Toxic Site," *Truthout*, https://truthout.org/articles/california-wildfire-likely-spread-nuclear-contamination-from-toxic-site/.
11. "Massive Woolsey Fire Began on Contaminated Santa Susana Field Laboratory, Close to Site of Partial Meltdown," https://www.psr-la.org/massive-woolsey

-fire-began-on-contaminated-santa-susana-field-laboratory-close-to-site-of-partial-meltdown/.

12. See Hal Morgenstern et al., *Epidemiologic Study to Determine Possible Adverse Effects to Rocketdyne/Atomics International Workers from Exposure to Ionizing Radiation* (Berkeley, Calif.: Public Health Institute, 1997). In addition to the increase in cancer rates, evidence suggests an increase in thyroid and autoimmune diseases among those living in proximity to SSFL.

INTRODUCTION

1. H. G. Wells, *The World Set Free* (1914; repr., Lexington, Ky., 2017), 72.
2. Wells, 73.
3. Wells, 72.
4. Gabriele Schwab, *Imaginary Ethnographies: Literature, Culture, and Subjectivity* (New York: Columbia University Press, 2012).
5. See Larsen and Kartchner, *On Limited Nuclear War*.
6. See Rob Nixon, *Slow Violence and the Environmentalism of the Poor* (Cambridge, Mass.: Harvard University Press, 2013).
7. I'm using this in the Foucauldian sense of an epistemological configuration. See Michel Foucault, *The Order of Things: An Archaeology of the Human Sciences* (New York: Routledge, 2005).
8. What I call the *nuclear unconscious* is elaborated in greater detail in chapter 1.
9. See also R. D. Laing, *The Divided Self: An Existential Study in Sanity and Madness* (New York: Penguin Books, 1990).
10. See Arundhati Roy, *War Talk* (Cambridge, Mass.: South End Press, 2003).
11. See Andrew Hoskins, "The Forgetting Conundrum," unpublished manuscript, p. 14. See also "The New War Imaginary: Why We Are Losing the Memory of Warfare," in *The Atomic Bombs and War Memories: Heritage of Peace in an Uncertain Age*, Research Report Series 33 (Hiroshima, Japan: Institute for Peace Science, Hiroshima University, April 2018), 63: "I argue that the 'western memory regime' [. . .] has forgotten nuclear war three times: [. . .] Firstly, after the bombing of Hiroshima and Nagasaki, the idea of 'total war' recedes sharply. Secondly, after the 1962 Cuban Missile Crisis the term nuclear war declines again. [. . .] And thirdly, 1979–1985 is associated with what has been called the 'Second Cold War' with rising tensions and rising investments in militaries by the US and the Soviet Union. Thereafter, there is a steep decline in the prominence of the term 'nuclear war,' and continuing to decline in the opening years of this century."
12. *Atomic Bombs and War Memories*, 63.
13. Henry A. Kissinger, "Force and Diplomacy in the Nuclear Age," *Foreign Affairs*, 1952, 357.
14. See Larsen and Kartchner, *On Limited Nuclear War*.
15. Quoted in Robert J. Lifton and Greg Mitchell, *Hiroshima in America: Fifty Years of Denial* (New York: Grosset and Putnam, 1995), 372.
16. Elaine Scarry, *Thermonuclear Monarchy: Choosing between Democracy and Doom* (New York: W. W. Norton, 2014), 7.

17. Scarry, 12.
18. Scarry, 8.
19. Scarry, 9.
20. Scarry, 10.
21. Scarry, 21.
22. Scarry, 11.
23. Scarry, 22.
24. See, e.g., Ian Lowe and Barry Brook, *Why vs. Why: Nuclear Power* (Sydney, Australia: Simon and Schuster, 2012).
25. For this and the following, see Jan Willem van Leeuwen, *Can Nuclear Power Slow Down Climate Change? An Analysis of Nuclear Greenhouse Gas Emissions* (Amsterdam, Netherlands: World Information Service on Energy, 2015).
26. Van Leeuwen, 12.
27. Van Leeuwen, 12. But even if one were to assume that nuclear power emits no greenhouse gases, which is not true, according to the scenarios projected by the nuclear industry, the nuclear mitigation share would grow only from the present level of less than 1 percent to at most 1.4 percent of the global greenhouse gas emissions by 2050–60. That is, these scenarios do not take into account greenhouse gases other than CO_2 emitted by nuclear power, nor do they include projections beyond 2060.
28. Van Leeuwen, 5.
29. Van Leeuwen, 5.
30. Van Leeuwen, 12.
31. Van Leeuwen, 12.
32. Van Leeuwen, 12.
33. For this and the following, see Caldicott, *Nuclear Power Is Not the Answer.*
34. Caldicott, 130.
35. Caldicott, 86.
36. Takashi Nagai, *We of Nagasaki: The Story of Survivors in an Atomic Wasteland* (New York: Duell, Sloan, and Pearce, 1951), 188–89. Quoted in Robert J. Lifton, *Death in Life: Survivors of Hiroshima* (New York: Random House, 1968), 309.
37. See Lifton, *Death in Life*, 309.
38. See Lifton, 371.
39. Kate Brown, *Plutopia: Nuclear Families, Atomic Cities, and the Great Soviet and American Plutonium Disasters* (Oxford: Oxford University Press, 2013), 337.
40. See Nixon, *Slow Violence.*
41. Brown, *Plutopia,* 337.
42. Litvinenko, who died of acute radiation syndrome, was the first known victim of poisoning by radioactive polonium-210. A public inquiry, concluded in 2016, established that Litvinenko's murder was the result of an operation by Russia's security service or spy agency, the FSB, most likely personally approved, as BBC News reported, by Vladimir Putin. I analyze this case in detail in chapter 5.
43. See Robert Mendick and Robert Verkaik, "Mystery Death of Ex-KGB Chief Linked to MI6 Spy's Dossier on Donald Trump," *Telegraph,* January 27, 2017,

http://www.telegraph.co.uk/news/2017/01/27/mystery-death-ex-kgb-chief-linked-mi6-spys-dossier-donald-trump/.

44. See Martin Cruz Smith, *Wolves Eat Dogs* (New York: Simon and Schuster, 2004). I discuss this novel in greater detail in chapter 5.

45. For this and the following, see Ellen Mitchell, "Trump Revealed Submarine Locations to Philippines President," *The Hill,* May 24, 2017, http://thehill.com/policy/defense/334969-trump-revealed-submarine-locations-to-philippines-president. According to an official transcript from the Philippine Department of Foreign Affairs, President Trump, in a phone call with Duterte on April 29, also addressed the possibility of a nuclear strike on North Korea, an alarming provocation that fueled tensions with North Korea, which eventually culminated in the verbal showdown between the two presidents before the intervention of South Korea and the rapprochement between the two Korean nations.

46. Aijaz Ahmad, *Lineages of the Present: Ideology and Politics in Contemporary South Asia* (London: Verso, 2000), 240.

47. For this and the following, see Amy Goodman, "Forget Russia. Is Provoking a Nuclear War with North Korea Grounds for Impeachment?," *Democracy Now!,* August 9, 2017, https://www.democracynow.org/2017/8/9/forget_russia_is_provoking_a_nuclear.

48. See also Noah Bierman, "President Takes War of Words Up a Notch," *Los Angeles Times,* August 11, 2017, front page. Tensions had grown in recent weeks after U.S. intelligence officials concluded that North Korea has produced a miniaturized nuclear warhead that can fit inside its missiles, leading the United Nations Security Council to impose a new round of sanctions against North Korea. The fallout of a nuclear strike on Guam would affect Japan, where senior officials are now pushing for long-range cruise missiles. For years there had been a consensus within the U.S. establishment and the military that military action against North Korea was unthinkable because North Korea could immediately devastate Seoul. But this all changed when Colonel Guy Roberts wrote an article in 2016 calling for the United States to adopt a first-strike nuclear policy, specifically mentioning North Korea. In 2017, Trump promptly nominated Roberts to be the assistant secretary of defense for nuclear policy.

49. The weapon's research and design laboratory in Los Alamos worked on uranium enrichment, paralleled by efforts to produce plutonium through irradiation and transmutation of uranium.

50. Joseph Masco, *The Nuclear Borderlands: The Manhattan Project in Post–Cold War Mexico* (Princeton, N.J.: Princeton University Press, 2006), 30.

51. Masco, 25–34.

52. See Masco, 236. The term *psychic toxicity* was coined by Herman Agoyo, an Indigenous antinuclear activist from New Mexico.

53. Masco, 237.

54. See Nixon, *Slow Violence.* Throughout *Radioactive Ghosts,* I argue that nuclear necropolitics includes both the spectacular violence of nuclear wars or catastrophes and the slow violence of long-term nuclear contamination with its health risks affecting planetary life for generations to come.

55. Cary Wolfe, "Wallace Stevens's Birds, or, Derrida and Ecological Poetics," in Fritsch et al., *Eco-Deconstruction: Derrida and Environmental Philosophy,* 334.

56. Wolfe, 333.
57. Quoted in Wolfe, 334.
58. See Mbembe, "Necropolitics."
59. Mbembe, 11.
60. See Ward Churchill, *Struggle for the Land: Native North American Resistance to Genocide, Ecocide, and Colonization* (San Francisco: City Lights Books, 2002); Valerie L. Kuletz, *Tainted Desert: Environmental and Social Ruin in the American West* (New York: Routledge, 1998); Masco, *Nuclear Borderlands*.
61. See Mike Davis, *Ecology of Fear: Los Angeles and the Imagination of Disaster* (New York: Vintage, 1999). While Mike Davis does not specifically address nuclear politics in the nuclear borderlands, his notion of an "ecology of fear" is pertinent to an analysis of nuclear necropolitics.
62. Mbembe, "Necropolitics," 12.
63. Mbembe, 14.
64. Eileen Welsome, *The Plutonium Files: America's Secret Medical Experiments in the Cold War* (New York: Dial Press, 1999).
65. See Rob Edwards, "The Radioactive Legacy of the Search for Plutopia," *New Scientist*, March 13, 2013, https://www.newscientist.com/article/mg21729082-500-the-radioactive-legacy-of-the-search-for-plutopia/.
66. It is important to remember that this was also the time when testing was outsourced, so to speak, and twenty nuclear weapons tests were conducted under the code name "Operation Crossroads" at the Bikini Atoll from 1946 to 1958, contaminating the twenty-three Pacific islands. Like the Manhattan Project, the tests at the Bikini Atoll clearly exhibit the neocolonial dynamic that Ward Churchill has called "radioactive colonization." Leslie Groves was against the tests because he saw the secrecy of the U.S. nuclear program compromised. There was little debate about the fact that the entire Indigenous population of 167 Micronesian citizens was forcibly resettled to the neighboring atoll of Rongerik, never able to return to their homeland.
67. Mbembe, "Necropolitics," 14.
68. Mbembe, 15.
69. See Lifton and Mitchell, *Hiroshima in America*, 351. I am also referring back to the Trump statement quoted at the beginning of the chapter.
70. Masco, *Nuclear Borderlands*, 55–56.
71. Mbembe, "Necropolitics," 16.
72. See Georges Bataille, *The Accursed Share: An Essay on General Economy*, vols. 2–3 (Berkeley, Calif.: Zone Books, 1991).
73. Georges Bataille, "Concerning the Accounts Given by the Residents of Hiroshima," trans. Alan Keenan, *American Imago* 48, no. 4 (1991): 497–514.
74. See John Heresy, *Hiroshima* (New York: Alfred A. Knopf, 1946).
75. Bataille, "Concerning the Accounts Given by the Residents of Hiroshima," 509.
76. Bataille, 497.
77. Bataille, 511.
78. Bataille, 506.
79. See Adi Ophir, *The Order of Evils: Toward an Ontology of Morals* (Berkeley, Calif.: Zone Books, 2005).

80. Bataille, "Concerning the Accounts Given by the Residents of Hiroshima," 508.
81. Bataille, 513.
82. Bataille, 509.
83. Bataille, 513.
84. Bataille, 506.
85. Bataille, 511.
86. See Gayatri Chakravorty Spivak, "Terror: A Speech after 9/11," *Boundary 2* 31, no. 2 (2004): 81–111.
87. I am deliberately using the male pronoun here because, as I argue in more detail later, the project of nuclear necropolitics is a deeply masculinist project fueled by male fantasies of sublime destruction.
88. Jayne Cortez, *Celebrations and Solitudes* (New York: Strata-East, 1974), 5.
89. Ayi Kwei Armah, *Two Thousand Seasons* (Senegal: Per Ankh, 2000), 170.
90. Bruno Latour, *Facing Gaia: Eight Lectures on the New Climate Regime* (Medford, Mass.: Polity Press, 2017), 226.
91. Robert Meister, *After Evil: A Politics of Human Rights* (New York: Columbia University Press, 2011), 36.
92. Jonathan Schell, *The Fate of the Earth; and, The Abolition* (Stanford, Calif.: Stanford University Press, 2000).
93. See Schell, 115.
94. Schell, 115.
95. Schell, 119.
96. Schell, 116.
97. See also Ursula K. Heise, *Imagining Extinction: The Cultural Meanings of Endangered Species* (Chicago: University of Chicago Press, 2016).
98. Schell, *Fate of the Earth*, 111.
99. Schell, 111.
100. William J. Hennigan and Tracy Wilkinson, "We're 30 Seconds Closer to 'Doomsday,'" *Los Angeles Times,* January 27, 2017, A3.
101. Stephen Schwartz was the former executive director of the group that founded the *Bulletin of the Atomic Scientists*.
102. Hennigan and Wilkinson, "We're 30 Seconds Closer to 'Doomsday.'"
103. Hennigan and Wilkinson.
104. See Lifton, *Death in Life*.
105. Scarry, *Thermonuclear Monarchy*, 8.
106. Scarry, 17.
107. Larsen and Kartchner, *On Limited Nuclear War*, xix.
108. Larsen and Kartchner, 83.
109. Larsen and Kartchner, 87.
110. Larsen and Kartchner, 89.
111. Larsen and Kartchner, 172.
112. Larsen and Kartchner, xxix.
113. Michael Walsh, "'Let It Be an Arms Race': Trump Doubles Down on Nuclear Proliferation," *Yahoo! News,* December 23, 2016, https://www.yahoo.com/news/let-it-be-an-arms-race-trump-doubles-down-on-nuclear-proliferation.

114. As he stated in a preelection interview with MSNBC's Chris Matthews, "the biggest problem we have is nuclear—nuclear proliferation, [. . .] and having some maniac, having some madman go out and get a nuclear weapon. That's in my opinion, that is the single biggest problem that our country faces right now." He then asserted that nothing was off the table when it came to nuclear weapons and asked point-blank why the United States makes them if it doesn't plan to use them. Matthews responded, "The trouble is, when you said that, the whole world heard it. David Cameron in Britain heard it. The Japanese, where we bombed them in '45, heard it. They're hearing a guy running for President of the United States talking of maybe using nuclear weapons. Nobody wants to hear that about an American president." Defiantly, Trump replied, "Then why are we making them? Why do we make them?"

At a news conference in February 2017, Trump offered the public another disturbing glimpse into his take on nuclear politics: "You know what uranium is, right? This thing called nuclear weapons like lots of things are done with uranium including some bad things. Nobody talks about that." After Trump proceeded by issuing the false claim that Hillary Clinton gave Russia 20 percent of the United States' uranium, he elaborated on the nuclear threat: "Don't forget, we're a very powerful nuclear country and so are they [the Russians]. I have been briefed. And I can tell you one thing about a briefing that we're allowed to say [. . .] nuclear holocaust would be like no other." While one might be tempted simply to dismiss these statements as overly trite and uninformed, their dangerous implications become blatantly obvious in the context of Trump's earlier emphatic proclamation about outlasting everybody in a new arms race.

On May 30, 2017, the *Los Angeles Times* featured an article by W. J. Hennigan and Ralph Vartabedian that stated, "As the global nuclear race heats up, debate rages in the U.S. over whether land-based missiles are needed." The cost of a nuclear race would be absolutely prohibitive and would certainly mean further cuts in social, educational, health, and civic services in a country where such services are already shamefully below the rest of the industrialized world's standards. Two years ago, the Pentagon estimated the costs for "a new ICBM system, known as the Ground-Based Strategic Deterrent," at $62.3 billion.

115. Trump's comments index an unfortunate end to the vision of a world without nuclear weapons, which John Kerry had invoked a year earlier in his speech at the United Nations headquarters in New York. Moreover, and perhaps most threateningly, Trump's very rhetoric of "outlasting them all" reaches far beyond the notion of a limited nuclear war that has in recent years been explored anew by defense analysts and specialists on nuclear policy. Extending back to the 1950s, the debates about limited nuclear war were seminal in the post–World War II era of the Cold War.

116. See also Elizabeth A. Povinelli's argument that one of the emerging figures of geo-ontopolitics (since Foucault's biopolitics) is the terrorist. Povinelli, *Geontologies: A Requiem to Late Liberalism* (Durham, S.C.: Duke University Press, 2016).

117. Mbembe, "Necropolitics," 17.

118. Mbembe, 18.

119. Svetlana Alexievich, *Voices from Chernobyl: The Oral History of a Nuclear Disaster*, trans. Keith Gessen (New York: Picado, 2005), 236.
120. Mbembe, "Necropolitics," 33.
121. More specifically, it started in response to the failure to impeach Richard (Dick) Wilson, head of the Bureau of Indian Affairs at Pine Ridge, whom residents accused of corruption, especially in relation to the selling off of tribal lands targeted for uranium mining.
122. Lifton and Mitchell, *Hiroshima in America*, 304.
123. Gregory Benford, *Deep Time: How Humanity Communicates across Millennia* (New York: HarperCollins, 1999).
124. Benford, 2.
125. Benford, 3.
126. Benford, 3.
127. Nevil Shute, *On the Beach* (New York: Random House, 1985).
128. Davis, *Ecology of Fear*, 339.
129. See also Davis, 354.
130. Davis, 47.

1. NO APOCALYPSE, NOT NOW

1. Alan Bass, *Difference and Disavowal: The Trauma of Eros* (Stanford, Calif.: Stanford University Press, 2000), 136.
2. Hans Loewald, "Psychoanalysis in Search of Nature: Thoughts on Metapsychology, 'Metaphysics,' Projection," *Annual of Psychoanalysis* 16 (1988): 50.
3. By referring to the notion of vibrant materiality, I am drawing from, yet modifying, recent feminist and posthumanist work in the new materialisms, most notably, from Jane Bennett, *Vibrant Matter: A Political Ecology of Things* (Durham, N.C.: Duke University Press, 2010). However, see also Stacy Alaimo, *Bodily Natures: Science, Environment, and the Material Self* (Bloomington: Indiana University Press, 2010); Karen Barad, *Meeting the Universe Halfway: Quantum Physics and the Entanglement of Matter and Meaning* (Durham, N.C.: Duke University Press, 2007); Rosi Braidotti, *Metamorphoses: Towards a Materialist Theory of Becoming* (Malden, Mass.: Polity Press, 2002); Braidotti, *The Posthuman* (Malden, Mass.: Polity Press, 2013); Mel Y. Chen, *Animacies: Biopolitics, Racial Mattering, and Queer Affect* (Durham, N.C.: Duke University Press, 2012).
4. Bass, *Difference and Disavowal*, 138.
5. Bass, 139.
6. See Bateson, *Steps to an Ecology of Mind*.
7. Loewald, "Psychoanalysis in Search of Nature," 50.
8. Loewald, 51. Loewald writes, "What is needed is a natural science that realizes that the interpretation of nature in terms of (individualistic) consciousness limits our view, granted that it has pragmatical validity for human conscious thought and action and appears to enhance man's domination of the world" (51).
9. Bass, *Difference and Disavowal*, 144.
10. Jacques Derrida, "No Apocalypse, Not Now (Full Speed Ahead, Seven Missiles, Seven Missives)," trans. Catherine Porter and Philip Lewis, *Diacritics* 14, no. 2 (1984): 23.

11. Schell, *Fate of the Earth*, 117.

12. This is, whether consciously or unconsciously, and at varying degrees of extremity, a belief held by many deep ecologists from the 1970s onward, especially in the insistence on population control. This is not to suggest that human population or its exponential growth are not important political questions, but often they are manifestations of sexist, classist, racist, and colonial anxieties, which are (re-)framed through specific, often holistic, constructions of Nature and the Nature–Culture distinction. See Christine J. Cuomo, "Ecofeminism, Deep Ecology, and Human Population," in *Ecological Feminism*, ed. Karen J. Warren, 88–105 (New York: Routledge, 1994); Greta Gaard, *Ecological Politics* (Philadelphia: Temple University Press, 2010).

13. Derrida, "No Apocalypse, Not Now," 20.

14. Derrida, 23.

15. Derrida, 21.

16. See Carl von Clausewitz, *On War*, trans. Michael Howard and Peter Paret (Oxford: Oxford University Press, 2007). A general of the Prussian army at the turn of the nineteenth century, Clausewitz was the first to posit that "war can be of two kinds, in the sense that either the objective is to *overthrow the enemy* [. . .] or *merely to occupy some of his frontier-districts* so that we can annex them or use them for bargaining at the peace negotiations. [. . .] This distinction between two kinds of war is a matter of actual fact. But no less practical is the importance of another point that must be made quite clear, namely that *war is nothing but the continuation of policy with other means*" (7). The notion that policy and peace, and peace achieved through policy, are continuations of war by other means has generated a significant amount of debate among twentieth-century proponents and critics of liberalism. See, e.g., the debates between Panajotis Kondylis, *Theorie des Krieges: Clausewitz—Marx—Engels—Lenin* (Stuttgart: Klett-Cotta/J. G. Cotta'sche Buchhandlung Nachfolger, 1988), and Raymond Aron, *Clausewitz: Philosopher of War*, trans. Christine Booker and Norman Stone (Englewood Cliffs, N.J.: Prentice Hall, 1985). See also Giorgio Agamben, *Means without End: Notes on Politics*, trans. Vincenzo Binetti and Cesare Casarino (Minneapolis: University of Minnesota Press, 2000); Gilles Deleuze and Félix Guattari, *A Thousand Plateaus: Capitalism and Schizophrenia*, trans. Brian Massumi (Minneapolis: University of Minnesota Press, 1987), esp. 351–423.

17. Elaborating upon his concept of the hyperobject, Timothy Morton hints toward this notion of a haunting from the future, as the hyperobject's "shadow looms out of the future into the present" (67) and "radiates temporality from the future into the present" (91). That it radiates and that Morton's elaborations on the *future future* of the hyperobject are often accompanied by mentions of the nuclear bomb, plutonium, and uranium are at least interesting to note. Timothy Morton, *Hyperobjects: Philosophy and Ecology after the End of the World* (Minneapolis: University of Minnesota Press, 2013).

18. Traci Brynne Voyles, *Wastelanding: Legacies of Uranium Minding in Navajo Country* (Minneapolis: University of Minnesota Press, 2015), 215.

19. Voyles, 217.

20. Barad, "Troubling Time/s," 226–27.

21. Derrida, "No Apocalypse, Not Now," 23.
22. Derrida, 24.
23. Derrida, 28.
24. Barad, "Troubling Time/s," 208.
25. For the "nuclear sublime," see Masco, *Nuclear Borderlands*.
26. Francesco M. Cataluccio, *Die Ausradierte Stadt: Tscherobyls Katastrophen*, trans. Sigrid Vagt (Vienna: Paul Zsolnay, 2012), 132. Cataluccio even titled his chapter on the disaster tourist economy of Chernobyl and Pripyat "The Disneyland of Radioactivity."
27. Derrida, "No Apocalypse, Not Now," 23.
28. Derrida, 23.
29. For "ethnographies of the future," see Schwab, *Imaginary Ethnographies*; Marilyn Strathern, *Reproducing the Future: Anthropology, Kinship, and the New Reproductive Technologies* (New York: Routledge, 1992).
30. Derrida, "No Apocalypse, Not Now," 27.
31. Derrida, 28.
32. Derrida, 28.
33. See Frank Kermode, *The Sense of an Ending: Studies in the Theory of Fiction* (New York: Oxford University Press, 2000).
34. Derrida, "No Apocalypse, Not Now," 28.
35. Derrida, 27–28.
36. Derrida, 27.
37. Samuel Beckett, *Happy Days: A Play in Two Acts* (New York: Grove Press, 1989), 13.
38. See Bruno Latour, *Politics of Nature: How to Bring the Sciences into Democracy*, trans. Catherine Porter (Cambridge, Mass.: Harvard University Press, 2004).
39. Derrida, "No Apocalypse, Not Now," 23.
40. Jacques Derrida, *Rogues: Two Essays on Reason*, trans. Pascale-Anne Brault and Michael Naas (Stanford, Calif.: Stanford University Press, 2005), 141.
41. Derrida, 144.
42. Derrida, 154.
43. Derrida, 155–56.
44. Derrida, 157.
45. Derrida, 157.
46. Schell, *Fate of the Earth*, 187.
47. Schell, 189.
48. Schell, 189.
49. Schell, 194.
50. Schell, 227.
51. Schell, 227.
52. Schell, 33.
53. Schell, 218.
54. Schell, 218.
55. Spivak, "Terror: A Speech after 9/11," 81.
56. Schell, *Fate of the Earth*, 137.

57. Derrida, *Rogues*, 158.
58. Derrida, 158.
59. Schell, *Fate of the Earth*, 66.
60. Ward Churchill, *A Little Matter of Genocide: Holocaust and Denial in the Americas 1492 to the Present* (San Francisco: City Lights Books, 1998), 346.
61. Svetlana Alexievich, *Voices from Chernobyl: The Oral History of a Nuclear Disaster*, trans. Keith Gessen (New York: Picador, 2005), 112.

2. NUCLEAR COLONIALISM

1. For a transcript of Gilbert's statement, see Petuuche Gilbert, "Petuuche Gilbert's Statement at the EPA Meeting in Gallup: NO MORE URANIUM MINING!!," *Earth Peoples* (blog), April 27, 2013, http://earthpeoples.org/blog/?tag=petuuche.gilbert.
2. Simon J. Ortiz, *Woven Stone* (Tucson: University of Arizona Press, 1992), 352–53.
3. Ortiz, 357.
4. See Churchill, *Struggle for the Land*. In the chapter titled "Radioactive Colonization," Churchill provides a detailed overview of the impacts of American nuclearism on the health of Indigenous communities in the Southwest.
5. See Churchill, esp. 239–91; Valerie L. Kuletz, *Tainted Desert: Environmental and Social Ruin in the American West* (New York: Routledge, 1998); Masco, *Nuclear Borderlands*. Ortiz's *Fight Back: For the Sake of the People, for the Sake of the Land* (1980), edited for and collected in *Woven Stone* alongside *Going for the Rain* (1976) and *A Good Journey* (1977), is divided into two parts, "Too Many Sacrifices" and "No More Sacrifices," respectively, with the first prose poem of part II titled "Our Homeland: A National Sacrifice Area."
6. Ortiz, *Woven Stone*, 358.
7. Ortiz, 352.
8. Of the Ghoomi, the main springs of the Aacqumeh hanoh valley, Ortiz writes, "The elders of the Aacumeh hanoh speak about the numbers of springs in the valley. In olden times. Now there are several minor wells pumped by windmills; water barely trickles into steel holding tanks and troughs. [. . .] Ghoomi has never been known to run dry, but it is watched anxiously." Ortiz, 340. Later, in poetic form, he explains,

> Our family hauled water
> in fifty-gallon drums
> for use as drinking water.
> My father built a sled on which we'd put the barrels.
> Over the barrels we stretched tarp
> as a cover.
> My mother said the people
> drank
> from the nearby river
> when she was a girl.
> But when I was a boy,

we used it only for washing clothes.
We could not drink it. (343)

Ortiz links this disruption to a long history of colonialism that connects the Spanish conquests of the seventeenth century to Anglo-American agricultural practices, water reclamation projects, and, of course, uranium mining during the twentieth century. Opening with "old and young people go by the springs frequently because the water from it is sweet and cold," Ortiz then switches to autobiographical and poetic form, writing, "The water in the cistern / on the northside of Srhakaiya / was not mountain cold. / It smelled / and tasted sour. But I was thirsty, / and I drank" (340). See Joni Adamson, *American Indian Literature, Environmental Justice, and Ecocriticism: The Middle Place* (Tucson: University of Arizona Press, 2001).

9. Simon J. Ortiz, *from Sand Creek* (Tucson: University of Arizona Press, 1981), 59.

10. See H. Josef Hebert, "Store Nuclear Waste on Reservation? Tribe Split," June 27, 2006, http://www.nbcnews.com/id/13458867/ns/us_news/t/store-nuclear-waste-reservation-tribe-split/.

11. Ortiz, *from Sand Creek*, 47.

12. Ortiz, 47.

13. For this and below, Leon Shenandoah, "Address to the General Assembly of the United Nations," October 25, 1985, http://light-seeds.com/Native-Prophecy.html.

14. Schell, *Fate of the Earth*, 189.

15. See Oren Lyons, "An Iroquois Perspective," in *American Indian Environments: Ecological Issues in Native American History*, ed. Christopher Vecsey and Robert W. Venables, 171–74 (Syracuse, N.Y.: Syracuse University Press, 1980).

16. Black Elk and John G. Neihardt, *Black Elk Speaks: Being the Life Story of a Holy Man of the Oglala Sioux*, Premier ed. (Albany: State University of New York Press, 2009).

17. *Los Angeles Times*, January 27, 2017, A15.

18. Democracy Now!, *Lakota Activist Debra White Plume from Pine Ridge: Why I Am a Water Protector at Standing Rock*, 2016, https://www.youtube.com/watch?v=ikNKhht0pt0.

19. Trump's contempt for Indigenous people also goes hand in hand with his unabashed contempt for women, revealed not only in the vulgarity of his words and actions but also in his attacks on reproductive health and health care more generally. Finally, it goes hand in hand with his unconcealed male fantasies of conquest that underwrite the iconicity of his very particular will to power as it is epitomized, for example, in his attempt to erect his phallic Trump Towers across the globe.

20. Peter Matthiessen, *In the Spirit of Crazy Horse* (New York: Viking Press, 1991), 593.

21. Matthiessen, 406.

22. Matthiessen, 406.

23. See Kevin Kamps, "The Great Lakes and a High-Level Radioactive Nuke

Waste Dump Don't Mix," *EcoWatch,* January 28, 2016, https://www.ecowatch.com/the-great-lakes-and-a-high-level-radioactive-nuke-waste-dump-dont-mix-1882160700.html.

24. Matthiessen, *In the Spirit of Crazy Horse,* 407.

25. Matthiessen, 409–10.

26. Derrida, "No Apocalypse, Not Now," 20.

27. Kuletz, *Tainted Desert,* 115.

28. Caldicott, *Nuclear Power Is Not the Answer,* 130.

29. Quoted in Klaus Theweleit, *Male Fantasies,* trans. Chris Turner, Carter Erica, and Stephen Conway (Minneapolis: University of Minnesota Press, 1987). It should be noted that Theweleit combines two portions of Canetti's original, appearing separately on pages 295 and 296 of *Crowds and Power* (New York: Farrar, Straus, and Giroux, 1984).

30. Herman Agoyo, "Who Here Will Begin This Story?," *Race, Poverty, and the Environment* 5, no. 3/4 (1995): 37.

31. While many Indigenous peoples first welcomed the fact that Los Alamos was a source of new work and income, they gradually discovered, as Agoyo vividly describes, the immensity of human costs: "We have slowly realized that this work which started out to harness an unimaginable power has in fact harmed human beings and the planet beyond any calculation. It has harmed us all by the sickness, death, and destruction that has been the ultimate product of this work." From this Indigenous perspective, the Manhattan Project is, as Joseph Masco argues, "a new moment in the colonial history of the Southwest, as ecosystems, bodies, and cosmologies have been transformed by their biological, social, and spiritual engagement with the plutonium economy" (101).

32. Agoyo, 102.

33. Masco, *Nuclear Borderlands,* 104.

34. Martin Cruz Smith, *Stallion Gate: A Novel* (New York: Ballantine Books, 1986), 148.

35. Smith, 152.

36. Smith, 166.

37. Smith, 174.

38. See Tanya H. Lee, "H-Bomb Guinea Pigs! Natives Suffering Decades after New Mexico Tests," March 5, 2014, https://indiancountrymedianetwork.com/news/environment/h-bomb-guinea-pigs-natives-suffering-decades-after-new-mexico-tests/.

39. Jean Comaroff and John L. Comaroff, *The Truth about Crime: Sovereignty, Knowledge, Social Order* (Chicago: University of Chicago Press, 2016).

40. Smith, *Stallion Gate,* 241.

41. Jimmy Santiago Baca, *Black Mesa Poems* (New York: New Directions, 1986).

42. Masco, *Nuclear Borderlands,* 290.

43. Masco, 228.

44. Gerald Vizenor, *Hiroshima Bugi: Atomu* (Lincoln: University of Nebraska Press, 2003), 78.

45. Vizenor, 78.

46. Vizenor, 92.
47. Vizenor, 87.
48. Vizenor, 87.
49. Vizenor, 86–87.
50. Vizenor, 171.
51. Vizenor, 56.
52. Vizenor, 95.
53. Vizenor, 203.

3. CRITICAL NUCLEAR RACE THEORY

1. See Tom Zoellner, *Uranium: War, Energy, and the Rock That Shaped the World* (New York: Viking Press, 2009), 2–14.
2. For this and the following, see Zoellner, 5–6.
3. Zoellner, 8.
4. Zoellner, 12.
5. Zoellner, 183.
6. Achille Mbembe, *Critique of Black Reason,* trans. Laurent Dubois (Durham, N.C.: Duke University Press, 2017), 2.
7. Mbembe, 170.
8. Mbembe, 4.
9. Mbembe, 136.
10. Mbembe, 137.
11. I discuss Lifton in detail in chapter 5.
12. Ngũgĩ wa Thiong'o, *Secure the Base* (Calcutta: Seagull Books, 2016), xiv.
13. Thiong'o, 106.
14. Thiong'o, 109.
15. Thiong'o, 110.
16. Arundhati Roy, *The Ordinary Person's Guide to Empire* (London: Flamingo, 2004), 8.
17. Vincent J. Intondi, *African Americans against the Bomb: Nuclear Weapons, Colonialism, and the Black Freedom Movement* (Stanford, Calif.: Stanford University Press, 2015).
18. Intondi, 21.
19. Intondi, 22.
20. Quoted in Paul Williams, *Race, Ethnicity, and Nuclear War: Representations of Nuclear Weapons and Post-Apocalyptic Worlds* (Liverpool: Liverpool University Press, 2011), 149.
21. Paul Robeson, *Paul Robeson Speaks: Writings, Speeches, and Interviews, a Centennial Celebration,* ed. Philip S. Foner (New York: Citadel Press, 1978), 169.
22. Quoted in Intondi, *African Americans against the Bomb,* 29.
23. Quoted in Intondi, 33.
24. Quoted in Intondi, 36.
25. Quoted in Intondi, 37.
26. Quoted in Intondi, 41.
27. Quoted in Intondi, 47.
28. Intondi, 60.
29. James Baldwin, *The Fire Next Time* (New York: Vintage Books, 1993), 53.

30. Quoted in Intondi, *African Americans against the Bomb*, 64.
31. For this and the following, see Intondi, 66–67.
32. Intondi, 68.
33. Quoted in Amy Swerdlow, *Women Strike for Peace: Traditional Motherhood and Radical Politics in the 1960s* (Chicago: University of Chicago Press, 1993), 92.
34. Huey P. Newton, *To Die for the People: The Writings of Huey P. Newton*, ed. Toni Morrison (New York: Writings and Readers, 1995), 7.
35. Quoted in Intondi, *African Americans against the Bomb*, 84.
36. Quoted in Intondi, 85.
37. Intondi, 87.
38. Quoted in Intondi, 90.
39. Intondi, 93.
40. Quoted in Intondi, 104.
41. Quoted in Intondi, 104.
42. Quoted in Intondi, 105.
43. Quoted in Intondi, 108.
44. Quoted in Intondi, 113.
45. Quoted in Intondi, 115.
46. For this and the following, see Intondi, 113–32.
47. Intondi, 118.
48. Intondi, 129.
49. Intondi, 131.
50. Intondi, 132.
51. Intondi, 131.
52. Quoted in Williams, *Race, Ethnicity, and Nuclear War*, v.
53. Malcolm X, *The Autobiography of Malcolm X* (London: Penguin Books, 2001), 373.
54. Albert E. Stone, *Literary Aftershocks: American Writers, Readers, and the Bomb* (New York: Twayne, 1994), 21.
55. Williams, *Race, Ethnicity, and Nuclear War*, 162.
56. Williams, 168.
57. Alice Walker, *In Search of Our Mothers' Gardens* (San Diego, Calif.: Harcourt Brace Jovanovich, 1988).
58. Walker, 342.
59. Williams, *Race, Ethnicity, and Nuclear War*, 168.
60. Mbembe, *Critique of Black Reason*, 183.
61. Barbara Smith, *Home Girls: A Black Feminist Anthology*, 2nd ed. (New Brunswick, N.J.: Rutgers University Press, 1983), xxxi.

4. THE GENDER OF NUCLEAR SUBJECTIVITIES

1. Brenda Wineapple, "The Politics of Politics; or, How the Atomic Bomb Didn't Interest Gertrude Stein and Emily Dickinson," *South Central Review* 23, no. 3 (2006): 43.
2. Gertrude Stein, "Reflection on the Atomic Bomb," in *The Previously Uncollected Writings of Gertrude Stein*, vol. 1, *Reflection on the Atomic Bomb*, ed. Robert Bartlett Haas (Los Angeles, Calif.: Black Sparrow Press, 1975).
3. See Melanie Klein, "Notes on Some Schizoid Mechanisms," *International*

Journal of Psycho-Analysis 27 (1946): 99–110; Robert Meister, *After Evil: A Politics of Human Rights* (New York: Columbia University Press, 2011).

4. Stein, "Reflection on the Atomic Bomb," 179.

5. Stein, 179.

6. Stein, 179.

7. Stein, 179.

8. Nuclear necropolitics and the nuclear unconscious have generated an entire range of experimental works, including Samuel Beckett's *Happy Days,* which I treat in the coda to *Radioactive Ghosts.* They have also generated a range of aesthetic works that approach nuclear politics in unconventional ways that cross the boundaries between genres and styles as well as high and popular culture. Apart from an entire series of graphic novels, popular culture renditions include, for example, Isao Takahata's highly acclaimed anime film *Grave of the Fireflies* (1988), which is inspired by his own traumatic experience as a child survivor of the United States' nuclear attacks on Japan.

9. Akira Mizuta Lippit, *Atomic Light (Shadow Optics)* (Minneapolis: University of Minnesota Press, 2005), 35–60.

10. See Masco, *Nuclear Borderlands,* 55–68.

11. "The Atomic Gardening Society," http://www.atomicgardening.com/1960/02/21/the-atomic-gardening-society/.

12. For this and the following, see B. S. Ahloowalia, M. Maluszynski, and K. Nichterlein, "Global Impact of Mutation-Derived Varieties," *Euphytica* 135, no. 2 (2004): 187–204.

13. *Dilbert,* August 29, 1989, http://dilbert.com/strip/1989-08-29.

14. Lippit, *Atomic Light,* 35–60.

15. Lisa Cartwright, "Women, X-Rays, and the Public Culture of Prophylactic Imaging," *Camera Obscura: Feminism, Culture, and Media Studies* 10, no. 2.29 (1992): 30.

16. Lisa Cartwright, *Screening the Body: Tracing Medicine's Visual Culture* (Minneapolis: University of Minnesota Press, 1995), 115.

17. Kate Moore, *The Radium Girls: The Dark Story of America's Shining Women* (Naperville, Ill.: Sourcebooks, 2017), 392.

18. For this and the following, see Moore, xvi.

19. For this and the following, see Moore, 4–10.

20. Moore, 8.

21. Moore, 387.

22. Moore, 392.

23. For this and the following, see Moore, 397–99.

24. Winston S. Churchill, *Memoirs of the Second World War* (Boston: Houghton Mifflin, 1959), 981.

25. Churchill, 980.

26. Marc Le Bot et al., *Le Macchine Celibi/The Bachelor Machines* (New York: Rizzoli, 1975), 22.

27. Quoted in Robert J. Lifton and Richard Falk, *Indefensible Weapons: The Political and Psychological Case against Nuclearism* (New York: Basic Books, 1982), 90.

28. Bel Mooney, *Over Our Dead Bodies* (London: Virgo Press, 1983), 6.

29. Ray Monk, *Robert Oppenheimer: A Life inside the Center* (New York: Anchor Books/Random House, 2014), 457.

30. Le Bot et al., *Le Macchine Celibi*, 22.

31. Thomas Pynchon, *Gravity's Rainbow* (London: Picador, 1975), 177. For a more detailed discussion of bachelor war machines and Pynchon, see Gabriele Schwab, *Subjects without Selves: Transitional Texts in Modern Fiction* (Cambridge, Mass.: Harvard University Press, 1994), 172–207.

32. See Denise Kiernan, *The Girls of Atomic City: The Untold Story of the Women Who Helped Win World War II* (New York: Simon and Schuster, 2013).

33. Charlene Spretnak, "Naming the Cultural Forces that Push Us toward War."

34. Simone de Beauvoir, *The Ethics of Ambiguity*, trans. Bernard Frechtman (Secaucus, N.J.: Carol/Citadel Press, 1997).

35. See Michelle Murphy, *Seizing the Means of Reproduction: Entanglements of Feminism, Health, and Technoscience* (Durham, N.C.: Duke University Press, 2012).

36. Catherine Eschle, "Gender and the Subject of (Anti)Nuclear Politics: Revisiting Women's Campaigning against the Bomb," *International Studies Quarterly* 57, no. 4 (2013): 715.

37. Linda Hogan, "Daybreak," in *Reweaving the Web of Life: Feminism and Nonviolence*, ed. Pam McAllister (Philadelphia: New Society, 1982), 354.

38. Hogan, 352.

39. Hogan, 353.

40. Hogan, 356.

41. Hogan, 356.

42. See Angie Zelter, *Trident on Trial: The Case for People's Disarmament* (Edinburgh: Luath, 2001), 11.

43. Eschle, "Gender and the Subject of (Anti)Nuclear Politics," 718.

44. Arundhati Roy, *War Talk* (Cambridge, Mass.: South End Press, 2003), 1.

45. Roy, 35.

46. Roy, 38.

47. Roy, 6.

48. Roy, 14.

49. Roy, 95.

50. Roy, 88.

51. Eschle, "Gender and the Subject of (Anti)Nuclear Politics," 717.

52. Masco, *Nuclear Borderlands*, 229.

53. I am taking the notion of "phantasms of the mutant body" as a specific instantiation of Jacques Lacan's "phantasms of the fragmented body" developed in his reflections on mirroring. See Jacques Lacan, *Écrits*, trans. Héloïse Fink and Russell Grigg (New York: W. W. Norton, 2006).

54. Masco, *Nuclear Borderlands*, 326.

55. Andy Newman, "In Baby Teeth, a Test of Fallout; a Long-Shot Search for Nuclear Peril in Molars and Cuspids," *New York Times*, November 11, 2003, sec. N.Y.

INTERLUDE

1. Alexievich, *Voices from Chernobyl*, 75.
2. Alexievich, 75.
3. Alexievich, 68.
4. Alexievich, 193.
5. See Teri Sforza, "'Beachfront Nuclear Waste Dump': Warring Sides Head to Settlement Talks over San Onofre," *Orange County Register*, April 7, 2017.

5. THE AFTERLIFE OF NUCLEAR CATASTROPHES

1. John Bradley, ed., *Atomic Ghost: Poets Respond to the Nuclear Age* (Minneapolis, Minn.: Coffee House Press, 1994), 3.
2. Masco, *Nuclear Borderlands*, 1.
3. Masco, 4.
4. Masco, 6.
5. Masco, 293.
6. Masco, 229.
7. Masco, 229.
8. Masco, 237.
9. Masco, 327.
10. Eleanor Wilner, "High Noon at Los Alamos," in Bradley, *Atomic Ghosts*, 185.
11. Bradley, *Atomic Ghosts*, 186.
12. Bradley, 187.
13. Lifton, *Death in Life*, 257.
14. Derrida, "No Apocalypse, Not Now," 23.
15. Lifton, *Death in Life*, 257.
16. Lifton, 351.
17. Lifton, 253.
18. Lifton, 254.
19. Lifton, 256.
20. Lifton, 259.
21. Lifton, 259.
22. Lifton, 457.
23. Lifton, 184.
24. Lifton, 184.
25. Lifton, 185.
26. Lifton, 189.
27. Lifton, 368.
28. Lifton, 368.
29. Lifton, 474.
30. Lifton, 470.
31. Lifton, 330.
32. Lifton, 329.

(Note 1 continued from previous page:) Region, https://www.nytimes.com/2003/11/11/nyregion/baby-teeth-test-fallout-long-shot-search-for-nuclear-peril-molars-cuspids.html.

33. Lifton, 329–30.
34. Christa Wolf, *Störfall: Nachrichten eines Tages* (Frankfurt, Germany: Suhrkamp, 1987).
35. Alexievich, *Voices from Chernobyl*, 236.
36. Adriana Petryna, *Life Exposed: Biological Citizens after Chernobyl* (Princeton, N.J.: Princeton University Press, 2003), 26.
37. Petryna, 203.
38. Petryna, 219.
39. See Churchill, *Struggle for the Land*; Kuletz, *Tainted Desert*; Masco, *Nuclear Borderlands*.
40. See Brad Evans and Henry Giroux, *Disposable Futures: The Seduction of Violence in the Age of Spectacle* (San Francisco: City Lights Books, 2015).
41. Alexievich, *Voices from Chernobyl*, 161.
42. Alexievich, 37.
43. Alexievich, 93.
44. Alexievich, 93.
45. Francesco M. Cataluccio, *Die Ausradierte Stadt: Tschernobyls Katastrophen*, trans. Sigrid Vagt (Vienna, Austria: Paul Zsolnay, 2012), 126.
46. Alexievich, *Voices from Chernobyl*, 52.
47. See Bennett, *Vibrant Matter*.
48. Alexievich, *Voices from Chernobyl*, 64.
49. Alexievich, 114.
50. Alexievich, 28.
51. Alexievich, 31.
52. Alexievich, 53.
53. Alexievich, 46.
54. Alexievich, 51.
55. Alexievich, 51.
56. Alexievich, 191.
57. Alexievich, 193.
58. Alexievich, 191.
59. Petryna, *Life Exposed*, 73.
60. Petryna, 213.
61. Alexievich, *Voices from Chernobyl*, 129.
62. Alexievich, 119.
63. Alexievich, 183.
64. Christa Wolf, *Accident: A Day's News*, trans. Heike Schwarzbauer and Rick Takvorian (Chicago: University of Chicago Press, 2001), 29. Originally published in 1989 by Farrar, Straus, and Giroux.
65. Wolf, *Störfall*, 38.
66. Wolf, *Accident*, 89.
67. Wolf, 108.
68. Wolf, 30.
69. Wolf, 55.
70. Wolf, 37.
71. Alexievich, *Voices from Chernobyl*, 38.

72. Alexievich, 40.
73. Alexievich, 47.
74. Alexievich, 41.
75. Alexievich, 46.
76. Alexievich, 47.
77. Alexievich, 49.
78. Alexievich, 50.
79. Alexievich, 53.
80. See Petryna, *Life Exposed,* 201–6.
81. Petryna, 146.
82. Petryna, 8.
83. Comaroff and Comaroff, *Truth about Crime,* 74.
84. Comaroff and Comaroff, 74.
85. Comaroff and Comaroff, 75.
86. Comaroff and Comaroff, 77.
87. Comaroff and Comaroff, 80.
88. Comaroff and Comaroff, 76.
89. For this and the following, see Kurtis Lee, "What We Know about Christopher Steele, the British Ex-Spy Who Wrote the Controversial Trump Dossier," *Los Angeles Times,* January 15, 2017, http://www.latimes.com/world/europe/la-fg-trump-russia-spy-2017-story.html.
90. Alexievich, *Voices from Chernobyl,* 236.
91. For this and the following, see Matthew Schofield, "Ruined Chernobyl Nuclear Plant Will Remain a Threat for 3,000 Years," McClatchy DC Bureau, April 24, 2016, http://www.mcclatchydc.com/news/nation-world/world/article73405857.html.
92. Schofield.
93. Schofield.
94. Schofield.
95. For this and the following, see Zhanna Bezpiatchuk, "The People Who Moved to Chernobyl," *BBC News,* October 12, 2018, https://www.bbc.co.uk/news/resources/idt-sh/moving_to_Chernobyl.
96. Bezpiatchuk, 8 of 12.
97. Lucy Birmingham and David McNeill, *Strong in the Rain: Surviving Japan's Earthquake, Tsunami, and Fukushima Nuclear Disaster* (London: St. Martin's Press, 2012), 97.
98. Birmingham and McNeill, 97–98.
99. Birmingham and McNeill, 102.
100. Birmingham and McNeill, 67.
101. Birmingham and McNeill, 76.
102. Birmingham and McNeill, 80.
103. Birmingham and McNeill, 169.
104. Birmingham and McNeill, 180.
105. Birmingham and McNeill, 169.
106. Schofield, "Ruined Chernobyl Nuclear Plant."
107. Schofield.

108. For this and the following, see Andreas Rosenfelder, "Fukushima: Alexander Kluge—'Wir Spielen mit einem Monstrum,'" *Die Welt,* March 14, 2011, https://www.welt.de/kultur/article12810989/Alexander-Kluge-Wir-spielen-mit-einem-Monstrum.html.

109. Rosenfelder. Translation mine.

110. See Tom James, "Hanford Nuclear Site Accident Puts Focus on Aging U.S. Facilities," Reuters, May 12, 2017, https://www.reuters.com/article/us-washington-nuclear/hanford-nuclear-site-accident-puts-focus-on-aging-u-s-facilities-idUSKBN1882TP.

111. James.

112. Robert Alvarez and Norman Solomon, with Robert Alvarez and Eleanor Walters, *Killing Our Own: The Disaster of America's Experience with Atomic Radiation* (New York: Random House/Delacorte Press, 1982).

113. Harvey Wasserman, "36 Years of Three Mile Island's Lethal Lies . . . and Still Counting," EcoWatch, March 27, 2015, https://www.ecowatch.com/36-years-of-three-mile-islands-lethal-lies-and-still-counting-1882023488.html.

114. Wasserman.

115. See Diane Cardwell and Jonathan Soble, "Westinghouse Files for Bankruptcy, in Blow to Nuclear Power," *New York Times,* December 22, 2017, https://www.nytimes.com/2017/03/29/business/westinghouse-toshiba-nuclear-bankruptcy.html.

116. Rob Nikolewski, "The Bankruptcy Shaking Nuclear Energy to the Core," *San Diego Union-Tribune,* April 9, 2017, http://www.sandiegouniontribune.com/business/energy-green/sd-fi-nuclear-woes-20170331-story.html.

117. I discuss Madsen's film in more detail in chapter 7.

6. HIROSHIMA'S GHOSTLY SHADOWS

1. See Heise, *Imagining Extinction.*

2. Linda Hogan, "Prayer for Men and Children," in Bradley, *Atomic Ghost,* 273.

3. Stephanie Strickland, "Shadow," in Bradley, 209.

4. Toge Sankichi, "The Shadow," trans. Richard Minear, in Bradley, 22–23.

5. Roy, *War Talk,* 2.

6. Alphonso Lingis, *Irrevocable: A Philosophy of Mortality* (Chicago: University of Chicago Press, 2018), 19.

7. Lippit, *Atomic Light,* 39.

8. Lippit, 1.

9. Lippit, 4.

10. Lippit, 48.

11. Lippit, 86.

12. Theodor W. Adorno and Max Horkheimer, *Dialectic of Enlightenment,* trans. John Cumming (London: Verso, 1997), 3.

13. Willem de Kooning, "What Abstract Art Means to Me," in *The Collected Writings of Willem de Kooning,* ed. George Scrivani (New York: Hanuman Books, 1988), 60.

14. Lippit, *Atomic Light,* 81.

15. See Ward Churchill, *Struggle for the Land*; Kuletz, *Tainted Desert*; Masco, *Nuclear Borderlands*.

16. Masco, *Nuclear Borderlands*.

17. Paul Virilio, *War and Cinema: The Logistics of Perception*, trans. Patrick Camiller (London: Verso, 1989), 81.

18. Virilio, 81.

19. Lippit, *Atomic Light*, 95.

20. Ray Bradbury, *The Martian Chronicles* (New York: Simon and Schuster, 2012), 222.

21. Quentin Meillassoux, *After Finitude: An Essay on the Necessity of Contingency*, trans. Ray Brassier (New York: Continuum, 2008), 112.

22. Meillassoux, 112.

23. Meillassoux, 116.

24. Dipesh Chakrabarty, "The Climate of History: Four Theses," *Critical Inquiry* 35, no. 2 (2009): 203.

25. Meillassoux, 116–17.

26. Ray Bradbury, "August 2016," in *The Martian Chronicles*.

27. Jorge Luis Borges, "The Library of Babel," trans. J. E. I., in *Labyrinths: Selected Stories and Other Writings*, ed. Donald A. Yates and William Gibson (New York: New Directions, 1964), 58.

28. Kent Johnson, "Trilobytes," in Bradley, *Atomic Ghost*, 20.

29. Beryle Williams, "Stragies for Survival," in Bradley, 269.

30. I use the term *experimental system* in the sense defined in Hans-Jörg Rheinberger, *Toward a History of Epistemic Things: Synthesizing Proteins in the Test Tube* (Stanford, Calif.: Stanford University Press, 2010). For a more detailed discussion, see Schwab, *Imaginary Ethnographies*.

31. See Schwab, *Imaginary Ethnographies*.

32. Vincent F. Ialenti, "When Deep Time Becomes Shallow: Knowing Nuclear Waste Risk Ethnographically," *Discard Studies* (blog), March 2017, https://discardstudies.com/2017/03/09/when-deep-time-becomes-shallow-knowing-nuclear-waste-risk-ethnographically/.

33. Ialenti.

34. E. Ann Kaplan, *Climate Trauma: Foreseeing the Future in Dystopian Film and Fiction* (New Brunswick, N.J.: Rutgers University Press, 2016), 120.

35. Kaplan, 123.

36. Kaplan, 121.

37. See Kaplan, 124.

38. Quoted in Kaplan, 126.

39. See James Clifford, *The Predicament of Culture* (Cambridge, Mass.: Harvard University Press, 1988), chapter 4.

40. Kaplan, *Climate Trauma*, 127.

41. See the detailed discussion of these pieces in Gabrielle Decamous, *Invisible Colors: The Arts of the Atomic Age* (Cambridge, Mass.: MIT Press, 2018), 12–13.

42. See Strathern, *Reproducing the Future*.

43. Amitav Ghosh, *The Great Derangement: Climate Change and the Unthinkable* (Chicago: University of Chicago Press, 2016), 31.

44. Ghosh, 82.
45. Ghosh, 84.
46. Morton, *Hyperobjects*, 120.
47. Morton, 121.
48. Morton, 121.
49. Morton, 15.
50. Morton, 122.
51. For this and the following discussion of the "spacing of time," see William Egginton, "On Radical Atheism, Chronolibidinal Reading, and Impossible Desires," *New Centennial Review* 9, no. 1 (2009): 204–7.
52. Martin Hägglund, "Chronolibidinal Reading: Deconstruction and Psychoanalysis," *New Centennial Review* 9, no. 1 (2009): 19.
53. Egginton, "On Radical Atheism," 205.
54. Egginton, 205.
55. André Leroi-Gourhan, *Gesture and Speech*, trans. Anna Bostock Berger (Cambridge, Mass.: MIT Press, 1993), 398.
56. Leroi-Gourhan, 406.
57. Leroi-Gourhan, 407.
58. Leroi-Gourhan, 408.
59. See Bennett, *Vibrant Matter*.
60. Morton, *Hyperobjects*, 122.
61. Chen, *Animacies*, 2.
62. Chen, 3.
63. Chen, 1.
64. Chen, 15.
65. Chen, 16.
66. Chen, 10.
67. Chen, 203.
68. Nikolas Rose, *The Politics of Life Itself: Biomedicine, Power, and Subjectivity in the Twenty-First Century* (Princeton, N.J.: Princeton University Press, 2009), 4.
69. I am drawing here from Nixon, *Slow Violence*; Mbembe, "Necropolitics."
70. See Deleuze and Guattari, *A Thousand Plateaus*, 208–31.
71. Roy, *War Talk*, 7.

7. POSTNUCLEAR MADNESS AND NUCLEAR CRYPTS

1. James Agee, "Dedication Day: Rough Sketch for a Moving Picture," *Politics* (1946), 121.
2. Agee, 122.
3. Agee, 123.
4. Agee, 124.
5. Agee, 124.
6. Agee, 125.
7. Günther Anders, ed., *Burning Conscience: The Case of the Hiroshima Pilot Claude Eatherly Told in His Letters to Günther Anders* (New York: Monthly Review Press, 1962).
8. Anders, xviii–xix.
9. Anders, xiv.

10. Quoted in Lifton and Mitchell, *Hiroshima in America*, 330.
11. Lifton and Mitchell, 302.
12. Lifton and Mitchell, 309.
13. Lifton and Mitchell, 309.
14. Lifton and Mitchell, 311.
15. Lifton and Mitchell, 313.
16. Michel Serres and Bruno Latour, *Conversations on Science, Culture, and Time*, trans. Roxanne Lapidus (Ann Arbor: University of Michigan Press, 1995), 17.
17. Serres and Latour.
18. Lifton, *Death in Life*, 224.
19. Lifton, 225.
20. Lifton, 274.
21. Lifton, 256.
22. Lifton, 256.
23. Lifton and Mitchell, *Hiroshima in America*.
24. Lifton and Mitchell, 338.
25. Lifton and Mitchell, 338.
26. Lifton and Mitchell, 340.
27. Lifton and Mitchell, 340.
28. Lifton and Mitchell, 136.
29. Lifton and Mitchell, 317.
30. Lifton and Falk, *Indefensible Weapons*, 87.
31. Lifton and Mitchell, *Hiroshima in America*, 352.
32. Lifton and Mitchell, 347.
33. Lifton and Mitchell, 347.
34. Lifton and Falk, *Indefensible Weapons*, 90.
35. Lifton and Falk, 95.
36. Lifton and Falk, 95.
37. Lifton, *Death in Life*, 508.
38. Lifton and Mitchell, *Hiroshima in America*, 374.
39. Günther Anders, "Reflections on the H-Bomb," *Dissent* (1956), 153.
40. Traci Brynne Voyles, *Wastelanding: Legacies of Uranium Mining in Navajo Country* (Minneapolis: University of Minnesota Press, 2015), 11.
41. In this context of a cultural imaginary preoccupied, if not fascinated, by extinction, see also Heise, *Imagining Extinction*.
42. Lifton and Mitchell, *Hiroshima in America*, 355.
43. Lifton and Falk, *Indefensible Weapons*, 278.
44. Lifton and Falk, 278.
45. Lifton, *Death in Life*, 526.
46. For this and the following, see the detailed discussion of transgenerational crypts in Schwab, *Haunting Legacies*.
47. Nicolas Abraham and Maria Torok, *The Shell and the Kernel: Renewals of Psychoanalysis*, vol. 1 (Chicago: University of Chicago Press, 1994).
48. Anders, "Reflections on the H-Bomb," 148.
49. Regarding the concept of vibrant matter, see also Bennett, *Vibrant Matter*.

50. Walter Benjamin, "Theses on the Philosophy of History, in *Illuminations*, trans. Harry Zohn (New York: Schocken Books, 1969), 249.

8. TRANSSPECIES SELVES

1. Franz Kafka, *The Metamorphosis*, trans. Susan Bernofsky (New York: Norton Critical Editions, 2016), 3.

2. Julio Cortázar, "Axolotl," in *Hopscotch; Blow-Up and Other Stories; We Love Glenda So Much and Other Tales*, trans. Paul Blackburn (New York: Alfred A. Knopf, 2014), 577.

3. Liu Sola, "The Last Spider," in *Blue Sky Green Sea*, trans. Martha Cheung (Hong Kong: The Chinese University of Hong Kong, A Renditions Paperback, 1993), 3.

4. Charis Cussins, "Confessions of a Bioterrorist," in *Playing Dolly: Technocultural Formations, Fantasies, and Fictions of Assisted Reproduction*, ed. E. Ann Kaplan and Susan Squier, 189–219 (New Brunswick, N.J.: Rutgers University Press, 1999).

5. I thank Christina García for introducing me to Fabelo's work. For a sustained discussion, see her dissertation "Touching Impenetrable Bodies: Material Ecologies in Cuban Literary and Visual Works" (PhD diss., University of California, Irvine, 2018), chapter 2.

6. Schell, *Fate of the Earth*, 62.

7. Schell, 68.

8. Schell, 85.

9. Hugh Raffles, *Insectopedia* (New York: Vintage Books, 2010), 29.

10. Raffles, 29.

11. Raffles, 29.

12. Astrid Schrader, "Abyssal Intimacies and Temporalities of Care: How (Not) to Care about Deformed Leaf Bugs in the Aftermath of Chernobyl," *Social Studies of Science* 45, no. 5 (2015): 1.

13. Cornelia Hesse-Honegger, *Heteroptera: The Beautiful and the Other, Or Images of a Mutating World*, trans. Christine Luisi (New York: Scalo, 2001), 24.

14. Raffles, *Insectopedia*, 31.

15. Raffles, 38.

16. Schrader, "Abyssal Intimacies and Temporalities of Care," 5.

17. See Hans Blumenberg, *The Legitimacy of the Modern Age*, trans. Robert M. Wallace (Cambridge, Mass.: MIT Press, 1985).

18. Schrader, "Abyssal Intimacies and Temporalities of Care," 5.

19. Schrader, 21.

20. Wilfred Bion, "Penetrating Silence," in *The Complete Works of W. R. Bion*, ed. Chris Mawson, vol. 15 (London: Carnac Books, 2014).

21. Quoted in Schrader, "Abyssal Intimacies and Temporalities of Care," 11.

22. Alphonso Lingis, *The Imperative* (Bloomington: Indiana University Press, 1998), 44.

23. Karen Barad, "Troubling Time/s and Ecologies of Nothingness," in *Eco-Deconstruction: Derrida and Environmental Philosophy*, ed. Philippe Lynes and David Woods (New York: Fordham University Press, 2018), 214.

24. Barad, 215.
25. Barad, 223.
26. Barad, 222.
27. Chen, *Animacies*, 1.
28. Chen, 1.
29. Quoted in Chen, 6.
30. Chen, 7.
31. Quoted in Chen, 8.
32. Chen, 8.
33. Chen, 10.
34. Chen, 16.
35. Chen, 17.
36. Chen, 203.
37. For this and the following, see Michelle Murphy, "Distributed Reproduction, Chemical Violence, and Latency," *S&F Online* 11, no. 3 (2013), http://sfonline.barnard.edu/life-un-ltd-feminism-bioscience-race/distributed-reproduction-chemical-violence-and-latency/.
38. For this and the following, see Jordy (Jordana) Rosenberg, "The Molecularization of Sexuality: On Some Primitivisms of the Present," *Theory and Event* 17, no. 2 (2014), https://muse.jhu.edu/article/546470.
39. Cortázar, "Axolotl," 8.
40. Cortázar, 9.
41. Alexievich, *Voices from Chernobyl*, 51.
42. Alexievich, 132.
43. See Alexander Kluge, *Die Wächter des Sarkophags: 10 Jahre Tschernobyl* (Hamburg, Germany: Rotbuch, 1996), 46.
44. For this and the following, see Kluge, 51.
45. Kluge, 49.
46. Kluge, 73.
47. Kluge, 88.
48. For this and the following, see Niamh McIntyre, "Experts Baffled as Robots Sent to Clean Up Fukushima Nuclear Site Keep Dying," *Independent*, March 5, 2017, http://www.independent.co.uk/news/world/robots-fukushima-nuclear-disaster-dying-probe-clean-up-tepco-toshiba-reactor-nuclear-radiation-a7612396.html.
49. Donna J. Haraway, *Staying with the Trouble: Making Kin in the Chthulucene* (Durham, N.C.: Duke University Press, 2016), 148.
50. Haraway, 149.
51. Haraway, 146.
52. Haraway, 164.
53. Haraway, 166.
54. Haraway, 168.
55. For a comprehensive description of *Deinococcus radiodurans*, see Edward O. Wilson, *The Future of Life* (New York: Vintage Books/Random House, 2002), 6–7.
56. Wilson, *Future of Life*, 7.

57. Jon Beckwith, *Making Genes, Making Waves* (Cambridge, Mass.: Harvard University Press, 2002), 98–115.

CODA

1. Sigmund Freud, "Civilization and Its Discontents," in *The Standard Edition of the Complete Psychological Works of Sigmund Freud, Volume XXI (1927–1931): The Future of an Illusion, Civilization and Its Discontents, and Other Works*, ed. Jim Strachey, trans. Joan Riviere (London: Hogarth Press/Institute of Psycho-Analysis, 1930), 76.

2. Freud writes, "This principle dominates the operation of the mental apparatus from the start. There can be no doubt about its efficacy, and yet its programme is at loggerheads with the whole world.... There is no possibility at all of its being carried through; all the regulations of the universe run counter to it. One feels inclined to say that the intention that man should be 'happy' is not included in the plan of 'Creation'" (76).

3. See William S. Burroughs, *Naked Lunch* (New York: Grove Weidenfeld, 1992).

4. See Beckett's remarks on failure in Samuel Beckett and Georges Duthuit, *Three Dialogues: Tal Coat—Masson—Bram Van Velde* (London: Transition Press, 1949).

5. Samuel Beckett, *Happy Days: A Play in Two Acts* (New York: Grove Press, 1989), 10.

6. Quoted in Peter Goin, *Nuclear Landscapes* (Baltimore: Johns Hopkins University Press, 1951), 7.

7. Ghassan Hage, *Alter-Politics: Critical Anthropology and the Radical Imagination* (Melbourne: Melbourne University Press, 2015), 3.

8. Hage, 3.

9. Lifton first developed the concept in *Death in Life*. I discuss Lifton in detail in chapter 5.

10. Beckett, *Happy Days*, 23.

11. Beckett, 27.

12. Beckett, 27.

13. See Louis Menand, "Now What I Wonder Do I Mean By That," *Slate*, August 21, 1996, http://www.slate.com/articles/news_and_politics/theater/1996/08/now_what_i_wonder_do_i_mean_by_that.html.

14. Lauren Berlant, *Cruel Optimism* (Durham, N.C.: Duke University Press Books, 2011).

15. See Tali Sharot, Christoph W. Korn, and Raymond J. Dolan, "How Unrealistic Optimism Is Maintained in the Face of Reality," *Nature* 14, no. 11 (2011): 1475–79.

16. Richard Powers, "What Does Fiction Know?," *Places Journal*, August 2, 2011, https://placesjournal.org/article/what-does-fiction-know/.

17. Within the traditions that formed this "old style," happiness used to be tied to understanding, predicting, and ultimately controlling the events and workings of nature. In Winnie's stage world, in which the destruction of natural ecologies and resources as well as a sustainable planetary future seems to be a

given, any belief in the control of nature is irrevocably shattered. Moreover, at least since the advent of the nuclear age, the power to control the workings of nature has succumbed to a necro- or thanatopolitical desire not only to create deathworlds but also to become, as Oppenheimer imagined himself, the God of destruction and apocalypse. How then may *Happy Days* challenge our notion of happiness in the face of disaster, catastrophe, and necropolitical desire?

18. Beckett, *Happy Days*, 28.
19. Beckett, 30.
20. Beckett, 16.
21. E. E. Gontarski, "Literary Allusions in 'Happy Days,'" in *On Beckett, Essays and Criticism,* ed. E. E. Gontarski (New York: Grove Press, 1986), 314.
22. Beckett, *Happy Days*, 29.
23. Beckett, 39.
24. Beckett, 29.
25. Jacques Derrida, *Archive Fever: A Freudian Impression,* trans. Eric Prenowitz (Chicago: University of Chicago Press, 1996), 33.
26. Derrida, 33.
27. Derrida, 34.
28. Beckett, *Happy Days*, 13.
29. Berlant, *Cruel Optimism*, 2.
30. Berlant, 3.
31. Berlant, 10.
32. See Christopher Bollas's introduction to Edward Said, *Freud and the Non-European* (London: Verso Books, 2014), as well as M. Ackbar Abbas, *Hong Kong: Culture and the Politics of Disappearance* (Minneapolis: University of Minnesota Press, 1997).
33. Beckett, *Happy Days*, 11.
34. Beckett, 11.
35. Beckett, 25.
36. Gontarski, "Literary Allusions in 'Happy Days,'" 316.
37. Beckett, *Happy Days*, 25. Reference identified in Gontarski, "Literary Allusions in 'Happy Days,'" 312.
38. See Schwab, *Subjects without Selves.*
39. See Bennett, *Vibrant Matter.*
40. Beckett, *Happy Days*, 40.
41. W. R. Bion, "Attacks on Linking," *Psychoanalytic Quarterly* 82, no. 3 (2013): 285.
42. Bion, 285.
43. For a detailed discussion of this Beckettian philosophy of language, see Schwab, *Subjects without Selves,* chapter 6.
44. W. R. Bion, *Second Thoughts: Selected Papers on Psychoanalysis* (London: Maresfield Reprints, 1984), 107.
45. See Steven Connor, "Beckett and Bion," http://www.stevenconnor.com/beckbion/.
46. This idea was inspired by Steven Connor's overview of Bion's concept of "attacks on linking," especially his notion that the mother acts for the infant

as a "screen or detoxifying repository of the terrors and horrors expelled from the self."

47. Richard Powers, "What does Fiction Know?," cited in Heather Hauser, *Ecosickness in Contemporary U.S. Fiction* (New York: Columbia University Press, 2014), 220.

48. See Wolfgang Iser, *Prospecting: From Reader Response to Literary Anthropology* (Baltimore: Johns Hopkins University Press, 1993), chapter 8.

INDEX

Aargau, 242–43
Abbas, Ackbar, 279
Abe no Sadato, 81
Abolition (Schell), 51
Abraham, Nicholas, xiii, 233, 234
"Abyssal Intimacies and Temporalities of Care" (Schrader), 250
abyssal intimacy, 250
Accident: A Day's News (Wolf), 161, 167
Acoma, 57, 61, 64, 78, 81, 133, 135, 139, 141, 142, 144; cancer rates and, 146; contamination and, 62
activism, 79; black, 91, 96; environmental, 231; gendered, 122–27; Indigenous, 59, 59 (fig.); peace, 88–89, 90, 93, 161, 218; political, 91. *See also* antinuclear activism
aesthetics, 108, 207, 246, 247, 248, 283; nuclear, 47, 81, 82, 83, 84, 110, 204, 213, 255
African Americans against the Bomb (Intondi), 91, 100
After Evil (Meister), 26
After Finitude (Meillassoux), 197
Agee, James, 217
Agency for Toxic Substances and Disease Registry, xxi
Agoyo, Herman, 19, 74, 233, 292n52
Ahmad, Aijaz, 15
AIM. *See* American Indian Movement
Albuquerque Tribune, 20
Aleph, The (Borges), 200
Alexievich, Svetlana, 32, 140, 154, 155, 162, 168, 171, 177, 260
Alter-Politics (Hage), 274
Alvarez, Robert, 183
American Indian Movement (AIM), 33, 59, 67

American Southwest, 71, 72, 85, 144; nuclear borderlands of, xvii, 4, 85, 87, 129; nuclear tests in, 13; sacrifice zones of, 61, 193
American Weekly, 117
Anders, Günther, xix, 4, 36, 122, 219, 221, 223, 230, 231, 234
Angel of Nuclear History, 234, 235
anima, 156
animacies, xx, 24, 253–59; hyperobjects and, 209–15; intimacy/extimacy of, 253
Animacies (Chen), 253
annihilation, 44, 46, 48, 52, 95, 161, 196, 229; phantasms of, 32
Anthropocene, xii, 198, 200, 209, 211
antinuclear activism, xvi, xviii, 9, 14, 36, 42, 56, 57, 78, 90, 92, 122, 123, 181, 219, 220, 242, 292n52
antinuclear movement, 7, 89, 90, 91, 93, 96, 98, 100, 102, 123, 125, 138, 244; civil rights movement and, xvii; feminist, 128–29, 160
"Antinuclear Politics and the Transcendence of Race" (Williams), 101
antinuclear resistance, 25, 39, 65, 79, 94, 96, 103, 104, 123, 220; African American, xvii, 89–90, 91, 92, 93; international movements and, 125
Anti-Nuke Rally, 102
Antiquiertheit des Menschen, Die (Anders), 122, 219
apocalypse, 35, 46, 49, 56, 79, 102, 165, 169, 259, 272
apocalyptic imaginary, 33, 34, 35–36, 45, 46, 48, 129, 228
Appel, Detlef, 177
Arapahos, 62, 67
Armah, Ayi Kwei, 25

Arms Control Association, 28
arms race, 2, 15, 30, 31, 42, 68, 71, 90, 103
art, 208; aesthetics and, 108; modernist, 237; representational, 246, 248; role of, xiv–xv; science and, 240
Artist's Institute, 208
assassinations, 20; covert, 174, 175–76
Atomic Age, 209
Atomic Energy Commission, xxi
Atomic Gardening Society, 111
atomic gardens, 110–18
atomic light, 13, 110, 156, 193, 205
Atomic Light (Lippit), 111, 113, 191–92
atomic rays, 111, 113, 118, 156, 192, 195
atomic trade, 188–96
Atomkraft, 138
Atomkraftwerk, 131
Atoms for Peace Program, 96–97, 111, 112
"August 2016: There Will Come Soft Rains" (Bradbury), xix, 196
Auschwitz, 220, 234
ausradierte Stadt, Die (Cataluccio), 163
Autoimmunity, 51
"Axolotl" (Cortázar), 238
axolotls, 238, 259

Baca, Jimmy Santiago, 79
bachelor's machine, xviii, 118–21, 122
Bailey, Mary, ix
Baj, Enrico, 56; painting by, 45 (fig.)
Baldwin, James, 94, 101
Bandung Conference, 90, 93
Barad, Karen, 45, 46, 57, 252–53
Basaglia, Franco, 237
Bass, Alan, 39, 40
Bataille, Georges, 4, 22, 23, 24, 25
Bateson, Gregory, xi
Battle of the Greasy Grass, 66
Battle of the Little Bighorn, 66, 67
BBC, 179, 291n42
Bear, Leon, 63
Beauvoir, Simone de, 123
Beckett, Samuel, xx, 49, 56, 267–84;

allegories and, 282; endgames and, 269, 275; nuclear holocaust and, 281–82; rhythms/moods of, 271; theater of cruelty and, 271
Beckwith, Jon, 264
Belafonte, Harry, 90, 94, 97
Belarussians, 141, 166, 167
Benford, Gregory, 34
Benjamin, Walter, 234, 282
Berlant, Lauren, 275, 278, 279
Bernstein, Paul, 30
Bertell, Rosalie, 56, 124
Bethe, Hans, 217
Between Two Ages (Brzezinski), 28
Beznau nuclear power plant, 244
Bhagavad Gita, 22, 195, 272
Bible, 278
biolingua, 271, 283
biology, 274–75; evolutionary, 269; transformational, 283
Bion, Winfred, 250; on attacks on linking, 282, 316n46
biopolitics, xi–xii, 32, 72, 213, 214, 256, 295n116
Birmingham, Lucy, 154, 179, 181
birth defects, 19, 168
Black Elk, Ben, 66
Black Elk, Seventh Generation and, 66
Black Elk Speaks, 66
Black Hills, 124, 125
Black Hills Alliance International Survival Gathering, 124
"Black Hills Survival Gathering, 1980" (Hogan), 124
Black Panther Party, 96
Blacks Against Nukes (BAN), 97
Blair, Tony, 125
Blinky, ix–xi, 289n2
Boeche, R. W., 81
Bollas, Christopher, 279
Borges, Jorge Luis, xix, 200
Bradbury, Ray, xix, 196, 199–200
Brathwaite, Edward Kamau, 85
Brown, Kate, 13, 20
Browne, Ronin, 80

Brutsche, Klaus, 137
Brzezinski, Mika, 30
Brzezinski, Zbigniew, 28
Bullcreek, Margene, 63
Bulletin of the Atomic Scientists, 28
Bumstead, Melissa, xxi
Burakumin (Outcast) Liberation Movement, 159
Bureau of Indian Affairs (BIA), 63, 296n121
Bürgerinitiative Lüchow-Dannenberg, 10
burial grounds, 134, 200, 202, 206
burials, ghostly, 201–7
Burning Conscience (Jungk), 220
Burroughs, William S., 268

Caldicott, Helen, 11, 72, 97, 125, 126
California Department of Toxic Substances Control (DTSC), xxi
California Public Utilities Commission, 184
Cameron, David, 295n114
"Camille Stories" (Haraway), 239, 261–65
cancer, 20, 131, 144, 147, 167, 177–78, 184, 244, 253, 290n12; Acoma and, 146; bone, 93, 117; childhood, xxi, 13, 137, 138; epidemic, 166; nuclear contamination and, 145; radiation-induced, 62
Canetti, Elias, 73, 301n29
Can Nuclear Power Slow Down Climate Change? (van Leeuwen), 10
capitalism, 50, 259, 274; corporate, 56; global, 20, 89; neoliberal, 54; sociopolitics of, 259
care: aesthetics of, 246; counterfeit, 158; ethics of, 170, 245, 250
Carrouges, Michel, xviii, 119, 120
Carter, Jimmy, 96
Cartwright, Lisa, 113
catachresis, 6, 49, 268, 269, 270, 271, 272, 282
Cataluccio, Francesco, 47, 163
Catastrophe (Beckett), 49

Center for Human Radiobiology, 117
Ceremony (Silko), 79
cesium-137, 171, 174, 178, 181
Chakrabarty, Dipesh, 197
Chen, Mel, xiv, 214, 256; animacies and, xx, 213, 253–54; molecular intimacies and, 254–55
Chernobyl, 3, 4, 11, 39, 42, 47, 50, 56, 72, 128, 130, 139, 140, 154, 161–78, 180, 182, 183, 242, 244, 245; aftermath of, 14, 161–77, 177–78; Fukushima and, 179; sarcophagus of, 146; survivors of, 32, 43, 45, 147, 155, 162–63, 170, 171, 232; tourism and, 111, 298n26
"Chernobyl" (Salter), 161
Cheyennes, 62, 67
Chicago Defender, 92
"Choices" (Baca), 79
"Chronolibidinal Reading" (Hägglund), 210
Churchill, Ward, xvii, 18, 72, 146, 293n66, 299n4
Churchill, Winston, 2, 118–19
Cirincione, Joseph, 100
civilization, xx, 34, 42, 196, 229, 268
Civilization and Its Discontents (Freud), 268
civil rights movement, xvii, 15, 25, 88–89, 90, 91, 94, 95, 102, 103, 104, 123
Clausewitz, Carl von, 297n12
Cleaver, Kathleen, 96
Clifford, James, 207
climate change, xii, 198, 209, 226, 256, 274, 284; nuclear energy and, 10, 11
Climate March, photo of, 59
"Climate of History, The" (Chakrabarty), 197
Climate Trauma (Kaplan), 204
Clinton, Bill, 69
Clinton, Hillary, 99, 295n114
Cold War, xvii, 7, 20, 28, 31, 39, 42, 51, 71, 86, 93, 122, 129, 153, 183,

218, 220, 231; end of, 88, 98; resurgence of, 123
Cole, Nat King, 94
colonialism, xvi, 43, 63–64, 90, 91, 93, 96, 253, 297n12; environmental, 68; as global issue, 103; Indigenous peoples and, 63; nuclear, 4, 19, 58, 62, 65, 69, 72, 80, 98, 101, 103, 104, 153, 154; racism and, 88; settler, 61, 258
colonization, xii, 32, 62, 92, 124; nuclear, xviii, 9, 60, 63, 80, 87, 101, 103, 104, 153; radioactive, 19, 57, 72, 77, 92, 103, 124, 232, 293n66
Comaroff, Jean, 77, 78, 172, 175, 176
Comaroff, John, 77, 78, 172, 175, 176
Committee for Sane Nuclear Policy (SANE), 94
Committee for State Security (KGB), 169, 174
Communist Party, 76, 77, 93
Communist Underground, 76
"Concerning the Accounts Given by the Residents of Hiroshima" (Bataille), 23
"Confessions of a Bioterrorist" (Cussins), 238
Connor, Steven, 316n46
Conrad, Joseph, 284
consciousness, 5, 6, 35, 39, 40, 218
corruption, 14, 161, 171, 172, 176; culture of, 171, 176
Cortázar, Julio, 238, 259
Cortez, Jayne, 25
cosmologies, 129, 153, 198, 301n31
Council on African Affairs, 92
Creation, 151, 315n2
"Creation" (Saenz), 151
crimes, 93, 161; corporate, 174; governmental, 174; against humanity, 78; politics and, 172–73
criminality, 173, 175; law and, 172
Crisis Without End (Caldicott), 126
critical nuclear race theory, xii, xvii, 15, 81, 85, 90, 91, 94, 103, 104, 125, 213
"Critical Nuclear Race Theory," xviii

Critique of Black Reason (Mbembe), xviii, 88, 102
cruel optimism, 206, 275, 276, 278, 279, 284
Cruz Smith, Martin, 14, 74, 171, 172, 174; collective memory and, 78–79; crime fiction of, 173; nuclear fiction and, 75–79. See also *Stallion Gate*; *Wolves Eat Dogs*
Cuban Missile Crisis, 7, 95, 290n11
cultural imaginary, 118, 119, 120, 122, 129, 130, 240, 283–84
culture, xi, 28, 30, 42, 47, 74, 113, 144, 169, 170, 230, 281, 304n8; Acoma, 136; Anishinaabe, 83; Cold War, 153; Japanese, 83, 159–60, 161; nuclear, xviii, 18, 121, 154–55, 222; popular, 35, 112; Pueblo, 74; Western, 278, 280
Curie, Marie, 15, 114, 116
curiositas, 250
Cussins, Charis, 238
Custer, George Armstrong, 67

Dakota Access Pipeline (DAPL), xvii, 59, 66, 68
Dali, Salvador, 281
Damsel Bugs from within Paul Scherrer Institute (Hesse-Honegger), 249 (fig.)
Dance of Radium (Huyghe), 208, 208 (fig.)
Dante, 278
DAPL. See Dakota Access Pipeline
Darwin, Charles, x
Das, Veena, 168
Daughtry, Herbert, 97
Davis, Angela, 95, 125
Davis, Mike, 19, 35, 95, 293n61
Davis, Sammy, Jr., 94
Day After, The (television film), 8
Day They H-Bombed Los Angeles, The (Williams), 257
death, 26, 33, 113, 141, 170, 195, 230, 280; atomic work of, 192, 208; double, 13; individual, 48, 88;

nuclear, 23, 33, 187; psychic, 13, 223; second, 26; social, 32, 168
death drive, 48, 51, 126
death-in-life, denials and, 223–30
Death in Life: Survivors of Hiroshima (Lifton), xix, 3, 156, 224, 225, 233, 315n9
death rays, 108, 110–18
deathworld, 3, 33, 80, 141, 165, 166, 179, 240, 274, 275, 280, 316n17
deception, 223; culture of, 60; epistemology of, 14; politics of, 8, 71, 86
Declaration on the Rights of Indigenous Peoples, 58
Dedication Day, 217, 218, 220
"Dedication Day: Rough Sketch for a Moving Picture" (Agee), 217
Deep Time (Benford), 34
Defenders of the Black Hills, 125
Deinococcus radiodurans, 263, 264, 265
de Kooning, Willem, 193
Deleuze, Gilles, 214, 258
denial, 17, 73, 159, 162, 164, 169; collective, 233; death-in-life and, 223–30; ecology of, xx, 104; epistemology of, 48; politics of, 48, 50
Derrida, Jacques, xvi–xvii, 4, 17, 36, 39–56, 71, 102, 109, 157, 191, 196, 205, 229, 272; abyssal intimacy and, 250; archive fever and, 278; culture/memory and, 47; death drive and, 51; death machine and, 43; nation-state sovereignty and, 50, 51; nuclear unconscious and, 39, 41; nuclear war and, 42, 46, 47, 48, 50; sovereignty and, 50
desire, 250; rearrangement of, 24, 54
destruction: archive of, 192, 196; environmental, 199; legacies of, 264; terror of, 49. *See also* nuclear destruction
Diablo Canyon, 182–85
Diacritics, 41
Dilbert, 112, 112 (fig.)
Diné Nation, 59

disarmament, nuclear, 53, 56, 89, 90, 95, 99
disaster tourism, 46, 111, 178, 298n26
discourse: antinuclear, 126, 129; gendering, xviii, 129; materialist, 128; nuclear, 6, 107, 108; scientific, 256; theoretical, 256
diseases, 13, 64, 93, 117, 136, 139, 238, 239, 254, 290n12
doubling, xiii, 88, 231, 248, 280, 281, 282; concept of, 227; psychic, 227
Dr. Strangelove (film), 122
Du Bois, W. E. B., 15, 90, 91, 92, 93, 94, 95, 100
Duras, Marguerite, 105
Duterte, Rodrigo, 14, 292n45

Earth, creation of, 151
earthquakes, 143, 185
Eatherly, Claude, xix, 9, 221–22, 223, 226, 229; mental illness of, 219–20
Ecodefense, 10
ecological issues, 15, 27, 29, 153, 207, 208, 226, 239, 284
ecology, 40, 45, 153, 256, 284; biopolitics and, xi–xii; mental, 224; natural, 317n17; nuclear, 154, 174, 239; planetary, 212; political, 129; psychic, 224, 232, 233; radioactive, 167
Ecology of Fear (Davis), 95
ecology of mind, xvi, 40
economic dependency, 61, 62, 104, 106
economic exploitation, 19, 153
economic justice, 89, 104
economic life, ecological life and, 153
economy, xvii, 54, 106, 173, 209; extractive, 69, 88; Native American, 70, 74; neoliberal, 50, 54; nuclear, 5–6, 56, 79, 86, 153, 184, 204; plutonium, 16, 17, 154, 301n31; political, 162; psychology and, 50; uranium, 85, 87; war, 56
ecopolitics, 129, 146
Edano, Yukio, 180

Effect of Gamma Rays on Man-in-the-Moon Marigolds, The, 112
Egginton, William, 210–11
Einstein, Albert, 2, 53, 219
Eisenhower, Dwight T., 96–97
Ellington, Duke, 92
Ellsberg, Daniel, 97
Emergency Committee of Atomic Scientists, 219
emotion, 116, 215, 222, 226, 230, 231, 275, 283
Endgame (Beckett), 49, 275
endgames, 155, 269, 275
end times, 48, 267, 268, 275, 278
entanglements, xii, xvii, xviii, 2, 3, 12, 18, 27, 53, 72, 85, 88, 91, 94, 103–4, 153, 164, 171, 198, 209, 240, 248, 254; transspecies, 130, 249, 265
environmental disasters, 15, 45, 144, 204, 209, 210, 212, 215, 254, 269, 274, 276, 284
Environmental Protection Agency (EPA), 58, 59
Envoy, Manidoo, 80, 82, 83
Erikson, Kai, 232, 233
Eschle, Catherine, 123, 128
Eternal Fuse, 217, 218
ethics, 23, 129, 172, 202, 203, 218, 230, 253; of care, xx, 170, 245, 249, 250, 262; transspecies, xiv, xv, 252, 265
eugenics movement, 264
European Parliament, 10
experimental systems, 208, 250, 310n30
extinction, 26–27, 33, 48, 52, 53, 88, 94, 188, 198, 200, 229, 259, 282; imagining, 27, 35, 48, 54, 153, 187, 207, 231, 233, 265; mass, 234, 262, 264; nuclear, 27, 52, 197, 199, 201; planetary, xx, 191, 199, 201, 207; specter of, 35

Fabelo, Roberto, 238–39, 313n5
fake peace, 81, 82
fake rain, 81
false dawn, 12, 13, 26, 60, 64, 79, 81
false death, 12, 13, 26
Fanon, Frantz, 94
fantasies, 41, 47, 239; apocalyptic, 157, 258; imperialist, 258; nuclear, 118–21, 157–58; survival, 45
Fate of the Earth, The (Schell), xvii, 41, 51
Fat Man, 75, 119, 182, 217
Faulkner, William, 217
fear, 161; ecology of, xx, 19, 48, 104, 226; internationalization of, 167; nuclear, 5, 6, 21, 26, 50, 95; politics of, 109; psychic ecology of, 226; reproductive, 232
"Fear Grows on O.C. Cities Near Nuclear Power Plant" (*Los Angeles Times*), 143
Federal Energy Commission, 69
feminism, 2, 102, 118–21, 122–27, 173, 209
fiction: nuclear, 48, 49–50, 75–79; science, 1–7
Figura atomica (Baj), 56
Fire Next Time, The (Baldwin), 94
Fischer, Michael, 202
Flint, water contamination in, 70
Folkkampanjen mot Kärnkraft-Kärnvapen, 10
"Force and Diplomacy in the Nuclear Age" (Kissinger), 7
Forsyth, Frederick, 175
Fort Laramie Treaties (1851 and 1868), 125
fossil fuel, 10, 11, 126, 139, 289n4
Foucault, Michel, 295n116
Frankfurt School, 225
Freud, Sigmund, 119, 223, 242, 268; conscious mind and, 40; on mental apparatus, 315n2
Friends of the Earth, 10
from Sand Creek (Ortiz), 62, 63, 82–83
FSB. *See* Russian Federal Security Service
Fukushima, xix, xxi, 3, 4, 6, 14, 39, 42,

50, 72, 126, 129, 130, 139, 140, 143, 145, 154, 162, 165, 169, 177, 183, 184; Chernobyl and, 179; death-worlds of, 179–82; survivors of, 43, 147, 232; tourism and, 111
Fukushima Daiichi, 179, 180, 181
Fuller, Loie, 208
fundamentalism, 89; nuclear, xix, 228, 229; psychological, 229; spiritual, 229
future: ecological, 78; ethnographies of, 177, 208, 298n29; haunting from, xviii–xix, 34; mourning of, 206; nuclear haunting from, 256, 232; sustainable, 315n17

gamma gardens, 111, 112
"Gathered at the River" (Levertov), 188
gender, 101, 104, 105–31; nuclear fantasies and, 118–21
General Atomics, 86
General Electric, 181
genetic engineering, 257, 264, 265
genocide, 18, 96, 118, 225, 226, 227, 228; nuclear, 73, 102
Gerasinov, Alex, 172
Gesture and Speech (Leroi-Gourhan), 211–12
Ghosh, Amitav, 207, 208, 209, 211, 214
Gilbert, Petuuche, 57, 58, 60; photo of, 59
Girls of Atomic City, The (Kiernan), 120–21
Global 2000: 10
global warming, 274; nuclear energy and, 10, 11–12, 72, 99
Glover, Edward, 22
Glückliche Tage/Happy Days/Oh les beaux jours (Beckett), poster for, 273 (fig.)
gold, 67, 86, 210
Goodman, Amy, 68
Gorbachev, Mikhail, 98
Gordon, Eugene, 93

Grand Canyon, 59, 145
Grants Uranium Belt, 58, 61
Grave of the Fireflies (film), 304n8
Gravity's Rainbow (Pynchon), 120
Gray, Thomas, 280
Great Derangement (Ghosh), 207
Great Law of Peace, 66
Great Law of the Iroquois Confederacy, 66
Great Sioux War (1876), 67
greenhouse gases, 10, 291n27
Gregory, Dick, 97
Griffin, Susan, 221
Groves, Leslie, 16, 76, 119, 293n66
Guattari, Félix, 214, 258
Gurin, Sergei, 56

Hage, Ghassan, 274
Hägglund, Martin, 210
hallucination, negative, xx, 72, 104, 263, 279, 283, 284
Hamai, Shinzo, 224
Hand of Mrs. Wilhelm Röntgen, The (Röntgen), 114 (fig.)
Hanford Nuclear Reservation, 4, 20, 182–85, 242
Hansberry, Lorraine, 90, 95
Happy Days (Beckett), xx, 49, 56, 267–84; theatrical realism and, 269
Haraway, Donna, 239, 261, 262, 263
Harlem Fight Back, 98
Harlequin Bug from Three Mile Island (Hesse-Honegger), 241 (fig.)
Harris, Erna, 90
Harrison, George, 119
Haul No protests, photo of, 59
Haunting Legacies (Schwab), xiii, 225
hauntings, nuclear, xx, 45, 83, 193
health care, 13, 226, 300n19
heart of darkness, 101, 284
heart of whiteness, 101
Hecker, Sig, 153–54
Hegel, G. W. F., 21, 22
heritage, 80; closed, 278; cultural, 74, 160–61; genetic, 257

Hersey, John, 23
Hesse-Honegger, Cornelia, xx, 241–42, 244–45, 251, 254, 255, 256, 259; defamiliarization and, 247; ethics of care and, 262; transspecies care and, 249–50; work of, 241 (fig.), 243 (fig.), 246, 247 (fig.), 248, 249 (fig.), 251 (fig.)
hibakusha, 13, 26, 57, 155–61, 181, 195, 253
"High Noon at Los Alamos" (Wilner), 155
Hiroshima, 3–9, 12, 17, 18, 22, 23, 29, 33, 39, 41, 50, 75, 79, 85, 90, 91, 92, 106, 119, 123, 124, 130, 141, 145, 154, 161, 165, 188, 189, 195, 196, 217, 219, 220, 230; aftermath of, 80, 137, 159, 181, 218; attack on, xiii, 105, 127, 181, 190, 224; black rain of, 180; collective memory of, 82; as deathworld, 80; destruction of, 82, 107, 122, 123, 192, 193; horrors of, 221; images of, 272; legacy of, xix, 13, 81, 160, 222, 225; numbing and, 225, 226, 227; poems, 68, 200–201; shadow images at, 156, 188; survivors of, 32, 43, 101, 103, 156, 223, 232; syndrome, 222; tourism and, 111; trace, 190–91; victims of, 62, 105; wounded bodies of, 83
Hiroshima (Hersey), 23
Hiroshima (Yamamoto), 157 (fig.)
Hiroshima, Mon Amour (Resnais), 105, 106, 122, 130
Hiroshima Bugi (Vizenor), 79–84, 85
Hiroshima in America (Bethe), 217
Hiroshima in America: Fifty Years of Denial (Lifton and Mitchell), xix, 33, 156, 222, 225, 228, 230
Hiroshima Peace Memorial Museum, 82, 191, 192
Hirsch, Daniel, xxi
Hitler, Adolf, 93, 106
Hogan, Linda, 79, 124, 188
Hollywood for SANE, 94

Holocaust, 105, 161, 162, 271; nuclear, 27, 72, 103, 127, 227, 276, 281–82, 284, 295n114
Home Girls (Smith), 102
Honor Our Pueblo Existence, 77
Horkheimer, Max, 193
Horney, Karen, 119
Horsey, David: cartoon by, 66, 67, 67 (fig.)
Hoskins, Andrew, 7
Howorth, Muriel, 111
Hughes, Langston, 101
humanity, 32, 46, 65, 78, 92, 173, 197, 211, 221, 232; death of, 89
humanoids, 167, 211, 237, 239, 259
human rights, 15, 90, 91, 102, 125, 126
Huyghe, Pierre: work of, 208, 208 (fig.)
hydrogen bombs, 219, 228
hyperobjects, 297n17; animacies and, 209–15
Hyperobjects (Morton), 209

Ialenti, Vincent F., 203, 204
imagination, xiv, xix, 19, 27, 40, 44, 46, 70, 82, 118, 135, 137, 141, 202, 203, 204, 207, 208, 214, 229, 240, 255; limits of, 245; moral, 223, 230, 231; scale/boundaries of, 154, 196–201
immortality, 22, 227, 229, 265
Imperative, The (Lingis), 252
imperialism, 90, 91, 98, 106
Imperial Japanese Army, 105
Indefensible Weapons (Lifton and Erikson), 232, 233
Independent, 261
"Indigenous Delegation to DC," screen capture from, 60 (fig.)
Indigenous peoples, 16–17, 25, 58, 65, 67, 68, 71, 77, 78, 125, 133, 136, 139, 145, 147, 153; antinuclear movement of, 42; colonialism and, xvii, 61, 63, 124; false dawn and, 60; Los Alamos and, 75–76, 301n31; Manhattan Project and, 74, 76; nuclear borderlands and,

20, 87; nuclear energy and, 72; nuclear politics and, xvii, 18, 19; protests by, 103, 144; radioactive toxins and, 73; uranium mining and, 124
Insectopedia (Raffles), 240, 245
insects: humanoid, 239; mutant, 240; radioactivity and, 239; republic of, 240
Institute for Radiation Breeding, 112
Institute of Zoology, 245
Intermediate-Range Nuclear Forces Treaty, 98
International Court of Justice, 8, 29, 125
International Criminal Court, 8, 54
International Energy Agency, 112
International Nuclear and Radiation Event (INES), 180
International Physicians for the Prevention of Nuclear War (IPPN), 126, 162
In the Spirit of Crazy Horse (Matthiessen), xvii, 69
Into Eternity (Madsen), xix, 185, 201, 202, 203, 204, 206, 207, 210
Intondi, Vincent J., 91, 93, 96, 98
IPPN. *See* International Physicians for the Prevention of Nuclear War
Ishihara, Sakutaro, 201
ITV News, 175
Ivanov, Pasha, 171–72
Ivanov, Pavel, 172

James, William, 97
Jardin des Plantes, 238
Johnson, Greg, 97
Johnson, Kent, 201
Johnson, Lyndon B., 77
Joliot-Curie, Irene, 115
Jornada del Muerto, 2, 60
Joyce, James, 48
Jungk, Robert, 219, 220

Kafka, Franz, 48, 238
Kakadu National Park, 87

Kan, Naoto, 180
Kant, Immanuel, 210
Kaplan, E. Ann, 204–5, 207
Kartchner, Kerry, 30
Kashparov, Valery, 178
ka'tsina clowns, 74, 75, 76
Katsumata, Chairman, 180
Keats, John, 78
Keepers of the Flame, 217–18
Kennedy, John F., 77, 221
Kernkraftwerk, 131
Kerr McGee Corporation, 61, 146
Kerry, John, 295n115
Keystone Pipeline, 59
KGB. *See* Committee for State Security
Kiernan, Denise, 120–21
Killing Our Own (Wasserman), 183
Kim Jong-un, 42
King, Coretta Scott, 90, 95, 97, 125
King, Martin Luther, Jr., 15, 90, 94, 95, 100, 101
Kissinger, Henry, 7
Kitsutsuki, 83
Klein, Melanie, 25, 26, 107, 280
Kluge, Alexander, 182, 260
knowledge, 5, 14, 49, 115, 167, 224
Kotov, Vanya, 169
Kovalenko, Survivor, 164, 165
Kovtun, Dmitry, 175
Kuletz, Valerie L., xvii, 18, 71, 72
Küssaburg, 242, 244

Lacan, Jacques, x, 81, 155, 165, 252, 305n53
Laguna and Acoma Coalition for a Safe Environment (LACSE), 57–58
Lagunas, 61, 123, 133, 141, 144
Lakotas, 59, 64, 66, 67, 70
La Morticella, Barbara, 155
language, 110, 205; boundaries of, 168, 215; literary, 208, 283; nuclear, 268
Larry King Live (CNN), 77
Larson, Jeffrey, 30
"Last Spider, The" (Liu), 238

Latour, Bruno, 25, 50, 223, 224
Latun, Victor, 141, 166
Lawrence, William, 119, 228
leaf bugs, 242, 244–45, 252, 254
Lee, Kurtis, 175
Leibstadt nuclear power plant, 242, 243, 244
Leroi-Gourhan, André, 211, 212
leukemia, xxi, 115, 117, 137, 138
Levertov, Denise, 188
"Library of Babel" (Borges), xix, 200
Life Exposed (Petryna), 162, 170
lifeworlds, 270, 277, 281, 282
Lifton, Robert J., 3, 4, 26, 33, 36, 62, 154, 156, 157, 159, 160, 218, 224, 225, 228, 230, 233; on counterfeit nurturance, 158; death in life and, 229; doubling and, 227; false death and, 13; Hiroshima and, 226; Hiroshima syndrome and, 222; moral inversion and, 220, 274; on nuclear fundamentalism, 229; nuclear threat and, 232; nuclear violence and, 88; numbing and, 223, 227; species self and, xiv, 248
Light, Michael, 44, 151, 193; photo by, 44 (fig.), 121 (fig.), 152 (fig.), 194 (fig.)
Lingis, Alphonso, 191, 252, 253
linking: attacks on, 282, 316n46; symbolic/cognitive, 282
Lippit, Akira, 111, 113, 191–92, 193, 214
Literary Aftershocks (Stone), 101
literature, xiv–xv, 162; modernist, 237, 240; postmodernist, 240
Little Boy, 75, 119, 120, 217
"Liturgy for Trinity, A" (La Morticella), 155
Litvinenko, Alexander, 14, 174, 175, 176, 291n42
Liu, Sola, 238
Loewald, Hans, 39, 40, 41, 296n8
Logan, Linda, 123–24
Lopez, Louise, 75
Lorenzo, June: photo of, 59

Los Alamos, 71, 289n3, 292n49; Indigenous peoples and, 75–76, 301n31
Los Alamos National Laboratory, 60, 79, 119, 120, 153, 183; truth about, 73–74
Los Angeles Times, 28, 66, 143, 175, 182, 184, 295n114
Lost Ones, The (Beckett), 49
Lugovoy, Andrey, 175
Lukachev, 166
Luminous Processes, 118
Lund, Anne: work of, 185 (fig.)

Macy, Joanna, 210
MAD. *See* mutually assured destruction
Madsen, Michael, xix, 185, 201, 202, 204–5, 206, 210
Making Genes, Making Waves (Beckwith), 264
Malcolm X, 96, 101
Malevich, Kazimir, 246
Mallarmé, Stéphane, 48
Manhattan Project, ix, xiii, xvi, 2, 3, 14, 39, 60, 63, 75, 77–79, 86, 118, 121, 151, 182, 224, 229; Indigenous peoples and, 74, 76; legacies of, xi, xvii, 13, 16, 28–36, 42, 71–74, 80, 90–91; male fantasies and, 120; sacrifice zones and, 193–94; secrecy of, 20, 73, 74; *Stallion Gate* and, 171
Manhattan Project National Historic Park, 183
Maralinga, 4
March of Dimes, 135, 139
Marx, Karl, xiv, 248
Masco, Joseph, xvii, 16–19, 72, 79, 111, 129, 152–54, 163, 301n31
Matthews, Chris, 295n114
Matthiessen, Peter, xviii, 69, 70, 71
Mbembe, Achille, xviii, 19, 20, 22, 31, 88, 102; necropolitics and, xii, xvi, 50; necropower and, 32–33; on nuclearism, 18; nuclear sovereignty

and, 24; resource extraction and, 32–33
McCarthy, Joe, 92
McCartys Day School, 133, 139, 142
McNab, Andy, 175
McNeill, David, 154, 179, 181
media, 6, 28, 29, 139, 163, 180
Meillassoux, Quentin, 197, 198, 199, 258
Meister, Robert, 26
Memoirs of the Second World War (Churchill), 118–19
memory, xviii, 47, 64, 250, 264, 276; collective, 223; unconscious, 242
Metamorphoses (Ovid), 265
metamorphosis, 24, 264; phantasms of, 237–53
metaphors, 266–68, 269
metempsychosis, 264, 265
Middle Passage, 101
Miko, 81, 82, 83
militarism, 22, 103, 111, 169; hypermasculinist, xviii; nuclear, 93, 96, 98
Mille Plateaux, 258
Milton, John, 278, 281
Minamisoma, 179, 180
mind: ecology of, 257, 271; nature and, 40; prepsychoanalytic conception of, 40
Ministerial Interfaith Association of Harlem, 97
Missile Envy (Caldicott), 126
Mitchell, Greg, xix, 33, 156, 218, 225, 228; doubling and, 227; Hiroshima and, 222, 226; numbing and, 223, 227
Mitscherlich, Alexander, 225
Mitscherlich, Margarete, 225
Miyazawa Kenji, 181
Mobilization for Survival, 97
modernism, 32, 102, 106–10, 152
Mohawks, 64, 65, 78
molecular, xiv, xv, xvi, xx, 213, 214, 257; notion of, 254–55
"Molecularization of Sexuality, The" (Rosenberg), 258

"Mont Blanc" (Brathwaite), 85
Mooney, Bel, 119
Moore, Kate, 116, 118
moral inversion, 104, 220, 222, 223, 228, 229, 230, 274
Morgan, Leona: photo of, 59
Morning Joe, 30
Morrison, Toni, 90, 97, 125
Morton, Timothy, 209, 210, 212, 213, 258, 297n17
Mount Brockman, 87, 88
Mount Taylor, 145
mourning, 35, 263, 264, 265
Multicultural Alliance for a Safe Environment, 57, 58
Mumford, Lewis, 228
Munch, Edvard, 205
Murphy, Michelle, xv, 130, 255; distributed reproduction and, xviii, 123, 129, 256
Museo de Bellas Artes, 238
mutant body, 83, 129, 255, 257; phantasms of, ix, x, xv, xx, 232, 289n1, 305n53
Mutation, 265
mutations, x, 184, 239, 242, 245, 254, 264; plant/animal, 178; transgenerational, 171
mutually assured destruction (MAD), 31, 51

Nagai, Takashi, 12
Nagasaki, xix, 3, 4, 5, 7, 9, 12, 17, 18, 22, 29, 33, 39, 41, 50, 75, 79, 80, 85, 90, 91, 92, 106, 119, 123, 130, 141, 145, 154, 155, 190, 195, 217, 218, 219, 220, 223; aftermath of, 13, 131, 159, 181; attack on, xiii, 127, 181, 224; destruction of, 107, 122, 192, 193; images of, 272; legacy of, 13; survivors of, 43, 103
Nairn, Allan, 15
"Naming the Cultural Forces that Push Us toward War" (Spretnak), 122
Naranjo, Marian, 77

Nasser, Gamal Abdel, 94
nationalism, 89, 106
National Socialist Party, 106
nation-states, sovereign, 50, 51, 52–53, 54, 56
natural history, 197, 198
natura naturans/natura naturata, 40
nature: control of, 316n17; culture and, 297n12; dominating, 40; mind and, 40; psychoanalytic theory of, 41
Navajo Nation EPA, 58
Navajos, 58, 61, 144
NBC News, 175
necropolitics, 31, 43, 101, 214, 316n17; neoliberal economy and, 50; nuclear, xi, xii, xv–xvi, xviii, 16–27, 33, 35, 48, 50, 51, 54, 71, 72, 77, 85, 88, 91, 95, 103, 109, 120, 126, 127, 128, 160, 171, 173, 199, 200, 202, 204, 215, 226, 231, 234, 245, 256, 257; nuclearism and, 49
"Necropolitics" (Mbembe), xvi, 18
necropower, 19, 22, 32–33
Neihardt, John, 66
neutron bombs, 96, 195
Newman, Andy, 130
New Mexico Environment Department, 58
Newton, Huey P., 96
New York Amsterdam News, 98
New York Post, 30
New York Times, 82, 130
Nichols, Kenneth D., 86
Night and Fog (Resnais), 105, 188
Night Scene Lit by a Lantern (play), 81
Nikolewski, Rob, 184
"No Apocalypse, Not Now" (Derrida), xvi–xvii, 22, 39, 41, 46
Nonproliferation Review, 28
Northeastern Pueblo, 74
North Korea, 15, 30
NPPs. *See* nuclear power plants
nuclear age, 5, 21, 41, 42, 59, 78, 86, 156, 201, 234, 240, 272; birth of, 151; children of, xviii, 82; cultural imaginary of, 130; false dawn of, 64; inauguration of, xvii; living in, 107; psychology of, 35; soul blindness and, 221
Nuclear and Industrial Safety Agency, 179
nuclear attacks, 3, 18, 46, 54, 75, 79, 98, 160, 190, 229; afterlife of, 153, 256; perpetrators of, 230; rogue, 42; survivors of, 13, 43, 101, 156, 161; threat of, 21
nuclear borderlands, 18, 77, 129, 232, 289n3, 293n61; Indigenous, 20, 57–64, 87
Nuclear Borderlands, The (Masco), 16, 152–53
nuclear contamination, x, 18, 79–80, 144, 234, 292n54; cancer and, 145; denial of, 140–41; risks/impacts of, x, 4. *See also* radioactive contamination
Nuclear Criticism, 41
nuclear crypts, xvi, 230–35
nuclear destruction, 2, 4, 7, 23, 24, 26, 35, 40, 41, 50, 63, 102, 156, 195–96, 201, 229, 230, 231, 234, 240; all-out, 190; fear of, 122; phantasms of, 42
nuclear disasters, xiii, 35, 39, 43, 47, 48–49, 50, 72, 93, 143, 153, 154, 231, 232, 233; aftermath of, 161–77, 178; fear of, 168; future, 44; rogue, 42
nuclear energy, xi, xix, 5, 9–12, 21, 42, 57, 111, 112, 126, 137, 144, 156, 224; climate change and, 10, 11; global warming and, 10, 11–12, 72; hazards of, 12, 29, 72; Indigenous peoples and, 72; nuclear weapons and, 97; production of, 145; promotion of, 139
nuclear explosions, 111, 165, 167, 214
Nuclear-Free Future Award, 125
nuclear gothic, 111, 115
Nuclear Guardianship, 210

nuclear imaginary, xvi, xvii, 3, 41, 43, 44, 46, 49, 102, 164, 239, 240, 254
nuclear industry, 9–10, 11, 12, 180, 184
Nuclear Information and Resource Service, 10
nuclearism, 4, 29, 39, 56, 71, 90; anxiety and, 231; dangers of, 26; Indigenous peoples and, xvii; legacies of, 7–15; manifestations of, xviii–xix; material effects of, 20; nation-state and, 50; necropolitical, 49, 95; politics/psychology and, 18; victims of, 153; violence of, 43
nuclear materials, 99, 210–13; half-life of, 210; long-range effects of, 211; psychic toxicity and, 16
nuclear-military-industrial complex, x, xi, xvi, xvii, xxi, 5, 12, 91, 153, 170
Nuclear Nonproliferation Treaty, 99
nuclear policy, 30, 98, 99–100, 292n48; poverty and, 96
nuclear politics, xii, xxi, 3, 4, 10, 12, 29, 35, 70, 72, 88, 89, 90–91, 104, 110, 126, 127, 175, 202, 223; bomb possession and, 7–8; centrality of, 6–7; defining, 14–15; Doomsday and, 28; Hiroshima and, 224; impact of, x–xi, 21; Indigenous peoples and, 18; macro/micropolitics and, 14; necropolitics and, 103; postcolonial, 126; psychological level of, 13; rise of, 28, 85; secrecy and, 14
Nuclear Posture Review, 99
nuclear power, 111, 124, 127, 163; capacity of, 118; extraction of, 88; managing, 182; slave labor and, 88
Nuclear Power Is Not the Answer (Caldicott), 11, 72, 126
Nuclear Power? No Thanks (Lund), 185 (fig.)
nuclear power plants (NPPs), 70, 88, 130–31, 137, 146, 180, 185, 243–44; advent of, 138; construction of, 10–11; inspection of, 143; maintaining, 184
nuclear reactors, 58, 87, 144, 245; meltdown of, 145; threats from, 182–85
nuclear reason, critique of, xii–xiii, xviii, 88–102
Nuclear Regulatory Commission, 58, 184
nuclear sublime, 22, 41, 46, 111, 118, 151, 152, 162, 163, 165, 166, 194
nuclear tests, 20, 72, 73, 93, 94, 99, 126–27, 130, 153
nuclear threats, xii–xv, 6, 17, 94, 182; forgetting, 7; global warming and, 99; transgenerational psychological impact of, 49–50
nuclear trauma, xiii, 43, 153, 162; *longue durée* of, 179; psychic half-life of, 234; psycho-ontological position of, 17; transgenerational, 43, 154
nuclear unconscious, xiii, xv, 4, 5, 6, 15, 39, 41, 290n8, 304n8; concept of, xvii; racially inflected, 104
nuclear violence, xix, 5, 17–19, 62, 77, 88, 128, 167, 233, 234, 240–41; children and, 13; structural, 4; transgenerational, 232
nuclear war, 9, 20, 27, 39, 43, 50, 56, 96, 97, 103, 127, 129, 156, 157, 162, 192, 226, 237, 239, 240; all-out, 7, 16, 18, 24–25, 26, 30, 35, 41, 72, 153, 191, 196, 204, 205, 222, 256; control over, 29, 46; discourses on, 42, 107; fear and, 95; future, 17, 32, 94; horrors of, 22; imaginary of, 1–7, 46, 48, 124; limited, 3, 7, 28–36, 56, 71, 72, 98; opponents of, 9, 93, 98, 103; phantasm of, 42; planetary survival and, 72; possibility of, 31, 35; self-referentiality and, 47; threat of, 7, 12, 43, 98
nuclear waste, 6, 34, 71, 203, 213, 240, 274; disposal of, 72, 182–83; half-life of, 40; proliferation of, 9,

268; relocating, 184; removal of, 145; repositories, 201, 202, 203, 205; risks of, 17, 202–3; storage of, 29, 47, 63, 210
nuclear weapons, 1, 13, 23, 33, 46, 47, 49, 57, 65, 73, 78, 87, 93, 94, 95, 100–101, 105, 107, 108–9, 110, 121, 122, 124, 127, 130, 144, 145, 153, 157, 160, 161, 218; abolition of, 28, 125, 126; afterlife of, 12; buildup of, 16, 31, 44, 47, 68–69, 86, 97, 101, 128; colonialism and, 98, 101, 154; construction of, 33, 77, 78, 91–92, 96, 97, 101, 217; controlling, 56; dangers of, 95, 107, 220; dependence on, 222; disposal of, 182–83; explosion of, 89, 142–43, 151, 192; first, 4, 60, 78, 100, 188, 192, 194, 195, 222; gender and, 129; illegality of, 8; impact of, 48, 52, 128; invention of, 51–52, 73, 91; location of, 14, 16; manufacturing, 14, 20, 92; modernizing, 30, 99–100; ontological crisis and, 158; power of, 8, 116, 224; psychohistory of, 79, 224; racism and, 98; radioactivity and, 118; rogue states and, 31, 42; sovereignty and, 52; stories about, 108, 137; struggle against, 90, 96, 123; testing, 20, 73, 93, 94, 99, 130; threat of, 20–21, 124; using, 28–29, 92, 230

Oak Ridge, 121, 144, 183, 222
Obama, Barack, 30, 69, 98–100; DAPL and, 66; START treaty and, 99
"Ode on a Distant Prospect of Eton College" (Gray), 280
Off-Limits für das Gewissen (Anders and Eatherly), 219
Olkiluoto Nuclear Power Plant, 201, 203
Oñate, Juan de, 63
100 Suns (Light), 44, 151, 194
Onkalo nuclear waste repository, 177, 185, 201, 202, 203, 205, 213

On Limited Nuclear War in the 21st Century (Larson and Kartchner), 30
On the Beach (Shute), 34
ontology, xiii–xiv, 5, 23, 35, 158, 257–59
Operation Crossroads, 293n66
Ophir, Adi, 23
Oppenheimer, J. Robert, 16, 22, 76, 77, 111, 151, 187, 195, 272, 316n17
oral histories, 162, 171, 174, 176, 232
Orange, James, 96
Ordinary Person's Guide to Empire, The (Roy), 89
orthoceras, 187–88, 191, 196
Ortiz, Alfonso, 74
Ortiz, Simon J., xviii, 62–63, 65, 73, 79, 82–83, 146–47; colonialism and, 61, 63–64; contamination and, 62; on false dawn, 60; poetry of, 146
"Our Own Atomic History," 264
Over Our Dead Bodies (Mooney), 119
Ovid, 265

Pacific Gas and Electric, 184
Pajarito Plateau, 74
PanGeo, 177
Paradise Lost (Milton), 281
Parents vs. SSFL, xxi
Parker, Charlie, 92
Patrushev, Nicolai, 175
Pauling, Linus, 9, 218, 219
Pechanga Reservation, 143
Peltier, Leonard, 69
Pena, Joe, 75
Petryna, Adriana, 162, 170, 171
phantasmagoria, 229, 238, 239, 240, 259
phantasms, 41, 42, 47, 165, 191, 232, 239, 257, 265; apocalyptic, 35; gendered/racialized, 6; nuclear, 229; unconscious, 238
Philippine Department of Foreign Affairs, 292n45
philosophy, 36, 81, 269

Physicians for Social Responsibility (PSR), xx, xxi, 126
Pine Ridge Reservation, xvii, 63, 66, 67, 68, 69, 125, 296n121; uranium mining and, 33
Pirella, Agostino, 237
planetary life, xv, 19–21, 34; destruction of, 19, 21, 126; ecological threats to, 27
Ploughshares Fund, 100
plutonium, 11, 16, 17, 75, 86, 99, 121, 182, 209, 210, 292n49, 297n17; experiments with, 20; half-life of, 73
Plutopia (Brown), 13
Poe, Edgar Allan, 176
Poitier, Sidney, 94
Pokhran nuclear tests, 127
polio, 133, 135, 139, 144
politics, 6, 15, 32, 36, 53–54, 91, 109, 176, 209, 242; antinuclear, 69, 101, 123, 207, 223, 224; Cold War, 31; crime and, 172–73; ecological, 207; energy, 59, 69, 70, 103, 147; environmental, 247; gender, xviii, 103, 104, 110, 123; genocidal/suicidal, 18, 95; global, 51, 110; psychic life and, 24; racial, 32; reproductive, xiv, xviii, 103, 122, 128–29, 130; water, 70
Politics of Life Itself, The (Rose), 214, 255
"Politics of Politics; or, How the Atomic Bomb Didn't Interest Gertrude Stein and Emily Dickinson" (Wineapple), 108
Politkovskaya, Anna, 175
polonium-210, 175–76, 291n42
Popular Front, 91
"Post–Cold War US Nuclear Strategy" (Bernstein), 30
posttraumatic stress disorder, 220
poverty, 29, 127, 144, 226; colonization and, 103; nuclear policy and, 96
Povinelli, Elizabeth, 295n116
Powers, Richard, 276, 284
Preciado, Beatriz, 258

Presidential Archives, 77
Priest, Nick, 175–76
Pripyat, 46, 47, 162, 164, 165, 172, 174, 178, 298n26
Program on Energy and Sustainable Development, 183
Program on Environmental and Nuclear Policy, xxi
Prophesy (documentary), 190
PSR. *See* Physicians for Social Responsibility
Psychiatric Hospital, 237
psychic, 13, 79, 81, 234, 274, 283
psychic automatism, 280, 281
psychic life, 4, 5, 17, 21, 154, 155, 233, 234; formation of, 34; nuclear age and, 3; politics and, 24
psychic numbing, 62, 223, 225, 226, 227, 231, 246; patterns of, 230; shell of, 230
psychic reality, 40, 41
psychic survival, 158, 280
psychoanalysis, xiii, 39, 40, 41, 242, 250, 278
"Psychoanalysis in Search of Nature" (Loewald), 39
psychohistory, 158, 224
psychology, xiii–xiv, 2, 3, 9, 18, 158, 161, 229, 280; economy and, 50; reverse, 109
psychopolitics, xi, xii, 33, 167, 223; nuclear, xiv–xv, 12
Puar, Jasbir, 254
public memory, 74, 79, 82
Pueblo, 74, 75, 76, 79
Pueblo uprising (1680), 63
Putin, Vladimir, 77, 99, 174–75, 291n42
Pynchon, Thomas, 120

"Queer Ecology" (Morton), 258
Quester, George, 30

race, 88, 101, 104
Race, Ethnicity, and Nuclear War (Williams), 100

racial justice, 15, 104
racism, 25, 31, 83, 89, 90, 94, 96, 102–3, 297n12; colonialism and, 88; environmental, xiii, 104; nuclear weapons and, 98
radiation, 105, 111, 112, 127, 130, 141, 163, 178, 192, 198, 205–6, 263; exposure, 114, 115, 261; impact of, 165–66; invisible, 195; levels, 261; victims of, 57, 165; waves of, 192
Radiation and Public Health Project Inc., 130
radiation sickness, 20, 117, 168, 192, 239
"Radioactive Colonization" (Churchill), 146
radioactive contamination, x, xii, xiv, 6, 9, 19, 20, 43–44, 58, 61–63, 72, 79, 103, 124, 130, 142, 157, 158, 163, 167–68, 173, 176, 224, 254, 256, 257, 260; impact of, 13, 32; indicators of, 165; sex lives/reproduction and, 169; transgenerational effects of, 128; zones of, 129. *See also* nuclear contamination
radioactive emissions, 72, 138
radioactive materials, 12, 176, 198, 199, 209, 234, 240, 253; assassinations with, 174; half-life of, 202, 256
radioactive poisoning, 176; assassination by, 14, 174, 175
radioactive waste, xxi, 58, 118, 235; archives of, 201; storage of, 177
radioactivity, xviii, 1, 40, 58, 110, 111, 112, 116, 143–44, 183, 196, 242, 243, 245, 253, 255; human-generated, 212; insects and, 239; nuclear weapons and, 118; reproduction and, 256; robots and, 259–61
radiobiology, 172
radium, 111, 116–17, 193, 208; death from exposure to, 117–18
"Radium Dance" (Fuller), 208

"Radium Girls" (*American Weekly*), 117 (fig.)
Radium Girls, The (Moore), 116
Radium Institute, 115
Raffles, Hugh, 240, 245, 247, 248
Rainbow Serpent, 87
Reagan, Ronald, 90, 97, 98
realism: biological, 53–54, 207; economic, 56; political, 53, 56; theatrical, 269, 277, 282, 283
Redhouse, John, 69
"Reflection on the Atomic Bomb" (Stein), 106–7, 110
Reflections on Hiroshima and Nagasaki (Hecker), 153
"Reflections on the H-Bomb" (Anders), 230
Reif, Kingston, 28
Renko, Arkady, 171, 172, 174
reproduction, 122, 239; distributed, xviii, 123, 256; gendered fantasies of, 119; politics of, 20, 118, 123, 128–31, 160; posthuman transspecies, 249; radioactivity and, 169, 256; technological, 177
reproductive health, 103, 128, 129, 167; damage to, 12, 130, 232
"Republic of Insects and Grass, A" (Schell), 239
resistance, 63, 66, 93. *See also* antinuclear resistance
Resnais, Alain, 105, 188
resources: environmental, 29; extraction of, 32–33, 92; natural, 89, 315n17; planetary, 207
responsibility, 202, 224, 232, 249; moral, 231; political, 198
Rheinberger, Hans-Jörg, 202
rhetoric, nuclear, x, 6, 31, 42, 46, 70, 110, 160, 218, 295n115
Roberts, Guy, 292n48
Robeson, Paul, 15, 90, 91, 92, 94, 95, 100
robots: alien, 261; bio-, 182, 260, 261; dead, 166, 182; green, 260; radioactivity and, 259–61

Rocky Flats Nuclear Guardianship, 210
Rogues (Derrida), 50, 51
rogue states, 30, 31
Ronin, 80, 81–82, 83, 84
Röntgen, Berthe, 113
Röntgen, Wilhelm Conrad, 113, 169; X-ray by, 114 (fig.)
Room of One's Own, A (Woolf), 106
Roosevelt, Eleanor, 94
Roosevelt, Franklin D., 2
Rose, Nicolas, 214, 255
Rosenberg, Jordy, 257–58, 259
Roy, Arundhati, 5, 6, 89, 125, 126, 127, 190, 215
Rubiyat of Omar Khayyam, The, 281
Russell, Bertrand, 94, 219
Russian Federal Security Service (FSB), 174, 175
Rustin, Bayard, 100

Sacred Secrets (Schecter and Schecter), 76
Sacred Stone Camp, 66
sacrifice zones, 18, 61, 71, 162, 174, 193–94
Saenz, Benjamin Alire, 151
Sakurai, Katsunobu, 179
Salter, Mary Joe, 161
Sand Creek massacre, 62, 63
SANE. *See* Committee for Sane Nuclear Policy
San Juan Pueblo, 74
San Onofre Plant, 143, 145, 182–85
Santa Clara Pueblo, 77
Santa Susana Field Laboratory (SSFL), xx, xxi, 290n12
Sarkophag, Der (Kluge), 182
Scarry, Elaine, 8–9, 29
SCE. *See* Southern California Edison
Scentless Plant Bug Environs Paul Scherrer Institute (Hesse-Honegger), 247 (fig.)
Schecter, Jerold L., 76
Schecter, Leona P., 76
Schell, Jonathan, xvii, 4, 36, 41, 51, 53, 54, 56, 65, 214; on extinction, 27; insects and, 239, 240; on nuclear weapons, 27, 52; second death and, 26; on sovereignty/war, 52
Schrader, Astrid, 245, 250
Schrei der Natur, Der (Munch), 205
Schuyler, George, 92
Schwarz, Stephen, 28
Schweitzer, Albert, 94
Scorpion Fly Near Nuclear Power Plant Leibstadt (Hesse-Honegger), 243 (fig.)
Scream, The (Munch), 205
Screening the Body (Cartwright), 113
Seale, Bobby, 96
Second Cold War, 7, 290n11
Second Wounded Knee, xvii, 33, 59, 68, 125
secrecy, 14, 20, 73, 172; culture of, 60, 74, 75, 77, 78, 176; politics of, 8, 43, 71, 86
Secure the Base (Thiongo'o), 85, 89
security, 157; national, 15, 98–99; nuclear, 129; ontological, 17, 161
Seeger, Pete, 97
self: apocalyptic, 227, 228; measured, 227; withdrawal of, 250; world and, 284
self-deception, 164, 171, 223
Sellafield, 242
Senate Internal Security Subcommittee, 219
"Serpentine Dance" (Fuller), 208
Serres, Michel, 4, 223, 224
Seventh Generation, 64–71, 73
shadow images, 156, 188, 189 (fig.), 190, 191
Shakespeare, William, 277, 278, 279
Shell and the Kernel, The (Abraham and Torok), 233
Shenandoah, Leon, 64–65
Shinkolobwe, uranium from, 85, 86
Shute, Nevil, 34
Silko, Leslie Marmon, 79, 123–24
Simpsons, The, ix, xi, 289n4; screen capture from, x (fig.)

Sitting Bull, 66
Six Nations, 65
Skull Valley, 63
slavery, 25, 32, 88, 101
Smith, Barbara, 102
Smithsonian Institution, 126
Sobolev, Sergei, 260
social justice, 89, 95, 102, 104
Social Security, 226
Soft Bug Near Nuclear Power Plant Gösgen (Hesse-Honegger), 251 (fig.)
Sortir du Nucléaire, 10
Southern California Edison (SCE), 143, 184, 185; nuclear waste and, 146; protests against, 144
sovereignty, 19, 25; national, 50, 52, 53, 56; nation-state, 50, 51, 52–53, 54, 56; necropolitical, 50, 174; nuclear, 22–23, 24, 25, 26, 31, 32, 52
Soviet Intelligence Archives, 76
Soviet Union, fall of, 7, 29, 98
Speakers for the Dead, 262
species-being, xiv, 248, 263, 264
species-life, 230–35, 240
Spivak, Gayatri Chakravorty, 24
splitting, 65, 109, 167, 168, 226, 227; ecology of, 104; horizontal, 26; moral psychology of, 26; politics of, 107, 108, 109; psychic, 5, 17, 25, 26, 107, 233, 280
Spretnak, Charlene, 122
Springfield Nuclear Power Plant, ix
Springfield Shopper, ix
SSFL. *See* Santa Susana Field Laboratory
Stallion Gate (Cruz Smith), 74, 75–79, 171
Standing Rock, xvii, 59, 64–71, 125
START treaty, 98, 99
Staying with the Trouble (Haraway), 261
Steele, Christopher, 14, 175
Stein, Gertrude, 106–10
Stevens, Wallace, 17
Stiletto (Veasey), 115 (fig.)

Stimson, Henry L., 118–19
Stingo, Ray, 75
Stockholm Peace Appeal, 92
Stone, Albert, 101
"Strategies for Survival" (Williams), 201
Strickland, Stephanie, 189, 190
Strong in the Rain (Birmingham and McNeill), 179
"Strong in the Rain" (Miyazawa), 181
strontium-90, 95, 130
Studiobühne, 270
subject-formation, xi, 40, 158, 162
subjectivity, ix, 24, 74, 75, 169, 171, 210, 211, 214, 247, 248, 250; boundaries of, 14, 21, 156, 212; female, 113, 123, 128; formation of, xi, 17, 41; post-Chernobyl, 162; postnuclear, 43, 155–61
Sumitomo Bank, 188; steps of, 189 (fig.)
surrealism: ethnographic, 207; nuclear, 111, 115, 131, 196–201
survival, 164, 168, 208; psychic, 158, 280; transspecies, 240
Survival (Fabelo), 238–39
Survival Gathering, 125
Sweet Honey in the Rock, 97, 125
symbionts, 262, 263, 264, 265
Szilard, Leo, 2

Tadodaho, 65
Tainted Desert, The (Kuletz), 71–72
Takahata, Isao, 304n8
technology, 2, 89, 252; apocalyptic, 45; masculine, xviii; nuclear, 97, 98; psychic, 279; renewable energy, 11; reproductive, 120
Telegraph, 14
Teller, Edward, 229
TEPCO. *See* Tokyo Electric Power Company
terrorism, 31, 51, 89, 317n46; nuclear, 11, 12, 25, 30, 32, 72, 79, 98, 129
Thacker, Eugene, 258
thanatocracy, 34–35

theater of cruelty, 269, 271, 284
theatricality, 270, 272, 282, 283
Theodorakopoulos, Tessa, poster by, 273 (fig.)
Thermonuclear Monarchy (Scarry), 8, 29
Thiong'o, Ngũgĩ wa, 85, 94
Three Mile Island, 4, 42, 154, 182–85, 242, 244
Time (magazine), 217
"Today We Reboot the Planet" (Rojas), 200
Toge Sankichi, 190
Tokyo Electric Power Company (TEPCO), 179, 180, 182
Tooth Fairy Project, 130
Torok, Maria, 233, 234; theory of the crypt and, xiii
toxicity, 1, 19, 45–47, 73, 129, 169, 214, 233, 255, 283–84; environmental, 254; linguistic, 168; psychic, 16, 26, 45, 79, 161, 167, 168, 172, 233
toxins, 58, 112, 174, 204, 214, 255; alien, 253; biopolitical impact of, 213; radioactive, 172, 180
transgenerational legacies, 33, 80, 170, 234
transmutation, 81, 83, 292n49
transspecies care, xv, 249–50, 262
transspecies encounters, 237–53, 263
transspecies selves, xvi, xx, 237, 253, 264
trauma, 62, 205; fatigue, 6; legacy of, 193; psychological responses to, 168; theory, 224; transgenerational, xiii, xv. *See also* nuclear trauma
Treaty on the Nonproliferation of Nuclear Weapons (NPT), 31
Trident on Trial (Zelter), 125
Trident Ploughshares, 125
"Trilobytes" (Johnson), 200–201
Trinity Test Site, 2, 60, 73, 75, 78, 111, 119, 120, 151, 154, 182, 193, 194, 272
"Troubling Time/s and Ecologies of Nothingness" (Barad), 252–53

Truman, Harry S., 100, 219
Trump, Donald, 14, 28, 67, 295n115; cartoon about, 66; DAPL and, 58–59, 68; Duterte and, 292n45; environmental policies and, 68; EPA and, 58; Indigenous people and, 300n19; North Korea and, 15; nuclear weapons and, 30, 31–32, 42, 72; Putin and, 175; scientific research and, 50; water rights and, 66
Trump as Custer (Horsey), 67 (fig.)
Truth about Crime, The (Comaroff and Comaroff), 77
"Two Cars in Every Garage and Three Eyes on Every Fish" (*Simpsons*), ix, xi, 289n2, 289n4; screen capture from, x (fig.)

Ukrainian Institute of Agricultural Radiology, 178
unconscious: apocalyptic, 284; cultural, 22, 35, 228, 230, 232, 237; economic, 5; political, 7, 16, 230; psychoanalytic theory of, 39
Union Minière, 86
United Nations, 8, 58, 85, 86, 125
United Nations Food and Agriculture Organization, 112
United Nations General Assembly, 8, 64–65
United Nations Security Council, 292n48
United Nuclear Corporation, 58
uranium, 11, 20, 70, 75, 85–86, 99, 120, 133, 134, 141, 177, 178; corporate capture of, 60–61; deadly force of, 62; energy production and, 145; enriched, 99, 292n49; impact study, 58; irradiation/transmutation of, 292n49; mining, xvii, 13, 33, 36, 44, 59, 72, 88, 92, 125, 142, 144, 145, 146, 240, 289n3, 296n121, 300n8
Uranium: War, Energy, and the Rock That Shaped the World (Zoellner), 85

uranium industry, 45, 144
U.S. Air Force, 9
U.S. Army, 66, 67
U.S. Army Corps of Engineers, 16
U.S. Atomic Energy Commission, 77
U.S. Department of Defense, 14, 69
U.S. Department of Energy, 69, 183
U.S. Department of Health, 176
U.S. Department of the Interior, 145
U.S. Seventh Cavalry, 66, 67

van Leeuwen, Jan Willem Storm, 10–11
Vartabedian, Ralph, 295n114
Veasey, Nick, 115; X-ray by, 115 (fig.)
Verkehrung ins Gegenteil (Freud), 223
vibrant matter, 187, 281, 296n3, 312n49
Villar Rojas, Adrián, xix, 200
violence, 51, 93, 125–26, 153, 234; biopolitical, 72; domestic, 170; mass, 225, 227; necropolitical, 18, 43; slow, 77, 103, 146, 168; structural, 94, 226. *See also* nuclear violence
Virilio, Paul, 195, 214
Vizenor, Gerald, 80, 81, 82, 83, 85
Voices from Chernobyl (Alexievich), 171, 177
Voyles, Traci, xvii, 45, 231

Wächter des Sarkophags, Die (Kluge), 260
Walker, Alice, 101, 102
"Wallace Stevens's Bird" (Wolfe), 17
Walsh, Michael, 30
WAND. *See* Women's Action for Nuclear Disarmament
war, 33, 91, 111, 122, 253, 257; genocidal, 118; sovereignty and, 52; war machines, 33, 35, 120, 126
War Resisters League, 94
War Talk (Roy), 5, 126, 190
Wasserman, Harvey, 183
watch dial factories, 116–17
water rights, 66

weapons: biological, 94; capitalization of, 42; industries, 126; out-of-ratio, 8; technological, 120; upgrading, 30–31
weapons of mass destruction, 30, 217
Wells, H. G., 1–7, 52, 228
Welsome, Eileen, 20
Welt Online, 182
"We're 30 Seconds Closer to 'Doomsday'" (Schwarz), 28
West, Nigel, 175
Western Shoshone, nuclear waste and, 72
Westinghouse Electric Company, 184
"What Does Fiction Know?" (Powers), 276
What Use Are Flowers? (Hansberry), 95
"When Deep Time Becomes Shallow" (Ialenti), 203
White Earth Reservation, 80
White Face, Charmaine, 125
White Plume, Deborah, 68
White Sands, 12, 64, 65, 142
"Who Here Will Begin This Story?" (Agoyo), 74
Williams, Beryle, 201
Williams, Paul, 100, 101
Williams, Robert Moore, 257
Wilner, Eleanor, 155
Wilson, Dagmar, 95
Wilson, Edward O., 263
Wilson, Richard (Dick), 68, 296n121
Wineapple, Brenda, 108, 110
Winnicott, W. D., 280
Winnie, 56, 267–84; burial of, 269, 274; psychic splitting and, 280; wonderful lines and, 49, 267, 270, 271, 276, 277–78, 280, 281, 284
Wolak, Frank, 183
Wolf, Christa, 161, 167, 168
Wolfe, Cary, 17
Wolves Eat Dogs (Cruz Smith), 14, 171, 173, 174
Women in Europe for a Common Future, 10

Women's Action for Nuclear Disarmament (WAND), 123, 126
Women's International League for Peace and Freedom, 90, 95
Women Strike for Peace, 90, 95
"Women, X-Rays, and the Public Culture of Prophylactic Imaging" (Cartwright), 113
Woolf, Virginia, 106
World Information Service on Energy, 10
World Set Free, A (Wells), 1, 2, 52, 228
Wounded Knee, 33, 63, 64–71, 80
Woven Stone (Ortiz), 79, 146
Wright, Frank Lloyd, 217
Wright, Richard, 93

X-ray machines, 112, 113, 134, 135, 138, 139
X-rays, xviii, 20, 113, 133, 134, 135, 136, 144; power of, 114–15

Yamamoto, Mutsumi, 254
Yamamoto Keisuke: painting by, 157 (fig.)
Yeats, William Butler, 278
Yucca Mountain, 63, 146, 185

Zelter, Angie, 125
053 GEORGE (Light), 152 (fig.)
072 OAK (Light), 121 (fig.)
061 HURON (Light), 44, 44 (fig.)
025 DIABLO (Light), 194 (fig.)
Zoellner, Tom, 85, 86–87
zombies, 44, 45, 257
Zone, 140, 141, 163, 166, 172, 174
zones of exception, 32, 50, 72
zones of exclusion, 3, 47, 162, 164, 165, 166, 171, 174, 178, 260

(continued from page ii)

47 *Elements of a Philosophy of Technology: On the Evolutionary History of Culture*
   Ernst Kapp

46 *Biology in the Grid: Graphic Design and the Envisioning of Life*
   Phillip Thurtle

45 *Neurotechnology and the End of Finitude*
   Michael Haworth

44 *Life: A Modern Invention*
   Davide Tarizzo

43 *Bioaesthetics: Making Sense of Life in Science and the Arts*
   Carsten Strathausen

42 *Creaturely Love: How Desire Makes Us More and Less Than Human*
   Dominic Pettman

41 *Matters of Care: Speculative Ethics in More Than Human Worlds*
   Maria Puig de la Bellacasa

40 *Of Sheep, Oranges, and Yeast: A Multispecies Impression*
   Julian Yates

39 *Fuel: A Speculative Dictionary*
   Karen Pinkus

38 *What Would Animals Say If We Asked the Right Questions?*
   Vinciane Despret

37 *Manifestly Haraway*
   Donna J. Haraway

36 *Neofinalism*
   Raymond Ruyer

35 *Inanimation: Theories of Inorganic Life*
   David Wills

34 *All Thoughts Are Equal: Laruelle and Nonhuman Philosophy*
   John Ó Maoilearca

33 *Necromedia*
   Marcel O'Gorman

32 *The Intellective Space: Thinking beyond Cognition*
   Laurent Dubreuil

31 *Laruelle: Against the Digital*
   Alexander R. Galloway

30 *The Universe of Things: On Speculative Realism*
   Steven Shaviro

29 *Neocybernetics and Narrative*
   Bruce Clarke

28 *Cinders*
Jacques Derrida

27 *Hyperobjects: Philosophy and Ecology after the End of the World*
Timothy Morton

26 *Humanesis: Sound and Technological Posthumanism*
David Cecchetto

25 *Artist Animal*
Steve Baker

24 *Without Offending Humans: A Critique of Animal Rights*
Élisabeth de Fontenay

23 *Vampyroteuthis Infernalis: A Treatise, with a Report by the Institut Scientifique de Recherche Paranaturaliste*
Vilém Flusser and Louis Bec

22 *Body Drift: Butler, Hayles, Haraway*
Arthur Kroker

21 *HumAnimal: Race, Law, Language*
Kalpana Rahita Seshadri

20 *Alien Phenomenology, or What It's Like to Be a Thing*
Ian Bogost

19 *CIFERAE: A Bestiary in Five Fingers*
Tom Tyler

18 *Improper Life: Technology and Biopolitics from Heidegger to Agamben*
Timothy C. Campbell

17 *Surface Encounters: Thinking with Animals and Art*
Ron Broglio

16 *Against Ecological Sovereignty: Ethics, Biopolitics, and Saving the Natural World*
Mick Smith

15 *Animal Stories: Narrating across Species Lines*
Susan McHugh

14 *Human Error: Species-Being and Media Machines*
Dominic Pettman

13 *Junkware*
Thierry Bardini

12 *A Foray into the Worlds of Animals and Humans*, with *A Theory of Meaning*
Jakob von Uexküll

11 *Insect Media: An Archaeology of Animals and Technology*
Jussi Parikka

10 *Cosmopolitics II*
Isabelle Stengers

9   *Cosmopolitics I*
    Isabelle Stengers

8   *What Is Posthumanism?*
    Cary Wolfe

7   *Political Affect: Connecting the Social and the Somatic*
    John Protevi

6   *Animal Capital: Rendering Life in Biopolitical Times*
    Nicole Shukin

5   *Dorsality: Thinking Back through Technology and Politics*
    David Wills

4   *Bíos: Biopolitics and Philosophy*
    Roberto Esposito

3   *When Species Meet*
    Donna J. Haraway

2   *The Poetics of DNA*
    Judith Roof

1   *The Parasite*
    Michel Serres

GABRIELE SCHWAB is distinguished professor at the University of California, Irvine. She holds appointments in the departments of comparative literature, anthropology, English, and European languages and studies. She received a PhD in literary studies from the University of Constance and a PhD in psychoanalysis from the New Center of Psychoanalysis in Los Angeles. She is the recipient of a Heisenberg Fellowship and a Guggenheim Fellowship. Her books in English include *Subjects without Selves: Transitional Texts in Modern Fiction*; *The Mirror and the Killer-Queen: Otherness in Literary Language*; *Haunting Legacies: Violent Histories and Transgenerational Trauma*; and *Imaginary Ethnographies: Literature, Culture, and Subjectivity*. She is editor of *Accelerating Possession: Global Futures of Property and Personhood* (with Bill Mauer); *Derrida, Deleuze, Psychoanalysis*; and *Clones, Fakes and Posthumans: Cultures of Replication* (with Philomena Essed).